TEMPLE AND CON[...]
God's Presence in the Cosmos, C[...]

Articles

Notes

Tradition & Traditions

CONTRIBUTORS

❧ Gary A. Anderson ❧

Gary A. Anderson is professor of theology, Old Testament and the Hebrew Bible at the University of Notre Dame. His books include: *The Genesis of Perfection: Adam and Eve in Jewish and Christian Imagination* (2001); *Literature on Adam and Eve Collected Essays*, ed. with Michael E. Stone, and Johannes Tromp (2000); *A Time to Mourn, A Time to Dance: The Expression of Grief and Joy in Israelite Religion* (1991); *Priesthood and Cult in Ancient Israel*, ed. with Saul M. Olyan (1991); and *Sacrifices and Offerings in Ancient Israel: Studies in their Social and Political Importance* (1987). His recent articles include: "The Iconography of Zion," *Conservative Judaism*, 54 (2002); "Ka'asher Shamanu, Ken Ra'inu," [in Hebrew] *Aqdamot* 12 (2002): "Joseph and the Passion of Our Lord," in *The Art of Reading Scripture*, eds. Ellen F. Davis and Richard B. Hays (2003); "The Culpability of Eve: From Genesis to Timothy," in *From Prophecy to Testament: The Function of the Old Testament in the New*, ed. Craig A. Evans (2004), 233–251; "Two Notes on Measuring Character and Sin at Qumran," in *Things Revealed: Studies in Early Jewish and Christian Literature in Honor of Michael Stone*, eds. Esther G. Chazon, David Satran, and Ruth A. Clements (2004); "Adam, Eve, and Us," *Second Spring* 6 (2004); "How to Think About Zionism," *First Things* (April 2005); "From Israel's Burden to Israel's Debt: Towards a Theology of Sin in Biblical and Early Second Temple Sources," in *Reworking the Bible: Apocryphal and Related Texts at Qumran*, eds. Esther G. Chazon, Devorah Dimant, and Ruth Clements (2005); "King David and the Psalms of Imprecation," *Pro Ecclesia* 15 (2006); "What Can a Catholic Learn from the History of Jewish Biblical Exegesis?" *Studies in Christian-Jewish Relations* 1 (2005–2006); "Mary in the Old Testament," *Pro Ecclesia* 16 (2007). Anderson's research concerns the religion and literature of the Old Testament and the early reception of those books in early Judaism and Christianity. He is finishing a book on metaphors for sin and forgiveness (tentative title: *Forgiving Israel's Debts: The Divine Economy in Early Judaism and Christianity* [Yale University, 2009]), and the function of the Tabernacle narratives in the Book of Exodus.

❧ Brant Pitre ❧

Brant Pitre is the Donum Dei Professor of Word and Sacrament at Our Lady of Holy Cross College in New Orleans, Louisiana. He received his Ph.D. in Theology from the University of Notre Dame, where he specialized in the study of the New Testament and ancient Judaism and graduated with highest honors. He is the author of several articles and a book, *Jesus, the Tribulation, and the End of the Exile* (2005). He is currently finishing a book, *Jesus and the Last Supper: Ancient Judaism and the Origin of the Eucharist*, to be published by Eerdmans.

❧ Michael Gielser ☙

Michael Gielser, a priest of Opus Dei, holds a doctorate in sacred theology (S.T.D.) and an advanced degree in philosophy. He is also the author of a trilogy of historical novels about the early Church of Rome: *Junia* (2002), *Marcus* (2004), and *Grain of Wheat* (2008). His numerous scholarly articles and essays on Scripture and spirituality have appeared in the *Gran Enciclopedia Rialp,* and in *Scripta Theologica, Nuestro Tiempo, Homiletic and Pastoral Review, This Rock, The Catholic Answer, The Priest*, and elsewhere. Among his teaching appointments, he has served as associate professor of biblical theology at the University of Navarre in Spain, and has given religious formation for inner-city minority youth in Chicago.

❧ Scott W. Hahn ☙

Scott W. Hahn, founder of the St. Paul Center for Biblical Theology, holds the Pope Benedict XVI Chair of Biblical Theology and Liturgical Proclamation at St. Vincent Seminary in Latrobe, Pennsylvania, and is professor of Scripture and theology at Franciscan University of Steubenville, Ohio. He has held the Pio Cardinal Laghi Chair for Visiting Professors in Scripture and Theology at the Pontifical College Josephinum in Columbus, Ohio, and has served as adjunct faculty at the Pontifical University of the Holy Cross and the Pontifical University, Regina Apostolorum, both in Rome. Hahn is the general editor of the *Ignatius Study Bible* and is author or editor of more than twenty books, including *Letter and Spirit: From Written Text to Living Word in the Liturgy* (2005); *Understanding the Scriptures* (2005), and *The Lamb's Supper: The Mass as Heaven on Earth* (1999). Yale University Press will publish his newest book, *Kinship By Covenant: A Canonical Approach to the Fulfillment of God's Saving Promises* in Fall, 2009.

❧ Raymond Corriveau, C.Ss.R ☙

Raymond Corriveau, C.Ss.R, is associate novice director for the North American Redemptorist Novitiate located in Glenview, Illinois. He obtained his Th. D in Moral Theology from the Academia Alfonsiana in Rome, and has taught moral theology and the ethics of St. Paul at the Toronto School of Theology. He has also served as a parish pastor and as Provincial Superior for his unit of the Redemptorists in Canada. He is the author of *The Liturgy of Life: A Study of the Ethical Thought of St. Paul in his Letters to the Early Christian Communities* (1970) and the co-editor, with Alberto de Mingo C.Ss.R. of *Readings on Redemption* (2006).

∽: Thomas Dubay, S. M. :∾

Thomas Dubay. S. M. is a retreat master and spiritual theologian. He has served as a professor at major seminaries and colleges and universities and has produced more than two hundred television and radio programs. Among his more than twenty-five books are: *Faith and Certitude* (1985); *The Evidential Power of Beauty: Science and Theology Meet* (1999); *Fire Within: St. Teresa of Avila, St. John of the Cross, and the Gospel On Prayer* (1989); *Authenticity: A Biblical Theology of Discernment* (1977); and *God Dwells Within Us* (1971).

∽: Denis R. McNamara :∾

Denis R. McNamara is assistant director and a member of the faculty of The Liturgical Institute, University of St. Mary of the Lake Seminary, Mundelein Seminary. He is the author of *Heavenly City: The Architectural Tradition of Catholic Chicago* (2005), *Shadow, Image and Reality: Beauty, the Bible and Catholic Church Architecture* (forthcoming, 2009) and articles and reviews in *Chicago Studies, Communio, The Priest, Homiletic and Pastoral Review, Assembly, Sacred Architecture,* and *Environment and Art Letter.* He holds a Ph.D. in Architectural History from the University of Virginia and has served on the Commission on Art and Architecture of the Archdiocese of Chicago.

∽: William A. Bales :∾

William A. Bales is a professor of sacred Scripture at Mount St. Mary's Seminary in Emmitsburg, Maryland. He holds a Ph.D. in New Testament from the Catholic University of America where he wrote his dissertation on the meaning and function of Ephesians 4:9–10. He is presently preparing a variety of articles for publication on such subjects as the idea of the "Gospel" in the Book of Acts; a reappraisal of the translation of Luke 4:22; a reassessment of "the least of these my brethren" in Matthew 25:31–46; and the function of Psalms 1 and 2 as unified introduction to the Psalter.

∽: Daniel Keating :∾

Daniel Keating is associate professor of Theology at Sacred Heart Major Seminary in Detroit, Michigan. He is the author of *Deification and Grace* (2007); *The Appropriation of Divine Life in Cyril of Alexandria* (2004), and the co-editor and contributor to *The Theology of St. Cyril of Alexandria: A Critical Appreciation* (2003); *Aquinas on Doctrine: A Critical Introduction* (2004), and *Aquinas on Scripture: An Introduction to His Biblical Commentaries* (2005). He has edited an edition of St. Thomas Aquinas' *Commentary on Colossians* (2006) and published scholarly articles and reviews in *Pro Ecclesia, Theological Studies, Journal of Early*

Christian Studies, Nova et Vetera, Henoch, and *Studia Patristica.* He earned his D.Phil in Theology from Oxford University in 2000.

~: John C. Cavadini :~

John C. Cavadini is the chair of the theology department at the University of Notre Dame and director of the university's Institute for Church Life. He is a scholar of patristic and early medieval theology, with special interests in the theology of Augustine and in the history of biblical exegesis. He is the author of *The Last Christology of the West: Adoptionism in Spain and Gaul, 785–820* (1993), and co-editor of *Who Do You Say That I Am: Confessing the Mystery of Christ* (2004). He is editor of *Miracles in Christian and Jewish Antiquity: Imagining the Truth* (1999); *Gregory the Great: A Symposium* (1996), and associate editor of *Augustine Through the Ages: An Encyclopedia* (Eerdmans, 1999). His articles have appeared in such journals as *Theological Studies, Religious Studies Review, Traditio, Augustinian Studies,* and *American Benedictine Review.*

~: Jean Cardinal Daniélou, S. J. :~

Jean Cardinal Daniélou, S. J. (1905–1974) was a theologian and patristics scholar who became a key figure in the mid-century theological renewal movement known as the *Ressourcement.* His classic work is the groundbreaking *The Bible and the Liturgy* (1956). Among his dozens of books are: *Holy Pagans of the Old Testament* (1957); *The Dove and the Darkness in Ancient Byzantine Mysticism* (1957); *The Lord of History: Reflections on the Inner Meaning of History* (1958); *From Shadows to Reality: Studies in the Biblical Theology of the Fathers* (1960); *Primitive Christian Symbols* (1964); and *The Theology of Jewish Christianity* (1964). His "The Sign of the Temple: A Meditation," is adapted from his 1958 monograph, *The Presence of God.*

~: Yves M.-J. Cardinal Congar, O. P. :~

Yves M.-J. Cardinal Congar, O. P. (1904–1995) was one of the most influential theologians of the twentieth century. His many books include *Tradition and Traditions: An Historical and a Theological Essay* (1966); *The Meaning of Tradition* (1964); *After Nine Hundred Years: The Background of the Schism between the Eastern and Western Churches* (1959); *I Believe in the Holy Spirit,* 3 vols. (1979–1983); *Lay People in the Church: A Study for a Theology of the Laity* (1957); *A History of Theology* (1968). His "The Eschatological Temple, the Kingdom, and the Church in History," is adapted from *The Mystery of the Temple, or, The Manner of God's Presence to his Creatures from Genesis to the Apocalypse* (1962).

Letter & Spirit 4 (2008): 7-12

INTRODUCTION

The singer of Psalm 73 is aggrieved and embittered. He is worn down from trying to reconcile the easy prosperity of the wicked, the constant afflictions of the
righteous, and the possibility of God's justice and providence. Nothing about the
world makes sense until he enters the Temple.

> When I thought how to understand this,
> it seemed to me a wearisome task.
> Until I went into the sanctuary of God—
> then I *perceived* their end. (Ps. 73:16–17)

In the Temple, the psalmist is finally given to understand the mystery of
the divine plan. The biblical word here—*bîn* in Hebrew, *syniēmi* in Greek—does
not refer to some ordinary kind of perception, the kind of conclusions that can be
reached by flesh and blood, by reason alone. Rather, the biblical word signals the
kind of insight that only comes by faith, an understanding of the secrets of the
kingdom given by the Father in heaven (Matt. 13:10–17). It is the understanding
that the young Christ displayed among the rabbis in the Temple, the understanding of the Scriptures that he revealed to his disciples in the upper room, in the
shadow of the Temple, on that first Easter night (Luke 2:47; 24:45).

In the sanctuary of God contemplation is brought to fruition by the gift of
divine Wisdom. The Temple is the seat of Wisdom and the dwelling place of the
Most High God. And the Temple, in many ways, can be seen as the unifying theme
of sacred Scripture. The apostolic writers noticed this, as did the early Fathers of
the Church. The classic expression of the theme is still Yves Congar's *The Mystery
of the Temple* (1958):

> [T]he essential point of God's plan ... could be well formulated
> in terms of a Temple built of living stones; for God's whole
> purpose is to make the human race, created in his image, a living,
> spiritual Temple in which he not only dwells, but to which he
> communicates himself and in turn receives from it the worship
> of a wholly filial obedience. ... Hence the story of God's rela-
> tions with his creation, and especially with man, is none other
> than the story of his ever more generous, ever deeper presence
> among his creatures.[1]

In the Temple we perceive the "end," the meaning of the salvation history
told in the Bible. It is the history of the Father's gracious self-revelation and sharing

---

1   *The Mystery of the Temple*, ix.

of his divine presence with his children. We see this "end" in the beginning, on the first pages of Scripture, where the world's creation is carefully depicted as the building of a cosmic Temple, a holy place for God to dwell with his people. In Scripture's final pages, we witness a new creation, described as a city come down from heaven, a city with no temple. "Its Temple is the Lord God the Almighty and the Lamb" (Rev. 21:22).

The dwelling of God with his people—first in the Tabernacle and Ark in the wilderness and later in Solomon's Temple at Jerusalem—shapes the narrative of the Old Testament even as it anticipates the revelation of the new covenant and the new Temple. Everything in the economy of salvation presses forward towards this end. The Temple is the substance of all that Israel longs for.

> One thing I ask of the Lord, this I seek:
> To dwell in the house of the Lord all the days of my life,
> that I may gaze on the loveliness of the Lord
> and contemplate his Temple. (Ps. 27:4)

Israel's hope is realized in the coming of Jesus Christ. In him, the Word of God "tabernacles" among us in the flesh (John 1:14). Presented in the Temple forty days after his birth to the Virgin Mary, his life proceeds by a mysterious impera-tive that he himself announced in the Temple at the age of twelve: "I must be in my Father's house" (Luke 2:49). Indeed, the "plot" of the Gospels unfolds against the backdrop of Jesus' pilgrimages to Jerusalem to celebrate the Temple feasts.

In his passion the body of Christ is revealed to be the new Temple, from which flows the new river of life. In offering his body and blood for the life of the world, he reveals himself as the new Lamb of sacrifice and the new High Priest, fulfilling in his person the deepest meanings of the sign of the Temple. Sending his Spirit at Pentecost, he establishes his Church, built on the cornerstone of Christ and the foundation of the apostles, as the true Temple, his Father's house of many mansions. In the Church, the promise of the Temple is realized. The Church is the house of prayer for all peoples, the holy mountain in which God is worshipped in Spirit and truth. Through the sacramental economy of the Church, the Spirit is given to dwell in believers—divinizing and deifying, making them living stones, Temples of the Holy Spirit.

The Temple theme is perhaps the richest in all of biblical theology, embrac-ing the mysteries of Christ, Church, and Kingdom; liturgy, sacraments, and priesthood; salvation, sanctification, and divine filiation. These are the beautiful mysteries we contemplate in this volume of *Letter & Spirit*.

In "To See Where God Dwells: The Tabernacle, The Temple, and the Origins of the Mystical Tradition," **Gary A. Anderson** explores a little-studied aspect of Israel's Temple traditions—how Israel came to believe that the holiness of God's invisible presence infused the architecture and furniture of God's dwelling, making these physical objects bearers of the divine presence. As Anderson shows, this belief played an important role in Israel's faith and devotional life. This belief also became influential in the development of early Christian thinking about the incarnation. As the Temple furniture was held to bring one into real contact with God, the early Church Fathers described how the divinized flesh of Christ made visible the glory of the invisible God. As to gaze upon the dwelling of God was to see God, to look upon Christ was to look upon God.

Anderson also sketches some of the early movements of the Christian mystical tradition. He shows how Moses' contemplation of the Tabernacle became a model for mystical prayer, beginning early in the Christian era. Again we see the influence of Jewish faith concerning the holy objects of the divine dwelling. Anderson quotes pseudo-Dionysius' reflections on Moses: "And yet he does not meet God himself, but contemplates, not him who is invisible, but rather where he dwells (Exod. 25). This means, I presume, that the holiest and highest of things perceived with the eye of the body or the mind are but the rationale which presupposes all that lies below the Transcendent One."

Brant Pitre's "Jesus, the New Temple, and the New Priesthood," is a bold investigation of the deep Old Testament figures that inform the self-understanding of Jesus as he is portrayed in the gospels. Pitre argues persuasively that the gospels reflect Jesus' awareness that he is the dwelling-place of God on earth, the foundation stone of a new Temple and a new creation, and the founder of a new, eschatological priesthood that offers a new sacrifice, the Eucharist. Pitre's work advances what he calls a *biblical mystagogy* of the Temple and the Jewish priesthood. As he sheds new light on the biblical origins of the priesthood and the sacramental economy, Pitre also opens up new possibilities for scholarly consideration of Jesus' "self-consciousness."

In "The Rejected Stone and the Living Stones: Psalm 118:22–23 and New Testament Christology and Ecclesiology," **Michael Giesler** seeks the origins of the most ancient christological and ecclesiological traditions in the Church. He explores the Church's belief that it is the Temple of God built upon the cornerstone of Christ. As Giesler shows, this ecclesiology is rooted in Jesus' own teaching, in which he applied to himself Old Testament traditions concerning the divine "stone." Giesler sees a deep connection between this "stone" christology and the Church's Temple ecclesiology. He traces this connection to Christ's words and acts designating Peter as "the rock" upon which he founded his Church. As Giesler notes in a close reading of 1 Peter, it is no coincidence that a New Testament writing attributed to Peter provides the most extended reflection upon the meaning of Christ as the cornerstone of the Church and the Church as a Temple of living stones.

Scott W. Hahn is also studying the Old Testament substrata that inform New Testament christology and ecclesiology. His "Temple, Sign, and Sacrament:

Towards a New Perspective on the Gospel of John," makes a fresh contribution to the study of John's christology and pneumatology, as well as John's understanding of the sacramental ministry of the Church. Through a close reading of John's narrative, Hahn argues that the evangelist is doing much more than portraying Jesus as the fulfillment of Israel's hopes concerning the Temple. According to Hahn, John envisions that fulfillment continuing in the Church's sacraments, exercised by the authority of Christ and the gift of the Holy Spirit. The sacraments, he argues, are among those "greater works" that Jesus promised the apostles they would perform: "If one follows the logic and symbolism of John's Gospel, the sacraments, primarily baptism and Eucharist, truly are the specific times and places where the believer continues to experience Christ as the new Temple."

Raymond Corriveau, C.Ss.R considers the influence of the Temple theme on early Christian moral teaching. "Temple, Holiness, and the Liturgy of Life in Corinthians" explores an under-appreciated aspect of St. Paul's teaching—his presentation of the Christian life as a daily offering of one's self in spiritual sacrifice to God. This cultic and liturgical understanding is tied closely to Paul's teaching that baptism establishes Christians as "temples" of the Holy Spirit. And, as Corriveau demonstrates, this Temple imagery is crucial to Paul's ideas about purity and holiness, as well as to his conception of the "priestly" nature of the believer who, "in the living out of his moral life, becomes a priest in the temple of his own body, dedicated to the service of God."

"The Indwelling of Divine Love: The Revelation of God's Abiding Presence in the Human Heart," by Thomas Dubay, S. M., explores the spirituality that flows from the New Testament teaching that the body is a temple, the dwelling place of the Trinity. Dubay retrieves the roots of this teaching through a spiritual interpretation of the "divine pedagogy" found in the Old Testament. He detects a pattern of ever increasing nearness and intimacy with God, preparing the way for Jesus' startling revelation—that God desires to dwell and abide in the hearts of believers. Dubay offers rewarding insights into the incarnation and the divine economy, while showing how the Temple theme furnishes a theological foundation for Christian prayer and contemplation.

We also present in this volume four specialized studies of key aspects of the Temple theme. Denis R. McNamara's "Living Stones in the House of God: The Temple and the Renewal of Church Architecture," explores the theological significance of the Temple for designing the church building as the *domus Dei*, or "house of God." The church, he maintains, is intended to be "an image of the heavenly Jerusalem" in which the building "fulfills the Temple typologies ... not as a shadowy copy of the true Holy of Holies, but as an image of the reality of heaven in true participation." William A. Bales' "The Mystery of His Will": Contemplating the Divine Plan in Ephesians" offers a close reading of a pivotal New Testament text (Eph. 1:8–10). Bales demonstrates the influence of Daniel's prophecy on Paul's presentation of the divine "mystery," which he understands to be God's plan to dwell with his people in an everlasting kingdom.

In "'You Are Gods, Sons of the Most High'": Deification and Divine Filiation in St. Cyril of Alexandria and the Early Fathers," **Daniel A. Keating** contributes to our understanding of the work of the sacraments, especially baptism, in bringing us the fruits of the incarnation—the gift of the Spirit and the sharing in the divine nature. In his beautiful recovery of the Church's traditional teaching, Keating shows the glorious "end" to which the economy of salvation tends—our "deification" as sons and daughters formed in the image of Christ, destined to live in communion with the Trinity. In "Scripture, Doctrine, and Proclamation: *The Catechism of the Catholic Church* and the Renewal of Homiletics," **John C. Cavadini** demonstrates how the "scriptural pedagogy" of the *Catechism* can be a powerful tool for the Church's preachers as they seek to proclaim the great mysteries of the Church and the Eucharist in the economy of salvation.

We conclude this volume of *Letter & Spirit* with excerpts from what we consider to be two of the most important modern expositions of the Temple theme. **Jean Cardinal Daniélou, S.J.'s** "The Sign of the Temple: A Meditation," is a poetic and patristic reading of the tradition drawn from his classic *The Presence of God*. Daniélou contemplates the mystery of the human purpose in the cosmic Temple of creation: "God has in some way left creation unfinished, and man's mission is to bring it to fulfillment ... [as] the mediator through whom the visible universe is gathered together and offered up."

Like Daniélou, **Yves J.-M. Cardinal Congar, O.P.**, sees the priestly work of God's children culminating in the heavenly liturgy of the new Jerusalem, which we participate in through the offering of the sacrifice of the Mass on earth. Congar's "Church, Kingdom, and the Eschatological Temple," excerpted from *The Mystery of the Temple*, is a fitting conclusion to our contemplation of the Temple. He writes: "If there is one obvious direction in the great story of God's presence to his creatures as it has been made known to us by revelation ... it is surely this—it begins by momentary contacts and visits, then passes through the stage of external mediations that draw God ever nearer to mankind, and finally reaches the state of perfectly stable and intimate communion."

Congar's reading of the Book of Revelation reminds us that the Temple is meant to be the template, the form and the model for our contemplation of the mysteries of God's kingdom. As Moses gazed on the divine plan of the Tabernacle and David on the heavenly pattern for the Temple, we too, like the psalmist, are meant to "contemplate the Temple."

In bidding farewell to his apostles, Jesus said he was going to prepare a place for them in his Father's house (John 14:2–3). Thus, he transfigured the mysterious sign of the Temple, revealing it to be an icon of the divine hospitality, the hospitality of God, that lies at the heart of salvation history. From the foundation of the world,

God's desire has been to set a table for his children in his kingdom, to prepare a place for us in his house of glory, the "household of God, which is the Church of the living God" (1 Tim. 3:15).

In the Temple we perceive God's saving plan as a soteriology that is trinitarian, covenantal, and sacramental. We perceive the "end" of that plan in our sharing in the divine nature. It is an intimacy established by Christ's new covenant, through which God bestows the blessings of his presence by sacramental signs, making us his children in the image of his Son. Here, in the state of grace, God comes to abide in us, making each of us a Temple of living stones, a holy place of his dwelling. In the state of glory, we will come to the Father's house to receive the inheritance prepared for us in the many mansions of the heavenly Temple. There we will dwell in the Trinity as now the Trinity dwells in us.

Letter & Spirit 4 (2008): 13–45

TO SEE WHERE GOD DWELLS:
The Tabernacle, the Temple, and the Origins of the Christian Mystical Tradition

~: Gary A. Anderson :~

University of Notre Dame

Scholars have long noted that the priestly instructions concerning the construction of the Tabernacle exceed the bounds of what would be ordinarily expected. The sheer volume of detail that is lavished on this building is uncommon for the priestly writer. Generally, he is prolix only when a theme is being introduced for the first time; should a return to the theme be warranted, he is more than capable of abbreviation.[1]

This general pattern of composition is not followed in regard to the Tabernacle. Especially striking is the tendency to repeat the list of appurtenances that are found within the Tabernacle (Exod. 30:26–30; 31:7–11; 35:11–19; 39:33–41; 40:2–15; 40:18–33). Six times these items are listed; the final three are perhaps most striking because they occur one right after the other. Indeed, one could say that the account of the Tabernacle ends with a concatenation of three lists of the materials for the Tabernacle and includes only enough extraneous material to keep the thread of a narrative from disappearing altogether.

As Menahem Haran has remarked, "The priestly writers find [this] subject so fascinating that ... [they are] prompted to recapitulate the list of its appurtenances time and again. Their tendency to indulge in technicalities and stereotyped repetitions has here reached its furthest limits."[2] I suggest that this is because the Tabernacle furniture was understood as possessing something of the very being of the God of Israel. As such, it bears careful and repeated repetition whenever the occasion arises, not unlike the piling of divine epithets in a psalm of praise or descriptions of the beloved that flow from the pen of the lover. While Mesopotamian

---

*   This essay was first given as a paper at the Ninth Orion Symposium at the Hebrew University, Jerusalem, Israel ("Text, Thought, and Practice in Qumran and Early Christianity"). A variant form of this essay will appear in the conference proceedings.

1   Compare, for example, the law regarding how to offer the sin and holocaust offerings in Lev. 5:8–9, 10a; the former law is long and detailed because none of the previous chapters have dealt with this type of offering; the latter is abbreviated because a law already exists to which it can refer (Lev. 1:14–17).

2   Menahem Haran, *Temples and Temple-Service in Ancient Israel: An Inquiry into Biblical Cult Phenomena and the Historical Setting of the Priestly School* (Winona Lake, IN: Eisenbrauns, 1985), 149.

scribes could mark temple accessories as divine by using the cuneiform *dingir* sign,[3] the Bible could indicate this by way of repetition.

I cannot consider all of the evidence from the biblical period, though some background will be necessary. My essay concerns the role that the Temple and its furniture assume in the Second Temple period (roughly 520 B.C. to 70 A.D.) and beyond. I hope to show the following: First, that the furniture of the Temple was treated as quasi-divine in both literary and iconographic sources during the Second Temple period; second, that the exalted estimation of these pieces of furniture made them dangerous to look at but at the same time, quite paradoxically, desirous or even compulsory to contemplate; third, that the impossibility of dividing with precision the house of God from the being of God led the early Christians to adopt this Jewish theologoumenon as a means of clarifying how it was that Jesus could be both God and man. Finally, I want to suggest how this Jewish tradition came to have a formative influence on the rise of Christian mysticism.

The Ark and the Realism of the Bible's Liturgical Language

Anyone who has worked on the problem of the cult in the Bible knows that there is a highly realistic quality to the liturgical language used therein. The Temple is God's home and hence the spot where he dwells among men. In order to breathe life into this belief, the Bible provides legislation for how to prepare the home for God's dramatic entrance, how to provide God with food in a way that befits his dignity, and finally, how to keep his home clean so that he will remain there and offer his blessings to the worshipers and pilgrims who desire to revere him.[4] Not unlike kings portrayed in other ancient Near Eastern literatures, the biblical king of kings will, from time to time, make a personal appearance. And, like other devout subjects of the imperial realm, Israelites are urged to appear before him periodically so as to demonstrate their fealty (Exod. 23:17 and parallels).[5]

---

3   On the Mesopotamian evidence, see below. The *dingir* sign is the cuneiform ideogram that marks a person or object as divine.

4   The best account of the "real presence" of God in the Tabernacle is that of Haran, *Temples and Temple Service*. For a fine treatment of the theme in Mesopotamia, see the classic essay of A. Leo Oppenheim, "The Care and Feeding of the Gods," in *Ancient Mesopotamia: Portrait of a Dead Civilization* (Chicago: University of Chicago, 1964), 183–198. On the statue itself, Elko Matsushima writes: "These statues played a central role in many important rituals and religious ceremonies in the temple area and sometimes even outside the temple. The cult statue of the god was fully identified with the god in question and was considered by the worshippers to be actually a living being, able to do whatever a human being does, for example, sleep, wake, or eat, even though the statue was always motionless and dumb." "Divine Statues in Ancient Mesopotamia: Their Fashioning and Clothing and their Interaction with the Society," in Elko Matsushima, ed., *Official Cult and Popular Religion in the Ancient Near East: Papers of the First Colloquium on the Ancient Near East—The City and its Life, Held at the Middle Eastern Culture Center in Japan (Mitaka, Tokyo), March 20–22, 1992* (Heidelberg: Universitätsverlag C. Winter, 1993), 209.

5   An appearance before a king was a sign of beatitude and favor. This point is driven home in the

This theophanic aspect is most vividly brought to light in the laws for the pilgrimage festivals. According to Exodus 23:17 and its parallels, Israelites must appear three times a year at the Temple in order "to see the face of the LORD." As noted already by Samuel David Luzzatto in his commentary on Isaiah, but seconded by Abraham Geiger, August Dillman, and most moderns, the decision of the Masoretic Hebrew text to vocalize the verbal stem *ra'ah* as a *niphal* ("to present oneself [before the face of the LORD]") is not likely the original reading.[6]

The most likely reading of this verse is that the Israelites must come "to see the face of the Sovereign" three times a year. But having made the case for such a reading we have created a new problem. If the command demands that Israel "see the face of God," how was that command fulfilled? The dramatic theophany that Israel was witness to at the completion of the Tabernacle (Exod. 40:34–35) was certainly not standard fare at every pilgrimage festival. What exactly did later pilgrims see when they ascended the mountain of the LORD?

The most obvious answer would be the Ark. As scholars have long noted, the Ark is regularly identified with the LORD's presence and at one time in its history was the subject of ceremonial processions. This is certainly implied by the liturgical refrain of Numbers 10:35–36. When the Ark was to set out, Moses would say:

> Advance, O LORD!
> May your enemies be scattered,

---

story of Absalom's banishment from the court of his father, King David. Begrudgingly David accedes to Joab's plea to normalize relations and allows Absalom to return. Nevertheless, David lets Absalom know that things are still not well by telling Joab: "Let Absalom return to his house; but *my face let him not see*. So Absalom returned to his house, but the face of the king he did not see" (2 Sam. 14:24). The expression, "my face let him not see," uses the exact same idiom as that found in Exod. 23:17. In Akkadian texts as well, the idiom *amaru pani*, "to see the face of PN," means to encounter either the king or the god in a face-to-face fashion. See Robert D. Biggs, ed., *The Assyrian Dictionary of the Oriental Institute of the University of Chicago*, 21 vols. (Chicago: Oriental Institute, 1964–2006), vol. 1, A, part 2:21–22. (Hereafter, *Chicago Assyrian Dictionary*.) In the case of an audience with the god, the idiom refers to beholding the cult statue.

6   See Luzzatto, *Sefer Yeshayahu* [The Book of Isaiah] (Padua: 1855) on Isa. 1:12. Geiger, *Ha-Miqra' we-turgemav* [The Bible and its Translations] (Jerusalem: Mosad Bialik, 1949), 218–19; August Dillmann, *Die Bücher Exodus und Leviticus* [The Books of Exodus and Leviticus] (Leipzig: S. Hirzel, 1897), 276. Luzzato notes the following problems: First, nowhere in the Bible do we find the expected combination of the passive stem "to appear" with an indirect object (*liphne* YHWH); rather this passive stem is somewhat anomalously conjoined to a direct object (*'et pene* YHWH or *pene* YHWH). And, more significantly, in every text where the context is some sort of personal appearance—with the exception of those involving God—we invariably find the infinitival form of the N-stem "to appear" spelled with a *heh* after the *lamedh* (for example, in 2 Sam. 17:17 or 1 Kings 18:2). But in Isa. 1:12, Exod. 34:24, and Deut. 31:11, texts that concern coming to the Temple, we find the infinitive spelled without the *heh*. Since the infinitive of N-stem is regularly spelled in a *plene* fashion in biblical texts and only in rabbinic Hebrew do we find regular elision of the intervocalic *heh*, the simplest solution is to assume that the Masoretes have wrongly vocalized these texts. And if these texts have been wrongly vocalized then there is a high probability that Exod. 23:17 has been as well.

And may your foes flee before you!

And when it halted he would say:

> Return, O LORD,
> Unto the ten thousands of Israel!

A similar identification of the Ark with the being of God is presumed by the entrance liturgy of Psalm 24:7–10, "O gates, lift up your heads! Up high, you everlasting doors, so that the King of glory may come in." According to Frank Moore Cross, this portion of Psalm 24 is "an antiphonal liturgy used in the autumn festival … [and it] had its origin in the procession of the Ark to the sanctuary at its founding, celebrated annually in the cult of Solomon and perhaps even of David. On this there can be little disagreement."[7]

The close nexus between God and this piece of cultic furniture is nicely illustrated in the story of the battle with the Philistines that would eventually lead to the Ark's capture. Having been routed badly in an initial exchange of hostilities, the Israelite militia regrouped to prepare a new strategy. "Let us fetch the Ark of the Covenant of the LORD from Shiloh," they decided, "[for] thus he will be present among us and will deliver us from the hands of our enemies" (1 Sam. 4:3). The response to the Ark's entry into the Israelite war camp reveals how close was the attachment of God's being to this piece of furniture.

> When the Ark of the Covenant of the LORD entered the camp, all
> Israel burst into a great shout, so that the earth resounded. The
> Philistines heard the noise of the shouting and they wondered,
> "Why is there such a loud shouting in the camp of the Hebrews?"
> And when they learned that the Ark of the LORD had come to
> the camp, the Philistines were frightened; for they said, "*God has
> come to the camp.*" And they cried, "Woe to us! Nothing like this
> has ever happened before. Woe to us! Who will save us from the
> power of this mighty God?" (1 Sam. 4:5–8).

The highly realistic tenor of the language here must not be overlooked. Though God is not fully reducible to or coterminous with the Ark, his presence is nevertheless so closely interwoven with it that one can point to the Ark as it approaches in military processions and say, "here comes God."

This entire scene—which demonstrates the rash and ill-considered efforts of the Israelites to misuse this divine image—must be contrasted with the story of David's ignominious retreat from Jerusalem in the wake of Absalom's revolt. As David departs, Zadok appeared along with a group of Levites bearing the

---

7   See his *Canaanite Myth and Hebrew Epic: Essays in the History of the Religion of Israel* (Cambridge, MA: Harvard University, 1973), 93.

Ark. Given that the odds in favor of David's reclaiming his kingdom did not seem high, Zadok drew the only possible conclusion: David's future would depend on divine assistance and the easiest way to assure this would be to bring God along for the departure.[8] David, however, will have none of this. Not because he views such a stratagem as rooted in a "magical" concept of the Ark. Quite the reverse, David believes himself to be in the process of paying the price for past sins (2 Sam. 12:7–15) and willingly takes upon himself this period of exile from his city and his God. His own words are most revealing: "Take the Ark of God back to the city. If I find favor with the LORD, he will bring me back and *let me see it* and its abode" (2 Sam. 15:25–26). Favor with the deity will be symbolized not only by restoration to his kingdom but by being granted the privilege of *seeing* the Ark.

"Seeing" the Deity

This high valuation on seeing the representation of the deity should not surprise anyone familiar with ancient Near Eastern practice. As early as 1924, and even before, Friedrich Nötscher[9] argued that references to seeing God in pilgrimage laws and the Psalter were to be understood against the background of the act of displaying the statue of the god or goddess in non-Israelite cultures. Although Israel's cultic life was without a direct and immediate representation of God himself, the Ark and other pieces of the Tabernacle furniture supplied an almost exact parallel.

No better witness to the close nexus between Temple appurtenance and the presence of God could be seen than in the priestly rules about how to disassemble the Tabernacle prior to the Israelite camp's moving to a new destination in the wilderness. The rules are carefully laid out with one goal in mind: the prevention of inappropriate Levitical groups from laying eyes on the holiest parts of this structure. "Let not [the Kohathites] go inside and witness the dismantling of the sanctuary," the writer warns, "lest they die" (Num. 4:20).[10] In this text, seeing the furniture is analogous to seeing the very being of God, which likewise would result in death.[11]

---

8   On the theological and political importance of the cult-image to the identity of a people, see Patrick D. Miller and J. J. M. Roberts, *The Hand of the Lord: A Reassessment of the "Ark Narrative" of 1 Samuel* (Baltimore: Johns Hopkins, 1977).

9   In his book *"Das Angesicht Gottes Schauen": Nach Biblischer und Babylonischer Auffassung* [Seeing the Face of God: Biblical and Babylonian Perspectives] (Würzburg: Becker, 1924).

10 In a representation of a procession from Palmyra, Syria, in the first century A.D., a portable sanctuary is borne by a camel that is covered by a piece of red cloth. The worshippers greet the artifact with upraised arms as though the deity himself sat astride the camel. See Othmar Keel, *The Symbolism of the Biblical World: Ancient Near Eastern Iconography and the Book of Psalms* (Winona Lake, IN: Eisenbrauns, 1997), 326.

11 See, for instance, Exod. 33:20. In one rabbinic tradition, this law was promulgated because the Kohathite clan was in the habit of "feasting their eyes on the *Shekinah*," who dwelt among the furniture. See *Bemidbar Rabbah* [Midrash on Numbers] 5:9. (For an English translation, see H.

Finally, I might mention Psalm 48, a text that describes in considerable detail the circumambulation of the city of Jerusalem after the destruction of enemy forces that foolishly attempted to overtake it. Having exhorted the inhabitants of Zion and the surrounding province of Judah to stream forth in pilgrimage to celebrate this event, the Psalmist urges them to make a close visual inspection of the architecture of the city. "Walk about Zion, go round about her," he urges, "number her towers, consider well her ramparts, go through her citadels; that you may tell the next generation that *this is God*, our God forever and ever" (Ps. 48:13–15).

It is the last line here that should occasion some surprise. Here our author seems to take his paean of praise to unimaginable heights. He claims that these buildings testify to the very being of God. Amos Hacham puts his finger directly on the pulse of this text when he writes, "[Regarding the phrase] 'this is God,' the word 'this' [*zeh*] is similar in meaning to 'look here.' It is an expression of palpable excitement and its point is that the one who sees the Temple in its splendor and glory feels within himself as if he saw, face to face, the glory (*kavod*) of the LORD. He cries, 'this [this building] is God, our God.'"[12]

I suggest that this language is not solely a result of the excess or superfluity that often characterizes the genre of praise (although obviously this is a factor). Rather, these texts exhibit ancient Israel's deeply held view that God really dwelt in the Temple and that all the pieces of that building shared, in some fashion, in his tangible and visible presence. To use a modern metaphor, one might imagine the Temple as a giant electrical generating plant that powered the land of Israel. In its core was a nuclear reactor in which the radioactive rods emitted divine energy that was absorbed by the entire infrastructure of the building. Though the glow was brightest at the center, even the periphery had to be entered and handled with caution. Not even the thickest cement wall or lead surface could prevent these divine energies from overwhelming their boundaries and radiating divinity upon whatever stood in its vicinity.

The Angelic Host and the Aura of God in his Temple

In understanding this biblical motif, Mesopotamian texts provide a very close parallel. "The aura of a god in his temple," W. G. Lambert writes, "could so attach itself to the temple, or architectural parts of it in particular, also to the implements he used, and to the city which housed the temple, in such a way that these various things also became gods and received offerings as a mark of the fact."[13]

Freedman and Maurice Simon, eds., *Midrash Rabbah*, 10 vols. [London: Soncino, 1983]). This illustrates nicely the attraction that the Temple appurtenances were felt to possess as well as their attendant danger.

12   *Sefer Tehillim* [Book of Psalms], Daat Ha-Miqra (Jerusalem: Rav Kook, 1990), 278.

13   W. G. Lambert, "Ancient Mesopotamian Gods: Superstition, Philosophy, Theology," *Revue de l'Histoire des Religions* 207 (1990): 129.

Not only was the statue of the god imbued with the veritable presence of the god it represented, but more remarkably, the divine aura was shared by even the furniture and other accessories dedicated to the temple.[14] The whole building pulsated with the presence of the god—the structure of the temple itself literally shared in the presence of the divine.[15]

As we will see, this deeply rooted ancient Near Eastern tendency to link the appurtenances of the building to the central cultic image had a vibrant afterlife in post-biblical Judaism. But perhaps even at this point some examples would be in order. In the *Songs of Sabbath Sacrifice*, from Qumran, there is regularly some confusion as to whether a particular title identifies the Holy One, the God of Israel, or one of his angelic host.[16] Such syntactic difficulties are regular enough that one has a hard time imagining that it is the gulf of many centuries between composition and commentary that is creating the problem. The text itself seems to enjoy the confusion it creates, from time to time, between the two categories.

The most likely explanation for this phenomenon is to be found in the Bible itself. As James Kugel has explained, in the course of a theophany, the angel of the LORD will frequently fade into the person of God himself.

> The fact that [this confusion occurs] in text after text (even if, after a time, it became conventional) suggests that there was something essential about this confusion. It represents the biblical authors' most realistic sense of the way things actually are. The spiritual is not something tidy and distinct, another order of being. Instead, it is perfectly capable of intruding into everyday reality, as if part of this world.[17]

---

14 Note the concluding observations of Gebhard Selz's remarkable essay, "The Holy Drum, the Spear, and the Harp: Towards an Understanding of the Problems of Deification in the Third Millennium Mesopotamia," in *Gods and their Representations*, Irving L. Finkel and Markham J. Geller, eds., Cuneiform Monographs 7 (Grönigen: Styx, 1997), 184: "A statue of a god was an independent entity, because it stood on a holy place, and had the name of a god, the appearance of a god, and so on. It was these qualities of a statue, including its partaking in certain rituals, which left no doubt that it was the god himself. *The same holds true for the 'cultic objects'; it is their function and their special attributes, including their participation in holy rites, which made them god-like.*" Emphasis added. Compare also the essay of K. van der Toorn, "Worshipping Stones: On the Deification of Cult Symbols," *Journal of Northwest Semitic Languages* 23 (1997): 1–14.

15 These Mesopotamian texts had a decisive grammatical advantage over their biblical brethren; they could mark the overflow of the divine energies by attaching a *dingir* sign to lists of temple furniture. See Selz, "The Holy Drum, the Spear, and the Harp," 176–179.

16 The text from Qumran includes a portrayal of a heavenly throne room and a liturgy of angels. See in particular the commentary of Carol Newsom on the seventh Sabbath Song in her *Songs of Sabbath Sacrifice: A Critical Edition*, Harvard Semitic Studies 27 (Atlanta: Scholars Press, 1985), 213–225. Note also her comment (at 24): "Many occurrences of *elohim* in the Shirot are ambiguous and might refer to God or to the angels."

17 James L. Kugel, *The God of Old: Inside the Lost World of the Bible* (New York: Free Press, 2003), 36.

But it is not only the case that angels bleed into God and vice versa; the same syntactic difficulties attend the sanctuary as well. As Carol Newsom has argued, these thirteen songs are organized around the important seventh song.[18] And, as in the two songs that flank this centerpiece (the sixth and seventh), the number seven is itself crucial to its compositional structure. The song opens with seven highly ornate exhortations to the angelic priesthood to commence their praise. Having done this, we move from voices of the angelic host to the sanctuary itself bursting into song.

> [And along with the seven groups of angels who were exhorted
> to sing praise][19] let all the [foundations of the hol]y of holies
> offer praise, the uplifting pillars of the supremely exalted abode,
> and all the corners of its structure. Sin[g praise] to Go[d who is
> dr]eadful in power[, all you spirits of knowledge and light] in or-
> der to [exa]lt together the splendidly shining firmament of [his]
> holy sanctuary. [Give praise to hi]m, O god-[like] spirits, in order
> to pr[aise for ever and e]ver the firmament of the upper[m]ost
> heaven, all [its] b[eams] and its walls, a[l]l its [for]m, the work of
> [its] struc[ture. The spir]its of holie[st] holiness, living god-like
> beings[, spir]its of [eter]nal holi[ness] above all the hol[y ones.[20]

The building itself breaks into song, dramatically eclipsing the difference between the angelic host and the building in which they serve. Even more striking is how the text vacillates over just what precisely is the object of praise. With the angels, one is never in doubt that they are the ones who must offer praise. However, the divinized Temple not only offers praise, but itself becomes the object of praise. "Give praise to him, O god-like spirits," the text exhorts, "in order to praise/confess (*le-hodot*) … the firmament of the uppermost heaven, all its beams and walls." Indeed the last sentence quoted above ("The spirits of holiest holiness.") is difficult to parse grammatically. How exactly is it related to its immediate antecedent, that is, to the list of architectural features of the Temple? Newsom's commentary is revealing:

> The expression *ruhey qodesh qodashim* may mean either "most
> holy spirits … or spirits of the holy of holies." However the title is
> construed, these angelic spirits are in some way associated with
> the heavenly sanctuary which has just been described, either as

---

18   Newsom, *Songs of Sabbath Sacrifice*, 13–17.

19   The use of *hallelu* as an imperative call to praise marks the beginning, middle and end of the seventh song (see 4QSongs of the Sabbath Sacrifice [4Q403] 1:30, 41 and 2:15). First the angels are called to offer praise, then the Temple itself, and finally, the chariots of the inner sanctum.

20   4Q403 1:41–45.

attendants or as the *animate spiritual substance of the heavenly Temple itself.*[21]

No matter which way we go with these two options we reach essentially the same destination. Either the Temple is such an overpoweringly holy structure that angelic spirits literally ooze from its various surfaces or those surfaces themselves slip into the realm of divine being itself. Hebrew constructions such as *elohim hayyim* ("the living God") that one would normally construe as divine titles now become attributes of the supernal Temple ("a living pulsating godlike [building]").

Although the end of the seventh song is fragmentary, enough remains for Newsom to conclude that the praise moves from the outer parts of the heavenly sanctuary to its inner sanctum and its furnishings. As such, the structure of this crucial middle song anticipates "to a certain extent the structure and content of the ninth through the thirteenth songs."[22]And not surprisingly, in these latter songs the structural edifice of the supernal Temple again comes to life so as to voice its praise. Strikingly, Newsom notes, the thirteenth and final song appears to conclude with a systematic list of the contents and structures of the heavenly Temple.

That the Sabbath songs seem to feel no embarrassment about ascribing divine qualities to the Temple provides a striking piece of data against which we can contextualize how the Samaritan version of the Pentateuch and the Septuagint handle several texts in Exodus that speak of "seeing" God. We have already mentioned the command to visit Jerusalem during the three pilgrimage festivals in order to fulfill the obligation of "seeing the face of the Sovereign, YHWH." The Masoretes smoothed over this arresting phrase by rendering "to see" in the passive "to be seen/appear."

The Samaritan translation found another way around the problem. Building on the common confusion of the Hebrew letters *daleth* and *resh*, it read the line: "to see the presence of the Ark (reading *aron* in place of *adon*) of the LORD." Though correctly dismissed by text-critics as a secondary reading, it is an invaluable piece of information for the scholar of early biblical exegesis.[23] Minimally, this reading demonstrates that for at least one strand of ancient Judaism, seeing the Ark was a close substitute to seeing God himself. Maximally, it may provide us with a piece of indirect evidence that, in the Second Temple period, pieces of the Temple furniture were taken out of the building and displayed before the eyes of earnest pilgrims.[24]

Though the Septuagint anticipates what the Masoretes will do with this verse by rendering the verb "to see" in the passive form, in a couple of other places

---

21   Newsom, *Songs of Sabbath Sacrifice*, 233. Emphasis added.

22   Newsom, *Songs of Sabbath Sacrifice*, 9.

23   The importance of this textual variant for the practices of Second Temple Judaism have already been noted by Israel Knohl, "Post-Biblical Sectarianism and the Priestly Schools," *Tarbiz* 60 (1991): 140–141.

24   See the argument of Israel Knohl below.

it replaces the difficult construction of "seeing God" with the notion of beholding the structure in which he dwells. Compare, for example, Exodus 25:8 where Moses is told that the entire purpose of building the Tabernacle is so "that I may dwell among [the people Israel]." The Septuagint replaces the idiom of dwelling with a reference to vision. Build the sanctuary, Israel is exhorted, "so that I may *be visible* among you."

Similarly, in Exodus 24:9–11, where the Masoretic text declares that Moses and the select group that ascended to the top of Mount Sinai "saw the God of Israel," the Septuagint introduces a rather significant qualification—"they saw *the place where* the God of Israel stood."

If we skip ahead to the Book of Revelation, it is perhaps significant that when the Kingdom of God is to be revealed at the end of time and the appearance of God in his full glory would seem to be at hand, what is described is something not unlike what Moses must have beheld at Sinai:

> Then the seventh angel blew his trumpet, and there were loud voices in heaven, saying, "The kingdom of the world has become the Kingdom of our Lord and of his Messiah, and he will reign forever and ever." Then the twenty-four elders who sit on their thrones before God fell on their faces and worshiped God, singing, "We give you thanks, Lord God Almighty, who are and who were, for you have taken your great power and begun to reign. The nations raged, but your wrath has come, and the time for judging the dead, for rewarding your servants, the prophets and saints and all who fear your name, both small and great, and for destroying those who destroy the earth." *Then God's Temple in heaven was opened, and the Ark of his Covenant was seen within his Temple*; and there were flashes of lightning, rumblings, peals of thunder, an earthquake, and heavy hail (Rev. 11:15–19).

The common denominator that binds all these examples together is that of gazing upon the architecture of the sanctuary as a fit replacement for seeing the face of God.

Pilgrimage and the Face of God

Turning to evidence from the post-biblical era, in Mishnah *Hagigah* (1:1),[25] we have a piece of *halakhah*, or Jewish legislation, concerning who must make the pilgrimage to Jerusalem:

---

25   The *Hagigah* ("The Festal Offering") dates from about 200–220 A.D. For an English translation of the Mishnah, see Herbert Danby, *The Mishnah* (Oxford: Clarendon, 1933); Jacob Neusner, *The Mishnah: A New Translation* (New Haven: Yale University, 1988).

All are subject to the command to appear [before the LORD] excepting a deaf-mute, an imbecile, a child, one of doubtful sex, one of double sex, women, slaves that have not been freed, a man that is lame or blind or sick or aged, and one that cannot go up [to Jerusalem] on his feet.

In the Tosefta,[26] we find a *baraita*, or oral-law tradition, that attempts to explain just how the various categories described are related to the biblical text which states simply that every male must go up to Jerusalem to see the face of God. According to Rabbi Yehudah (d. 219), "even the blind man [is exempt] because Scripture states that '[every one of your males] must *see* [the face of God] (Exod. 23:17).'"[27] The striking detail here, is the reading of *ra'ah* as a verb in the *qal* stem. This prompts the intervention of a rabbi who presumes that the verb should be read in the *niphal* and cites in his support 1 Samuel 1:22, the only text in the Bible where the *niphal* reading is unambiguous in regard to the pilgrimage to the Temple.[28] This unit of the Tosefta comes to a close with the notice that the sages were inclined to tip the scales of judgment in favor of Rabbi Yehudah's rendering.

In addition to considering how the biblical text is used in relationship to several other rabbinic texts, Shlomoh Naeh has a very illuminating remark as to just what all of this might mean historically.

It is possible that the cause for the textual differences is not solely due to *tikkune soferim*[29] but is also rooted in historical practice. Perhaps what is seen here are two ancient customs or conceptualizations of the command to go up for pilgrimage and "see." According to one, the pilgrims entered the Temple building and received the presence of the *Shekinah*; according to the other they were not authorized to enter the Temple proper but to bring a sacrifice and "appear" in the courtyard. A similar

---

26 A supplementary compilation of Jewish oral law, composed perhaps a generation after the Mishnah, in the late third century.

27 Tosefta *Hagigah* 1:1-2. For an English translation of the Tosefta, see Jacob Neusner, *The Tosefta in English*, 6 vols. in 2 (Peabody, MA: Hendrickson, 2002).

28 I am not following the text as printed but rather the reconstruction of Shlomoh Naeh, "Ha-im em la-Massoret?" [Did the Tannaim Interpret the Script of the Torah Differently from the Authorized Reading?] *Tarbiz* 61 (1992): 413. What is remarkable here, as Naeh takes considerable care to point out, is that there is no discussion of a dispute between the *ketiv* and *qere*, that is, between what is written in the consonantal text and what is read in the Masoretic text. Rather the ambiguity of the consonantal text is the subject of dispute and Rabbi Yehudah believes that the simplest reading—the *qal*—has the added advantage of providing a scriptural support for a piece of Mishnaic legislation. Unless Israel is obligated "to see God," how are we to understand the Mishnah's exemption of the blind? Certainly the blind were able "to appear" before God if that is what the Torah demanded.

29 A quasi-technical term to refer to the "emendations of scribes."

dispute regarding the participation of the gathered throng of pilgrims at the Temple liturgy during the festival existed between the Pharisee/Sages party and the various sects at the close of the Second Temple period (see Sussman and Knohl[30]). It is likely that this dispute was a longstanding one inasmuch as it reflects two of the most fundamental positions regarding Temple worship and its place in the life of the community. It is possible that the Talmudic terminology *re'iyyat panim* [seeing the face (of God)] and *re'iyyat qorban* [appearing with a sacrifice] reflects these two variant conceptualizations.[31]

In a recent article, Israel Knohl has taken this idea of "seeing God" a step further. He begins with a citation of Mishnah *Kelim* (1:8–9):[32]

> The court of the priests is more holy (than the court of the Israelites) for the Israelites cannot enter therein except to fulfill sacrificial obligations such as the laying on of hands, slaughter, and hand waving. The area between the porch and the altar is more holy (than the court of the priests) for no priest who is blemished or has unkempt hair can enter therein.

These boundaries are transgressed during the pilgrimage festivals. First of all, the Temple vessels which normally belong solely to the inner sanctum move out to the courtyard, and the people who generally are restricted to the outer court can now move into the more sacred area in order to view the vessels.

How do we know that the vessels were displayed in this fashion? Here things are a bit more ambiguous and require some development. In Mishnah *Hagigah* (3:8), the question is asked: "How did they enter upon the cleansing of the Temple court? They immersed the vessels that were in the Temple and said to them: 'take care not to touch the table [or lamp] so as to render them unclean.'"[33] This Mishnah is quite unclear about just what is meant. Both the Jerusalem and Babylonian Talmuds, however, provide a plausible context. They declare that it was customary on festival days to bring the table out of the Temple into the courtyard and to display it to the pilgrims.[34] As Knohl observes, this ritual is at variance with scriptural law.

---

30   Yaakov Sussman, "The History of the Halakhah and the Dead Sea Scrolls," *Tarbiz* 59 (1990): 65–68 and Knohl, "Post-Biblical Sectarianism and the Priestly Schools."

31   Naeh, "Ha-im em la-Massoret?" 417.

32   Knohl, "Post-Biblical Sectarianism and the Priestly Schools." Mishnah *Kelim* [Vessels] comes from the sixth order of the Mishnas and concerns the cleanliness of the sacred vessels.

33   Mishnah *Hagigah* [The Festal Offering] comes from the second order of the Mishnah dealing with the Jewish feasts.

34   Jerusalem Talmud *Hagigah* [The Festal Offering] 3.8 (79d); Babylonian Talmud *Hagigah* 26b. For English translations of the two Talmuds, see Jacob Neusner, ed. *The Talmud of the Land*

For, according to Numbers 4:18–20, even the Levitical priests who had greater privileges than the laity to enter sacred space, put their lives at risk when they gazed upon the sacred furniture of the Tabernacle. Knohl's explanation of this problem is suggestive.

> It seems to me that the sages departed from convention and permitted the display of the Temple furniture before the pilgrims so as to allow them to fulfill their obligation "to see the face." Or, to put it another way, the presentation of these holy items before the large assembly created the experience of a public theophany. The Israelites who had longed for the Temple courts and asked "when may I come to see the face of God," went up to the Temple at the pilgrimage feast and gazed upon the vessels of the Temple-service that were brought out of hiding. In this way their spiritual thirst was slaked and they fulfilled the commandment of the Torah that "three times a year each male must see the face of the Sovereign, the LORD, the God of Israel (Exod. 34:23)."[35]

A Most Radical Form of Anthropomorphism

However we might wish to assess the historical problem as to whether the Temple appurtenances were put on display or not, we can certainly conclude that one significant strand of rabbinic literature assumes as much. And in doing so, these rabbinic texts involve themselves in a logical contradiction. On the one hand the furniture itself, owing to the divine power that was infused within them (see Num. 4:18–20), were extraordinarily dangerous. If persons without priestly status were to catch even a glimpse of them they would be struck dead.

As Daniel Schwartz has argued, one midrashic tradition employed this idea to explain how the Israelite armies in Numbers 31:6 were able to defeat the Midianites.[36] When the Midianites attacked Israel, Phinehas displayed the Ark before them and the Midianites, being unworthy of its sight, were instantly slain. A similar understanding is found in the Masoretic text of 1 Samuel 6:19, a text that appears secondary and probably reflects a late scribal attempt to bring the traditions of Numbers 4 into alignment with the care needed when taking the Ark into a public domain.[37] However that might be, the lesson is clear: the Ark is not

---

of Israel, 35 vols. (Chicago: University of Chicago, 1982–1994); Jacob Neusner, *The Talmud of Babylonia: An American Translation*, 75 vols., Brown Judaic Studies (Atlanta: Scholar's Press, 1984–1995).

35 Knohl, "Post-Biblical Sectarianism and the Priestly Schools," 140–41.

36 Daniel Schwartz, "Viewing the Holy Utensils (P. Ox V, 840)," *New Testament Studies* 32 (1986): 155–56.

37 According to 1 Sam. 6:19, when the Philistines had tired of holding the Ark, they sent it back with the indemnity penalty of the notorious "golden hemorrhoids." But when the Ark had made

just a symbol for God; in some very real sense it is so closely linked to God that gazing indiscreetly upon it is an occasion for instant death.

Yet for all their cognizance of the dangers improper viewing of the ark posed for the Israelite community, the rabbis were content at times to ignore them altogether within the context of the religious festival. According to *Yoma*, the Babylonian Talmud's tractate on the Day of Atonement (54a):

> [A] Rabbi Judah contrasted the following passages: "And the ends of the staves were seen" and it is written "but they could not be seen without" (1 Kings 8:8)—how is that possible?—They could be observed, but not actually seen. Thus was it also taught: "And the ends of the staves were seen." One might have assumed that they did not protrude from their place. To teach us [the fact] Scripture says: "And the staves were so long." One might assume that they tore the curtain and showed forth; to teach us [the fact] Scripture says: "They could not be seen without." How then? They pressed forth and protruded as the two breasts of a woman, as it is said: "My beloved is unto me as a bag of myrrh, that lieth betwixt my breasts" (Song 1:13).

> [B] Rabbi Kattina said: Whenever Israel came up to the festival, the curtain would be removed for them and the cherubim were shown to them, whose bodies were intertwined with one another, and they would be thus addressed: Look! You are beloved before God as the love between man and woman.

This remarkable text engages in the most radical form of anthropomorphism. In the first unit [A] the Ark of the Covenant is imagined as the veritable body of God that beckons the Israelite forward through the power of erotic attraction. Only the veil prevents a full frontal view of a radically feminized form of the deity. Having quickened these carnal desires, the veil is thrown aside [B] so that the pilgrim might behold his God, here described not as an invisible being who sits upon the Ark ("enthroned above the cherubim" in biblical parlance) but rather as one of the cherubim themselves. God is, for the purposes of this text, this particular golden artifact. There is no danger in viewing the Godhead here; quite the contrary, this unveiling of the Godhead seems to be the central rite of the pilgrimage festival itself.

---

its way back to Beth-shemesh the local townsmen, according to the Masoretic text, made the mistake of gazing upon it. "[The Lord] struck at the men of Beth-shemesh," the text explains, "because they looked into the Ark of the Lord; He struck down seventy men among the people [and] fifty thousand men."

It is tempting to read this in parallel with a tradition found in the *Mekilta of Rabbi Ishmael*.[38] In view of the command (Exod. 20:23) not to make "gods of silver or gods of gold" to stand "beside the LORD," the *Mekilta* moves in a surprising direction. One might expect that the normal invective against idols would be standard here. And indeed the *Mekilta* begins its discussion of this verse with traditions precisely of this sort. But at the conclusion of its rather lengthy discussion of this verse, the *Mekilta* abruptly turns in another, quite surprising, direction.

The reference to "gods of silver and gods of gold" is no longer understood in terms of idolatrous images pure and simple. It now refers to aberrant means of producing the cherubim. Lest one presume to fashion them out of silver in place of gold, the Torah declares: "don't make beside me gods of silver." Moreover, should one entertain the idea of making four cherubim instead of two then he would commit the sin of making "gods of gold." The turn taken by the *Mekilta* regarding the last phrase of the verse is most striking.

> "[Gods of gold] do not make for yourselves." This is written so that you would not think that because the Torah has given permission to make them for the Temple so I will make them for the synagogues and houses of study. Accordingly, the Torah teaches: "do not make [these gods of gold] for yourselves."[39]

Now admittedly in my translation, I have reconstructed in brackets the object of the verb "to make" in accord with the only possible antecedent provided by the biblical text—*elohe zahav*. One could, however, read the text as Rashi[40] does and supply a different object—the cherubim— so that there is no mistaking what is intended. I sincerely doubt whether the author of the unit in the *Mekilta* would reprove Rashi for this explanatory gloss. For certainly *"elohe zahav"* does not mean "God conceived of as a piece of gold"; that would be idolatry pure and simple. But it is striking, just the same, that the *Mekilta* is not as worried as Rashi seems to be about the ambiguity of the antecedent.

Indeed this whole unit of the *Mekilta* only works if we presume that the line between "a portion of God's being represented in golden form" and a "god of gold" is a rather fine one.[41] I see no reason why one could not gloss the turn taken by the *Mekilta* this way: "a golden object that partakes of the divine essence do not

---

38   A commentary on the book of Exodus. See *Mekhilta de-Rabbi Ishamel*, eds. Hayim S. Horowitz and Israel A. Rabin (Frankfurt: J. Kaufmann, 1931), 241.

39   *Mekilta* on Exod. 20:23.

40   The French rabbi and biblical interpreter (d. 1105). For the text and a translation see Abraham M. Silbermann, *Chumash with Rashi's Commentary* (New York: Feldheim, 1934), 106a.

41   It offers an intriguing parallel, perhaps, to Rabbi Judah Ha-Levi's somewhat apologetic reading of the sin of the golden calf (*The Kuzari* 1:92). Israel, he argued, was expecting Moses to bring down some sort of visible token toward which they could "direct their gaze during their devotions." Israel's problem, on this view, was not so much the act of venerating a material thing

make for yourselves [that is, to put in your synagogues]." The usage here is a prosaic adaptation of the more poetic language of the Sabbath Songs that did not shrink from describing the supernal Temple as *elohim hayyim* ("the living God").

This text comes tantalizingly close to making explicit what was implied by the Babylonian Talmud's *Yoma* (54a). The cherubim that have been placed in the Holy of Holies are, in some real sense, representations of God's true presence in the Temple. The historian of religion will wish to ask how different this is from the Mesopotamian practice of marking the divinity of temple furniture with the *dingir*-sign? Or, for that matter, from the words of the psalmist who exclaimed when gazing upon the architecture of Jerusalem: "This is God!" (Ps. 48:14).

Carrying the Table of the Presence

Perhaps most striking of all the examples is a tradition found in the Midrash *Mishle*, on the Book of Proverbs. Here the Israelite is defined as the individual who gazes upon the face of God.

> The Queen of Sheba brought circumcised and uncircumcised persons before Solomon. They were of similar appearance, height, and dress. She said to him, "Distinguish for me the circumcised from the uncircumcised." Immediately Solomon gestured to the High Priest and he opened the Ark of the Covenant. Those who were circumcised bent over half-way but no more so that their faces might be filled with the radiance of the *Shekinah*. The uncircumcised promptly fell to the ground upon their faces. Solomon said to her, the former ones are the circumcised and the latter are the uncircumcised. She said how do you know this? He said to her, "Is it not written about Balaam, 'he who gazes upon the sight of the Almighty, [fallen (partly over) but with eyes unveiled]?' (Num. 24:4). Had he fallen completely to the ground, he would not have seen anything."[42]

How then are we to understand this radical disjuncture between a highly-charged Ark of the Covenant that spells immediate death for anyone who would cast eyes upon it and the definition of an Israelite as one who can gaze directly at its center? Certainly Knohl's suggestion is appropriate here—namely, that during the pilgrimages, all Israel is temporarily raised to the status of priest so that they can behold the sacred furniture. Evidently, however, not all Second Temple circles were of one mind on this matter. As Knohl observes, Talmudic tradition has it that

---

as it was attributing "divine power to a creation of their own." In Judah Ha-Levi, *The Kuzari*, ed. Avraham Yaakov Finkel (Scranton, PA: Yeshivath Beth Moshe, 2000).

42   Burton L. Visotzky, ed. *Midrash Mishle: With Variant Readings and Commentary* (New York: Jewish Theological Seminary, 1989), 6.

the Sadducees and Boethusians opposed the display of Temple furniture before the laity. Confirmation of the historical accuracy of a charge such as this can be found in the Temple Scroll from Qumran that emphatically rules out the ritual act of carrying the Table of Presence from its home within the Temple-building itself.[43]

Additional confirmation of the practice of displaying the furniture can be gathered from a puzzling piece of tradition found in *Papyrus Oxyrhynchus 840*. The text reads,

> And having taken them he brought them into the place of puri-
> fication and was walking in the Temple. And having approached,
> a certain Pharisee, a chief priest, whose name was Levi, joined
> them and said to the Savior: Who gave you permission to enter
> this place of purification and to see these holy vessels, when you
> have not washed yourself, nor have your disciples surely bathed
> their feet? But you, in a defiled state, have entered this Temple,
> which is a pure place that no one enters nor dares to view these
> holy vessels without having first washed themselves and changed
> their clothes.
>
> And immediately the Savior stopped, and standing with his
> disciples answered: Are you then pure in your present state here
> in the Temple? And he replied to him: I am pure, for I have
> washed myself in the pool of David, and having descended by
> one staircase I came up by another; and I have put on white and
> pure clothes, and only then did I come and lay eyes on these
> holy vessels. The Savior answered him saying: Woe unto you, O
> blind one.[44]

---

43 Within a list of the Temple appurtenances we read: "[... the altar of] incense; but the table ... *shall not depart from the Temple*. And its bowls shall be of pure gold." *11QTemple Scroll* [11Q19], 3:10–12. Emphasis added.

44 This intriguing document is a fragment of a purported "gospel" that details a conversation between Jesus and a chief priest in the Temple. For the text and translation, see François Bovon, "Fragment Oxyrhynchus 840, Fragment of a Lost Gospel, Witness of an Early Christian Controversy over Purity," *Journal of Biblical Literature* 119 (2000): 705–728. Bovon makes a very strong case that the text should not be read as a window into the world of first century Palestine and hence another piece of information relevant to the quest for the historical Jesus. All of the pieces of this text fit better within the realm of the emerging second or third-century Church. Though I would agree, in the main, with his assessment that every detail in the text that looks Jewish is better understood in the framework of early Christianity, there is one piece of data which just does not work: the presumption that gazing on the sanctuary vessels is a holy act (at 720). There is simply no Christian liturgical counterpart that even remotely parallels it. In private conversation, Bovon confirmed that the parallels he adduced are not quite satisfactory.

As Schwartz has argued, the key point in this text is the claim that only persons of sufficient purity should be allowed to enter the Temple precincts to view the sacred vessels. Like Knohl, Schwartz is inclined to see this argument as to who may view the vessels and under what sort of conditions as rooted in an inner-Jewish dispute over the display of the Temple vessels to the laity.

"On this background," Schwartz concludes, "it is not unreasonable to assume that [the] practice associated with festive celebrations in the Temple, the exhibition of Temple utensils before the crowds of pilgrims, should be understood in [this] way: it was an attempt [by the Pharisees] to let the public share in what priests had claimed as their own prerogatives."[45] The fact that Jesus desires to see the Temple vessels in this text leads Schwartz to the conclusion that we have before us "another rare instance of Jesus' participation in Pharisaic criticism of the same overemphasis on the part of the priests."[46]

Pompey's Seeing of the Temple Utensils

But from the perspective that I have adopted in this essay, the most interesting part of Schwartz' article derives from his discussion of Josephus. For in Josephus we have a writer who claims a very good priestly pedigree. Schwartz observes that, when writing about the entrance of Pompey into the Temple in 63 B.C., Josephus stresses that Pompey was able to glimpse the Temple utensils.

> [I]ndeed, he states that "of all the calamities of that time none so deeply affected the nation as the exposure to alien eyes of the holy place, hitherto screened from view" (*Wars of the Jews*, Bk. 1, Chap. 7, 6, 152). Here, indeed, he is speaking of the sanctuary or the Holy of Holies; nevertheless, the emphasis on sight rather than entry is remarkable. This point is further developed with specific reference to the holy utensils, in the parallel account in *Antiquities of the Jews* (Bk. 14, Chap. 4, 4, 71–72) (although this development is counterbalanced by some new compliments for Pompey): "And not light was the sin committed against the sanctuary, which before that time had never been entered or seen. For Pompey and not a few of his men went into it and saw what it was unlawful for any but the High Priests to see. But though the golden table was there and the sacred lampstand and the libation vessels."[47]

Nor indeed is this the only occurrence of this remarkable point of emphasis. In some half-dozen examples one can point to a similar interest in gazing upon

---

45   Schwartz, "Viewing the Holy Utensils," 156.
46   Schwartz, "Viewing the Holy Utensils," 157.
47   Schwartz, "Viewing the Holy Utensils," 154.

the Temple and its furniture as over against an interest in physical entry or even touch.

The emphasis that Josephus puts on "seeing" can best be set in perspective through the evidence of Jewish coinage from the early second century, A.D. In a recent article on the typology reflected in coins hailing from the revolt of Bar Kokhba, Dan Barag writes:

> In a series of large and important silver coins, Bar Kokhba stamped the image of a Temple-façade along with the words, "Jerusalem" or "Shimon." On the reverse side he stamped an image of a lulav and etrog along with the words, "Year one of the redemption of Israel." ... The Temple that appears on these coins ... has four pillars. In the middle of the façade is an object whose identity remains a riddle. It is obvious that this object or symbol possessed tremendous significance, for in contemporary coins of this period we frequently find images of the Temple in whose center is stationed a god or goddess.[48]

Indeed, we can be even a bit more emphatic here. The god or goddess so depicted is the patron of the Temple in question and as such was represented in those temples by his or her statue. As Martin Price and Bluma Trell remark, the statue of the god was normally out of view of the worshipers and so the coins do not reflect what one would have seen if one went to the respective cities and compared the image on the face of the coin to the Temple façade itself.

Indeed the artist often has to widen "the space between the central columns ... to accommodate the image which usually identifies the shrine with no possible ambiguity."[49] So, one purpose of bringing the statue forward was to signify just whose town this coin hailed from and under which divine auspices it drew its authority. But equally important, Price and Trell observe, is the manner by which this identification of god and temple takes place—the presentation of the god at the door of the Temple "would suggest the age old custom of [an] epiphany, a god appearing in person before his worshipers."[50]

Barag concludes that the symbolism of the Bar-Kokhba coins is unambiguous: the Table between the two columns on the front side of the coin "symbolizes the renewal of the liturgy of regular Temple-service: 'You shall set the bread of presence upon the Table before me on a regular basis' (Exod. 25:30; Lev. 24:8) and

---

48 Dan Barag, "The Table of the Bread of Presence and the Façade of the Temple upon the Coins of the Bar Kokhba War," *Qadmoniot* 20 (1987): 22. The lulav, the frond of a date palm tree, and the etron, a citron fruit, are part of the Jewish ritual for the feast of Sukkot.

49 Martin Price and Bluma Trell, *Coins and their Cities: Architecture on the Ancient Coins of Greece, Rome, and Palestine* (Detroit: Wayne State University, 1977), 19.

50 Price and Trell, *Coins and their Cities*, 19.

the lulav and etrog on the reverse side of the coin represent the aspiration to renew the pilgrimage festivals, and in particular, that of Sukkot."[51]

In a subsequent exchange of letters, Asher Grossberg mentions the Talmudic interpretations of the Mishnah in *Hagigah* 3:1, as well as the supporting evidence of the *Papyrus Oxyrhynchus 840*.[52] In Grossberg's opinion, the two sides of the coins represent a single reality. The Table was paired with the lulav and ethrog because the Table was that piece of Tabernacle furniture that was displayed before pilgrims during the feast of Sukkot. These coins denote a longing to fulfill the commandment of seeing the presence of God during Sukkot.

In Barag's opinion, however, the Talmudic evidence that Grossberg cites (a set of texts that overlap with those cited by Knohl) is purely aggadic or homiletic in character and bears no historical or legal weight. Although Barag correctly notes that the Mishnah in *Hagigah* is by no means a clear reference to the practice of showing the Table to pilgrims (indeed Chanoch Albeck saw the text in a much more pedestrian fashion: the warnings were issued solely to priests attending to the pieces of furniture and had nothing to do with the festivals proper), it is hard to deny the fact that the coins have placed the Table exactly where statues of the god would go in nearly all of the parallel coins found in pagan contexts.[53]

This reading is suggested further by the combination of evidence from *Papyrus Oxyrhynchus 840*, the Temple Scroll, as well as more circumstantial evidence such as the Samaritan version of Exodus 23:17, the importance the Septuagint puts on seeing the Tabernacle as a means of seeing God, and the witness of Josephus to the importance of seeing the appurtenances of the Temple.

Though Josephus does not, as Barag observes, mention the ritual of displaying the furniture on festivals, he does remark that the curtains of the Tabernacle were constructed in such a way that they could be pulled back to permit an unobstructed view. Since the Torah gives no hint of such a thing, where would

---

51   Barag, "The Table of the Bread of Presence," 24.

52   See Grossberg's response to Barag's article in *Qadmoniot* 21 (1988): 81–82.

53   It is worth noting as well that Josephus, in his description of the Tabernacle, remarks that the veils could be pulled aside on festivals so that they would not obstruct the view. As the biblical text itself offers no reason to suggest such things, many historians have cited this passage as an indication that viewing the Temple furniture was a well-known custom of the Second Temple period. The text in question (*Antiquities of the Jews*, Bk. 3, Chap. 6, 124–25, 127–128) reads: "The Tabernacle was covered with curtains woven of fine linen, in which the hues of purple and blue and crimson were blended. Of these the first (veil—*paroket*) measured ten cubits either way and was spread over the pillars which divided the Temple and screened off the sanctuary; this it was which rendered the latter invisible to the eyes of any. ... A second (veil—*masak*), corresponding to the first in dimensions, texture and hue, enveloped the five pillars that stood at the entrance, supported by rings at the corner of each pillar, it hung from the top to the middle of the pillar; the rest of the space was left as a passage for the priests entering beneath it. Above this was another covering of linen, of the same dimensions, which was drawn by cords to either side, the rings serving alike for curtain and cord, so that it could either be outspread or rolled together and stowed into a corner, in order *that it should not intercept the view* above all on the great days." Emphasis added.

Josephus have derived such a detail if not from some sort of contemporary practice? However we might sort out the historicity of the Talmudic sources about the display of Tabernacle furniture—it would be fair to say that the image of the Table of Presence at the door of the Temple indicates for the person who struck this coin that this piece of furniture bore some resemblance to the identity of the God who dwelled therein. If we set this coin next to the rabbinic evidence we can at least say that a goodly number of rabbinic materials imagine that the furniture shares enough of the divine presence that seeing it constitutes a fulfillment of the command, "to see the face of God."

The Incarnation and the Temple of Christ's Body

Scholars have long been aware that the New Testament and early Christianity thought of the person of Jesus Christ and the community that he founded in terms of the Temple. As to the former, no text could be clearer than the Gospel of John. Early in his ministry when Jesus is asked for a sign to authorize his teaching and actions he declares: "Destroy this Temple and in three days I will raise it up." His interlocutors puzzle over this declaration and wonder how a building that has been under constructions for some forty-six years could be quickly reestablished. At this point the narrator intervenes with an important clarification: "But Jesus was speaking of the Temple of his body. After he was raised from the dead, his disciples remembered that he had said this; and they believed the Scriptures and the word that Jesus had spoken" (John 2:21-22).[54]

The early New Testament community was viewed as an eschatological Temple that represents the perduring body of Christ after his resurrection and ascension. This can be seen in Paul's declaration, "Do you not know that you are God's Temple and that God's Spirit dwells in you? If anyone destroys God's Temple, God will destroy that person. For God's Temple is holy, and you are that Temple" (1 Cor. 3:16-17).[55]

But my purpose is not to survey the literature about how the Temple serves as a metaphor for Jesus' person or of the community he founded. Rather, I would like to limit myself to how the metaphor of the Temple is associated with the notion of sight—such that looking at the physical body of Jesus becomes tantamount

---

54 For a recent survey of the issue, see Alan R. Kerr, *The Temple of Jesus' Body: The Temple Theme in the Gospel of John*, Journal for the Study of the New Testament Supplement Series 220 (Sheffield: Sheffield Academic, 2002). Still very useful is the magisterial survey of Yves Congar, *The Mystery of the Temple* (London: Burns and Oates, 1962).

55 See also 2 Cor. 6:16; Eph. 2:20–22; Heb. 13:15–16; 1 Pet. 2:5; 4:17; and Rev. 3:12; 11:1–2. The literature on this matter is considerable. For a brief review see, Richard Bauckham, "James and the Gentiles (Acts 15:13–21)," in *History, Literature, and Society in the Book of Acts*, ed. Ben Witherington III (Cambridge: Cambridge University, 1996), 165–168. An older survey of the problem can be found in Bertil E. Gärtner, *The Temple and the Community in Qumran and the New Testament: A Comparative Study in the Temple Symbolism of the Qumran Texts and the New Testament* (Cambridge: Cambridge University, 1965).

to beholding the very person of God. And for these purposes there is no better text than John 1:14: "And the Word became flesh and dwelt among us and we saw his glory, the glory as of the Father's only Son, full of grace and truth."

The key clause in establishing that this text speaks to the matter of the Temple is the phrase, "he dwelt among us." The Greek verb *skēnoō* is clearly borrowed from the story of the Tabernacle in Exodus and served to translate the Hebrew word *shakan/mishkan*. As Raymond Brown remarks, "we are being told that the flesh of Jesus Christ is the new localization of God's presence on earth, and that Jesus is the replacement of the ancient Tabernacle."[56] This idea dovetails nicely with another major feature of this Gospel, namely, that Jesus is "the replacement of the Temple (2:19–22)," which, as Brown adds, is simply "a variation of the same theme."

Brown also notes the very important connection between the "tenting" of the Word and its becoming visible to the naked eye. "In the Old Testament," he observes, "the *glory* of God (Hebrew: *kabod*; Greek: *doxa*) implies a visible and powerful manifestation of God to men." Then, having reviewed several biblical texts that describe the appearance of God at the site of the Temple, he concludes: "It is quite appropriate that, after the description of how the Word set up a Tabernacle among men in the flesh of Jesus, the prologue should mention that his *glory* became visible."[57]

Brown's observation, however, was made solely on the basis of the Exodus narrative and as such grounds the theology of the prologue in a singular act—the moment when the glory of the LORD filled the Tabernacle on the day of its completion. What we have shown in this article is that this momentous theophany was routinized in the daily life of the cult. It was not only the Israelites of Moses' day who saw God as he entered his newly dedicated Tabernacle; all Israelites could see God as they ascended to the Temple to participate in the rite of the furniture.[58] What the post-biblical Jewish materials we have examined provide is a more phenomenological, or even cultic, background against which we can set John's own theology of a visible and Tabernacle-like presence of the *Logos*.[59]

---

56 Raymond E. Brown, *The Gospel according to John I–XII*, Anchor Bible 29 (Garden City, NY: Doubleday, 1966), 33. Three recent works have treated this theme at great length, Craig A. Evans, *Word and Glory: On the Exegetical Background of John's Prologue*, Journal for the Study of the New Testament Supplement Series 89 (Sheffield: Sheffield Academic, 1993), 77–113; Kerr, *The Temple of Jesus' Body*; and Craig R. Koester, *The Dwelling of God: The Tabernacle in the Old Testament, Intertestamental Jewish Literature, and the New Testament*, Catholic Biblical Quarterly Monograph Series 22 (Washington, DC: Catholic Biblical Association, 1989), 100–115.

57 Brown, *Gospel according to John I–XII*, 34.

58 No study of the prologue to John's Gospel and Jewish Tabernacle/Temple traditions has evidenced any knowledge of the role the Temple furniture played in Jewish sources. Compare, for example, the recent and exhaustive survey of Koester, *The Dwelling of God*, 100–115.

59 I should emphasize that the Jewish background I have proposed here does not by any means exhaust the levels of meaning that are inscribed to the faculty of "sight" in John's prologue. As Rudolph Bultmann articulated, the notion of sight in John has at least three discrete meanings (*The Gospel of John: A Commentary* [Philadelphia: Westminster, 1971], 69, n. 2): "1. That of the

As is well known, the theme of God being visible to the eye was extremely important to Philo. One of his favorite definitions of the Jewish people is that of a people who have the unique gift of being able to see God.[60] So salient was this definition for Philo, that Gerhard Delling concludes: "[W]hoever says 'Israel' says 'seeing God.' The etymology of the name Israel opens the possibility for Philo to express that which is specific of the Jewish religion in a siglum that points to the special relationship between the one God and the Jewish people. For him it attests to the uniqueness of the revelation of God and with it the uniqueness of knowing, of seeing God, that it accords."[61]

What is perhaps worthy of further study is how Philo relates this ability to see God to the revelation of God within the Temple. One of Philo's proof texts for this concept derives from Exodus 24:11, a text in which the Israelites who have ascended the heights of Mount Sinai are said to see God amid their festal meal.[62] But more to our point is how Philo relates the *Logos* to the Tabernacle structure.

> What is the meaning of the words, "Thou shalt set apart the veil between the Holy of Holies" (Exod. 26:33b)? I have said that the simple holy (parts of the Tabernacle) are classified with the sense-perceptible heaven, whereas the inner (parts), which are called the Holy of Holies (are classified) with the intelligible

---

perception of earthly things and happenings accessible to all men (1:38, 47; 9:8, etc); 2. of the perception of supernatural things and events accessible only to a limited number of men (1:32, 33, 34; 20:12, 14, etc.). Whereas in both these cases what is referred to is perception with one's physical eyes, 'seeing' is used, 3. of the perception of matters not visible to the organs of sight. The object of such 'seeing' is the revelation-event, or alternatively the person of Jesus the Revealer." Bultmann, himself, sees John 1:14 as falling under the third category as the perception of Jesus as "God" cannot originate in the physical object of sight itself but must be the subject of a specific moment of revelation. Although this understanding should not be rejected, I would argue that at the same time John compares the presence of God to that of a Temple which was visible to the naked eye. I do not think the inner contradiction would have bothered John just as it does not bother St. Athanasius in the text I will discuss below.

60   See Gerhard Delling, "The 'One who Sees God' in Philo," in *Nourished with Peace: Studies in Hellenistic Judaism in Memory of Samuel Sandmel* (Chico, CA: Scholars Press, 1984), 27–41. Also see the comprehensive survey of this problem in Ellen Birnbaum, *The Place of Judaism in Philo's Thought: Israel, Jews, and Proselytes* (Atlanta, GA: Scholars Press, 1996). Especially useful is Chapter Two, "'Israel' and the Vision of God" and chapter three, "'Israel' and the Ones who Can See."

61   Delling, "The 'One who Sees God,'" 41.

62   The text in question (*On the Confusion of Tongues*, 56) reads: "For we are the 'race of the Chosen ones of that Israel,' who sees God, 'and there is none amongst us of discordant voice' (Exod. 24:11), that so the whole world, which is the instrument of the All, may be filled with the sweet melody of its undiscording harmonies." The notion of "seeing God" only works in light of the Masoretic Text; the verb in the Septuagint is a passive. Perhaps Philo has in mind both verses 10 and 11, for in verse 10 the Septuagint declares that the elders could see *the spot wherein God dwells*, that is, they could contemplate the Temple and its furniture but not God himself. Text in *The Works of Philo: Complete and Unabridged in One Volume* (Peabody, MA: Hendrickson, 1993), 234–252.

world. *The incorporeal world is set off and separated from the visible one by the mediating Logos as by a veil.* But may it not be that this *Logos* is the tetrad, through which the corporeal solid comes into being? For this is classified with the invisible intelligible things while the other (part of the Tabernacle) is divided into three and is connected with sense-perceptible things, so that there is between them something (at once invisible and visible of substance).[63]

This remarkable text notes that the Tabernacle neatly divides what is perceptible to the senses (the *three* pieces of furniture that sit in the "holy") from what is beyond all vision (that is, the being of God himself who resides in the Holy of Holies). Upon four pillars (the tetrad) rests a veil that represents the *Logos* and as such the *Logos* mediates in visible form what remains invisible to the naked eye. This veil would have been seen every day by the priests appointed to tend the menorah and the incense altar. Can we extrapolate from this text that Philo's definition of Israel as a nation that can see God includes the notion that through the cult the *Logos* has become a mediator in visual form of the Holy One of Israel who is beyond all human knowledge?[64]

The Appearance of God in the Flesh

The Johannine theme that God became visible in the flesh of Jesus had an extraordinary influence in early Christianity. For St. Irenaeus, writing in about 180, the primary reason for God becoming man was that the world could see him.[65] To see God was to be drawn into the divine realm.

Tertullian (d. 222) reaches the same destination but via a slightly different path.[66] He was bothered by the fact that God regularly makes himself visible to Israel in the Old Testament yet says at the same time that anyone who gazes upon his face will die (Exod. 33:20). How can these be reconciled? For Tertullian, the Gospel of John provides the key; for while it affirms that no human being has seen the Father (John 1:18), it concedes that human beings can see the Word (1:14). When one reads, then, in the Old Testament of appearances of God to various holy individuals, these are to be understood as nothing other than appearances of the

---

63   Philo, *Questions and Answers on Exodus*, 2:94. Emphasis added. Text in *Philo, Supplement 2: Questions and Answers on Exodus*, ed. Ralph Marcus, The Loeb Classical Library (Cambridge, MA: Harvard University, 1953).

64   Compare the lengthy treatment of the concept in Jonathan Z. Smith's essay, "The Prayer of Joseph," in his *Map is Not Territory: Studies in the History of Religons* (Chicago: University of Chicago, 1978), 37–39.

65   Irenaeus, *Against the Heresis*, Bk. 4, Chap. 20. Text in *The Anti-Nicene Fathers*, vol. 1, eds. Alexander Roberts and James Donaldson (Peabody, MA: Hendrickson, 2004).

66   Tertullian, *Against Praxeas*, Chaps. 14–16. Text in *The Anti-Nicene Fathers*, vol. 3, eds. Alexander Roberts and James Donaldson (Peabody, MA: Hendrickson, 2004).

Word of God prior to his full incarnation. As with Irenaeus, Tertullian sees the purpose of the incarnation as to make God visible to human eyes.

Perhaps even more emphatic about this theme was St. Gregory of Nyssa (d. 395). He writes:

> If everyone had the ability to come, as Moses did, inside the cloud, where Moses saw what may not be seen; or to be raised above three heavens as Paul was and to be instructed in Paradise about ineffable things that lie above reason; or to be taken up in fire to the ethereal region, as zealous Elijah was; and not be weighed down by the body's baggage, or to see on the throne of glory, as Ezekiel and Isaiah did; the one who is raised above the cherubim and glorified by the Seraphim—then surely if all were like this, there would be no need for the appearance of our God in flesh.[67]

Why then did Jesus become flesh according to John 1:14? For Gregory the answer resides in what Jewish thought would call *hiddardarut ha-olam* ("the gradual decline of the world"). Because of the overall weakness of the human race at this time, no one could any longer see as Moses saw. Therefore, like a physician matching his cure to the infirmity of the patient, God took dramatic measures and became visible in human flesh.

There is one more twist in the story though that is worth attending to. If Jesus inhabits flesh the way God will inhabit the Temple, just how might we understand the relationship of the Godhead to the building in which it rests. Is the relationship an intrinsic one? By this I mean: is the entire body of Jesus, in all its carnality, divinized by this indwelling? Or to use the Jewish metaphors we have followed: Is the body of Jesus like the Temple walls in the Sabbath Songs, that is, so infused with the divine energies that they come to life and are called *elohim hayyim* ("*the living God*" or "*living divine beings*") during moments of angelic praise? Or is it like the Table of Presence presented before the pilgrims in order to fulfill their obligation to see God; or, like the veil that separates the visible portions of the Temple from the invisible? All of these Jewish metaphors bespeak an intrinsic relation in as much as it is not possible to divide or separate fully the being of God from the objects he inhabits.

The other option is to consider the relationship of the Word to Jesus as more extrinsic in nature. The carnal flesh of Jesus, on this view, is a dispensable vehicle through which the divine medicine has been administered; as such, it can and

---

67   *To Theophilus, Against the Apollinarians.* Text in Friedrich Müller, ed., *Gregorii Nysseni Opera Dogmatica Minora, Pars 1* [Gregory of Nyssa, Minor Dogmatic Works, Part 1] (Leiden: E.J. Brill, 1958), 123–24. The translation here is courtesy of my colleague, Brian Daley, who has granted me permission to use it.

indeed must be ignored by spiritual adepts in order to attend to true source of divinity, namely, the *Logos* that resides within. This issue, of course, is not an idle matter; the proper way of rendering John 1:14 became one of the major forks in the road for early Christianity.[68]

For St. Athanasius, writing in the fourth century, there was only one answer to that question: the flesh of Jesus *participates* in the divinity of the indwelling *Logos*. In order to drive home this point, Christian thought would declare that what was predicated of the fleshly-person of Christ could also be predicated of God as well as the reverse (the so-called "communication of properties" or *communicatio idiomatum*).

The manner by which Athanasius arrives at this conclusion depends on a construal of the biblical Temple as a structure that *physically* participates in the life of the God who inhabits it. Athanasius is concerned about the readiness of the Arians "to divide" the person of Christ into two, his human side and his divine side. To do so, Athanasius argues, would be idolatrous because when Christians prostrate themselves before Jesus they do so before the whole person, flesh and body.

If the two are divisible then the act of venerating the person Jesus results in the worship of a creature. "And we do not worship a creature," Athanasius declares. "And neither do we divide the body from the Word and worship it by itself; nor when we wish to worship the Word do we set him far apart from the flesh, but knowing ... that 'the Word was made flesh' (John 1:14) we recognize him as God also, after having come in the flesh."

How does Athanasius justify his argument from the standpoint of sacred Scripture? By attending to the practice of the Jewish pilgrimage feasts.

> But we should like your piety to ask [the Arians] this question.
> When Israel was ordered to go up to Jerusalem to worship at

---

68   On the one side of the fence was the docetic option that claimed that the Word did not so much become flesh as it was made manifest in the flesh. For the problem of rendering the Greek, see Georg Richter, "Die Fleischwerdung des Logos im Johannesevangelium" [The Incarnation of the *Logos* in the Gospel of John] *Novum Testamentum* 13 (1971): 81–126 and 14 (1972): 257–76. He argues that John 1:14 declares that the Word truly became flesh. See also the response of K. Berger, "Zu 'das Wort ward Fleisch' Joh. 1:14a" ["The Word became Flesh"] *Novum Testamentum* 16 (1974): 161–66. For Berger, the meaning of the Greek is the opposite of what Richter maintains: "Erscheinen in einer Gestalt, ohne damit diese zu 'werden'" ["to appear in a form without becoming it"]. He compares this extrinsic connection of *Logos* to flesh to the way God inhabits a Temple (at 164): "Das Erscheinen des Christus im Fleisch und das Wohnen unter/in der Gemeinde bedeutet also nicht, dass der Kyrios mit diesen Menschen identisch wird, sondern dass er in ihnen als in einem heiligen Tempel wohnt (so wie man es sonst vom Pneuma sagt)." ["The appearance of Christ in the flesh and the dwelling in the community does not mean that the Lord becomes identical with these human beings but that he dwells among them as if in a Temple (just as one speaks of the Spirit)"] This precise question, whether God appeared in the flesh or became that very flesh, was the subject of enormous disagreement in the fourth and fifth-century christological controversies.

the Temple of the Lord, where the Ark was, "and above it the cherubim of glory overshadowing the mercy-seat" (Heb. 9:5), did they do well or not? If they were in error, how is it that those who despised this law became liable for punishment? For it is written that "if a man make light of this command and not go up, he shall perish from among his people" (Num. 9:13). But if they were correct in this practice and so proved themselves well-pleasing to God, then are not the Arians abominable and the most shameful of any heresy, even many times more worthy of destruction?

For they approve the former people [the Jews] for the honor paid by them to the Temple, but they will not worship the Lord who is in the flesh as a God indwelling a temple ... And [the Jews] did not, when they saw the Temple of stones, suppose that the Lord who spoke in the Temple was a creature; nor did they set the Temple at nought and retire far off to worship. But they came to it according to the Law, and worshipped the God who uttered his oracles from the Temple. Since this was so, how can it be other than right to worship the body of the Lord, all-holy and all-reverend as it is, announced by the Holy Spirit and made the vestment of the Word. ... Therefore, he that dishonors the Temple dishonors the Lord in the Temple; and he that separates the Word from the body sets at nought the grace given to us in him.[69]

Athanasius' point is crystal clear. Just as the Jews had complete justification in prostrating themselves before a building of stone and not dividing the God from the house in which he dwelt—for though they knew God was not limited to the stones nor the furniture, at the same time they did not use that limitation as license for not going up to Jerusalem—so the Christian has complete justification in prostrating himself before Jesus and not dividing the indwelling God from the flesh that contains him.

Given the importance of Athanasius in Church history one might have expected that this "Temple-theology" would have had a long afterlife itself. But in fact it ends with Athanasius himself. This is because of what happens within the school of Antiochene Christianity. There, already with the figure of Theodore of

---

69 *To Adelphius, Against the Arians*, Letter 60: 7–8. Text in *Patrologiae Cursus Completus. Series Graeca*, ed. J. P. Migne (Paris: Garnier and J. P. Migne, 1857–1891), 26, 1080–1082. Hereafter abbreviated *PG*. English translation in *A Select Library of Nicene and Post-Nicene Fathers of the Christian Church*, vol. 4, eds. Philip Schaff and Henry Wace (Grand Rapids, MI: Eerdmans, 1998), 575.

Mopsuestia, it is propounded that God abandons Jesus at his passion and lets the man suffer on his own.

Though the textual justification for the position of Theodore is grounded in a textually problematic verse from Hebrews (Heb. 2:9; for more on this, see note 71 below), the larger thematic argument comes from the metaphor of a Temple. For though God can indwell the Temple such that his presence infuses even the furniture and masonry, he can also depart from the Temple and go into exile.[70] Pursuing this model to its logical end, Theodore, and later, most notoriously Nestorius (early fifth century), argued that the indwelling of God in Jesus' body like a Temple was a wholly extrinsic affair. In some parts of the Gospel story, they argued, we see only the weak human body that Jesus inhabits, in others the deity bursts on to the scene; at the crucifixion, God literally departs from his Temple and leaves the man Jesus to die on his own.[71] Hence, to be consistent with the New Testament evidence, Theodore declared, we must be able to divide the human figure from the divine being who indwells him.

In the aftermath of the Nestorian controversy we see the rejection of the Temple metaphor as a means of understanding the incarnation[72] and its transferral

---

70   See the discussion of Theodore in his commentary on the Nicene Creed (*Homily* 6, 6). Throughout this text he distinguishes what happened to the man Jesus—here described as the material framework of the Temple—in contrast to God who resided within him, here understood as comparable to the glory of the LORD that sits atop the Ark and is free to come and go as it pleases. "It is not divine nature that received death, but it is clear that it was that man who was assumed as a temple to God the Word which was dissolved and then raised by the one who had assumed it. And after the crucifixion it was not divine nature that was raised but the temple which was assumed, which rose from the dead, ascended to heaven, and sat at the right hand of God; nor is it to divine nature—the cause of everything—that it was given that every one should worship it and every knee should bow, but worship was granted to the form of a servant which did not in its nature possess (the right to be worshipped). While all these things are clearly and obviously said of human nature, he referred them successively to divine nature so that his sentence might be strengthened and be acceptable to hearers. Indeed, since it is above human nature that it should be worshipped by all, it is with justice that all this has been said as of one, so that the belief in a close union between the natures might be strengthened, because he clearly showed that the one who was assumed did not receive all this great honor except from the divine nature which assumed him and dwelt in him." For photographs of the Syriac original see Raymond Tonneau, *Les homélis catéchétiques de Théodore de Mopsueste* [The Catechetical Homilies of Theodore of Mopsuestia] (Vatican City: Biblioteca Apostoloica Vaticana, 1949), 140–143.

71   Theodore grounded this remarkable assertion in a textual variant of Heb. 2:9. "And in order to teach us why he suffered and became 'a little lower [than the angels],' he said: '*Apart from God* [in place of, 'by the grace of God'] he tasted death for every man.' In this he shows that divine nature willed that he should taste death for the benefit of every man, and also that the Godhead was separated from the one who was suffering in the trial of death, because it was impossible for him to taste the trial of death if (the Godhead) were not cautiously remote from him."

72   Pope St. Leo the Great, *Sermon* 2, 1 [3,1]: "For this wondrous child-bearing of the holy Virgin produced in her offspring one person which was truly human and truly divine, because neither substance so retained their properties that there could be any division of persons in them; *nor was the creature taken into partnership with its Creator in such a way that the one was the in-dweller, and the other the dwelling (nec sic creatura in societatem sui Creatoris est assumpta, ut ille habitator,*

to the person of the Virgin Mary.[73] For with Mary, the extrinsic element of the Temple metaphor is altogether apt and fit. She does not become God but she does "house" God in the most intimate way imaginable.[74] Here, the extrinsic manner of relating God to Temple is put to good use. In late Byzantine hymns to Mary the Tabernacle/Temple imagery reaches new heights.[75] The cult of Mary in the medieval period is greatly indebted to this development of the Temple figure.

Seeing God in the Temple: A Summary of the Evidence

It has often been stated that because of Israel's radically anti-iconic stance, it came to prefer forms of revelation that were mediated by word rather than sight. This assertion, like all such truisms, is to some extent accurate. Nevertheless, as we have seen in this article, it should not be assumed that because Israel rejected the

---

et illa esset habitaculum; sed ita ut naturae alteri altera misceretur); but so that the one nature was blended with the other. And although the nature which is taken is one, and that which takes is another, yet these two diverse natures come together into such close union that it is one and the same Son who says both that, as true man, 'He is less than the Father,' and that as true God 'He is equal with the Father.'" For Leo it is crucial that there be no division between God and man in the person of Jesus Christ. As a result, the Temple-metaphor as deployed by the Antiochene school is allowed no place at the table. In Leo's mind, Nestorius had effectively divided the in-dweller (God the Son) from the dwelling (Jesus as man) and hence ruled out any direct comparison of Jesus to the Temple. For the Latin original, see *Sermons [de] Léon le Grand* [Sermons of Leo the Great], ed. René Dolle, Sources Chrétiennes 22 (Paris: Éditions du Cerf, 1964), 94–99. The note appended by Dom René Dolle, the editor of the text, is worth citing (at 97, n. 3): "C'était là, en effet, une expression employée par Nestorius pour caractériser l'union du Verbe divin avec l'homme Jésus. Dans une letter à S. Cyrille, il écrivait:: 'Il est exact et conforme à la tradition évangélique, d'affirmer que le corps du Christ est le temple de la divinité' (PG 77, 49), texte qui pouvait certes s'entendre dans un sens orthodoxe mais qui prenait un sens très particulier dans le contexte de pensée nestorienne." [(The Temple-metaphor) was, in effect, an expression employed by Nestorius for characterizing the union of the divine Word with the human Jesus. In a letter to St. Cyril, he wrote: "It conforms exactly to the Gospel tradition to affirm that the body of Christ is the Temple of the Divinity," a text that can be heard in an orthodox fashion but which assumes a very peculiar sense in the context of Nestorius' thought.] English translation in *St. Leo the Great: Sermons*, trans. Jane Patricia Freeland and Agnes Josephine Conway, The Fathers of the Church 93 (Washington, DC: Catholic University of America, 1996), 88.

73 Leo the Great, *Sermon* 22, 2, "For the uncorrupt nature of him that was born had to guard the primal virginity of the Mother, and the infused power of the divine Spirit had to preserve in spotlessness and holiness *that sanctuary which he had chosen for himself:* that Spirit (I say) who had determined to raise the fallen, to restore the broken, and by overcoming the allurements of the flesh to bestow on us in abundant measure the power of chastity: in order that the virginity which in others cannot be retained in child-bearing, might be attained by them at their second birth." For the Latin, see *Léon le Grand*, 80–81. English translation in *St. Leo the Great: Sermons*, 82.

74 On this theme, see my essay, "Mary in the Old Testament," *Pro Ecclesia* 16 (2007): 33–55.

75 The florid use of Temple imagery to fill out the figure of Mary is nicely illustrated in the collection of homilies from the seventh century and later assembled by Brian Daley, *On the Dormition of Mary: Early Patristic Homilies* (Crestwood, NY: St. Vladimir's Seminary, 1998). What had once been standard predications of Christ (see the text of Athanasius above) now become standard for the figure of the Virgin.

representation of God in statuary form in the Temple, it thereby rejected all linkages of God to a specific physical domain.

As Haran has pointed out with such clarity, the realistic language of the cult—that is, the providing of the Deity with light, a pleasing aroma, and food—presume that some aspect of the Deity has actually taken up residence within the confines of the Tabernacle. Moreover, according to the priestly narrative, he sits astride the Ark of the Covenant and is veiled from view by both the darkness of his inner cella and the outstretched wings of the cherubim that stand in front of him.

Because his presence was thought to be localized in precisely this location, the effect of this theologoumenon on the entire Tabernacle compound was almost exactly that of what we find in other ancient Near Eastern settings. The aura of the Deity's presence was so overwhelming that all parts of the Temple-compound came to share in its effulgence. There is ample biblical proof that this was believed to be the case: first, the injunction one finds in the psalms "to gaze" upon the Temple or the presence of God within the Temple; second, the original form of the pilgrimage laws which most certainly commanded that Israelites "see the face of the LORD"; and third, the priestly fascination with the architectural detail of the Tabernacle, a fascination that leads him to repeat the list of its appurtenances whenever his narrative will allow him.

And again, as we have seen, this evidence is greatly extended when we move into the Second Temple period. The Samaritan and Septuagint versions alter the Masoretic text at several occasions to inform the reader that seeing God means seeing either the place where he dwells (the structure of the Tabernacle itself) or the Ark itself. Josephus strikingly emphasizes in numerous places that the entrance of non-Israelites into the Temple confines was not problematic because of the danger of encroachment on sacred space but because they thereby viewed what pagan eyes were forbidden to see. And most striking is the ritual of taking the Temple vessels out of the Temple so that they can be viewed by pilgrims. This was done, no doubt, with the intention of allowing these individuals the opportunity of fulfilling the mitzvah of *re'iyyah*, or "seeing" while they were in Jerusalem.

As Knohl has suggested, the ruling of the Temple Scroll that these vessels ought to remain within and not be subject to such movement provides strong evidence that this ritual was more than simply a product of rabbinic imagination. Nothing more strongly suggests the close nexus between God and the house he inhabits than this practice. If God is not somehow fused with the very furniture of this building how could viewing it fulfill the mandate for the pilgrim?

Michael Wyschogrod has argued that the Temple provides a close, though not exact, analogy to what Christianity means by the doctrine of incarnation: "The God of Israel is a God who enters the world of humanity and in so doing does not shun the parameters of human existence that include spatiality."[76] Indeed, when

---

76   Michael Wyschogrod, "A Jewish Perspective on Incarnation," *Modern Theology* 12 (1996): 195–209.

God assumes residence in the Tabernacle, he so ties his personal identity to that building that praise of the building can come close to praise of God himself.

This close continuity of God and Temple would seem to be radically compromised by its destruction in 587 B.C. and 70 A.D. Some Christian apologists were certainly alert to this fact and used the Temple's destruction as a basic building block in their argument that God had permanently abandoned the Jews. But, in fact, just the opposite occurs. As the Temple vessels are removed from the building just prior to this catastrophic end, God's presence and future promise of restoration becomes tied to where these vessels are interred and when they shall be revealed. The attachment of God to his home continues even after that home is destroyed.

This analogy of the Temple to the incarnation was not lost on early Christianity. Beginning with John 1:14 we see an attempt to describe the tabernacling presence as God's becoming present in Jesus such that he can be "seen" among men and women. For decades after the appearance of John's Gospel, debate raged, however on just how God was attached to this person.

Did he actually become the (now divinized) flesh of Jesus Christ, the claim of nascent orthodoxy, or did he simply make use of the ordinary human flesh as the occasion to manifest himself in a way that only those with the proper esoteric knowledge could ascertain, as the Gnostics claimed? To answer this question, St. Athanasius turned to a set of logical relations that would have been most at home in Second Temple Judaism. He asked whether the pilgrims to Jerusalem, when they prostrated themselves in veneration before the building distinguished between the invisible God who dwelled there and the very brickwork that enclosed him. At some theoretical level, of course, a distinction could and must be made, but the manner in which the Deity overtook the space in which he was housed was so overwhelming that any distinction at the phenomenological level of human experience was not possible. As God became one with his furniture so God became one with flesh.

The Tabernacle and the Mystical Turn

But the story of Christian exegesis is not exhausted by this specific christological turn. The narratives about the Tabernacle, narratives so beholden to technical detail that they become nearly unintelligible to modern readers, became a favorite site for mystic contemplation for many spiritual writers.

Blessed John of Ruusbroeck, a fourteenth century Flemish mystic wrote an extensive commentary on this portion of the Bible entitled, *The Spiritual Tabernacle.* "Although its heavily allegorical character may not be attractive to modern readers," a recent commentator remarks, "it seems to have been very popular in Ruusbroeck's own day, at least if we deduce this from the fact that more manuscripts of this treatise are extant than those of any other of his writings."[77]

---

77 *John Ruusbroec: The Spiritual Espousals and Other Works,* introd. and trans. James A. Wiseman,

The impetus to accord such importance to the biblical material on the Tabernacle begins with St. Gregory of Nyssa's *Life of Moses*. In this work, the ascent of Moses to the top of Mount Sinai to contemplate the heavenly Tabernacle became the very model for the life of serious prayer and contemplation. Moses, as the first mystic adept, has paved the way for the rest of humanity to follow.

But more important than Gregory was the influence of pseudo-Dionysius the Areopagite, active in the fifth and sixth centuries and the undisputed father of Western mystical tradition.

> It is not for nothing that the blessed Moses is commanded to submit first to purification and then to be separated from those who have not undergone this (Exod. 24:15–18). When every purification is complete (his forty days of fasting) he hears the many-voiced trumpets (Exod. 20:18). He sees the many lights, pure and with rays streaming abundantly. Then, standing apart from the crowds and accompanied by chosen priests, he pushes ahead to the summit of the divine ascents. *And yet he does not meet God himself, but contemplates, not him who is invisible, but rather where he dwells* (Exod. 25). This means, I presume, that the holiest and highest of things perceived with the eye of the body or the mind are but the rationale which presupposes all that lies below the Transcendent One. *Through them* (that is, the *physical* appurtenances of the Tabernacle in Exod. 25), however, his unimaginable presence is shown, walking the heights of those holy places to which the mind at least can rise.[78]

The striking line here is how Dionysius understands the function of all the textual detail in Exodus 25–40. Moses is called to the top of Mount Sinai for an intimate audience with God, yet the direct vision of God is something that no human person is able to withstand.

How was God to mediate his presence to this budding novice of the religious life? According to Dionysius, who is clearly following the lead of the biblical text, Moses does not see God himself but rather confronts the next best thing. He is allowed to contemplate the invisible God in the visible form of his domestic furniture. For, as he argues, it is through this furniture that "his unimaginable presence is shown." To paraphrase Dionysius, we cannot see God face to face but he has graciously consented to let us see where he dwells.[79]

The Classics of Western Spirituality (New York: Paulist, 1985), 24.

78 This text is taken from Paul Rorem, "Moses as Paradigm for the Liturgical Spirituality of Pseudo-Dionysius," in *Studia Patristica* 18:2, ed. Elizabeth A. Livingstone (Kalamazoo, MI: Cistercian, 1989), 275–279.

79 Before closing I should adduce one modern parallel that might make this abstract concept

more concrete. Two of the most heavily visited tourist sites in the United States are the Oval Office and Graceland Mansion—the former being the office of the President and the latter the home of the performer, Elvis Presley. Now even in this visual age, where photographs and film-clips (readily available on youtube.com) of these two men are a dime a dozen, it is striking to hear what tourists say when they can lay their physical eyes on the furniture used by them. Numerous persons report an intimacy that overwhelms the senses. It is as though an unimagined part of that person came vividly to life. Somehow the possessions themselves and the way they are configured in a room conveys something crucial to their being. An explanation for this is not difficult to find. If the identity of a person we love and admire is always elusive no matter how often we see them, then our best chance to achieve a fuller knowledge is to avail ourselves of every possible clue to their identity. Non-verbal cues are often as good and sometimes even better than verbal ones. There is much to be learned from how someone dresses and comports himself. Equally revealing are decisions about one's domicile and how to organize the domestic space within. For individuals such as the President or Elvis, where there is little or no opportunity for face to face contact, perhaps one of the best ways of learning about who they are is seeing how they arrange their most intimate living spaces. If I have been successful in this essay, I will have advanced the thesis that the same holds true for God himself.

Letter & Spirit 4 (2008): 47–83

JESUS, THE NEW TEMPLE, AND THE NEW PRIESTHOOD

~: Brant Pitre :~

Our Lady of Holy Cross College

Almost fifty years ago, in his excellent but often-overlooked book, *The Mystery of the Temple*, the great Dominican theologian Yves Congar highlighted a paradox present in the gospels—a mystery of sorts:

> When the gospel texts are read straight through with a view to discovering the attitude of Jesus towards the Temple and all it represented, two apparently contradictory features become immediately apparent: *Jesus' immense respect for the Temple*; his very lively criticism of abuses and of formalism, yet above and beyond this, *his constantly repeated assertion that the Temple is to be transcended*, that it has had its day, and that it is doomed to disappear.[1]

With these words, Congar put his finger on one of the most puzzling aspects of Jesus' relationship to the Judaism of his day. For it is of course true that the Gospels contain numerous statements of Jesus in which he esteems the Temple as the dwelling place of God, and others in which he explicitly denounces the Temple and declares that it will eventually be destroyed. For example, on the one hand, Jesus says, "he who swears by the Temple, swears by it and by him who dwells in it" (Matt. 23:21). On the other hand, he denounces the city of Jerusalem for opposing the prophets of God and says to her: "Behold, your house [the Temple] is forsaken and desolate" (Matt. 23:38). How do we explain this seeming paradox? How can Jesus both revere the Temple and at the same time declare its eventual destruction?

In order to answer this question, I will focus on four aspects of the Jewish Temple that are widely known but have not been sufficiently highlighted in the historical study of Jesus. Although most students of the Bible have a basic knowledge of the importance of the Temple at the time of Jesus, our appreciation of ancient Jewish Temple *theology* is still somewhat under-developed.[2] In this paper, I will

---

1   Yves Congar, *The Mystery of the Temple*, trans. Reginald F. Trevett (Westminster, MD: Newman, 1962), 112 (emphasis added).

2   Thankfully, this situation appears to be changing. In recent years, there has been an explosion of research into the liturgical and theological symbolism and significance of the Temple. Much of this is discussed in the exhaustive bibliography of G. K. Beale's excellent work, *The Temple*

try to move beyond the obvious visible, political, and national significance of the Temple to its deeper theological and liturgical significance. From a theological and liturgical perspective, for a first-century Jew, the Temple was at least four things: (1) the dwelling-place of God on earth; (2) a microcosm of heaven and earth; (3) the sole place of sacrificial worship; (4) the place of the sacrificial priesthood.[3]

As I hope to show, when these four Jewish beliefs about the Temple are given due emphasis, Jesus' strange combination of criticizing others for abusing the Temple and prophesying its destruction makes eminent sense. The reason: *Jesus saw all four of these aspects of the Temple as being fulfilled in himself and his disciples.* Indeed, the evidence in the Gospels strongly suggests that Jesus saw his own body as (1) the dwelling-place of God on earth; (2) the foundation stone that would be the beginning of a new Temple and a new creation; and (3) the sole place of sacrificial worship in the new covenant. Moreover, there are also good reasons to believe that he saw himself and his disciples as constituting (4) the new, eschatological priesthood that had been spoken of by the prophets.[4]

Because of this, the old Temple was destined to pass away and be replaced by a new Temple, a greater Temple, one "not made with hands," and the old priesthood with a new. In this essay, I hope to offer the beginnings of what might be called a *biblical mystagogy* of both the Jewish Temple and the Jewish priesthood, one which has the potential to shed enormous light on Jesus' view of himself and his disciples. But in order to see all this, we will need to examine how the Temple was viewed in first-century Judaism, in order to root our understanding in ancient Jewish practice and belief.

The Importance of the Temple in Ancient Judaism

It should go without saying that the ancient Jewish Temple, as the liturgical and sacrificial center of Second Temple Judaism, was extremely important.[5] Although

---

and the Church's Mission: A Biblical Theology of the Dwelling Place of God (Downers Grove, IL: InterVarsity, 2004). See also Jonathan Klawans, Purity, Sacrifice, and the Temple: Symbolism and Supersessionism in the Study of Ancient Judaism (Oxford: Oxford University, 2006), esp. 111–144.

3   By "sacrificial priesthood" I am referring here to those ordained priests who ministered in the Temple cult. There was of course a sense in which the entire people of Israel was called to be "a kingdom of priests and a holy nation" (Exod. 19:5–6), but this universal priesthood is not the object of our present study.

4   This essay is drawn from a book I am currently writing on Jesus and the Jewish roots of the Last Supper. For further details, see Brant Pitre, *Jesus and the Last Supper: Judaism and the Origin of the Eucharist* (Grand Rapids, MI: Eerdmans, forthcoming).

5   The Second Temple period ranges from roughly 520 B.C. to 70 A.D. On the Jewish Temple, see especially the concise but amazingly thorough article by Johann Maier, "Temple," in *Encyclopedia of the Dead Sea Scrolls*, 2 vols., eds. Lawrence H. Schiffman and James C. VanderKam (New York: Oxford University, 2000), 2:921–926. See also Beale, *The Temple and the Church's Mission*; Carol Meyers, "Temple, Jerusalem," *Anchor Bible Dictionary*, 6 vols, ed. David Noel Freedman (New York: Doubleday, 1992), 6:350–369; E. P. Sanders, *Judaism: Practice and Belief 63BCE–66 CE* (Philadelphia: Trinity Press International, 1992), 47–145; Emil Schürer, *The History of the*

modern readers often consider those sections of the Bible which describe the Temple and its sacrificial rituals to be rather dull (if not downright repugnant), this was most certainly not the case for practicing Jews in the first century. For the vast majority of them, the Temple was arguably the center of their religious life. As N. T. Wright has said:

> The Temple was the focal point of every aspect of Jewish national life. Local synagogues and schools of Torah in other parts of Palestine, and in the Diaspora, in no way replaced it, but gained their significance from their implicit relation to it. *Its importance at every level can hardly be overestimated.*[6]

E. P. Sanders is in agreement:

> *I think that it is almost impossible to make too much of the Temple in first-century Jewish Palestine.* Modern people so readily think of religion without sacrifice that they fail to see how novel that idea is.[7]

These modern sentiments find confirmation in ancient Jewish texts. To cite but one famous example: according the Mishnah, Simeon the Just, who was high-priest during the third century B.C., used to say:

> By three things the world is sustained: by the Law, *by the [Temple]-service*, and by deeds of loving-kindness.[8]

In this ancient Jewish text, "the service" (Hebrew *'abodah*) is a technical term for the sacrificial worship offered to God by his priests in the Temple.[9] For Simeon the Just, then, the importance of the liturgy of the Jerusalem Temple is not simply

---

Jewish People in the Age of Jesus Christ (175 B.C.—A.D. 135), 3 vols., rev. and ed. Geza Vermes, et al. (Edinburgh: T. & T. Clark, 1973, 1979, 1986, 1987), 2:237–313; Menahem Haran, *Temples and Temple Service in Ancient Israel* (Oxford: Clarendon, 1978); Joachim Jeremias, *Jerusalem in the Time of Jesus*, trans. F. H. Cave and C. H. Cave (Philadelphia: Fortress, 1969), 21–27, 84–86, 147–221; H. H. Rowley, *Worship in Ancient Israel* (London: S.P.C.K, 1967), 71–110; Congar, *The Mystery of the Temple*. For a beautifully illustrated introduction to the Temple as described in rabbinic literature, see Israel Ariel and Chaim Richman, *Carta's Illustrated Encyclopedia of the Holy Temple in Jerusalem*, trans. Yehoshua Wertheimer (Jerusalem: Carta, 2005).

6   N. T. Wright, *The New Testament and the People of God* (Minneapolis: Fortress, 1992), 224. Emphasis added.

7   E. P. Sanders, *The Historical Figure of Jesus* (London: Penguin, 1994), 262. Emphasis added.

8   Mishnah *Aboth* [The Fathers], 1:2. The Mishnah, a compilation of the Jewish oral law dates to roughly 200 A.D. See *The Mishnah*, trans. Herbert Danby (Oxford: Oxford University, 1933), 446. My translation here modifies Danby's slightly.

9   See Jacob Neusner, *The Mishnah: A New Translation* (New Haven: Yale University, 1988), 673, who likewise translates the term as "the Temple service."

national, but *cosmic*: it is one of the three things that "sustains the world." We will return to this cosmic dimension shortly.

For now, the basic point is that the Temple was of central significance for Judaism at the time of Jesus. This is important to stress because of a long-standing tradition, both in popular Christian consciousness and in some New Testament scholarship, of depicting the Jewish Temple in entirely negative terms: as an out-moded system of external rituals and legalistic regulations; or as an oppressive tool of economic exploitation used and abused by the widely-despised priestly hierarchy; or simply as a primitive expression of sacrificial religion, destined to be transcended by a purely spiritual worship.[10] Other authors are not so harsh, but rather tend to downplay the significance of the Temple by suggesting that in Jesus' day it had already been eclipsed by the emergence of the local gathering place of worship, the synagogue.[11] Neither of these approaches does justice to the immense reverence and respect which most Jews of Jesus' day had for the Temple. With this basic point in mind, let us turn now to four specific aspects of the Temple that will play an important role in our study—*the Temple as the dwelling-place of God; the Temple as a microcosm of heaven and earth; the Temple as the sole place of sacrifice;* and *the Temple as the place of the sacrificial priesthood.*

The Temple as the Dwelling-Place of God

The first aspect of the Jewish Temple, one which marked it out as different from all other buildings, is the fact that it was the dwelling place of God. Above all, it was the presence of God that made the Temple a place "set apart": in Greek, that is what the word "temple" (*hieron*) means.[12] Although ancient Jews recognized

---

10   Sanders gives an excellent catalogue of such views in New Testament scholarship at the beginning of his study. See *Jesus and Judaism* (Philadelphia: Fortress, 1985), 23–60.

11   See, for example, Luke Timothy Johnson, *The Writings of the New Testament: An Interpretation*, rev. ed. (Minneapolis: Fortress, 1999), 59, who asserts that "in the first century … the Temple was not the center of piety in the way that synagogue and home were." This totally ignores the centrality of sacrifice in worship (which, as we will see, could only be carried out in Jerusalem), and that Jewish synagogues themselves reflected their subordination to the Temple by the fact that they were oriented toward the Temple, so that "the people prayed standing with their faces turned toward the Holy of Holies, towards Jerusalem." See Schürer, *The History of the Jewish People*, 2:449, citing Mishnah *Berakoth* [Firstlings] 4:5–6, and Tosefta *Megillah* [The Scroll of Esther] 3:21–22: "The minister of the synagogue faces the holy place, and all the people face the sanctuary," and "the doors of the synagogue open only eastward, for so we find concerning the sanctuary that it was open eastward." Translated by Jacob Neusner, *The Tosefta: Translated from the Hebrew, with a New Introduction*, 2 vols. (Peabody, MA: Hendrickson, 2002), here at 650. Johnson's error reflects an anachronistic tendency to read back some of the later features of rabbinic Judaism (which lacked a Temple and was hence wholly focused on the synagogue) into the period of the Second Temple. At the risk of oversimplifying, it may nevertheless be helpful to make the point that later rabbinic Judaism is much more like Protestantism (that is, non-sacrificial, with no cult and a rabbinate), and Judaism at the time of Jesus was much more like Catholicism (sacrificial, with both cult and priesthood).

12   See, for example, N. T. Wright, *Jesus and the Victory of God* (Minneapolis: Fortress, 1996), 406–407; Meyers, "Temple, Jerusalem," 351–352; Craig R. Koester, *The Dwelling of God: The Tabernacle*

that the transcendent God of the universe could not be "contained" by any earthly dwelling, they nevertheless maintained that he had chosen in some unique way to dwell with his people in the Temple in Jerusalem.

This belief runs like a golden thread through the writings of the Old Testament. Any knowledgeable Jew would have been familiar with the unforgettable account of the building of the Temple by King Solomon. On the day of its dedication, after the priests of Israel bring the Ark of the Covenant into the holy place, the presence of God descends from heaven in the form of the "glory cloud"—what the rabbis later referred to as the *Shekinah*[13]—to make the Temple his dwelling place:

> And when the priests came out of the holy place, a cloud filled the house of the LORD [that is, the Temple], so that the priests could not stand to minister because of the cloud; *for the glory of the* LORD *filled the house of the* LORD. Then Solomon said: "The LORD has set the sun in the heavens, but has said that he would dwell in thick darkness. *I have built thee an exalted house, a place for thee to dwell forever.*" Then the king faced about, and blessed all the assembly of Israel, while all the assembly of Israel stood.
> (1 Kings 8:10–14)

Although Solomon himself goes on to acknowledge that "heaven and the highest heaven cannot contain" God, much less a man-made "house," (1 Kings 8:27), this does not negate the fact of God's presence in the Jerusalem Temple. Through an act of divine condescension, the God of the universe deigns to dwell among his people, and pours out the glory of his presence upon this sacred place, set apart for him. As Josephus says in his account:

> This cloud [the glory cloud] so darkened the place, that one priest could not discern another; but *it afforded to the minds of all a visible image and glorious appearance of God's having descended into this Temple, and of his having gladly pitched his Tabernacle there.*[14]

Although by the time of Jesus, the Ark of the Covenant—which was the principal symbol of God's glorious presence—had been lost, the belief persisted

---

    in the Old Testament, Intertestamental Jewish Literature, and the New Testament, Catholic Biblical Quarterly Monograph Series 22 (Washington, DC: Catholic Biblical Association of America, 1989).

13   On the *Shekinah,* see Congar, *The Mystery of the Temple,* 93–94 (with bibliography).

14   Josephus, *The Antiquities of the Jews,* Bk. 8, Chap. 4, 106, in *The Works of Josephus,* trans. William Whiston (Peabody, MA: Hendrickson, 1994), 219.

that God was present in a special way in the Temple.[15] This is what we find re-corded in the Gospels:

> He who swears by the altar, swears by it and everything on it; and he who swears by the Temple, swears by it and by *him who dwells in it*. (Matt. 23:16–21)

Jesus' words fit quite squarely into the matrix of ancient Jewish belief. In light of such texts, Sanders concludes:

> *The Temple was holy not only because the holy God was worshipped there, but because he was there.* ... Jews did not think that God was there and nowhere else, nor that the Temple in any way confined him. Since he was creator and Lord of the universe, he could be approached in prayer at any place. Nevertheless, he was in some special sense present in the Temple.[16]

Hence, the divine presence, the presence of God in the Temple, lays the foundation for all of its other aspects. Once this is clear, we can ask ourselves: what light does the Temple as the dwelling-place of God shed on Congar's paradox? How does it illuminate the mystery of Jesus' relationship to the Temple?

To attempt to answer these questions takes us straight into the heart of the debate over Jesus' messianic "self-understanding."[17] For, in what must be consid-ered one of the most striking passages in all the Gospels, Jesus not only identifies himself with the Temple, but asserts that he is in fact *greater than the Temple*:

> At that time Jesus went through the grainfields on the Sabbath; his disciples were hungry, and they began to pluck ears of grain and to eat. But when the Pharisees saw it, they said to him, "Look, your disciples are doing what is not lawful to do on the Sabbath." He said to them, "Have you not read what David did, when he

---

15   See 2 Macc. 2. See also the first-century work, *The Lives of the Prophets* (2:8–19) regarding Jeremiah and the removal of the Ark from the Temple. Text in *The Old Testament Pseudepigrapha*, 2 vols., ed. James H. Charlesworth, The Anchor Bible Reference Library (New York: Doubleday, 1983, 1985), 2:387–389.

16   Sanders, *Judaism*, 70–71.

17   For recent affirmations that Jesus saw himself as Messiah by two giants of New Testament scholarship, see Martin Hengel, "Jesus, the Messiah of Israel: the Debate about the 'Messianic Mission' of Jesus," in *Authenticating the Activities of Jesus*, eds. Bruce Chilton and Craig A. Evans, New Testament Tools and Studies 28:2 (Leiden: Brill, 1999), 323–349; Ben F. Meyer, "Jesus' Ministry and Self-Understanding," in *Studying the Historical Jesus: Evaluations of the State of Current Research*, eds. Bruce Chilton and Craig A. Evans (Leiden: Brill, 1994), 337–352. For a full-length exploration and defense of Jesus' messianic self-understanding, see Michael F. Bird, *Are You the One Who Is To Come? The Historical Jesus and the Messianic Question* (Grand Rapids, MI: Baker Academic, forthcoming).

was hungry, and those who were with him: how he entered the house of God and ate the Bread of the Presence, which it was not lawful for him to eat nor for those who were with him, but only for the priests? Or have you not read in the Law how on the Sabbath the priests in the Temple profane the Sabbath, and are guiltless? *I tell you, something greater than the Temple is here.* And if you had known what this means, "I desire mercy, not sacrifice," you would not have condemned the guiltless. *For the Son of Man is Lord of the Sabbath.* (Matt. 12:1–8)[18]

While there are many aspects of this fascinating text that could be explored, for our purposes here we will focus on only one: Jesus' words, "Something greater than the Temple is here." As the context makes clear, this is a veiled reference to *himself*. Should there be any doubt about this, he uses similar language elsewhere to refer to himself as prophet and king: "Something greater than Solomon is here" (Matt. 12:42; Luke 11:31) and "Something greater than Jonah is here" (Matt. 12:41; Luke 11:32). In our text, Jesus is not only identifying himself as a temple—as if this were not striking enough—but as *greater* than the Temple in Jerusalem.

This identification immediately raises a question of no little importance: *if, to an ancient Jew, the Temple is the dwelling place of God on earth, then what could possibly be greater than it?* Although some commentators have tried to avoid the obvious, the only adequate answer is, of course, God himself, present in person, "tabernacling" in the flesh.[19] In confirmation of this, Jesus' second enigmatic self-reference—"the Son of Man is Lord of the Sabbath"—points in the same direction. For again, to a first century Jew, there can be only one "Lord of the Sabbath": the maker of the Sabbath, the Lord of creation (see Gen. 1; Exod. 20). With these words—to use the somewhat infelicitous categories of twentieth-century theology—we find a christology that is very "high," but very *Jewish*: Jesus himself is the true Temple, where God dwells on earth. And, as the messianic "Son of Man," he

---

18   Compare Mark 2:23–38; Luke 6:1–5. Unless otherwise noted, all translations of the Bible contained herein are from the Revised Standard Version.

19   It is fascinating to observe that many modern commentators do not even attempt to wrestle with the implications of Jesus' identification of himself as "greater than the Temple." The verse is all but ignored in the otherwise extremely thorough work of W. D. Davies and Dale C. Allison, *The Gospel According to Saint Matthew* (Edinburgh: T. & T. Clark, 1991), 2:314–315. Similarly, the verse receives no discussion at all in Rudolf Schnackenburg, *The Gospel of Matthew* (Grand Rapids, MI: Eerdmans, 2002), 111–112. It is also lacking in works on Jesus, such as the (otherwise massive) work of James D. G. Dunn, *Jesus Remembered* (Grand Rapids, MI: Eerdmans, 2003), 566–569 who totally ignores it in his discussion of Matt. 12:1–8; Mark 2:23–28; Luke 6:1–5, and does not mention it anywhere else in his book. Even Ben Witherington's book, *The Christology of Jesus* (Minneapolis: Fortress, 1990), 66–71, never even mentions this verse in his discussion. It should be noted that this cannot be because there is a strong case for the inauthenticity of the verse, since we have already seen that it strongly coheres with Jesus' words about being "greater than Solomon" (Matt. 12:42; Luke 11:31) and "greater than Jonah" (Matt. 12:41; Luke 11:32).

has authority over creation itself and the Sabbath covenant. The divine identity and prerogative in both these statements is implicit but undeniable.[20]

But this is not the only evidence that Jesus identifies himself with the Temple as the dwelling-place of God. There is another key text, which is perhaps more suggestive because it focuses not so much on the earthly Temple as on its heavenly counterpart. (Although we do not have time to study it in depth, I should note here in passing that it was widely understood in ancient Judaism that the earthly Temple in Jerusalem was a replica of the heavenly Temple—where God "really" dwells.[21]) It is this heavenly Temple that forms the subject of Jesus' response to Nathanael's famous confession of him as "Son of God" and "King of Israel" (John 1:43–51). After Jesus mentions having seen Nathanael under the fig tree, he says:

> Jesus answered him, "Because I said to you, I saw you under the fig tree, do you believe? You shall see greater things than these." And he said to him, "Amen, amen, I say to you, *you will see heaven opened, and the angels of God ascending and descending upon the Son of Man.*" (John 1:50–51)[22]

Again, the key to understanding this strange image lies in the Old Testament. With these words, Jesus is combining two heavenly visions: Daniel's famous vision of the heavenly "son of Man" (Dan. 7:14), and Jacob's famous vision of the "staircase" to the heavenly Temple (commonly known as "Jacob's Ladder"):[23]

---

20 The fact that both these statements are often discarded by scholars as creations of the early Church shows just how lofty their christology is, although it is rarely noted by such scholars that the terminology is strikingly unique: the early Church itself never anywhere speaks of Jesus as "greater than the Temple" or "the Lord of the Sabbath." It is arguable that the reason for this is that these expressions were distinctively used by Jesus himself. Compare Craig Keener's comments, who remarks that Jesus' words are "veiled enough to prevent accusations of blasphemy—especially since his opponents would not expect him actually to claim what he was claiming—but obvious enough to enrage them." See Craig S. Keener, *A Commentary on the Gospel of Matthew* (Grand Rapids, MI: Eerdmans, 1999), 356.

21 See Congar, *The Mystery of the Temple*, 65, 91 n. 2; Beale, *The Temple*, 134–135; Maier, "Temple," 921–922; Meyer, "Temple, Jerusalem," 367; Schürer, *The History of the Jewish People*, 2:522 n. 31. George Foot Moore, *Judaism in the First Centuries of the Christian Era: The Age of the Tannaim*, 3 vols. (Cambridge: Harvard University, 1927), 1:404: "As the divine king, God received a worship that was more than royal homage; his palace was a temple in which angelic choirs perpetually intoned his praises and incense was burned upon the altar by a celestial priesthood." Also important is George Buchanan Gray, *Sacrifice in the Old Testament* (New York: KTAV, 1971 [1925]), 148–178, on the "sacrificial service in heaven."

22 For arguments favoring the authenticity of this text, see Craig L. Blomberg, *The Historical Reliability of John's Gospel: Issues and a Commentary* (Downers Grove, IL: InterVarsity, 2001), 82–85, not least of which is the use of the title "Son of Man," which is widely recognized as "both distinctive and characteristic" of Jesus.

23 As Raymond Brown notes, this link between John 1:51 and Gen. 28 goes back at least as far as the time of Augustine. See Brown, *The Gospel according to John*, 2 vols., Anchor Bible 29–29a (New York: Doubleday, 1966, 1970), 1:89.

I saw in the night visions, and behold, *with the clouds of heaven there came one like a son of man,* and he came to the Ancient of Days and was presented before him. And to him was given dominion and glory and kingdom that all peoples, nations, and languages should serve him. His dominion is an everlasting dominion which shall not pass away … (Dan. 7:13–14).

Jacob left Beer-sheba, and went toward Haran. And he came to a certain place, and stayed there that night, because the sun had set. Taking one of the stones of the place, he put it under his head and lay down in that place to sleep. *And he dreamed that there was a stairway*[24] *set up on the earth, and the top of it reached to heaven; and behold, the angels of God were ascending and descending on it!* And behold, *the* LORD *stood above it* and said, "I am the LORD, the God of Abraham your father and the God of Isaac …" Then Jacob awoke from his sleep and said, *"Surely the* LORD *is in this place;* and I did not know it." And he was afraid, and said, "How awesome is this place! This is none other than *the house of God,* and this is *the gate of heaven."* (Gen. 28:10–18)

First, it should be made clear that Jacob is having a vision, not simply of a "ladder" (as the English translations frequently suggest), but of *a* heavenly temple. In the ancient Near East, temple sanctuaries frequently consisted of several levels of ascending staircases; here Jacob sees the angels ascending and descending upon the staircases of the Temple, engaged in liturgical worship.[25] Second, this Temple is characterized by the presence of God. Not only is "the LORD" depicted as standing at the apex of the Temple, but Jacob is awestruck primarily because "the LORD is in this place"; for this reason, he names the place "the house of God" (Hebrew: *beth 'el*) and "the gate of heaven."

Once this Old Testament background is clear, Jesus' words to Nathanael take on a whole new depth, for it appears that *Jesus is fusing the heavenly Temple of Jacob's vision and the heavenly Son of Man of Daniel's vision into one.* If this is correct, the implications are weighty: no longer is the earthly sanctuary the dwelling place of the LORD; soon Nathanael will see the Son of Man revealed as "the house of God" and "the gate of heaven." Although, as before, Jesus does not make an explicit claim to divine identity, this is as close as it comes for a first-century Jew, since in Jacob's vision, the angels appear to ascend to God, whereas in Jesus' vision, the

---

24 Most translations have "ladder," but this English term distorts what is clearly a vision of the staircases that were often part of temples in the ancient Near East. See E. A. Speiser, *Genesis,* Anchor Bible 1 (New York: Doubleday, 1962), 218.

25 See Roland De Vaux, *Ancient Israel: Its Life and Institutions* (Grand Rapids, MI: Eerdmans, 1997 [1961]), 274–329; Speiser, *Genesis,* 218–220.

only visible heavenly being is the Son of Man.[26] As Raymond Brown puts it, with these words: "Jesus as Son of Man has become *the locus of divine glory*, the point of contact between heaven and earth."[27]

To sum up what we have seen so far: it was a standard belief in ancient Judaism that the Temple was the dwelling place of God. In both the synoptic Gospels and in John, Jesus, by contrast, transfers this belief to himself, thereby identifying himself as the true Temple of God. He is not only greater than the present Temple, the dwelling-place of God on earth, but at the revelation of the Danielic Son of Man he will be shown to be the heavenly Temple of God—the dwelling place of "the LORD" that was revealed to the patriarch Jacob. In light of such statements, Congar's question begins to see its resolution: it is no wonder that Jesus both reveres the Temple and awaits its destruction. The old Jerusalem Temple must make way for the unveiled glory of the divine presence that will be manifest in the coming of the heavenly Son of Man.

The Temple as a Microcosm of Heaven and Earth

The second aspect of ancient Jewish Temple theology that will prove important to our study is the belief that the Temple was not simply the dwelling place of God; it was also a microcosm of heaven and earth. Indeed, for ancient Judaism, the Temple not only had religious and cultic significance, it had *cosmic* significance: it was a miniature replica of the universe.[28]

It is worth noting here that for much of the twentieth century this cosmic dimension of the Temple was largely ignored.[29] Nevertheless, as recent scholarship has shown—and I am thinking here especially of G. K. Beale's book, *The Temple and the Church's Mission* (2004)—there is overwhelming evidence for this cosmic temple symbolism in both Scripture and Judaism at the time of Jesus. Indeed, the Old Testament, the Second Temple literature, and the rabbis all bear witness

---

26   If we had more space, we could explore the fact that in one version of Daniel's vision of the Son of Man, the Son of Man is not coming "to" the Ancient of Days but appearing "*as* the Ancient of Days." See the Septuagint translation (hereafter, LXX) of Dan. 7:13–14. Compare Rev. 1:12–16, where the Son of Man appears as the Ancient of Days, with "head and hair white as snow." I owe this fascinating insight to my colleague, Michael Barber.

27   Brown, *The Gospel according to John*, 1:91. Emphasis added.

28   See especially Beale, *The Temple and the Church's Mission*, 29–80, for abundant primary and secondary resources. See also Klawans, *Purity, Sacrifice, and the Temple*, 111–144; Meyers, "Temple, Jerusalem," 359–360; Sanders, *Judaism*, 249; Margaret Barker, *The Gate of Heaven* (London: SPCK, 1991), 104–132; Koester, *The Dwelling of God*, 59–63; Jon D. Levenson, *Sinai and Zion* (San Francisco: Harper & Row, 1985), 111–184; Raphael Patai, *Man and Temple* (New York: KTAV, 1976), 54–139.

29   This is no doubt due, at least in part, to the post-Kantian collapse of metaphysics, the materialism of modernity, as well as the widespread influence of Rudolf Bultmann's program of "demythologizing"—which at its core was really about "de-*cosmologizing*" the Bible. See Congar, who at the beginning of the 1960s can only cite Joachim Jeremias and one other German scholar as having highlighted this cosmic significance. *The Mystery of the Temple*, 94, n. 9.

to the fact that the Jerusalem Temple—like the Tabernacle before it, and other temples in the ancient Near East—was designed and decorated to represent the entire universe: the heavens, the earth, the sea, the stars. Take the following quotes as examples:

> [God] built *his sanctuary* [the Temple]
> *like the high heavens, like the earth,*
> which he has founded for ever. (Ps. 78:69)

> If anyone without prejudice, and with judgment, look upon these things [in the Tabernacle], he will find *they were in every one made in way of imitation and representation of the universe.* When Moses distinguished the Tabernacle into three parts, and allowed two of them to the priests, as a place accessible and common, he denoted *the land* and *the sea*, these being of general access to all; but he set apart the third division for God, because *heaven* is inaccessible to men. (Josephus, *Antiquities of the Jews*)[30]

> The house of the Holy of Holies is made to correspond to *the highest heaven.* The outer holy house was made to correspond to *the earth.* And the courtyard was made to correspond to *the sea.* (Rabbi Phinehas ben Ya'ir, second century A.D.)[31]

In addition to this overall cosmic symbolism, the specific *features* of the Temple, down to its architectural details, appear to have been constructed so as to conjure up images of all creation.[32] For example, the famous "bronze sea"—which contained some thousand gallons of water—was actually meant to represent "the sea" (1 Kings 7:23–24; 1 Chron. 18:8; Jer. 52:17). Moreover, the seven lamps of the menorah inside the holy place were interpreted by some Jews as representing the seven visible planets (Exod. 25:31–40; 37:17–24). Finally, Josephus even states that the veil in the Temple had cosmic significance:

---

30 *The Antiquities of the Jews*, Bk. 3, Chap. 7, 81, text in *The Works of Josephus*, 90.

31 The quotation is from Beale, *The Temple*, 46 n. 36.

32 Meyer, "Temple, Jerusalem," 359: "Other symbols constitutive of the cosmic order made visual and vital in the Temple can be identified in the exhuberant presence of floral and faunal motifs in the interior decoration of the building and in the construction and decoration of its appurtenances. The trees carved on the walls, the groves on the Temple mount, and perhaps even the sacred lampstands, are part of the symbolic expression of the mythic Tree of Life that stood on the cosmic mountain, and in the paradisiacal garden at creation. Similarly, the waters of the molten sea and the great fountains of the deep present in God's habitation on Zion (Ps. 46:4) contribute to the notion of the Temple as a cosmic center."

> It was a Babylonian curtain, embroidered with blue, and fine
> linen, and scarlet, and purple, and of a contexture that was truly
> wonderful. Nor was this mixture of colors without its mystical
> interpretation, but was a kind of *image of the universe*. ... This
> curtain had also embroidered upon it *a panorama of the heavens*.
> (Josephus, *The Wars of the Jews*) [33]

This will prove significant momentarily; for now, we can conclude by stating that for many ancient Jews, the Temple represented the heavens and the earth. [34] It was quite literally, a "micro-cosmos," a little universe. This may be one reason why the high priest Simeon (and the rabbis after him) taught that "the Temple service" was one of the three things which "sustained the world." [35]

Once this cosmic significance of the Temple is clear, another piece of the puzzle can be fitted into its place to illuminate two important episodes from the Gospels: (1) Jesus' prophecies of the Temple's destruction and restoration; and (2) his identification of himself as the "cornerstone" of the new Temple.

The first of these is important to emphasize. As the Gospels repeatedly attest, Jesus anticipated and spoke of the eventual destruction of the earthly Temple in Jerusalem, and also taught that it would be replaced by a new Temple, an eschatological Temple (see Matt. 23:37–39; Luke 13:34–35). [36] We see this both in his teaching and in the account of his trial before the Sanhedrin:

> And as he came out of the Temple, one of his disciples said to
> him, "Look, Teacher, what wonderful stones and what wonder-
> ful buildings!" And Jesus said to him, "Do you see these great
> buildings? *There will not be left here one stone upon another, that
> will not be thrown down.*" (Mark 13:1–2)

---

33   *The Wars of the Jews*, Bk. 5, Chap. 5, 212–214, in *The Works of Josephus*, 707 (slightly altered). See Beale, *The Temple*, 46–47, for abundant references to the ancient literature, especially Philo and Josephus.

34   So too Carol Meyers, an expert on the Temple: "The symbolic nature of the Jerusalem Temple, as for all major shrines in the ancient world, depended upon a series of features that, taken together, established the sacred precinct as being located at the cosmic center of the universe, at the place where heaven and earth converge. ... Zion, and the Temple built there, is the cosmic mount. The Temple building, on a mountain and a platform, replicates the heavenly mountain of Yahweh (compare Ps. 48:1–4) and also its earlier manifestation at Sinai. It also reaches back to the beginning of time, to the creation of the world. ... The foundation of the Temple thus becomes a protological event, going back to the beginnings of time." "Temple, Jerusalem," 358.

35   See Mishnah *Aboth* [The Fathers] 1:3.

36   This is widely recognized in modern scholarship: see especially Sanders, *Jesus and Judaism*, 61–90. See also Dunn, *Jesus Remembered*, 514–515, 628–634; Craig A. Evans, "Jesus and Predictions of the Destruction of the Herodian Temple," in *Jesus and His Contemporaries: Comparative Studies* (Leiden: Brill, 2001), 367–380; Paula Fredriksen, *Jesus of Nazareth, King of the Jews* (New York: Vintage, 1999), 226–228; Wright, *Jesus and the Victory of God*, 510–527.

> Now the chief priests and the whole Sanhedrin sought testimony
> against Jesus to put him to death; but they found none. ... And
> some stood up and bore false witness against him, saying, "We
> heard him say, '*I will destroy this Temple that is made with hands,
> and in three days I will build another, not made with hands.*'" (Mark
> 14:55–58)

In the first passage, we see Jesus clearly prophesying the destruction of the
Temple in Jerusalem—something which did indeed take place forty years later, in
70 A.D., when the Romans came and demolished the city of Jerusalem. In the second
text, we find important evidence for the fact that Jesus expected there to be a new
Temple, an eschatological Temple—a temple "not made with hands." Although
the testimony that he would destroy the Jerusalem Temple is called "false," there
is no reason to doubt that some error has been mixed with some truth: Jesus did
expect a new Temple "not made with hands" to be erected after "three days"; but
he did not say that he would destroy the earthly Temple.[37] Most important for our
purposes is that by speaking of the new Temple as being erected "after three days,"
he (implicitly) identified himself as the new Temple, that would replace the old.

Now, what is fascinating about this identification, given our interest in the
cosmological significance of the Temple, is that Jesus' image of the new Temple being "not made with hands" (Mark 14:56) draws directly on a famous Old Testament
prophecy. I am speaking here of the book of Daniel, which describes the coming of
a mysterious "stone" that is "cut by no human hand" (Dan. 2:31–35). In the Danielic
interpretation of the image, the identity of this stone is revealed:

> *And in the days of those kings the God of heaven will set up a king-
> dom which shall never be destroyed,* nor shall its sovereignty be
> left to another people. *It shall break in pieces all these kingdoms
> and bring them to an end, and it shall stand for ever; just as you saw
> that a stone was cut from a mountain by no human hand,* and that
> it broke in pieces the iron, the bronze, the clay, the silver, and
> the gold. A great God has made known to the king what shall
> be hereafter. The dream is certain, and its interpretation sure.
> (Dan. 2:44–45)

---

37 While it is true that the evangelist refers to this accusation as "false testimony," its falsity
    probably resides in only the accusation that Jesus himself would destroy the Temple; the rest
    of their accusation coheres quite well with Jesus' prophecies of the Temple's destruction, and
    is probably accurate. For discussions of this material, see Craig Evans, *Mark 8:27–16:20*, Word
    Biblical Commentary 34b (Nashville: Thomas Nelson, 2001), 445–446; Sanders, *Jesus and
    Judaism*, 71–76, although the latter seems to think that Jesus said that he himself would destroy
    the Temple, while I think that this is the element of the testimony which the evangelists (rightly)
    regarded as false.

Although there is much that could be said about this important passage, three points must suffice. First and foremost, the image of a "stone" cut from the mountain "by no human hand" is evocative of *the stones of the Temple*.[38] For, according to several Old Testament passages, the Temple altar was supposed to be "an altar of unhewn stones, upon which no man has lifted an iron tool" (see Josh. 8:31, drawing on Exod. 20:25; Deut. 27:6). Hence, the image of a stone cut "by no human hand" is a designation for a sacred stone, a cultic stone (compare 1 Kings 6:7).[39] Second, given the fact that the Temple was a microcosm of creation, the stone cut by no human hand is not only an image of an eschatological Temple, but of a "new creation." This implicit cosmic dimension becomes explicit when the little stone becomes a "great mountain" and fills "the whole earth" (Dan. 2:35–35).[40]

Hence, the little stone is not simply the beginnings of a new Temple, but of a new cosmos. Third and finally, and perhaps most striking of all, as Wright has pointed out, "from at least as early as the first century," the Danielic stone "not cut by human hand" was taken in ancient Jewish literature "to refer to the Messiah, and to the kingdom that would be set up through him."[41] In light of this ancient messianic interpretation of the stone, the polyvalence of the image is readily apparent: the stone represents the Messiah, the eschatological Temple, and the eschatological creation.

When Jesus' words about the new Temple "not made with hands" are given due weight, his basic point seems clear: he not only expected the destruction of the earthly Temple in Jerusalem, but he expected that earthly Temple to be replaced by a new Temple, an eschatological Temple—Daniel's prophecy of the Temple that would be built "by no human hand"—a prophecy which he apparently applied to himself. This interpretation coheres well with what we find elsewhere in the Gospels:

> Jesus said to them, "Have you never read in the Scriptures: *'The stone which the builders rejected has become the head of the corner; this was the LORD's doing, and it is marvelous in our eyes'* [Ps. 118:22–23]? ... And *he who falls on this stone will be broken*

---

38   See Dunn, *Jesus Remembered*, 631, n. 89.

39   Beale, *The Temple and the Church's Mission*, 153.

40   "Temples were symbolically the 'embodiment of the cosmic mountain' representing the original hillock first emerging from the primordial waters at the beginning of creation; these waters themselves were symbolized in temples together with fertile trees receiving life from such waters. ... Daniel's picture of an expanding mountain is compatible with ancient Near Eastern cosmogonies that sometimes portray a hillock arising amidst the chaos seas as the bridgehead of a new creation." Beale, *The Temple and the Church's Mission*, 53, 148, citing abundant secondary literature in support of this interpretation.

41   Wright, *Jesus and the Victory of God*, 500, citing 4 Ezra 13:25–38 as an example. See also Joachim Jeremias, "*Lithos*" in *Theological Dictionary of the New Testament*, 10 vols., ed. Gerhard Kittel (Grand Rapids, MI: Eerdmans, 1967), 4:272–273, for later rabbinic texts that explicitly identify the stone as the "Messiah."

to pieces; but when it falls on any one, it will crush him." (Matt. 21:42–44)[42]

Here we see quite clearly that Jesus is applying the image of the Danielic stone (as well as the Temple stone of Psalm 118) to himself. In light of this parallel, there should be no doubt that "the idea of the 'stone' is closely linked with the idea of the new eschatological Temple," and that Jesus applied this idea to himself.[43]

But, one might object: where could Jesus have gotten the (admittedly strange) idea that the entire Temple—not to mention creation itself—could be embodied in a single individual? Is it really plausible to believe that he could have identified himself with both the eschatological Temple and the beginnings of the new creation? Although to answer this question in full would take us too far afield, it is critical to note here that in ancient Judaism, there was one person who was viewed as embodying in himself both the Temple and the cosmos. That person was *the Jewish High Priest*, whose liturgical vestments were meant to replicate both the Temple and the universe.[44] As Josephus states, the colored "garments of the High Priest" were woven to match "the fabric of the Tabernacle."[45] And on those same garments were woven figures of the universe:

> For upon [the High Priest's] long robe *the whole world was depicted*,
> and the glories of the fathers were engraved on the four rows of stones,
> and your majesty on the diadem upon his head. (Wis. 8:24)

> Then [Moses] gave [the priests] their sacred vestments, giving to his brother [Aaron, the High Priest] the robe which reached down to his feet, and the mantle which covered his shoulders, as a sort of breast-plate, being *an embroidered robe, adorned with all kinds of figures, and a representation of the universe.* (Philo, circa 50 A.D.).[46]

---

42 Compare Mark 12:10–11; Luke 20:17–18. On the interpretation and authenticity of this passage, see the stunning article by Craig A. Evans, "God's Vineyard and Its Caretakers," in *Jesus and His Contemporaries*, 381–406. See also Seyoon Kim, "Jesus—the Son of God, the Stone, the Son of Man, and the Servant: The Role of Zechariah in the Self-Identification of Jesus," in *Tradition and Interpretation in the New Testament: Essays in Honor of E. Earle Ellis*, eds. Gerald F. Hawthorne and Otto Betz (Tübingen: Mohr-Siebeck, 1987), 134–148.

43 So Wright, *Jesus and the Victory of God*, 499.

44 See Beale, *The Temple and the Church's Mission*, 47–48; Sanders, *Judaism*, 249.

45 *Antiquities of the Jews*, Bk. 3, Chap. 7, 80, in *The Works of Josephus*, 90; compare Exod. 26:1; 28:5–6.

46 *The Life of Moses* Bk. 2, 143. Text in C. D. Yonge, trans., *The Works of Philo: Complete and Unabridged* (Peabody, MA: Hendrickson, 1993), 503.

We will return to the connections between the Temple and the priesthood in our final section below. For now, it is simply necessary to point out that in an ancient Jewish context, the notion that both the Temple and the cosmos could somehow be embodied in a single individual had a ready example in the figure of the High Priest. As the first-century Jewish philosopher Philo says: the High Priest "represents the world" and is a "microcosm" or "little world" (*brachys kosmos*).[47] Indeed, one could even suggest that for ancient Judaism, the cosmos was a macro-temple, the Temple was a microcosm, and the High Priest, when he donned his priestly vestments, was both a micro-temple *and* a microcosm, summing up all things—the "twelve tribes" and "the whole world"—in himself.

In light of what we have seen so far, we can now draw the following conclusion: a second key to the mystery of Jesus' relationship with the Temple has to do with the fact that the Jerusalem Temple was not simply a building; it was a microcosm of the universe. Moreover, the Gospels suggest that while Jesus expected the old Temple to be destroyed and replaced by a new Temple, he did not expect the new Temple to be a building of bricks and mortar. It would not be "made with hands"—that is, it would not be of this world, but of supernatural origin.

Sanders concludes: "We should probably think that [Jesus'] expectation was that new Temple would be given by God from heaven."[48] This is extremely important: to the extent that the Temple represented the cosmos, the destruction of the old Temple represented the demise and passing away of the old creation. Likewise, to the extent that the Temple represented all creation, any talk of a new Temple—especially one "not made with hands"—would signal the onset of the new creation. Great as the earthly Temple was, in the eschatological age, there would be no place for the Jerusalem Temple of stone and mortar, a Temple "made with hands." If Jesus was truly awaiting the coming of a new Temple, then his reverence for the earthly Temple and his prophecies of its demise make perfect sense; for it would be transcended by a new Temple and a new creation that would be made "by no human hand."

This interpretation finds confirmation in the gospel accounts of Jesus' crucifixion and death.[49] There we find an implicit connection between the death of Jesus, the demise of the Temple, and the destruction of the cosmos:

---

47 *Life of Moses* Bk. 2, 135. "Priestly attire was a microcosm of the Temple itself, which was also a small model of the entire cosmos." Beale, *The Temple and the Church's Mission*, 48.

48 Sanders, *Jesus and Judaism*, 73.

49 For an excellent study of Jesus' passion and death as an eschatological event with both cultic and cosmic ramifications, see Dale C. Allison, Jr., *The End of the Ages Has Come: An Early Interpretation of the Passion and Resurrection of Jesus* (Philadelphia: Fortress, 1985), 30–33. He points out that in Ps. 104:2; Isa. 40:22, and in the Babylonian Talmud, *Baba Metsia* [The Middle Gate] 59a, the sky is compared to a "curtain" or "tent."

> Now from the sixth hour there was darkness over all the land until the ninth hour. And about the ninth hour Jesus cried with a loud voice, "Eli, Eli, lema sabachthani?" that is, "My God, my God, why hast thou forsaken me?" And some of the bystanders hearing it said, "This man is calling Elijah." ... And *Jesus cried again with a loud voice and yielded up his spirit*. And behold, *the veil of the Temple* was *torn* (*eschisthe*) in two, from top to bottom; and the *earth shook and the rocks were torn* (*eschisthesan*); the tombs also were opened, and many bodies of the saints who had fallen asleep were raised, and coming out of their tombs after his resurrection they went into the holy city and appeared to many. (Matt. 27:45–53)

Notice the twofold consequence of Jesus' death: with the yielding up of his spirit, it is *the Temple* and *the earth* that are both "torn asunder" (Greek: *schizo*). In other words, the effects of his death are both *cultic* and *cosmic*. With his crucifixion, the Temple of the old creation and indeed, creation itself, are not only thrown into a state of upheaval, but arguably begin the process of "passing away." Should there be any doubt about this suggestion, recall what we learned earlier and what every first-century Jew would have known: on the Temple veil was depicted "the panorama of the heavens."[50] Hence, with the tearing of the Temple veil and the earthquake—the whole universe, "heaven and earth," were symbolically being torn asunder. And because the Jerusalem Temple was the sign and symbol of this universe, it was now destined to share the same fate. The old Temple would be replaced by a new, and the old world—as Isaiah had said so long ago—would be replaced by "a new heavens and a new earth" (Isa. 65:17; 66:22). And all this, according to Jesus, would begin "on the third day."

The Temple as the Sole Place of Sacrifice

The third ancient Jewish belief that can shed light on the mystery of Jesus and the Temple is that the latter was regarded as the sole place of sacrificial worship.[51] Now, it is true some Jews, such as the Essenes, at various times rejected the sacrifices in the Temple as illegitimate or ritually impure. And it is also true that outside the land of Israel, in the Jewish diaspora, some Jews may have departed from the Torah and officiated at their own sacrificial services.[52] Nevertheless, the fact remains that

---

50   Josephus, *Wars of the Jews*, Bk. 5, Chap. 5, 214. So Allison, *The End of the Ages Has Come*, 33.

51   On these points, see discussion in Sanders, *Judaism*, 47–54.

52   For criticisms of the Second Temple and even the rejection of the Temple as defiled, see, for example, 1 *Enoch* 90:28–29; *Damascus Document* (CDa) 5:6–7; Josephus, *Antiquities of the Jews* 18:9; Craig A. Evans, "Opposition to the Temple: Jesus and the Dead Sea Scrolls," in *Jesus and the Dead Sea Scrolls*, ed. James H. Charlesworth, Anchor Bible Reference Library (New York: Doubleday, 1992), 235–253; Maier, "Temple," 923–924.

for what Sanders has called "common Judaism," the Temple in Jerusalem was the only place where God could be licitly worshiped through the offering of sacrifice.[53] This belief was of course rooted in the divine Law given to Moses:

> You shall seek the place which the LORD your God will choose out of all your tribes to put his name and make his habitation there; thither you shall go, and thither you shall bring your burnt offerings and your sacrifices, your tithes and the offering that you present, your votive offerings, your freewill offerings, and the firstlings of your herds and of your flock; and there you shall eat before the LORD your God, and you shall rejoice, you and your households, in all that you undertake, in which the LORD your God has blessed you. ... Take heed that you do not offer your burnt offerings at every place you see; but at the place which the LORD will choose in one of your tribes, there you shall offer your burnt offerings, and there you shall do all that I am commanding you. (Deut. 12:5–14)

For Jews living at the time of Jesus, this text meant that while God could be honored through prayer, song, and Scripture reading in the local synagogues, the essence of religious worship—*sacrifice*—took place only in the Temple. Hence, for what Sanders calls "common Judaism," the Temple in Jerusalem was the only place sacrificial worship could be offered to God. Indeed, the Mishnah prescribes excommunication for anyone who "offers up [an offering] outside [the Temple court]," placing such an action on par with Sabbath-breaking, incest, blasphemy, idolatry, and child-sacrifice.[54] In contrast to the pagan world, whose landscape was littered with a host of temples to a pantheon of various deities, first-century Judaism explicitly restricted sacrificial worship of the one God to only one place: the Jerusalem Temple.

For Jesus and his contemporaries, this restriction of sacrificial worship to the Temple had important liturgical consequences, especially during major sacrificial feasts. According to witnesses such as Josephus and Philo, at such times, thousands of Jews would converge upon Jerusalem in order to offer animal sacrifices there in the Temple. Particularly striking is Josephus' description of how many pilgrims came to Jerusalem at Passover each year. He describes them as "an innumerable multitude," who had come from far and wide "in order to worship God."[55] When the time came, they would offer the Passover sacrifice "with cheerful willingness."

---

53   On these points, see discussion in Sanders, *Judaism*, 47–54.
54   Mishnah *Kerithoth* [Uprootings] 1:1, in *The Mishnah*, 563.
55   Josephus, *Antiquities of the Jews*, 17:213–214, in *The Works of Josephus*, 465.

At this time "they are required to slay more sacrifices in number than at any other festival."[56] He even gives us a precise description of the liturgical multitude:

> So these High Priests, upon the coming of their feast which is called the Passover, when they slay their sacrifices, from the ninth hour [about 3 p.m.] to the eleventh [about 5 p.m.], but so that a company not less than ten belong to every sacrifice (for it is not lawful for them to feast singularly by themselves), and many of us are twenty in a company, found the number of sacrifices was 256,500; which, upon the allowance of no more than ten that feast together, amounts to 2,700,200 persons that were pure and holy.[57]

Even if somewhat exaggerated, this is a staggering figure: over 200,000 lambs for some 2 million people. For the modern reader, who probably has never witnessed a single animal sacrifice, much less several thousand, it is difficult to imagine two hundred thousand lambs being slaughtered at the Passover feast, and just *how much blood* would have been spilled. Indeed, the Mishnah tells us that a drainage canal had to be built to allow for the flow of blood from the altar:

> At the south-western corner [of the Altar] there were two holes like two narrow nostrils by which *the blood that was poured* over the western base and the southern base *used to run down and mingle in the water-channel and flow out into the brook Kidron.*[58]

One can only imagine what this would have looked like during a major feast like Passover. With some 200,000 lambs being slaughtered and their blood being poured out upon the altar, the brook of the Kidron Valley must have looked like a veritable river of blood and water, flowing out from the altar of the Temple. We will return to this image shortly; for now, we need only stress that all this was so because the Temple was the sole place of sacrifice. Indeed, according to the Pentateuch, there was no other place the blood could licitly be poured out in sacrificial worship.

With this important background in mind, we can now turn to passages in the Gospels that bear on Jesus' relationship with Temple sacrifice. As mentioned above, there should be no doubt that, during the greater portion of his public ministry,

---

56 Josephus, *Antiquities of the Jews*, 17:213, in *The Works of Josephus*, 465.

57 Josephus, *The Wars of the Jews*, 6:423–427, in *The Works of Josephus*, 749.

58 Mishnah *Middoth* [Measurements] 3:2. For other mentions of this drainage channel, see Mishnah tractates *Yoma* [The Day of Atonement] 5:6; *Zebahim* [Sacrifices] 8:7ff.; *Temurah* [Exchange] 7:6; *Tamid* [Always] 5:5. It is fascinating to note that the same channel that was used to drain the blood into the river was also used for pouring out "drink-offerings" of wine; see Mishnah *Meilah* [Sacrilege] 3:3.

Jesus himself not only participated in the Jewish feasts, but also directed others to offer the appropriate sacrifices in the Temple.[59] One thinks here of course not only of his parents traveling to Jerusalem to keep the Passover when he was twelve years old (Luke 2:41–51), but of his words to the leper who was cleansed: "Go, show yourself to the priest, and offer the gift that Moses commanded, for a proof to the people" (Matt. 8:4; see also Mark 1:44; Luke 5:14). However, all this changes when, during his last days in Jerusalem, he performs one of his most memorable prophetic signs: the so-called "cleansing of the Temple." Although this episode is well known, I cite it here to highlight the sacrificial implications of his action:

> And they came to Jerusalem. And he entered the Temple and began to drive out those who sold and those who bought in the Temple, and *he overturned the tables of the money-changers and the seats of those who sold pigeons; and he would not allow any one to carry anything through the Temple.* And he taught, and said to them, "Is it not written, 'My house shall be called a house of prayer for all the nations'? But you have made it a den of robbers.'" (Mark 11:15–16)[60]

Contrary to common opinion, Jesus' action in the Temple is not merely a spontaneous outburst of righteous indignation at the extortion of pilgrims by greedy money-changers.[61] Much less is it, as S. G. F. Brandon once suggested, an attempt at enacting a full-scale "takeover" of the Jerusalem Temple.[62] Instead, I would submit, it is quite clearly a symbolic action, a prophetic sign, carried out in the tradition of biblical prophets like Isaiah, Jeremiah, and Ezekiel.[63] The meaning of this sign is evident from its *effect*: by overturning the tables of the money-changers and by driving out those who were buying and selling the animal sacrifices, Jesus temporarily causes a *cessation of sacrifice*. As Wright states:

---

59 It is intriguing to note, along with Congar, that "the Gospels say nothing of any sacrifice offered by Jesus" in the Jerusalem Temple. Congar, *The Mystery of the Temple*, 116–117. I doubt, however, whether this silence should be taken to suggest that Jesus never offered sacrifice in the Temple— something which would have arguably put him in the position of breaking the Mosaic Law which he came not to abolish but to fulfill (Matt. 5:17). The question of whether he ever offered a sin offering, however, is something worthy of christological reflection and speculation. Compare Mary's offering in Luke 2:22–24, done out of obedience to the Law.

60 For an exhaustive survey of competing opinions and interpretations, see Jostein Ådna, *Jesu Stellung zum Tempel* [Jesus' Stand against the Temple], Wissenschaftliche Untersuchungen zum Neuen Testament 119 (Tübingen: Mohr Siebeck, 2000).

61 No hard evidence for such extortion has ever been produced, and the money-changers served an essential role to pious pilgrims. See Sanders, *Jesus and Judaism*, 61–71.

62 See S. G. F. Brandon, *Jesus and the Zealots* (Manchester: Manchester University, 1967).

63 Sanders actually uses the terminology of "symbolic demonstration"; I find "sign" more precise and more helpful because it is actually utilized in the biblical texts. Compare Sanders, *Jesus and Judaism*, 69

I suspect that the answer [to the question of the meaning of Jesus' actions] lies closer to the mechanics of what actually happened in the Temple. ... Without the right money, individual worshippers could not purchase their sacrificial animals. Without animals, sacrifice could not be offered. *Without sacrifice, the Temple had lost its raison d'être. The fact that Jesus effected only a brief cessation of sacrifice fits perfectly with the idea of a symbolic action.* He was not attempting a reform; he was symbolizing judgment.[64]

In short, in the "cleansing of the Temple," Jesus is performing a small-scale symbolic demonstration of what will eventually happen to the Temple as whole: the sacrifices will cease when the Temple is destroyed (compare Dan. 9:25–27).

The question this should raise for us, is, of course: if Jesus symbolized the cessation of sacrifice in the Temple, did he think it would be restored? Would the sacrificial worship of God cease altogether? Or would it be superseded by something greater? To answer this question, I turn to one of the great Jewish scholars of the twentieth century: Jacob Neusner. In his interpretation of the cleansing of the Temple, he states:

[The overturning of the money-changers' tables] would have provoked astonishment, since it will have called into question the very simple fact that the daily whole offering [known as the *tamid*] effected atonement and brought about expiation for sin, and God had so instructed Moses in the Torah. Accordingly, only someone who rejected the Torah's explicit teaching concerning the daily whole offering could have overturned the tables—or, as I shall suggest, someone who had in mind setting up a different table, and for a different purpose: for the action carries the entire message, both negative and positive. ... The overturning of the moneychangers' tables represents an act of rejection of the most important rite of the Israelite cult, the daily

---

64   Wright, *Jesus and the Victory of God*, 423. See also John Dominic Crossan, *The Historical Jesus* (San Francisco: HarperCollins, 1991), 357: "[Jesus'] action is not, of course, a physical destruction of the Temple, but it is a deliberate symbolic attack. It 'destroys' the Temple by 'stopping' its fiscal, sacrificial, and liturgical operations." Although Sanders' interpretation of Jesus' actions as a "symbolic demonstration" have been criticized by some, the strongest arguments for this interpretation is based on the fact that Jesus' actions did not—indeed, they could not—actually cause the buying and selling of sacrifices in the Temple to cease entirely. As Sanders rightly points out, the Temple complex was huge; if Jesus had really intended to stop all buying and selling, this would have taken an army of men. All Jesus can do alone is temporarily interrupt the offering of sacrifice. Hence, anyone witnessing the event would have recognized it is the symbolic action of a prophet, intended to make a point. See Sanders, *Jesus and Judaism*, 70.

whole-offering, and, therefore, a statement that there is a means
of atonement other than the daily whole offering, which is now
null. *Then what was to take the place of the daily whole-offering? It
was to be the rite of the Eucharist: table for table, whole offering for
whole offering.*[65]

This is a fascinating conclusion: for Neusner, Jesus' actions did not just symbolize the cessation of just any sacrifice, but of the cessation of the *tamid*, the daily
whole burnt offering, which was believed to effect atonement (see Num. 28:1–8).
Moreover, when Jesus' actions in the Temple are combined with his actions in the
upper room, they lead a Jewish scholar like Neusner to the conclusion that he
intended the sacrifices of the Jerusalem Temple to be replaced by "the rite of the
Eucharist."

Should there be any doubt about Neusner's suggestion, we need only turn
to the account of the Last Supper, and pay particular attention to the sacrificial
language and imagery utilized by Jesus in the words of institution:

Now, as they were eating, Jesus took bread, and blessed, and
broke it, and gave it to the disciples and said, "Take, eat; *this
is my body*." And he took a cup, and when he had given thanks
he gave it to them, saying, "Drink of it, all of you; for this is
my *blood of the covenant*, which is *poured out for many* for *the
forgiveness of sins*. (Matt. 26:26–28)[66]

As Joachim Jeremias pointed out some fifty years ago, by utilizing the
combined imagery of "body" and "blood," any ancient Jew would have recognized
that Jesus "is applying to himself *terms from the language of sacrifice*."[67] This is
especially true of the image of "blood" being "poured out"; such language is clearly
sacrificial imagery drawn directly from the liturgy of the Temple (Lev. 4:5–7; Deut.
12:26–27).

---

65   Jacob Neusner, "Money-Changers in the Temple: The Mishnah's Explanation," *New Testament Studies* 35 (1989): 287–290 (here 289–90, emphasis added), cited in Jostein Ådna, "Jesus' Symbolic Action in the Temple (Mark 11:15–17): The Replacement of the Sacrificial Cult by His Atoning Death," in *Gemeinde ohne Tempel* [Community without Temple], eds. Beate Ego, Armin Lange, and Peter Pilhofer (Tübingen: Mohr Siebeck, 1999), 461–473 (citation 472, n. 6). For similar conclusions, "Jesus as the Founder of a Cult: the Last Supper and the Primitive Christian Eucharist," in Gerd Theissen and Annette Merz, *The Historical Jesus: A Comprehensive Guide* (Minneapolis: Fortress, 1998), 405–439.

66   Compare Mark 14:22–24; Luke 22:19–20; 1 Cor. 11:23–25. On the authenticity of words of institution, see Wright, *Jesus and the Victory of God*, 559–562.

67   Joachim Jeremias, *The Eucharistic Words of Jesus*, trans. John Bowden (London: SCM, 1966), 222.

Once these parallels are clear, Jesus' actions during his last days in Jerusalem—both in the cleansing of the Temple and at the Last Supper—begin to make a great deal of sense, and indeed mutually illuminate one another. By temporarily causing the cessation of sacrifice in the Temple, Jesus points forward to the day when "sacrifice and offering" will "cease" in the Jerusalem Temple, as the prophet Daniel had foretold (see Dan. 9:27).

But at the same time, this does not mean that sacrificial worship will be entirely brought to an end. Rather, it is the very "pouring out of blood," which was formerly confined to the Temple, that will now be transferred to the rite of the Last Supper, and, through the command for it to be repeated, to the early Eucharist of the disciples. Indeed, when the Jewish background is properly taken into account, it becomes clear that *it is precisely the Jewish notion of one single locus of sacrificial worship that lays the foundation for Jesus' prophecy of the Temple's destruction.* Once the offering of the "blood of the covenant" is transferred from the Temple sacrifices to the offering of his own body and blood, there can no longer be any room for Jerusalem Temple cult. Its time has come to an end. There can be only one Temple of sacrifice: the body of Jesus.

Again, while this paper is primarily focused on Jesus' own teachings and actions, it is important not to let confirmation from the accounts of crucifixion pass us by. There is in fact one aspect of his passion and death that is well-known, although its possible connection to the Temple sacrifice is frequently overlooked.[68] I am speaking of the Gospel of John's description of the piercing of Jesus' side, from which blood and water flow:

> Since it was the day of Preparation, in order to prevent the bodies from remaining on the cross on the Sabbath ... the Jews asked Pilate that their legs might be broken, and that they might be taken away. So the soldiers came and broke the legs of the first, and of the other who had been crucified with him; but when they came to Jesus and saw that he was already dead, they did not break his legs. *But one of the soldiers pierced his side with a spear, and at once there came out blood and water.* He who saw it has borne witness—his testimony is true, and he knows that he tells the truth—that you may also believe. (John 19:31–35)

---

68 Compare, for example, Brown, *The Gospel according to John*, 2:946–952, whose lengthy and detailed discussion of the historicity and meaning of the flow of blood and water from Jesus' side fails to record any witnesses in connection with the Temple.

What is the meaning of this unforgettable scene, and why does John step into the narrative to insist on the veracity of his eyewitness testimony to the event?[69] In light of what we have learned about Temple sacrifice, I suggest that John is calling attention to the fact that *Jesus' crucified body has now become the locus of sacrifice; his body is the new Temple.* Should there be any doubt about this, recall what we learned earlier: it was from the altar of sacrifice in the Temple that a stream of blood flowed, mixing with the waters of the Kidron to form a river of blood and water.

If this is the background which John has in mind—and I submit that it is—then the obvious implication is that *it is no longer the Temple in Jerusalem from which the blood of sacrifice will flow. The Temple has now been replaced by the immolated body of Jesus.* Not only does Jesus replace the Temple sacrifices with the bread and wine of the Last Supper—which he identifies as his "body" and "blood"—but the very body and blood of the crucified Messiah is now revealed as the true Temple of God. And because, as every first-century Jew would have known, there could be only one place of sacrifice, Jesus' body now replaces the Temple in Jerusalem. He fulfills the purpose of the Temple in himself; what he began in the upper room is completed on the wood of the cross, and the mystery of his identity with the Temple is now fully revealed. In this light, the words of John from earlier in his gospel now make sense:

> The Jews then said to him, "What sign have you to show us for doing this?" Jesus answered them, *"Destroy this Temple, and in three days I will raise it up."* The Jews then said, "It has taken forty-six years to build this Temple, and will you raise it up in three days?" But he spoke to them of *the Temple of his body.* (John 2:18–21)

The Temple as the Place of the Sacrificial Priesthood

The fourth and final aspect of the ancient Jewish Temple that has the power to illuminate the mystery of Jesus' relation to it is the identity of the Temple as the place of the sacrificial priesthood.[70] If, for an ancient Jew, it would have been absurd to speak of religious worship without sacrifice, then it would be equally absurd to

---

69   See now Richard Bauckham, *Jesus and the Eyewitnesses: the Gospels as Eyewitness Testimony* (Grand Rapids, MI: Eerdmans, 2006), 358–383.

70   On the priesthood and the Temple, see esp. Sanders, "The Ordinary Priests and Levites: At Work in the Temple," in *Judaism,* 77–102; and Schürer, "Priesthood and Temple Worship," in *The History of the Jewish People,* 2:237–313. See also Haran, *Temples and Temple-Service in Ancient Israel;* Haran, "Priest and Priesthood," in *Encyclopedia Judaica,* 16 vols. (New York: KTAV, 1971), 13:1076–1088; Joachim Jeremias, *Jerusalem at the Time of Jesus,* trans. F. H. Cave and C. H. Cave

speak of sacrifice without priesthood. Indeed, the two are almost synonymous: the Temple is the locus of the priesthood because it is the sole place of sacrifice, and it is the sole place of sacrifice because it is the locus of the priesthood. The place of "the priests, the ministers of the LORD," is "between the vestibule and the altar"—that is, in the Temple (Joel 2:17). Hence, any attempt to understand Jesus' relationship to the ancient Jewish Temple must eventually raise the question of his relationship to the ancient Jewish priesthood.

And yet, when we turn to recent studies of Jesus and Judaism, we find a strange situation: If there is any single subject which modern historical scholarship on Jesus has almost completely neglected, it is the subject of Jesus and the Jewish priesthood.[71] Although one finds over and over again the assertion that Jesus expected a new Temple, one searches even the most in-depth monographs on Jesus in vain for any detailed treatment of whether he expected this eschatological Temple to be in any way tied to an eschatological priesthood.

This is true, despite the fact that it is widely acknowledged that the Dead Sea Scrolls have proven beyond the shadow of a doubt that Jews in the first century were not only waiting for a new Temple, but for a priestly Messiah.[72] Indeed, several major scholars categorically deny even the possibility that Jesus saw himself as a priestly Messiah, much less that he sought to establish an eschatological priesthood.[73] Remarkably, this is even true of studies that are otherwise very interested in the ancient Jewish context of Jesus' words and deeds. Such works leave one with the distinct (but historically puzzling) impression that while Jesus had a great deal

---

(Philadelphia: Fortress, 1969), 147–221; de Vaux, *Ancient Israel*, 274–515; Gray, *Sacrifice in the Old Testament*, 179–270.

71   The most notable exception is the excellent pair of articles by Crispin H. T. Fletcher-Louis, "Jesus as the High Priestly Messiah: Part 1," *Journal for the Study of the Historical Jesus* 4:2 (2006): 155–175; "Jesus as the High Priestly Messiah: Part 2," *Journal for the Study of the Historical Jesus* 5:1 (2007): 57–79. For others, see Albert Vanhoye, S.J., *Old Testament Priests and the New Priest*, trans. J. Bernard Orchard, (Petersham, MA: St. Bede's, 1986), 47–59; André Feuillet, *The Priesthood of Christ and His Ministers*, trans. Matthew J. O'Connell (New York: Doubleday, 1975); Oscar Cullman, *The Christology of the New Testament*, trans. Shirley C. Guthrie and Charles A. M. Hall (London: SCM, 1959), 83–89. It is notable that none of these appear in major historical monographs on Jesus.

72   See James C. VanderKam and Peter Flint, *The Meaning of the Dead Sea Scrolls: Their Significance for Understanding the Bible, Judaism, Jesus, and Christianity* (San Franciso: HarperCollins, 2002), 265–273; John Collins, *The Scepter and the Star: The Messiahs of the Dead Sea Scrolls and Other Ancient Literature*, Anchor Bible Reference Library (New York: Doubleday, 1995), 74–101.

73   See, for example, Dunn, *Jesus Remembered*, 654; Jürgen Becker, *Jesus of Nazareth*, trans. James E. Crouch (New York: Walter de Gruyter, 1998), 215; James D. G. Dunn, "Messianic Ideas and their Influence on the Jesus of History," in *The Messiah: Developments in Earliest Judaism and Christianity*, ed. James H. Charlesworth (Minneapolis: Fortress, 1992), 373; Geza Vermes, *Jesus the Jew: A Historian's Reading of the Gospels* (Philadelphia: Fortress, 1973), 153. See Fletcher-Louis, "Jesus as the High Priestly Messiah: Part 1," 155, n. 1.

to say about the Jewish Temple, he had almost nothing to say about the Jewish priesthood.

In this final section, I would like to challenge this widespread assumption and suggest instead that if Jesus expected a new, eschatological Temple, then it stands to reason that he also expected a new, eschatological priesthood.[74] From a first-century Jewish perspective, the Temple cult and the sacrificial priesthood were inextricably intertwined. Although I cannot develop the arguments at length here,[75] several of the texts we have already examined regarding Jesus and the new Temple also suggest that Jesus not only awaited an eschatological priesthood but also saw in himself and his disciples a new priesthood. Indeed, it is no coincidence that *in the very texts wherein Jesus speaks about the eschatological Temple, he also speaks of the eschatological priesthood.*

Take, as our first example, the famous account of the cleansing of the Temple. As we saw above, Jesus' act of overturning the tables of the moneychangers is widely recognized as a prophetic sign of the destruction of the Jerusalem Temple and its eventual replacement by a new Temple. But what often goes overlooked is that in one of the Old Testament prophecies cited by Jesus, Isaiah not only speaks of an eschatological Temple; he also speaks of *a new priesthood*, in which not only Levites but *Gentiles* will offer sacrifice and act as priests. Compare the texts:

> And [Jesus] entered the Temple and began to drive out those who sold and those who bought in the Temple, and he over-turned the tables of the money-changers and the seats of those who sold pigeons; and he would not allow any one to carry any-thing through the Temple. And he taught, and said to them, "*Is it not written, 'My house shall be called a house of prayer for all the nations'?* But you have made it a den of robbers." (Mark 11:15–16)

> And *the foreigners who join themselves to the* LORD, *to minister to him*, to love the name of the LORD, and to be his servants ... *these I will bring to my holy mountain*, and make them joyful in my house of prayer; *their burnt offerings and their sacrifices will be accepted on my altar; for my house shall be called a house of prayer for all peoples.* (Isa. 56:6–8)

---

74   I am building here on the excellent work of Fletcher-Louis, "Jesus as the High Priestly Messiah," but taking his insights in a different direction. See also his book: Crispin H. T. Fletcher-Louis, *All the Glory of Adam: Liturgical Anthropology in the Dead Sea Scrolls*, Studies on the Texts of the Desert of Judah 57 (Leiden: Brill, 2002).

75   I refer the reader here to my forthcoming volume, *Jesus and the Last Supper*, where I will treat this in much greater depth.

As many commentators have recognized, the prophecy of Isaiah that is cited by Jesus is one of the most striking in the Old Testament. For in it, Isaiah clearly depicts Gentiles ("foreigners") as not only being brought by God into the Temple (the "house of prayer") to worship. He also depicts them acting as priests—offering their "burnt offerings" and "sacrifices" on the "altar"—something only priests were allowed to do.[76] Should there be any doubt about this interpretation, Isaiah makes the point a second time, in the final chapter of the book, where God declares that the Gentile "nations" will bring the lost tribes of Israel to the new Jerusalem, but that he will take "some of them" to be "priests and Levites" (Isa. 66:20–21).

It is hard to overestimate how striking these prophecies would have been to any Jewish reader living in the first-century. For at the time Jesus, every practicing Jew would have known that it was not only totally prohibited for a Gentile to act as priest, but even the majority of Israelites—all twelve tribes, with the exception of the tribe of Levi—were prohibited from acting a priests. Since the time of the golden calf incident, the priesthood had been taken away from the twelve tribes as a whole and given to only one: the tribe of Levi (see Exod. 32).

The upshot of this background is simple: by speaking of a future "house of prayer" for all nations where Gentiles act as "priests and Levites," Isaiah is clearly describing not only a new Temple, but a radically new priesthood—*an eschatological priesthood*. The fact that Jesus chooses and cites this particular prophecy when he performs his sign of the Temple's destruction is not inconsequential: it demonstrates that he is not only awaiting a new Temple, but a new priesthood, in which both Israel and the Gentiles will act as priests in the eschatological age.

Should there be any doubt that this was possible in an ancient Jewish context, it is worth pointing out that this is exactly what is described in the ancient writing known as the *Testament of Levi*, which contains an amazing description of the coming of a priestly Messiah who inaugurates an eschatological priesthood.[77]

---

76 See Beale, *The Temple and the Church's Mission*, 135, citing E. J. Young, *The Book of Isaiah* (Grand Rapids, MI: Eerdmans, 1996), 535. Intriguingly, Beale suggests that "the reason that the Gentiles will be included as priests is because now the place of true worship and Temple service is not geographically located in the old, temporal Jerusalem, but throughout the entire earth, where 'all mankind will come to bow down before me' for ever (Isa. 66:23)." Beale, *The Temple and the Church's Mission*, 137–138.

77 Although there continues to be debate about the Jewish origin of the *Testaments of the Twelve Patriarchs*, of which the *Testament of Levi* is a part, Howard Clark Kee dates the Jewish elements to the second century B.C., especially given the fact that fragments of an Aramaic Testament of Levi were found among the Dead Sea Scrolls. For discussion, see Kee's introduction in *The Old Testament Pseudepigrapha*, 1:775–781. See also Collins, *The Scepter and the Star*, 86–89, who points out that while the current Greek testaments are "Christian in their present form," they are "widely thought to incorporate an older Jewish work," such as that found at Qumran. See the discussion in Gerbern S. Oegema, *The Anointed and His People: Messianic Expectations from the Maccabees to Bar Kochba*, Journal for the Study of the Pseudepigrapha Supplement Series 27

Although the passage is long, it is the most explicit ancient description of the hope for a priestly Messiah and a messianic priesthood, and is worth citing in full:

> When vengeance will have come upon them from the Lord, *the priesthood will lapse. And then the Lord will raise up a new priest, to whom all the words of the Lord will be revealed."* ... And the angels of glory of the Lord's presence will be made glad by him. *The heavens will be opened and from the Temple of glory sanctification will come upon him, with a fatherly voice, as from Abraham to Isaac.* And the glory of the Most High shall burst forth upon him. And the spirit of understanding and sanctification shall rest upon him in the water. For he shall give the majesty of the Lord to those who are his sons in truth forever. *And there shall be no successor for him from generation to generation forever. And in his priesthood the Gentiles shall be multiplied in knowledge upon the earth,* and they shall be illumined by the grace of the Lord. *In his priesthood sin shall cease* and lawless men shall rest from their evil deeds, and righteous men shall find rest in him. *And he shall open the gates of Paradise; he shall remove the sword that has threatened since Adam, and he will grant to the saints to eat of the Tree of Life.* The spirit of holiness shall be upon them. And Beliar shall be bound by him. And he shall grant his children the authority to trample on wicked spirits.[78]

Although much could be said about this important text, for now we need only make the following point: according to the *Testament of Levi*, there was an expectation that in the last days God would send a distinctively priestly Messiah, "an eschatological High Priest,"[79] who would not only restore the "lapsed" priesthood of the last days, but inaugurate a new priesthood in which "the Gentiles" would somehow participate. It is also worth noting, given what we have seen about the supernatural Temple, that the new priesthood of the Messiah does not appear to be focused on the earthly Jerusalem, but on "the Temple of glory" in "the heavens." Finally, this priesthood—this eschatological priesthood—will be ordered toward a definitive atonement for sin: "in his priesthood, sin shall cease."

With this in mind, we can turn to our second example from the Gospels: Jesus' response to the Pharisees' objection to his disciples plucking grain on the

---

(Sheffield: Sheffield Academic, 1998), 75–81, who treats the description of the priestly Messiah as representing the Jewish version of the document.

78 *Testament of Levi* 18:1–14, in *Old Testament Pseudepigrapha*, 1:794–795.

79 Collins, *The Scepter and the Star*, 89.

Sabbath. As we saw above, Jesus' justification for his disciples' actions rests above all on his identification of himself as "greater than the Temple" (Matt. 12:6). Again, however, Jesus' identification of himself with the Temple is not floating in mid-air: it is inextricably tied to his identification of himself with David and his disciples with *priests in the Temple*, as a justification for their "working" on the Sabbath. Consider the text a second time, this time focusing on the priestly imagery:

> At that time Jesus went through the grainfields on the Sabbath; his disciples were hungry, and they began to pluck ears of grain and to eat. But when the Pharisees saw it, they said to him, "Look, your disciples are doing what is not lawful to do on the Sabbath." He said to them, *"Have you not read what David did, when he was hungry, and those who were with him: how he entered the house of God and ate the Bread of the Presence, which it was not lawful for him to eat nor for those who were with him, but only for the priests? Or have you not read in the Law how on the Sabbath the priests in the Temple profane the Sabbath, and are guiltless?* I tell you, something greater than the Temple is here. And if you had known what this means, "I desire mercy, not sacrifice," you would not have condemned *the guiltless.* For the Son of Man is Lord of the Sabbath. (Matt. 12:1–8)

Admittedly, Jesus' argument here is somewhat dense. In order to properly understand it, we must turn again to the Old Testament background of his words, in which he alludes to two key texts, both of which are related to the weekly sacrifice of the Bread of the Presence.

First, he is alluding to passages in the Pentateuch which command the priests to offer the "Bread of the Presence"—a mysterious bread that was kept perpetually in the Tabernacle, and later, in the Temple (Exod. 24:59; 26:35)—on the Sabbath:

> [God said to Moses:] "And you shall take fine flour, and bake *twelve cakes* of it. ... And you shall set them in two rows, six in a row, upon the table of pure gold. ... *Every Sabbath day Aaron shall set it in order before the* LORD *continually on behalf of the sons of Israel as an everlasting covenant.* And *it shall be for Aaron and his sons, and they shall eat it in a holy place,* since it is for him a most holy portion out of the offerings by fire to the LORD, a perpetual debt." (Lev. 24:5–9)[80]

---

80   RSV, slightly adapted.

Here we see quite clearly the Bread of the Presence was not simply kept in the Tabernacle as a sign of God's "everlasting covenant" (Hebrew: *berith 'olam*) with the twelve tribes of Israel (the "twelve cakes"). It was also offered as an offering "every Sabbath day" by the priests ("Aaron and his sons"), with the requirement that the priests—and they alone—eat it in the Tabernacle (the "holy place"). The reason this is important is that it is sometimes forgotten that, in the Old Testament, the Sabbath was not just a day of rest from work: it was a day of *worship*, and worship was constituted by sacrifice. And there was one sacrifice that was unique to the Sabbath alone: the offering of the Bread of the Presence, which was accompanied by an offering of wine.[81] Each Sabbath day, the priests in the Temple would offer and eat the bread and wine of the Presence which, though "unbloody,"[82] was nevertheless a sacrifice in the true sense.[83] It is this sacrifice of bread and wine to which Jesus refers when he speaks of the "priests in the Temple" profaning the Sabbath by working, but remaining "guiltless."

Second, Jesus is also alluding to a time *when David and his disciples acted like priests* by going into the Tabernacle and actually eating the "Bread of the Presence," even though only priests were supposed to eat it (1 Sam. 21:3–6). In this episode, David and his men are on the move, in flight from Saul, and come to the Tabernacle and the priest Ahimelech. David asks the priest for "five loaves of bread, or whatever is here," to feed his men. The priest answers David by pointing out that he has "no common bread at hand," but only "holy bread"—and insists that the men cannot eat it unless they have abstained from sexual relations. Such temporary abstinence was required of priests in the Old Testament while serving in the Temple (Exod. 19:15; Deut. 23:9–13). David responds by pointing out that sexual abstinence was always practiced while on a military "expedition"—that is, he and his men are in a state of priestly purity—and Ahimelech therefore acquiesces:

> So the priest gave him the holy bread, for there was no bread
> there but the Bread of the Presence, which is removed from

---

81 See Exodus 25:39, which describes the Bread of the Presence being accompanied by "flagons and bowls with which to pour libations; of pure gold you shall make them" (likewise Exod. 37:16).

82 Compare *Testament of Levi* 3:6, which speaks of a "bloodless oblation," in *Old Testament Pseudepigrapha*, 1:789.

83 "Regarded from the standpoint of material used, sacred offerings fall into two broad classes: (1) the animal or bloody offering; (2) the vegetable or bloodless offering." Gray, *Sacrifice in the Old Testament*, 398. The bloody sacrifices are sometimes referred to by the Hebrew terms *zebah* and *'olah*, while the unbloody sacrifices are referred to by the Hebrew term *minhah* (at 401). The Bread of the Presence falls into the latter category. For further discussion, see Paul V. M Flesher, "Bread of the Presence," in *The Anchor Bible Dictionary*, 6 vols., Anchor Bible Reference Library (New York: Doubleday, 1992), 1:780–81.

before the LORD, to be replaced by hot bread on the day it is taken away [that is, the Sabbath]. (1 Sam. 21:6)

Again, the main thrust of this story is that in eating the Bread of the Presence, David—as elsewhere in the books of Samuel and Chronicles—acts as *a priest*. As Crispin Fletcher-Louis says, "The way Jesus tells the Old Testament story, *David* plays the role of the priest who enters the sanctuary on the Sabbath to collect the old bread and distribute it to his fellow priests."[84]

Once this background is in place, Jesus' overall response to the Pharisees becomes clear: they accuse his disciples of working on the Sabbath by plucking grain. Jesus responds by giving two examples of biblical cases where people appear to break the Mosaic Law: first, when David and his disciples enter the Tabernacle to eat the Bread of the Presence, and second, when the priests in the Temple offer the Bread of the Presence on the Sabbath, but remain "guiltless." The obvious implication of his parallel between the "guiltless" priests (Matt. 12:5) and his "guiltless" disciples (Matt. 12:7) is that both have priestly prerogatives when in the Temple. Again, Fletcher-Louis states:

> Jesus justifies his disciples breach of the Sabbath because he claims to be a sacral king and high priestly Son of Man. Where *he* is, in that place there is the transcendent liturgical space and time of the true Temple in which his disciples can legitimately act as priests for whom the Sabbath prohibition does not apply.[85]

But why does Jesus choose such obscure Old Testament examples? Although we can only speculate, one cannot help but wonder if the reason is because at the Last Supper he will institute a ritual in which the twelve disciples—most of whom were apparently not Levitical priests[86]—will be commanded *to repeat the very priestly act of offering sacrificial bread and wine of a new "covenant"* (Matt. 26:28;

---

84   Fletcher-Louis, "Jesus as the High Priestly Messiah: Part 2," 76. On the priesthood of David, see Carl E. Armerding, "Were David's Sons Priests?" in *Current Issues in Biblical and Patristic Interpretation: Studies in Honor of Merrill C. Tenney Presented by his Former Students*, ed. Gerald F. Hawthorne (Grand Rapids, MI: Eerdmans, 1975); Anthony Phillips, "David's Linen Ephod," *Vetus Testamentum* 19 (1969): 458–487.

85   Fletcher-Louis, "Jesus as the High-Priestly Messiah: Part 2," 77.

86   Although there is some speculation that John, the son of Zebedee was of a priestly family, and good reasons to believe that Matthew (Matt. 9:9; 10:3) was of Levitical heritage (he is also called "Levi" in Mark 2:15; Luke 5:27) there is no evidence to my knowledge that any of the other Twelve were of priestly descent. The theory about the priestly identity of John was recently given a very visible supporter in Joseph Ratzinger (Pope Benedict XVI), *Jesus of Nazareth*, trans. Adrian J. Walker (New York: Doubleday, 2007), 224–225, following Henri Cazelles, "Johannes. Ein

Mark 14:24; Luke 22:20; 1 Cor. 11:23). In the old Temple of the old covenant, this would constitute a grave sacrilege, as well as a violation of the Law. But, as we will see in a moment, in the new Temple—the Temple of Jesus' "body"—it appears that a new "Bread (and Wine) of the Presence" will constitute the center of the eschatological priesthood of the restored twelve tribes of Israel.

Once again, should this seem implausible in a first-century Jewish context, it is critical to recall that there is strong evidence that other Jews at the time of Jesus were thinking along the same lines. Particularly important in this regard is the testimony of the Dead Sea Scrolls, which provide so many insights into Jewish practice and belief at the turn of the era. It is well known that the authors of the scrolls were waiting for a new Temple in the eschatological age: indeed, one of the most famous scrolls is known as the *Temple Scroll*; it is an extremely long description of exactly what this new Temple and its new cult would be like.[87] It is also well-known that they were waiting for a priestly Messiah. But it is often missed that in at least one scroll, known as *The War Scroll*, the vision of the last days not only contains the expectation of an eschatological Temple but also an eschatological priesthood:

> They shall arrange *the chiefs of the priests* behind *the High Priest* and of his second (in rank), *twelve chiefs to serve in perpetuity before God*. And the twenty-six chiefs of the divisions shall serve in their divisions and after them *the chiefs of the Levites to serve always, twelve, one per tribe*. And the chiefs of their divisions shall each serve in his place. *The chiefs of the tribes*, and after them the fathers of the congregation, *shall take their positions in the gates of the sanctuary in perpetuity*. ... These shall take their positions at the holocausts and the sacrifices, in order to prepare pleasant incense for God's approval, to atone for all his congregation, and *to satisfy themselves in perpetuity before him at the table of glory*.[88]

Above all, two parallels stand out between this vision of the new Temple and the new priesthood and Jesus' own. First and foremost, it envisions an eschatological priesthood which consists both of the "High Priest" and twelve "chief priests"—one for each tribe—who will offer sacrifice in the eschatological Temple.

Sohn des Zebedäus. 'Priester' und Apostel" [John. A Son of Zebedee. 'Priest' and 'Apostle'] *Internationale Katholische Zeitschrift Communio* 31 (2002): 479–484.

87   See Otto Betz, "Jesus and the Temple Scroll," in *Jesus and the Dead Sea Scrolls*, ed. James H. Charlesworth, Anchor Bible Reference Library (New York: Doubleday, 1992), 75–103.

88   *1QWar Scroll* [1QM] 2:1–6, translation in Florentino García Martínez and Eibert J. C. Tigchelaar, *The Dead Sea Scrolls Study Edition*, 2 vols. (Leiden: Brill, 1997, 1998), 1:115.

The parallel between this numerical arrangement and Jesus and "the Twelve" is striking. Second, and equally important, the Scroll emphasizes that these twelve chief priests will not only offer normal animal sacrifices, but—in particular—they will feast on *the sacrificial Bread of the Presence*. When the Scroll says that they will feast at "the table of glory" (*shulhan kabod*), this is a clear reference to the golden "table" (*shulhan*) of the Bread of the Presence, which was in the Tabernacle sanctuary, and which could only be eaten by the priests (see Exod. 25:23–30; compare 1QM 2:6). In light of this connection, one cannot help but think of Jesus' words to the disciples at the Last Supper:

> As my Father appointed a kingdom for me, so do I appoint for you *that you may eat and drink at my table in my kingdom*, and *sit on thrones, judging the twelve tribes of Israel*. (Luke 22:29–30)

It seems that in both the Dead Sea Scrolls and in the Gospels, we find not only the vision of a new Temple, but of an eschatological priesthood that is focused on the sacrificial offering of the Bread of the Presence and the "table" of glory.

This connection brings us to our third and final example from the Gospels: Jesus' words and deeds at the Last Supper.[89] As we saw above, scholars such as Neusner have argued that by identifying the bread as his body and the wine as his blood, Jesus was deliberately replacing the sacrificial cultus of the Jerusalem Temple with the ritual of the Eucharist. But, again, what has often been overlooked is the distinctively *priestly* nature of his actions. By referring to his blood being "poured out" (Matt. 26:28; Mark 14:24; Luke 22:20) and commanding his disciples to "do this" (Luke 22:19; 1 Cor. 11:24–25), *Jesus deliberately institutes the repetition of a sacrificial rite of the Last Supper by the disciples, who would thereby act as eschatological priests.* In order to see this, we need to recall, again, that the "pouring out" of blood in a cultic context was a sacrificial act performed by priests.[90] Although laymen could slaughter the animal, it was only the priests who could "pour out" the blood at the altar:

---

89   On the Last Supper, see Dunn, *Jesus Remembered*, 229–231, 512–513, 771–773, 795–796, 804–805, 815–818; Theissen and Merz, *The Historical Jesus*, 405–436; Wright, *Jesus and the Victory of God*, 554–562; Barry D. Smith, *Jesus' Last Passover Meal* (Lewiston, NY: Edwin Mellen, 1993); Ben F. Meyer, "The Expiation Motif and the Eucharistic Words: A Key to the History of Jesus?" *Gregorianum* 69 (1988): 461–487.

90   See Exod. 29:12; Lev. 4:7, 18, 25–26, 30, 34; 8:15; 9:9; Deut. 12:25–27; 2 Kings 16:15. Lev. 17:1–6 is very explicit that if a layman "pours out" the blood of an animal as a sacrificial offering outside the Tabernacle, he incurs bloodguilt and shall be "cut off" from his people (Lev. 17:13; Deut. 12:16). I owe this point about the cultic nature of "pouring out" blood to Evans, *Mark*, 394. See also Jeremias, *The Eucharistic Words of Jesus*, 222, n. 5: "He is applying to himself terms from the language of sacrifice ... in the case of the participle *ekchunnomenon* ('poured out', Mark 14:24). *'Ekchein haima* is used in the LXX, apart from its use of murder or the domestic slaughter of cattle, only when speaking of sacrifice."

> And *the anointed priest* shall take some of the blood of the bull and bring it to the tent of meeting ... and *the priest* shall put some of the blood on the horns of the altar of fragrant incense before the LORD which is in the tent of meeting, and *the rest of the blood* of the bull *he shall pour out at the base of the altar.* (Lev. 4:5–7)

Thus, with Jesus' command to the disciples to "do this"—to offer his body and his blood in the form of bread and wine—he is commissioning them to perform a priestly action. Should there be any doubt about this, as Jeremias noted long ago, the injunction to "do this" was "an established expression for the repetition of a rite."[91] When this background is combined with the fact that Jesus' terminology of "remembrance" (*anamnesis*) was also linked to the repetition of the "Passover sacrifice" (compare the Septuagint translation of Exod. 12:14), it strains credulity to suggest that he did not see himself as instituting a sacrificial rite to be repeated by his priestly circle of disciples.

Lest there remain any doubt about this as well, we bring one final text to bear on our subject. As is widely recognized, Jesus' language of "blood" of the "covenant" (Matt. 26:28; Mark 14:24; Luke 22:20; 1 Cor. 11:25) is a direct allusion to a pivotal Old Testament event: the sacrificial liturgy of Moses and the elders of Israel atop Mount Sinai.[92] As most scholars recognize, Jesus' allusion draws a parallel between the sealing of the covenant with blood on Mount Sinai and his inauguration of the new covenant in the upper room. But what often goes unrecognized is the striking parallels between the priestly hierarchy of the Sinaitic liturgy and the various circles of Jesus' own disciples. Compare the following texts:

> And [the LORD] said to Moses, "Come up to the LORD, *you and Aaron, Nadab, and Abihu, and seventy of the elders of Israel,* and worship afar off. Moses alone shall come near to the LORD; but the others shall not come near, and the people shall not come up with him. And he [Moses] rose early in the morning, and built *an altar* at the foot of the mountain, and *twelve pillars, according to the twelve tribes of Israel.* And he sent *young men of the people of Israel, who offered burnt offerings and sacrificed peace offerings of oxen to the* LORD. And Moses took half of the blood and put

---

91 Jeremias, *The Eucharistic Words of Jesus,* 249–250. See Exod. 29:25; Num. 15:1–16; 1QRule of the Community [1QS] 2:19; compare 1QS 1:1–2:18; Jeremias points out that "All of these texts have kakah (LXX houtos) with a jussive form of 'assah (LXX poiein)." *The Eucharistic Words of Jesus,* 249, n. 4.

92 See Dunn, *Jesus Remembered,* 516.

it in basins, and half of the blood he threw against the altar. ... And Moses took the blood and threw it on the people, and said, "Behold, *the blood of the covenant* which the LORD has made with you in accordance with all these words." *Then Moses and Aaron, Nadab, and Abihu, and seventy of the elders of Israel went up, and they saw the God of Israel*; and there was under his feet as it were a pavement of sapphire stone, like the very heaven for clearness. And he did not lay his hand on the chief men of the people of Israel; *they beheld God, and ate and drank.* (Exod. 24:1–11)

If one carefully compares the numbers and divisions of this priestly hierarchy of Mount Sinai with the various circles of Jesus' own disciples, the parallels are quite striking:

Old Covenant Priesthood	*Jesus and his Disciples*[93]
Moses	Jesus
The 1: the High Priest, Aaron	The 1: Peter, chief of the Apostles
The 3: Aaron, Nadab, Abihu	The 3: Peter, James, and John
The 12: Twelve Pillars/"Young Men" of the Twelve Tribes	The 12: Twelve Apostles of the Twelve Tribes
The 70: Priestly Elders of Israel	The 70: Appointed and Sent Out

These parallels—which to my knowledge continue to go undetected by Jesus scholarship—are striking. What are we to make of them? Is it possible that Jesus was unaware of the numerical correspondence between his own disciples and the priestly mediators at Mount Sinai? I think not. Rather, they strongly suggest that *Jesus deliberately organized the various circles of his disciples to signify the imminent eschatological restoration of the sacrificial priesthood.*[94]

---

93 See Matt. 10:1–4; 16:13–20; 17:1; Luke 10:1–16.

94 Should there be any doubt about this, these parallels go a long way toward providing a historical explanation for the opposition Jesus met with from one particular ruling body within Second Temple Judaism: the Great Sanhedrin. For while modern scholars often miss the significance of Jesus' gathering and commissioning seventy disciples, the *seventy* members of the Jerusalem Sanhedrin would have certainly gotten the point. Jesus' gathering of priestly followers was a direct challenge to their authority and their Temple and a threat to their existence. See Mishnah *Sanhedrin* [The Council] 1:5–6: "The greater Sanhedrin was made up of one [the High Priest] and seventy and the lesser [Sanhedrin] of three and twenty. Whence do we learn that the greater Sanhedrin should be made up of one and seventy? It is written, 'Gather unto me seventy men of the elders of Israel' [Num 11:16]." To my mind, this parallel alone demolishes the position that Jesus had no intentions of establishing some kind of priestly hierarchy. This position is ultimately based on ignorance of (or inattention to) the priestly hierarchy of the Old Testament

In summary: although much more could be said, it seems clear that when Jesus' words and actions that reflect his anticipation of a new Temple are examined closely in light of their ancient Jewish background, they not only reveal his expectation of an eschatological Temple—which would consist of himself and his disciples—but of an eschatological priesthood as well. Although I am well aware that this conclusion swims against the tide of most twentieth-century scholarship on Jesus and that it may come as a surprise to some readers, it really should not. For anyone familiar with Second Temple Judaism at the time of Jesus—for that matter, anyone familiar with the Old Testament—knows that the Temple cult and the Temple priesthood were inextricably intertwined with one another. They existed in a living, symbiotic relationship. To the extent that Jesus did not come to "abolish" the Torah and the Prophets but to "fulfill" them (Matt. 5:17), one must ask and attempt to answer the important historical question of whether Jesus expected a new Temple and a new priesthood. And the answer that seems forthcoming from a close study of the sources is a resounding "yes."

The Mystery of the Temple: Some Conclusions

We end by returning to the initial paradox posed by Yves Congar in his masterful work, *The Mystery of the Temple*. How is it that we find in Jesus a combination of both deep respect for the Jewish Temple and at the same time a prophetic pronouncement of its ultimate demise? In this essay, I have tried to utilize four Jewish beliefs about the Temple—as the dwelling-place of God, a microcosm of heaven and earth, the sole locus of sacrifice, and the place of the sacrificial priesthood—to shed light on several sayings and deeds of Jesus.

As our study suggested, Jesus seems to have repeatedly tapped into these various beliefs about the Jewish Temple, but transferred them to himself, and, by extension, to his disciples. The implication of this transferal is quite simple: Jesus did not simply see himself—as he is so often portrayed nowadays—as a mere "eschatological prophet"—much less as a moralizing teacher of prudential wisdom. Rather, he saw himself as the new Temple, the eschatological Temple that had been spoken of by the prophets and was awaited by many Jews of his day.

The implications of these conclusions are significant. First, they suggest that Jesus believed that the sacrificial worship of the old covenant was coming to its end. The time of animal sacrifice was now being brought to a close, to be replaced not only by the sacrificial death of Jesus, but by the memorial of that sacrifice which he instituted in the upper room.

---

and ancient Judaism, as well as modern (often Protestant) prejudices against the concept of priesthood and sacrifice. Any scholarly denial of Jesus' priestly vision will have a hard time explaining why Jesus sent precisely the opposite message to his Jewish followers and audiences by organizing his disciples as he did.

Second, the growing scholarly recognition that Jesus intended to establish a new Temple cult—one focused on his body, focused on the Eucharist—needs to be complimented by the recognition that he also appears to have sough to establish a new priesthood, an eschatological priesthood. Although the study of this issue is still in its infancy, when the evidence from the Gospels is situated in the context of ancient Jewish liturgy and ancient Jewish eschatology, the conclusion seems unavoidable, and its implications weighty. In the twentieth century, it was very popular to see Jesus as the "apocalyptic prophet" who thought (wrongly) that history would come to its end in his lifetime.[95] But if Jesus not only deliberately organized his disciples into a priestly hierarchy, but commanded their twelve chiefs to repeat the sacrificial ritual of offering his body and blood, then this picture needs to be radically called into question. Indeed, the Last Supper strongly suggests that Jesus envisioned a future time when the eschatological priesthood would be in force after his death, and that he sought to establish it in his absence.

Third, when the cosmic significance of the Temple is taken into account, Jesus' identification of himself as the new Temple also reveals that for Jesus—like many other Jews of his day—the coming of the new Temple would not simply be an event of national (or even international) significance. Rather, it would impact the cosmos itself. Because the Temple was a miniature replica of the universe, and because—as the rabbis contended—the "whole world" was sustained by its liturgy, the destruction of the Jerusalem Temple meant nothing less than that the age of "this world" was coming to its end, and the age of the "world to come"—the messianic age—would be objectively inaugurated. Jesus apparently saw his death as thus ushering in the beginnings of a new creation.

Fourth, and finally, and by no means least significant, Jesus' identification of himself with the Temple provides us with a penetrating insight into the mystery of his self-understanding. While the twentieth century was characterized by a great deal of scholarly wrangling over "low christology" (supposedly represented by the synoptics) and "high christology" (supposedly located only in John), our study of the Jewish Temple has made one thing abundantly clear. If Jesus did indeed refer to himself as "something greater" than the earthly Temple and identified himself as the heavenly Temple of the "Son of Man," then he was claiming nothing less than to be God dwelling with us. Indeed, he thereby identified his own body as "the house of God" and the "gate of heaven." If this is correct, then contemporary christological discussions of Jesus' self-understanding may want to revisit the issue and pay closer attention to the insights that can be gained from Jesus and the mystery of the Jewish Temple.

---

95   Most famously, Albert Schweitzer, *The Quest of the Historical Jesus*, trans. William Montgomery (New York: Macmillan, 1968 [1906]).

Letter & Spirit 4 (2008): 85–105

The Rejected Stone and the Living Stones:
Psalm 118:22–23 and New Testament
Christology and Ecclesiology

~: Michael Giesler :~

Wespine Study Center

The dramatic climax of the Gospel of Matthew begins with Jesus' triumphant entry into Jerusalem. The events that follow in Matthew 21 are filled with Old Testament imagery and allusions. His entrance into the city deliberately evokes the coronation of the son of David, Solomon, who similarly rode in upon David's mule to the joyous celebration of the crowds (1 Kings 1:32–40).

Matthew asserts almost explicitly that Jesus is fulfilling the royal-messianic prophecies of both Isaiah (62:11) and Zechariah (9:9), and he depicts the crowd paying Jesus royal homage, laying their garments on the ground for him to walk on (compare 2 Kings 9:13). The evangelist also has the crowds singing the last of Israel's great Hallel ("thanksgiving") psalms in praise of Jesus: "Hosanna to the Son of David! Blessed is he who comes in the name of the Lord! Hosanna in the highest" (Matt. 21:9; Ps. 118:26).[1]

The action continues with a series of symbolic words and deeds from Jesus, again all colored by Old Testament associations. He cleanses the Temple of money-changers and heals the blind and the lame; and he delivers a series of pointed parables that underscore the hostility and rejection of Israel's religious leaders—the chief priests, the scribes, and the Pharisees.

The chapter concludes with Jesus himself appealing to a "scriptural proof text from the Psalms"[2]:

> Jesus said to them, "Have you never read in the Scriptures: 'The very stone which the builders rejected has become the head of the corner; this was the Lord's doing, and it is marvelous in our eyes.' Therefore I tell you, the Kingdom of God will be taken away from you and given to a nation producing the fruits of it.

---

1 The "Hallel" psalms are Psalms 113–118. On the patterns of Davidic fulfillment in Matthew see Brian M. Nolan, *The Royal Son of God: The Christology of Matthew 1-2 in the Setting of the Gospel*, Orbis Biblicus et Orientalis 23 (Fribourg: Éditions Universitaires, 1979)

2 W. D. Davies and Dale C. Allison, *A Critical and Exegetical Commentary on the Gospel according to Matthew*, 3 vols., The International Critical Commentary on the Holy Scriptures of the Old and New Testaments (Edinburgh: T. & T. Clark, 1988), 3:184.

And he who falls on this stone will be broken to pieces; but when it falls on any one it will crush him. (Matt. 21:42–44)

Jesus here quite explicitly applies Psalm 118:22 to himself. In bold fashion, he declares that he is the "stone" rejected by the "builders," whom he identifies with Israel's leaders. He also here seems to apply this psalm to his passion and resurrection. His rejection is his passion and death, which is vindicated by the "marvelous" work of God who will raise him from the dead and make him the cornerstone of some new building or temple.

All three synoptic Gospels attest to Jesus quoting Psalm 118:22 in association with his final teaching at Jerusalem (see Mark 12:10; Luke 20:17). And this exegetical reading—that Jesus is the "stone" and that his rejection represents his passion while his resurrection and ascension mark his establishment as the cornerstone of the Church—was a commonplace in the early Church, beginning within the pages of the New Testament (see Acts 4:11; 1 Pet. 2:7–9).

From the beginnings of the Christian interpretative tradition, then, Jesus' quotation of Psalm 118 was understood both christologically and ecclesiologically. That is to say: Jesus was understood to be here saying something about himself as Israel's Messiah, as well as describing the Church as the Temple or building of God, built-up by the apostles upon the foundation of him as the corner-stone.

This exegesis—begun in the New Testament, developed in the writings of the Fathers, and affirmed by successive ecumenical councils over the centuries—has in turn become the authoritative interpretation of the Catholic Church, articulated most recently by the Second Vatican Council (1963–1965) and by the post-conciliar *Catechism of the Catholic Church* (1993):

> The Lord compared himself to the stone which the builders rejected, but which was made into the cornerstone. On this foundation the Church is built by the apostles and from it the Church receives solidity and unity. This edifice has many names to describe it ... especially, the holy Temple. This Temple, symbolized in places of worship built out of stone, is praised by the Fathers and, not without reason, is compared in the liturgy to the Holy City, the New Jerusalem. As living stones we here on earth are built into it. It is this holy city that is seen by John as it comes down out of heaven from God when the world is made anew, prepared like a bride adorned for her husband.[3]

---

3   Second Vatican Council, *Lumen Gentium* [The Light of Nations], Dogmatic Constitution on the Church (November 21, 1964), 6, in *The Documents of Vatican II*, ed. Walter M. Abbot (Piscataway, NJ: New Century, 1966); compare *Catechism of the Catholic Church*, 2d. ed. (Vatican City: Libreria Editrice Vaticana, 1997), no. 756.

My purpose in this article is to return to the biblical sources of this ancient ecclesiological teaching of the Church. Through a biblical-theological reflection on the scriptural texts, I hope to illuminate the development of this self-understanding of the Church's identity and mission. As I hope to show, this self-understanding of the Church as a holy Temple is, to a certain extent, rooted in Christ's own self-understanding as expressed in his use of Psalm 118:22–23.

My method will be as follows: I will begin by attempting to recover the original context and meaning of Psalm 118. I also want to look at the broader "theology of the stone" evidenced in the Old Testament—especially in the prophets—and consider the relation of this tradition to the stone imagery of Psalm 118. Following that, I will outline some general observations about the use of the Psalter in the New Testament before examining in detail the context for Jesus' use of Psalm 118:22–23 in Matthew 21. Finally, I will explore the beginnings of the interpretative history of Psalm 118:22–23 in the New Testament, focusing in particular on the interpretation of this text in 1 Peter 2:4–10. I will conclude with a few observations about New Testament christology and ecclesiology as suggested by this study.

Psalm 118 and Nehemiah's Rebuilding of the Walls

Almost all modern exegetes agree that Psalm 118 is a "song of thanksgiving" intended to be sung by the Hebrew community as a whole. Its purpose is to celebrate and give thanks for God's salvation of the people from some national distress. The structure of the psalm dances between the individual and the community, both of whom express their thanksgiving to God for favors received. There is a strong indication of a festal procession and of a hero being acclaimed from the Temple, a hero who has been harassed by personal enemies or the nation's enemies or both.

Scholarly agreement ends there. There are more than two dozen serious proposals as to the possible original setting and circumstances of the psalm. It is beyond my purposes here to evaluate these various options.[4] For the purposes of this article, I suggest that while the psalm may have originated in the context of the monarchy, and hence before the destruction of the kingdom and the exile, its importance for the New Testament opens up when it is understood in association with the Tabernacle feast of 444 B.C. after the restoration of Jerusalem's walls following Israel's return from exile (Neh. 6:15–16; 8:13–18; 12:27). The cornerstone verse in the psalm, I believe, may have been an addition by Nehemiah himself, the post-exilic governor of Judea and rebuilder of Jerusalem's walls.

Historically, the rebuilding of the walls would have proven to both Israel and its neighbors that God was on their side. The much maligned and rejected people had managed to find victory against all odds and had rebuilt their Temple and city.

---

4   For an overview of the various scholarly proposals, see Andrew C. Brunson, *Psalm 118 in the Gospel of John: An Intertextual Study on the New Exodus Pattern in the Theology of John*, Wissenschaftliche Untersuchungen zum Neuen Testament 158. (Tübingen: J. C. B. Mohr Siebeck, 2003), 23–26.

In addition to the historical similarities of concern, in both the original Hebrew and in the Septuagint translation there are particularly rich spiritual and linguistic points of contact between the biblical memoir of the rebuilding in Nehemiah and psalm.[5]

The stone rejected by the builders which proved to be the keystone is realized on many different levels among the Jews of Nehemiah's time. The stone could mean the Jews as a people, the Law, the walls restored, and even Nehemiah himself as a person. Thus, the psalm verse both reflects and is reflected in the life of the people and their faith.

Psalm 118 speaks of a stone rejected, while Nehemiah tells us that the Samaritans ridiculed the Israelites' efforts to rebuild Jerusalem's walls. Indeed, Nehemiah 4:2 reports the taunt of a certain Sanballat: "What are these feeble Jews doing? … Will they revive the stones out of the heaps of rubbish, and burned ones at that?" I suggest that the psalm may be alluding to that historical situation. The stones are probably the charred and half-destroyed walls of Jerusalem at that time.

The psalm goes on to sing of the rejected stone becoming the keystone and that this remarkable turn of events marked a "day which the LORD has made" (Ps. 118:24). Nehemiah 6:15 affirms that the walls, despite the Samaritans' scorn, were finished on a certain day and that in all they had taken only fifty-two days to re-build—a marvelous achievement that apparently astonished surrounding peoples. Compare the summary text in Nehemiah to the psalm passage quoted by Christ:

> So the wall was finished on the twenty-fifth day of the month Elul, in fifty-two days. And when all our enemies heard of it, all the nations round about us were afraid and fell greatly in their own esteem; for they perceived that this work had been accomplished with the help of our God. (Neh. 6:15–16)

> The stone which the builders rejected has become the head of the corner. This is the LORD's doing; it is marvelous in our eyes. (Ps. 118:22–23)

---

5   For the details of my argument for an original setting of 444 B.C., after the repair of the Jerusalem walls, see my *Christ the Rejected Stone: A Study of Psalm 118, 22–23, Biblical and Ecclesiological Implications* (Pamplona: Ediciones Universidad de Navarra, 1974), 31–61. Other scholars who agree with this setting for the psalm are: Alexander F. Kirkpatrick, *The Book of Psalms*, 3 vols., The Cambridge Bible for Schools and Colleges (Cambridge: Cambridge University, 1903), 3:693; Friedrich Baethgen, *Die Psalmen* [The Psalms], 2d ed. (Göttingen, Vandenhoeck & Ruprecht, 1897), 347; Michel Berder, *"La Pierre Rejetée par les Bâtisseurs": Psaume 118, 22–23 et son Emploi dans las Traditions Juives et dans le Nouveau Testament* ["The Stone Rejected by the Builders": Psalm 118:22–23 and its Use in Jewish Traditions and in the New Testament] Études Bibliques 31 (Paris: Gabalda, 1996), 89, 105; John James Steward Perowne, *The Book of Psalms*, 2 vols. (London: Bell and Daldy, 1868), 2:287.

To reconstruct the walls of a large city in such a short time is truly a marvel, especially given that the Jews were undermanned and had to remain constant on the alert for enemy attacks. When Psalm 118 speaks of the "marvelous work" of God, it might very well be referring to the rebuilding of the walls.

We also know from Nehemiah's memoirs that the successful completion of the wall was a motive for a great celebration in Israel—in the form of a procession along the walls, which took place near the time of the Feast of Tabernacles (Neh. 12:27–43). Psalm 118 has the literary form of a triumphal procession and contains specific allusions to tents and procession branches, suggesting an autumn harvest feast or specifically, Tabernacles. We know, too, from later Israelite history, that this psalm was particularly associated with Tabernacles.

The psalm speaks of people shouting from the Temple and the hero entering it; that hero very well could have been Nehemiah. Although there is no perfect historical correspondence, like the "hero" depicted in the psalm, Nehemiah was pressed by his enemies and then saved. Like the hero in the psalm, his victory is celebrated by a procession and a passing through the gates. These associations are also supported by the grammatical connections in both the Hebrew and Septuagint texts between Nehemiah's original prayer in Nehemiah 1:11 (O Lord … give success to your servant today) and the petition in Psalm 118:25 (O Lord … give us success!).[6]

My point in this quick comparison of Nehemiah and Psalm 118 is that whatever its original setting, the psalm was likely used at Nehemiah's liturgical celebration of the dedication of the wall of Jerusalem. There could well have been earlier post-exilic historical occasions for the psalm's use, such as the foundation ceremony of the Temple in Zerubbabel's time (Ezra 3:6–7, 10–13; Zech. 4:7; Hag. 2:3–5) or the actual completion of the Temple (Ezra 6:15). But what is also clear is that the life and work of the Jews in Nehemiah's time constitute an authentic historical incarnation of the cornerstone referred to in Psalm 118:22–23. The psalm, then, could represent Nehemiah's celebration of his own victory over his enemies with God's help.

This Nehemian context helps us to make some suggestions as to the meaning of the cornerstone alluded to in Psalm 118:22–23. The key is the phrase "it is marvelous (*niphᵉlâ'th*) in our eyes." *Niphᵉlâ'th* has a two-fold meaning. It is something difficult (Jer. 32:37; Zech. 8:4–6) and it is something marvelous (2 Sam. 1:26). The prophecies of Jeremiah and Zechariah about the impossibility yet the marvel of Israel's renovation seem culminated in the *niphᵉlâ'th* of Psalm 118:22–23. The

---

6   Others have noted the connections between Neh. 1:11 and Ps. 118:25. Brunson, who argues for an original setting for the psalm in the period of the monarchy, suggests that Nehemiah "echoes the well-known psalm as a paradigm for his own situation." In general, Brunson believes that while Ps. 118 was likely used at Nehemiah's Tabernacles festival, it was not "created especially for that festival." See *Psalm 118 in the Gospel of John*, 25, n. 20.

cornerstone captures the whole idea of abandonment then life, rejection then glory. Yet only the eyes of faith can see it.

Here we see still another meaning for the rejected stone—the Jews themselves as the chosen people who are restored to their land after exile and ridicule. Their sureness in their election helps them to see the events around them as signs of favor from God. The vision of the surrounding nations at their successful reconstruction of the walls is one of astonished envy (see Neh. 6:16). Yet for the Jews it is one of wonder and thanksgiving (Ps. 118:22–23). If there is a real historic connection between Nehemiah 6:16 and our psalm verse, the so-called "stone" would be the same for both peoples: namely, the successful reconstruction of the walls. But the peoples' reactions are completely different. While both recognize that the event is from God, the Jews are glad, but the surrounding peoples can only be envious and afraid.

The "Rock" of Salvation and Stumbling

If the historical setting of Psalm 118 cannot be established with absolute certainty, by the time of the New Testament the psalm has clearly taken on a "messianic" interpretation. Jesus' use of the psalm in Matthew is definitely "messianic"—interpreting the psalm in light of his own person and mission. The question, historically, is how the psalm came to be understood in this light. Andrew Brunson states the historical problem succinctly:

> There is no extant pre-rabbinic interpretation of Psalm 118:22 that is explicitly messianic or eschatological. ... It is possible that this verse was interpreted messianically prior to its use in the New Testament, and it would be somewhat surprising for it to gain such importance in the early apologetic if there was no messianic association to begin with; but as there is no clear evidence, it is difficult to draw firm conclusions.[7]

The issues involved are complicated and should not detain us here. All that we can establish with certainty is that Psalm 118 was significant in the liturgy of Israel, especially in celebrating Tabernacles and Passover. For our purposes I think it will suffice to presume that throughout the Second Temple period, Psalm 118 increasingly came to be associated with a cluster of other biblical texts in which the image of a *stone* figures prominently. In the prophets, especially in Isaiah, this image increasingly came to take on messianic importance. Indeed, as we will see, Jesus joins his quotation of Psalm 118:22–23 to a stone image likely drawn from Isaiah and Daniel—an image that was widely understood as having messianic

---

7   Brunson, *Psalm 118 in the Gospel of John*, 41.

meaning.[8] Thus, we need to examine these stone metaphors before turning to the New Testament.

Throughout the Old Testament, God is associated with the title "Rock." God is the Rock of sure foundation upon which Israel must place its trust. God is the Rock who begets his child Israel (Deut. 32:18) and feeds them with water in the desert (Exod. 17:3–7; Isa. 48:21). Though the people forget him, he remains the true strength of Israel (Deut. 32:30). This theme of God as the Rock in the sense of being a bulwark and fortress runs throughout the Psalter.[9]

As the Rock may be a father and protector of his people, God is also a stone that destroys. In the Book of Daniel, King Nebuchadnezzar in a dream sees a stone that breaks away, untouched by human hands, and which destroys a huge statue made of gold, bronze, iron, and clay. The wind blew away all these elements but the stone remained, growing into a great mountain and filling the earth (Dan. 2:35). Daniel, in answer to the king's demand, interprets the dream. The stone, he says is the kingdom which God will found, that will shatter and absorb all previous earthly kingdoms, itself never being destroyed (Dan. 2:44).

Thus, the stone spoken of here is essentially eschatological and is most notable for its impending universal influence. The stone in Daniel is a symbol of the future—it will fall upon, destroy, and supplant earthly kingdoms and fill the world with the Kingdom of God. As we will soon study at length, Christ, in using Psalm 118 as a parable to the Pharisees, concludes with this image of the crushing, eschatological stone—most probably derived from Daniel's prophecy, which was well known to the Jews of his day.

Isaiah, too, associates the "Rock" of God with a judgment—especially on those in Israel who do not believe him. Isaiah 8:14–15 reads:

> And he will become a sanctuary, and a stone of offense, and a
> rock of stumbling to both houses of Israel, a trap and a snare to
> the inhabitants of Jerusalem. And many shall stumble thereon;
> they shall fall and be broken; they shall be snared and taken.

Read in the context of Israel's political misfortunes at the time, the threat of an Assyrian invasion in the eighth century B.C., the text evidently means that, for those who trust in his providence despite the difficult circumstances, God will be a sanctuary. Those who do not trust in him and refuse to see beyond the human or the political, will find God to be a stumbling stone. Those who do not see God in current events, those who are blind to his demands on their lives, will stumble. God who wanted to be a true sanctuary and a firm rock for his people, will instead be for them a cause of ruin and confusion.

We find a similar use of the stone metaphor in Isaiah 28:16:

---

8   Isa. 8:14–15; Dan. 2:34–35, 44–45.

9   See Pss. 18:3; 27:5, 6; 31:3; 40:1–3; 62:3.

> Behold, I am laying in Zion for a foundation a stone, a tested stone, a precious cornerstone, of a sure foundation: "He who believes will not be in haste."

The rock here can be interpreted on a purely physical level. For instance, Isaiah seems to be referring to the great, solid foundation stones of Solomon's Temple (1 Kings 5:17). We can also read this passage in a more spiritual way. The "stone" is the remnant of chosen people whom God founds in Zion. For those who are not founded on this faith in God, Isaiah foretells a "crushing" defeat—"When the overwhelming scourge passes through, you will be beaten down by it" (Isa. 28:18).

The consequences for rejecting the rock are analogous, then, to those mentioned in Isaiah 8:14–15. Yet it is worthwhile to note that the rock itself mentioned in Isaiah 28:16 is not God himself, but is *laid by him*. In a more general way, though, both oracles agree: one must have faith in God if he is to stand.

The stone in both of these passages has a double meaning, which complements the meaning of the cornerstone in Psalm 118 in power and depth. The stone for Isaiah is both a source of stumbling (Isa. 8:14–15) and a foundation stone (Isa. 28:16). Isaiah's profound message is similar to Psalm 118's—the need for supernatural vision in the face of history. Those who do not trust in God and who think only humanly in times of crisis shall fall and be broken upon the very God they did not trust.

What is the relation between the cornerstone of Psalm 118 and the stone of Isaiah? In Isaiah, the rock is more "existential," so to speak. It is not so much a question of the vision of faith, but rather an entire life of faith. The stone in Isaiah 8:14–15 is used almost as an anti-symbol against the Jews themselves, whereas the cornerstone in our psalm verse could symbolize the Jews in a positive and triumphant sense. Yet both passages are imbued with the notion of rejection (compare Isa. 30:12). Self-sufficiency and deceit are the real cause of the Jews' blindness, according to Isaiah, making God a rock of stumbling and self-ruin rather than a sanctuary.

The stone as a source of life; the stone as protector of the people; the stone as firmness for the believer; the stone as occasion of ruin. All of these Old Testament images are in some way connected with the basic attitude of the people of Israel toward God, and of God toward them. The stone as "kingdom to come" and "cornerstone of the universe" are said to be the future work of God's power. All these meanings of the messianic stone were in play when New Testament times arrived with the birth of Christ.

The Psalms and the Self-Consciousness of Jesus

As scholars have long noticed, the psalms represent the single most quoted portion of the Old Testament in the New Testament writings.[10] No doubt this reflects the importance of the psalms in the liturgical life of devout Jews. This is not the place to explore the implications of this evidence except to note that the Gospels depict Christ himself quoting from the Psalter on numerous occasions.[11]

In his final days in Jerusalem, he deploys such quotations to dramatic effect. In his debate with the Pharisees, he applies to himself Psalm 110:1, an enthronement psalm associated with the coronation of Davidic kings. In the process, he leaves his opponents speechless and strongly suggests his own divinity (Matt. 22:21–46).

During his trial, when the High Priest presses him to confess whether or not he is the Christ, Jesus answers that "from this time onward you will see the Son of Man seated at the right hand of Power and coming on the clouds of heaven" (Matt. 26:64). Here he is quoting from Psalm 110:1 indirectly ("The LORD said to my Lord: sit at my right hand"). Again the allusion serves as a statement of his divine identity. The words of the psalm are to be crystallized in his future glory, which will reveal him as the divine Son and Davidic savior and king anticipated by Israel.

On the cross, in the hour of his greatest desertion and aloneness, he chooses to cry out in a psalm verse:

> From the sixth hour there was darkness over all the land until the ninth hour. And about the ninth hour, Jesus cried out in a loud voice, "Eli, Eli lama sabachthani?" that is, "My God, My God, why have you deserted me?" (Matt. 27:45–46; Ps. 22:1).

Jesus consciously uses the psalms throughout his life, according to the Gospel testimony. He draws them out on many occasions and for many purposes—to clarify, to rebuke and silence, to predict his own glorious future, to express his deepest affliction, to exemplify and add power to his teaching, to refer to himself and the Kingdom of God, and to sing and give praise to God like any other pious Jew (see Matt. 26:30–32).

We also need to note that Psalm 118, along with Psalm 110, has been identified as the most significant in New Testament citations. Some argue that it is the most quoted psalm in the New Testament—quoted at least eleven times, with

---

10   A recent study determined that of the Scripture quotations in Mark, 21 percent are from the psalms; 18 percent of the quotations in Matthew are from the psalms; 31 percent in Luke; and 76 percent in John. The number of allusions and other intertextual echoes point to an even greater influence for the psalms. See the discussion in Margaret Daly-Denton, *David in the Fourth Gospel: The Johannine Reception of the Psalms*, Arbeiten zur Geschichte des Antiken Judentums und des Urchristentums 47 (Leiden: Brill, 2000), 22–57; the statistical overview is at 34.

11   See, for instance, Matt. 5:4 (Ps. 37:11); Matt. 5:33–35 (Ps. 48:3); Matt. 21:15–16 (Ps. 8:2; Wis. 10:20–21).

thirteen more allusions made to it.[12] But more than statistically significant, the psalm is decisive for the developing of christology and, as we will see, ecclesiology. Klyne Snodgrass has argued that the section of the psalm that concerns us in this article, Psalm 118:22–26, is among the three Old Testament texts that "provided the framework for Jesus' understanding of his ministry."[13] I agree with Snodgrass, and I believe our study of the New Testament usage will bear that out.

Psalm 118 in Matthew 21

It is in this larger context that we have to seek the meaning of his use of Psalm 118:22–23 in Matthew 21:42–43. It must be noted that the deployment of the psalm comes at the conclusion of a section of the book, Chapter 21, which is entirely overlaid with messianic themes and Old Testament imagery and pivots on Jesus' conflict with the religious authorities of Israel.

The entire chapter from the first verse has clear messianic overtones, which spring from the theme of rejection and glorious recognition. By deliberately entering Jerusalem on a donkey, Christ was indicating his messianic identity. Zechariah's prophecy of the king on the donkey (Zech. 9:9) would have been well known to the Pharisees and was commonly accepted in those days as a sign of the Messiah. His opponents and supporters alike would have known that the man who purposefully attempted to fulfill that prophecy was indirectly proclaiming himself Messiah.[14] Hence the crowd's knowing enthusiasm and the Pharisees' bitter envy. To add to the messianic cast of the chapter, the crowds are depicted as honoring him with a title that was widely recognized as messianic ("Son of David").[15]

As in the original setting of Psalm 118, in Matthew 21 the people and their joy play a central role. The entire scene seems to be a repetition of the psalm, with the

---

12   For a helpful review of all the quotations and allusions, see Brunson, *Psalm 118 in the Gospel of John*, 2. Reviewing the scholarly claims about the importance of the psalm, Brunson comments: "Such claims, if true, would suggest that Ps. 118 should rank among the most important Old Testament passages quoted in the New Testament. Among its occurrences in the New Testament, it is linked with the Son of Man in the passion predictions, voiced in Jesus' lament over Jerusalem, quoted in the entrance to Jerusalem narrative, and is key to understanding the parable of the wicked tenants."

13   According to Snodgrass, the other decisive Old Testament texts for Jesus' self-understanding are Isa. 61:1–13 and Dan. 7:13–14. See his "The Use of the Old Testament in the New," in *The Right Doctrine from the Wrong Texts?: Essays on the Use of the Old Testament in the New*, ed. G. K. Beale (Grand Rapids, MI: Baker, 1994), 29–51, at 40. See also on Ps. 118:222–23, Snodgrass' *The Parable of the Wicked Tenants: An Inquiry into Parable Interpretation*, Wissenschaftliche Untersuchungen zum Neuen Testament 27 (Tübingen: J. C. B. Mohr, 1983).

14   S. L. Edgar, "New Testament and Rabbinic Messianic Interpretation," *New Testament Studies* (1958), 47–54.

15   For specific testimonies from the Talmud and Midrash, see Hermann Leberecht Strack and Paul Billerbeck. *Kommentar zum Neuen Testament aus Talmud und Midrasch* [Commentary on the New Testament from Talmud and Midrash], 4 vols., 3d ed. (München: Beck, 1951–1956), 842.

celebrants in Jerusalem, as in the psalm, bringing out branches in a festal procession and crying out: "Hosanna! Blessings on he who comes in the name of the LORD!" (Matt. 21:9; Ps. 118:26). The people of Jerusalem here sing the psalm as part of their manifest recognition of Jesus as the Messiah, giving exuberant thanksgiving to God. Indeed, on a spiritual, historic, and linguistic level Psalm 118 is fulfilled in Matthew 21—the acclaim of the crowds for their hero, the procession and the branches, the way Christ "cuts down" (Ps. 118:10) his adversaries in a series of very biting encounters (the expulsion of the dealers from the Temple, the withering of the fig tree, the parables of the two sons and the wicked tenants).

The fact that Jesus, at the end of this series of words and deeds, applied Psalm 118 to himself probably did not escape his audience. Hence, we must conclude that Jesus understood the psalm in a messianic sense, in the same way that he understood his symbolic actions in the Temple and his parables. His driving out the merchants and money-changers from the Temple had clear messianic implications, as Jesus makes clear by quoting from the prophets.[16] He heals the blind and the lame, too, in likely another messianic and royal-Davidic act.[17]

The scene provokes a confrontation with the religious authorities that becomes the context for his cursing of the fig tree and his series of parables delivered against Israel's leaders. But first Jesus is depicted quoting another psalm. He uses Psalm 8:2, which speaks of babies and infants glorifying God. Again, his use of the psalm is associated with his sense of his own identity. He seems clearly to be saying that the children of Jerusalem, like the children of the psalm, are declaring the majesty of God who is in their midst in his person.

But he also seems to be evoking the immediate context of the psalm, which would have been known by both him and his audience. The very next verse of Psalm 8 speaks of God founding a bulwark to confound his enemies and to put his adversaries to silence. This, of course, is what Jesus will go on to do in the prophetic withering of the fig tree and in the confrontation with the elders over his authority (Matt. 21:23–27).

The fig tree episode that follows (Matt. 21:18–22), in which Christ curses the tree for not bearing fruit, is often interpreted as symbolizing Israel, which was not prepared for the Messiah.[18] And as the drama unfolds throughout Matthew 21, Jesus' words and actions build on a pattern of rejection followed by glory, culminating in the dramatic prediction that the "son" of the vineyard owner will be killed by the wicked tenants (Matt. 21:39). The lesson is an obvious one and is certainly

---

16　See Matt. 21:12–17; compare Isa. 56:3–8; Jer. 7:4, 8–10.

17　Compare Matt. 21:14; 2 Sam. 5:6, 8. See the discussion in Davies and Allison, *The Gospel of Matthew*, 140.

18　Manuel de Tuya, *Evangelios* [The Gospels], Biblia Comentada 5 (Madrid: Editorial Católica, 1964), 462.

not lost on the Pharisees, priests, and scribes: they have refused to recognize the Messiah's inherent authority and power, and their days are now numbered.

Matthew records that Christ told a double parable about the vineyard: the parable of the two sons and the parable of the wicked husbandmen. Both end on the same obvious implication: the kingdom would be lost or taken from the religious authorities and given to others. These "others" in the first parable are the tax collectors and prostitutes, who "are making their way into the Kingdom of God" before the so-called leaders of the people. In the second parable, the "others" are those who will be given the vine to produce its fruit. So there is rejection for some, divinely granted privilege for others. The ones most despised (tax collectors) and most persecuted (the only son of the vineyard owner) would be the true heirs of the Kingdom of God.

In the parable of the wicked husbandmen, just as in the parable of the vine-yard laborers, the vineyard itself does not change, although its caretakers do. God is consistent in his promises to the true Israel, which is his vineyard so lovingly planted long before (compare Isa. 5:1–7). But the vineyard tenants can become perverse and can reject the owner and his just claims for payment. Like the barren fig tree, the tenants, the authorities of Israel, give no fruit and end up rejecting and killing the owner's son.

That Jesus identifies himself in this parable with the rejected "son," links this parable to his "parable-like" use of the cornerstone metaphor in the verses that immediately follow. The same pattern is used—rejection of God's servant (or stone) results in punishment. As the wicked tenants are dispatched to a "miserable death," those who reject the "stone" are crushed and destroyed by it. There are many eschatological suggestions here, both of punishment for the Jewish leaders and Christ's final glory, as the rejected stone becomes the keystone.[19]

The Pattern of Rejection and Glorification

This is the immediate context in which we must look for the meaning of Christ's use of Psalm 118:22–23. As we have seen, Jesus' quotation of the psalm is the culmination and crowning phrase of the preceding series of teachings and sym-bolic actions that emphasize the theme of rejection and glorification. Specifically, his use of the psalm is tied to the immediately preceding parable of the tenants, with its deep allegorical overtones. The meaning could not be clearer: a new people would supplant Israel's elders as the shepherds of the Kingdom of God, just as new

---

19 Joachim Jeremias interprets Christ's use of the cornerstone phrase as intentionally eschatological. The glorious keystone is to crown the heavenly Temple of the future; this Temple is a figure of the saved people of God at the end of time. Apart from being a keystone he will also be a punishment for his enemies, for Christ is also a stone to fall upon and be crushed, as Matt. 21:44 attests. See Jeremias, "*Lithos, Lithinos* [Stone]," in *Theological Dictionary of the New Testament*, 10 vols., ed. Gerhard Kittel, trans. and ed. Geoffrey W. Bromiley (Grand Rapids, MI: Eerdmans, 1964–1985), 4:268–280.

husbandmen would be chosen for the vineyard. The same meaning is intended by his use of Psalm 118 in the verses that follow this parable.[20] We see the same basic theme—the ingratitude of Israel and God's punishment. The son who is killed in the parable is left unnamed, as is the identity of the "stone"; but the context points to Jesus as the referent in both cases.

Throughout this passage, too, we have an odd mixing of metaphors—of the vineyard and the stone. Hence, Jesus tells the parable of the vineyard (Matt. 21:33–41), then follows that parable immediately with the quotation of our psalm (Matt. 21:42). Immediately after quoting the psalm, he returns to the vineyard metaphor about "producing the fruits" of the kingdom (Matt. 21:43). After that the metaphor shifts back again to that of the stone:

> And he who falls on this stone will be broken to pieces; but when
> it falls on any one, it will crush him. (Matt. 21:44)

In his use of the psalm, Jesus appears to evoke a proverb in vogue in those days, attributed to a Jewish rabbi of the second century B.C.:

> If the rock falls on the dish, poor dish!
> If the dish falls on the rock, poor dish![21]

In other words, if one refuses the rock he will be crushed. Beneath this surface meaning, deeply embedded in the Old Testament, was the entire "theology of the Rock" that we alluded to earlier. Indeed, Jesus appears to be evoking both Isaiah's prophecy that many shall fall and be broken upon the divine "Rock" (Isa. 8:14–15), and the prophecy of Daniel 2:34–44, which foretold the crushing of God's opponents by a stone "not cut out by human hand" and the establishment of a "kingdom which shall never be destroyed." Both prophecies of the stone are thereby connected with the rejected stone of Psalm 118:22–23. And the "cornerstone" of our psalm is likewise associated with the "sanctuary" of Isaiah 8:14 and the "kingdom" of Daniel 2:44.

The reference to Daniel also helps us to see another important dimension of the metaphors of the stone and the vineyard in Matthew 21. The wording of the cornerstone verse, taken exactly from the Septuagint translation by Matthew, is in a "rebuilding" context. As in Psalm 118, a stone which has been discarded is reestablished and remounted. In itself this biblical theme evokes a great number of sentiments—of renewed trust in God, of conversion, of suffering then deliverance. Jesus' use of this psalm, then, is not random. The words are rich in biblical

---

20 That Christ was fully aware of the consequences behind Psalm 118 and that he had actually lived them and foretold them is particularly noted by Johannes Betz in his article, "Christus-Petra-Petrus, [Christ, Rock, Peter]" in *Kirche und Überlieferung* [Church and Tradition], Johannes Betz and Heinrich Fries (Freiburg: Herder, 1960).

21 Strack and Billerbeck, *Kommentar zum Neuen Testament* 1:877.

resonance, and the basic principles of rejection followed by glorification are simply extended and completed in the person of Jesus and in his life—although they are also mysteriously projected to an unknown future intervention of God in favor of his Son.

The builders of the people of God, Israel's leaders, like the tenants in his parable, had rejected their foundation and future, Israel's cornerstone and heir. For this reason they will be cut off—either killed as were the tenants in the vineyard parable, or crushed with the rock as in Jesus' stone metaphor. As the parable and the psalm imply the identity of Jesus as "son" and "stone," so both the parable and the psalm herald the rise of a new people.

Hence, we detect a close connection in both his parable and his quotation of the psalm between the Kingdom of God and the people God has chosen. Matthew 21:43 speaks of a new people (*ethnos*) to whom the Kingdom of God is given. This *ethnos* is the same as the *ethnos hagion* ("holy nation") of 1 Peter 2:9. In Matthew, as in 1 Peter, the people of the covenant are involved. Indeed the text of the epistle (which we shall study at length below) shows a similar polemic against unbelieving Judaism, against which judgment is proclaimed in an allusion to Isaiah 8:14 (compare 1 Pet. 2:7).

The central notion in the epistle text is the very idea that Matthew seems to draw from our parable: in the very act of rejection by the unbelievers, God has laid the cornerstone of his house, his Temple—the new chosen race, the royal priesthood, the *ethnos hagion*, the people of his new covenant.

A corollary of this interpretation is that the people to whom the vineyard is now entrusted will share in the glory of their chief cornerstone. Just as Christ himself was rejected then glorified, so will his people be persecuted and then glorified and raised in Christ, their chief cornerstone and keystone. It is a religious phenomenon deeply embedded in Old Testament history—how Israel herself was despised but then exalted. The fact that Christ's rejection and glorification are here expressed in material terms (stone and builders) does not take away from the fact that a true human community is at stake.

The Cornerstone and the Rock: Beginnings of the Church

The intimate identification of Jesus with this new *ethnos* is represented by his relationship with the man he designates as the "rock" upon whom he will build his Church. This is not the place to rehearse the long literature on the place of Peter in the New Testament. What I want to suggest here is that in renaming Simon as *Petros*, or "rock," Jesus established a set of connections that would influence the New Testament's understanding of the "rejected stone" psalm and consequently the Church's own self-understanding.

The expression "to build upon a rock" is only found in two places in the Gospels—both on the lips of Christ himself. One, of course, is his famous commissioning of St. Peter: "upon this rock I will build my Church" (Matt. 16:18). The second passage is found at the end of the Sermon on the Mount.

> Every one then who hears these words of mine and does them will be like a wise man who built his house upon the rock; and the rain fell, and the floods came, and the winds blew and beat upon that house, but it did not fall, because it had been founded on the rock. And every one who hears these words of mine and does not do them will be like a foolish man who built his house upon the sand; and the rain fell, and the floods came, and the winds blew and beat against that house, and it fell; and great was the fall of it. (Matt. 7:24–27)

The passage is quite clear. Only the man who listens and acts on Christ's word will be building on a rock—only his construction will last. The implication here is that it is not sufficient to simply listen to Christ's word, nor simply to cry out "Lord, Lord," if one truly wants to be built up into Christ and to build in Christ. This is one aspect of Christ's promise to Peter that should be kept in mind. Christ builds in Peter; Peter himself does not build.

Speaking of Christ's foundation of his Church, Michael Schmaus notes that it is difficult to pinpoint any one solemn act by which the Church was established. In fact, suggestively, he sees that "the Church grew throughout Jesus' life according to his creative will. Everything he did was like a stone laid in the house of God, which is the Church, and as such is willed and desired by him."[22]

What then is the true relation between Christ and Peter as the Bible portrays it? The Greek grammar suggests something of the answer. Note that the expression in Matthew 16:18 "upon this rock" (*epi tautē tē petra oikodomēso*) is in the dative, the relative sense. Peter as a rock is intrinsically dependent on the real Rock, the cornerstone. The man who listens to Christ's words and lives them builds his life on a rock that is ontologically firm for itself (*epi tēn petran*; Matt. 7:24). Peter, despite the great authority Christ promises him, will always be dependent on Christ's own ontological firmness. Thus Christ can build both on Peter's greatness or his littleness, but ultimately the Church depends on Christ's own greatness. In a certain sense, Christ's power is most clearly seen when he builds an invincible Church upon a "little rock"—*petros*.[23]

---

22 Michael Schmaus, *Katolische Dogmatik*, 5 vols. (Müchen: Max Hueber Verlag, 1960–1963), 4:167. My translation. English: *Dogma*, 6 vols. (New York: Sheed & Ward, 1968–1977).

23 Heinrich Stephan, Theobaldus Fix, Karl Bendict Hase, Ludwig Dindorf, Wilhelm Dindorf, and G. R. Lud. de Sinner, *Thesaurus Graecae Linguae*, vol. 7 (Graz: Akademische, 1954), 1017, 1020.

Living Stones and the New Temple

It is interesting, then, that it is in a New Testament writing attributed to St. Peter that we find the most extended reflection upon the reality of Christ as the cornerstone of the Church. Peter alone of all New Testament authors shows the greatest interest in developing and charismatically applying the cornerstone image.[24]

> Come to him, to that living stone, rejected by men but in God's sight chosen and precious; and like living stones be yourselves built into a spiritual house, to be a holy priesthood, to offer spiritual sacrifices acceptable to God through Jesus Christ. For it stands in Scripture:

> "Behold, I am laying in Zion a stone, a cornerstone chosen and precious, and he who believes in him will not be put to shame."

> To you therefore who believe, he is precious, but for those who do not believe, "The very stone which the builders rejected has become the head of the corner," and "A stone that will make men stumble, a rock that will make them fall"; for they stumble because they disobey the word, as they were destined to do.

> But you are a chosen race, a royal priesthood, a holy nation, God's own people, that you may declare the wonderful deeds of him who called you out of darkness into his marvelous light. Once you were no people but now you are God's people; once you had not received mercy but now you have received mercy. (1 Pet. 2:4–10)

---

24 Whatever be the relation between 1 Pet. 2:4–7 (see Mark 12:10 and parallels) and Rom. 9:33, the apostle Peter would have had special interests in the stone-motif because of his own new name "Cephas-Peter-Rock" and because of Jesus' statement to him, "You are Peter, and upon this rock I will build my church" (Matt. 16:16). Luke corroborates Peter's interest in this theme by recording that Peter used the same saying about Jesus as the rejected cornerstone (or capstone) in one of his early sermons (Acts 4:11). The uniqueness of 1 Pet.'s exegesis for the Christian community is emphasized by Gundry: "The Petrine concept of Christians as living stones in relation to Christ, the living stone *par excellence*, has no parallel in the other stone-passages and may well derive from Peter's own experience, namely, his being named *Petros* because of his disciple relationship to Christ." Indeed, throughout 1 Pet. we find key passages directly linked with sayings of the Lord and events in Peter's own life in union with Christ. Thus, the peculiar experience and psychology of Peter can be traced in the epistle. See Gundry, "'Verba Christi' in 1 Peter: Their Implications concerning the Authorship of 1 Peter and the Authenticity of the Gospel Tradition," *New Testament Studies* 13 (1966–1967): 336–350, at 346. C. F. D. Moule has also argued that the stone tradition in 1 Pet. is rooted in Peter's naming by Christ as *Petros* and his designation as *petra* (rock). See "Some Reflection on the 'Stone' Testimonia in Relation to the Name Peter," *New Testament Studies* 2 (1955–1956): 56–58.

The development of the stone metaphor in 1 Peter 2:4–10 is the most ample treatment of Christ as "the Rock" and the Church as the new Temple of God in all of the New Testament. In turn, we see in this passage how this metaphor became important for the self-understanding of the early Church, a self-understanding that, as we said at the outset, continues to be reflected in the Church's official teaching. In developing this metaphor, Peter unites in one incisive vision Psalm 118:22–23 and the Isaianic tradition concerning God as the stone, applying them both to Jesus and his teaching. In addition, he inherently connects the identity of the new people of God as a new Israel through the use of Jesus' cornerstone imagery and the image of the Church as a new Temple of God built upon that cornerstone.

Jesus Christ in 1 Peter 2:4–10 is the "living stone" (*lithon zōnta*). The people built upon him are "living stones" (*lithoi zōntes*). To apply the term "living" to an inert object like a stone may seem a bit strange at first. But one need only recall the Bible's own use of the term "rock" in Deuteronomy 32, where the rock is said to "engender his people" (Deut. 32:18).

In the same sense, the verb that Peter uses, *oikodomeisthe* ("built into"), can mean the "building" of a person—as God was said to have "built" Eve out of the bone of Adam.[25] This living construction is an action proper to God, and seems to have been implied in Christ's saying to Peter, "upon this rock I will build my Church."[26] In this case, the living stones are being built-up on the foundation of the living stone, Christ, into a new Temple, a "spiritual house" (*oikos pneumatikos*). The building of his Church, which is something living and divine, is a marvel which God has done and which Peter openly announces in this passage.

Christ, the living stone, is said to be chosen by God (*eklekton*) but rejected by men (*hypo anthrōpōn men apodedokimasmenon*). The Greek term *eklekton* will also be applied to the new people of God, who are a "chosen race" (*genos eklekton*; 1 Pet. 2:9). The living stone, too, is said to be "rejected," an obvious allusion to Christ's application of Psalm 118:22–23 to himself. However, here the antagonists—the rejecters of the stone—are not the Jewish elders as they are in Jesus' initial reading of the psalm and in the preaching of Peter reflected in Acts 4:11. Instead, they are "men," or humanity in general (*anthrōpōn*). Peter may here have altered the phrase to adapt Christ's image and message to his flock, since they may have been suffering persecution at the time of Peter's writing (compare 1 Pet. 3:13–17). Peter's message, then, would be that Christ, the living stone, was also rejected and persecuted by men just as the Christians were suffering for the sake of his name. The living and suffering quality of the rejected stone, then, has been transferred to the people.

---

25   Compare the Septuagint translation of Gen. 2:22.

26   God's building through one man can be especially appreciated in Isa. 51:1–2, where Abraham is called a rock and his people proceed through God's guidance: "Listen to me, you who pursue integrity, who seek the Lord. Consider the rock you were hewn from, the quarry from which you were cut. Consider Abraham your father and Sarah who gave you birth. For he was alone when I called him, but I blessed and increased him."

The living stones are being built into a spiritual house (*oikos pneumatikos*). This imagery is familial in the sense of a "household" of God. But it is also evocative of the Temple. This new Temple reading is reinforced by the designation of the new people of God as a holy priesthood (*eis hierateuma hagion*) responsible for offering spiritual sacrifices (*anenegkai pneumatikas thysias*) pleasing to God through Christ.

The language here is all priestly and sacrificial—emphasizing the identity of the new people as being a new Temple and a new priesthood, offering a new kind of sacrifice, "spiritual sacrifices." Again, the identity of this new people is tied intimately to the identity of Christ. As the new Temple is joined to the cornerstone of Christ, the new priesthood can only offer sacrifices "through Christ," that is, in union with the priesthood of Christ.

After proclaiming the marvelous identity of this new people of God, Peter "proves" this identity through a creative appeal to the Old Testament, deploying a singularly inspired combination of Isaiah 28:16, Isaiah 8:14, and Psalm 118:22–23—all of which are united in the person of Jesus or his teaching. As an explanation of the holy priesthood of the faithful, Peter adduces the foundation stone phrase of Isaiah 28:16. The implication is that Christians can offer spiritual sacrifices, acceptable to God, because they are grounded on the foundation stone of Zion, Jesus Christ. Of course, the explicit reference to Zion associates Christ again with the Temple.[27]

In Peter's usage, the cornerstone (*lithon akrogōniaion*) is seen here in a double connotation we discussed in considering the original texts in Isaiah. It is both a foundation stone and stumbling stone at the same time. Archeologically it has been shown that the cornerstones of old were huge rocks which served to unite two walls of a building or temple, and which jutted out and often caused people to trip.[28] Peter in the same way sees Christ as the cornerstone of the New Temple, which served to unite the two walls of the new people of God—the Jew and Gentile—and to support the entire structure of the Church. But in addition, Christ is the stone that makes men stumble—those men, that is, who do not believe him. This double effect of the one and only stone is developed metaphorically by Peter in the subsequent verses (1 Pet. 2:7–9).

In interpreting Christ as both cornerstone and stumbling block, Peter follows Isaiah and Jesus in linking Psalm 118 with Isaiah 8:13–14. The implication, again, is that one and the same stone will have two different effects: it will be a cause of joy and honor for some (Ps. 118:23), and a cause of ruin and defeat for others (Dan. 2:34 and Isa. 8:14).

---

27 Compare Isa. 30:20: "Go to the mountain of the LORD, to the Rock of Israel." For the Zion traditions, see John H. Elliott, *1 Peter: A New Translation with Introduction and Commentary*, The Anchor Bible 37B (New York: Doubleday, 2000), 424–425.

28 *Biblia Comentada V* (Evangelios) Manuel de Tuya, O.P., 473. Compare *Revue Biblique* (1920), 488.

After recalling the unfortunate reality of the stumbling of some, he refers immediately to the joy and privilege of the new chosen people. Peter identifies the Church as the new Israel, or rather, as the fulfillment of the covenant promises made to Israel at Mount Sinai (1 Pet. 2:9–10). Peter here draws on the covenantal formulation of Exodus 19:3–8 and applies to the living stones, the new people of God, all the titles that God once gave the Israelites in establishing them as his chosen people. The Church is to be a "royal priesthood (*basileion hierateuma*), a holy nation (*ethnos hagion*), and a people for God's own possession" (*laos eis peripoiēsin*).

The people themselves are connected to their cornerstone by the adjective "chosen" (*eklekton*). They are a chosen people (*genos eklekton*) just like their Savior was chosen by God (*lithos ... eklekton para de Theō*). The new people of God does not "replace" the old. Instead, the Church inherits the prerogatives and responsibilities given to Israel in its original election by God and the covenant made following the Exodus. In this, the Church fulfills the prophecy of Isaiah for a "new Exodus," a restoration from exile and the reestablishment of a chosen people:

> Behold, I am doing a new thing;
> now it springs forth, do you not perceive it?
> I will make a way in the wilderness
> and rivers in the desert. ...
> to give drink to my chosen people,
> the people whom I formed for myself
> that they might declare my praise. (Isa. 43:19–21)

This prophecy is the other scriptural foundation underlying 1 Peter 4:9. The Church is the new people that God has formed for himself. And this "new thing," this new Exodus that Isaiah alludes to, is evoked most fully in the faith in Jesus, and God's marvelous action on behalf of his people.

The Church, then, is tantamount to a new creation. Peter makes this clear when again he applies messianic texts to the Church. The living stones, the holy nation, the chosen race, and royal priesthood, is a new people created out of a "no people."

> Once you were no people but now you are God's people; once
> you had not received mercy but now you have received mercy.
> (1 Pet. 2:10; compare Hosea 1:9–10; 2:23–24)

Again we see the pattern of rejection and glorification. A people who were once "no people," by the mercy of God have been made "God's people." And again the Church fulfills the prophecy of old:

> I will say to No-people-of-mine, "You are my People";
> and he will answer "You are my God." (Hos. 2:24)

Some Implications for Ecclesiology

Thus we see that in 1 Peter, the self-designation of Christ as the cornerstone in Psalm 118 serves to ground a deep reading of the reality of the Church in light of the Old Testament. And we find Peter's exegesis consistent with the stone and cornerstone imagery used throughout the New Testament writings.

For the New Testament writers, the cornerstone prophecy, as we have analyzed it in the Old Testament, is fulfilled and brought to bear in the person and works of Jesus Christ. At the same time, the reality of rejection is applied to the leaders of the chosen people (Matt. 21:42–43), but is also extended to all men and women (1 Pet. 2:4).

The term *apodokimazein* ("rejected") can refer both to the rejection of Christ by Israel's priests (Luke 9:22), or by the people who are included in the more general "this generation" (Luke 17:25). The root word itself, *dokimē*, refers to a concrete historic test with salvific consequences (Rom. 12:12; Phil. 1:10). In this case, the test is Christ himself. Christ, the cornerstone, is seen as the source of stumbling and confusion for those in Israel who do not believe (Rom. 9:33). The reason for rejecting Christ remains the same as in the Old Testament—pride and self-sufficiency.

In all the New Testament passages there is a notable deepening with respect to the interconnection between God the rejected One and the people he founds and supports. Christ is not only a cornerstone in the sense of a foundation; he is also a keystone or capstone in the sense of being his people's chief glory. St. Peter describes this mysterious bond when he speaks of Christians as living stones built on the living rock, which is Christ (1 Pet. 2:5). The Christians, who were once a non-people, have become the people of mercy.

St. Paul sees both Jew and Gentile as united upon one foundation, which is Christ. He alludes to this union as a living structure which "grows" into a holy Temple (Eph. 2:19–22), and which is rooted in the mystery of God's eternal love for man (Eph. 2:4–5). The Church, then, is a spiritual edifice built upon the cornerstone of Christ and the foundation of the apostles. To "build upon" the cornerstone of Christ, believers must possess doctrinal fidelity and personal humility (compare Col. 2:7; 1 Cor. 3:9–11). To build-up or "edify" one another as Christians, mutual charity is necessary (1 Cor. 8:1; 1 Thess. 6:11).

Christ constitutes a life-giving stone as well as a testing stone (1 Cor. 10:4), thus uniting in his person those aspects of divine power which had been revealed in the Old Testament—God as the rock that begets his child (Deut. 32:18), the Rock that gives water to a thirsty people (Exod. 17:3–7).

St. John, in the Apocalypse, though he does not quote Psalm 118 directly, represents the final triumphant state of Christ the rejected stone. The image of Christ as the living stone and the Church as the new Temple of living stones culminates in the vision of the new Jerusalem coming down from heaven in glory. After the enemies of God and his people are fully conquered and destroyed, the glorious kingdom of the Lamb and his Father will be established. The heavenly city of

Jerusalem is built upon twelve foundation stones (Rev. 21:14). It is the final victory of Christ and his people. As both had been rejected and persecuted, now both are reinstated in love and glory. Their kingdom will fill the world in the eschatological sense of the stone in Daniel 2:34 and the cosmological sense of Job 38:6.

None of these passages, of course, are isolated in themselves. They all point to and depend upon the central reality of Christ and his people, both of whom are rejected yet reigning. Indeed, there are many references to Christ's rejection by his own people (Matt. 21:42–44; 1 Pet. 2:8). Instead of being a rock of life and sureness, he has become a stumbling stone (Isa. 8:14).

There is, then, an obvious ontological and ecclesiological import behind Psalm 118:22–23—one of the many Old Testament passages that are uplifted and transformed in the reality of the Word incarnate. "The stone which the builders rejected has become the cornerstone" thus entails a complete New Testament reality. It is the revelation about Christ and his people which is extended into time, and affords an interesting characteristic about the nature of the Church—its participation in the rejection and glory of her founder. Nevertheless, at the same time, the second part of the psalm passage—"This is God's work and it is wonderful to see"—speaks of the need of faith to fully grasp the meaning of that relationship. I have tried in this article to show how a rejection-glory pattern lies behind the events narrated in Matthew 21 and its parallels. There is a continuous tension between those who reject Christ and those who accept him.

With regard to the ecclesiological significance of the Scripture verses under study, we may conclude that the image of Christ the Rock has many facets—all of which point to key relations between Christ and his people, between his people and the world. Christ himself is a foundation stone for those who believe in him, while he is a stumbling stone for unbelievers. In his person and his teaching he is rejected not only by persecutors and unbelievers, but also by the proud or self-sufficient within the chosen community. In the end, however, he is glorified and his true people rejoice with him, since he is the cornerstone and keystone of their existence.

Upon Christ, the stone rejected yet reigning as the cornerstone, a source of stumbling yet the source of security, his Church is aligned and grows in holiness. His people are the living stones attached to him and bound in love and mutual edification. To remain firmly founded and organically attached upon this foundation, one must be humble and remain doctrinally faithful.

The Church's members, hence, are intrinsically united to Christ, and share in their Master's rejection and glorification. At the end of time, Christ and his people will finally triumph over evil—their enemies will be definitively crushed and broken upon him—and Christ will become the cornerstone and keystone of the universe, in which God will be "all in all" (1 Cor. 15:28).

Letter & Spirit 4 (2008): 107–143

Temple, Sign, and Sacrament:
Towards a New Perspective on the Gospel of John

~: Scott W. Hahn :~
St. Paul Center for Biblical Theology

The significance of the Jerusalem Temple in John's Gospel has been the subject of a large number of monographs in the last decade. As a result of this work, scholars now generally accept not only that the Temple is a central theme in the Fourth Gospel, but that John is advancing what might be characterized as a "Temple christology"—that is, John wishes to show how the Temple and its liturgy find their fulfillment in Jesus Christ, especially in his death and resurrection.[1]

However, if our interpretation of John stops with that scholarly consensus—that John portrays Jesus as the fulfillment of the Temple—we are left with an apparently disconcerting situation; for, since Christ is now ascended, our Temple must be gone. And if this is true, the Church's situation would be not unlike that of Judaism after 70 A.D. and the destruction of the Temple.[2] But John's Temple christology is not conceived so narrowly as to limit it to Christ's immediate person and earthly ministry. Rather, the evangelist insists that Jesus' ministry continues in and through the intermediaries of the Spirit and the apostles.

In this article, I want to pursue these broader lines of the Temple fulfillment theme in John. In particular, I want to explore how John envisions Christ's fulfillment of the Temple and its festivals through the sacraments celebrated by the power of the Spirit, especially the sacraments of baptism and the Eucharist.[3] I

---

1   See, for example, Mary L. Coloe, *God Dwells With Us: Temple Symbolism in the Fourth Gospel* (Collegeville, MN: Liturgical Press, 2001); Johannes Frühwald-König, *Tempel und Kult: Ein Beitrag zur Christologie es Johannesevangeliums* [Temple and Cult: A Contribution to the Christology of the Gospel of John], Biblische Untersuchungen 27 (Regensburg: Friedrich Pustet, 1998); Paul M. Hoskins, *Jesus as the Fulfillment of the Temple in the Gospel of John*, Paternoster Biblical Monographs (Carlisle: Paternoster, 2006); Alan Kerr, *The Temple of Jesus' Body: The Temple Theme in the Gospel of John*, Journal for the Study of the New Testament Supplement Series 220 (Sheffield: Sheffield Academic, 2002); Mark Kinzer, "Temple Christology in the Gospel of John," *Society of Biblical Literature Seminar Papers* 37:1 (Missoula, MT: Scholars Press, 1998): 447–464; Lucius Nereparampil, *Destroy This Temple: An Exegetico-Theological Study on the Meaning of Jesus' Temple-Logion in Jn 2:19* (Bangalore: Dharmaram, 1978); Gunnar H. Østenstad, *Patterns of Redemption in the Fourth Gospel: An Experiment in Structural Analysis*, Studies in the Bible and Early Christianity 38 (Lewiston, NY: Edwin Mellen, 1998); Antony Therath, *Jerusalem in the Gospel of John: An Exegetical and Theological Inquiry into Johannine Geography* (New Delhi: Intercultural Publications, 1999); Stephen T. Um, *The Theme of Temple Christology in John's Gospel*, Library of New Testament Studies 312 (Sheffield: Sheffield Academic, 2006).

2   Coloe, *God Dwells With Us*, 216.

3   On the presence of sacramental symbolism in John, see Raymond E. Brown, "The Johannine Sacramentary" in *New Testament Essays* (Milwaukee: Bruce,1965), 51–76; Alf Correll, *Consummat-*

present this article as more exploratory than demonstrative. That said, by bringing together some of the most fruitful findings of Johannine scholarship, I hope this reading of John will offer a new perspective on the many signs Jesus performed in the presence of his disciples and the relationship of those signs to the new life that John wishes to communicate by his writing (see John 20:30–31).

I will begin by briefly reviewing the depiction of the Temple in the Old Testament and its significance for the old covenant People of God. This will enable us to better understand how John's first-century Jewish readers would have received his identification of Jesus as the replacement of the Temple and its festivals.

Following that, I will examine the first Passover narrative in John (2:13–3:21). This will show three things: First, that John depicts Jesus as the "new Temple" at the outset of his public ministry, a theme he pursues throughout his gospel. Second, that Jesus performs his "signs" in the context of this broader fulfillment of the Temple and the Temple festivals. Third, that in the dialogue with Nicodemus, Jesus moves from his "signs" to the sacrament of baptism, that is, rebirth by the Spirit (John 3:3, 5).

I will then consider John's narratives of the second Passover (John 6) and the Feast of Tabernacles (John 7–9). I hope to show that in these accounts, too, Jesus functions as new Temple, that the Temple festivals are the context for Jesus' "signs," and that the "signs" he performs point forward to the sacraments of baptism and the Eucharist.

Moving to the third and final Passover narrative of the gospel (John 11:55–20:31), I will focus on Jesus' last discourse (John 13–17), in which he confers on the disciples his own "Templeness" and commissions them to continue his mission—indeed, to perform "greater works than these." I will suggest that the

---

um Est: Eschatology and Church in the Gospel of St. John (New York: Macmillan, 1958); Oscar Cullmann, Early Christian Worship, trans. A. Stewart Todd and James B. Torrance, Studies in Biblical Theology 10 (London: SCM, 1953); Frederick W. Guyette, "Sacramentality in the Fourth Gospel: Conflicting Interpretations," Ecclesiology 3 (2007): 235–250; Francis J. Moloney, "When is John Talking about the Sacraments?" in "A Hard Saying": The Gospel and Culture (Collegeville, MN: Liturgical Press, 2001), 109–130; P. Paul Niewalda, Sakramentssymbolik im Johannesevangelium? Eine Exegetisch-Historische Studie [Sacramental Symbolism in the Gospel of John? An Exegetical-Historical Study (Limburg: Lahn-Verlag, 1958); Bruce Vawter, "The Johannine Sacramentary," Theological Studies 17 (1956): 151–166. Johannine scholars range from the anti- or non-sacramental to the ultra-sacramental. Writing near the end of his life Raymond Brown claimed: "Most scholars recognize some form of sacramentalism" (An Introduction to the Gospel of John, ed. Francis J. Moloney [New York: Doubleday, 2003], 231). Brown's own moderate approach, outlined in "The Johannine Sacramentary" and pursued in his various commentaries, recommends itself for its exegetical common sense. Ironically, it is from Baptist scholar David Aune that one finds one of the most forceful defenses of sacramental and liturgical allusions in John: "It would therefore be incorrect to claim … that basic elements of congregational life, worship, sacraments and the ministry play only insignificant roles in the Fourth Gospel. Such elements do not receive explicit treatment precisely because they are the presuppositions of the ecclesial context out of which the gospel arose." See The Cultic Setting of Realized Eschatology in Early Christianity, Supplements to Novum Testamentum 28 (Leiden: Brill, 1972), 73. Emphasis mine.

sacraments fall under this category of "greater works," and that this interpretation is supported by consideration of John 19:34, which symbolically depicts the sacraments flowing from the death and resurrection of Christ, and John 20:22–23, in which the apostles receive the Spirit in order to perform the "greater work" of remitting sins.

This exploration will allow me to suggest the following conclusion: that, if one follows the logic and symbolism of John's Gospel, the sacraments, primarily baptism and Eucharist, truly are the specific times and places where the believer continues to experience Christ as the new Temple. Having established this central thesis, I will make some corollary conclusions in a brief theological reflection.

The Embodiment of God's Covenant with David

The literature on both the historical role of the Temple in Israel and its literary importance in the Scriptures is enormous.[4] From this literature, I want to stress the following points:

First, the Temple was *the embodiment of God's covenant with David.*[5] The central text of the Davidic covenant (2 Sam. 7:8–16), focuses on a son of David who will build a "house" for God (that is, the Temple), and for whom God will build a "house" (that is, a dynasty). The immediate, though penultimate, fulfillment of this covenant was found in David's son, Solomon, who, like David, was an "anointed"

---

4   See, for example, the brief reviews by Coloe, *God Dwells With Us*, 31–63; and Hoskins, *Jesus as the Temple*, 38–107, and longer treatments by G. K. Beale, *The Temple and the Church's Mission: A Biblical Theology of the Dwelling Place of God*, New Studies in Biblical Theology 17 (Downer's Grove, IL: InterVarsity, 2004); Jon D. Levenson, "The Temple and the World," *Journal of Religion* 64 (1984): 275–298; John M. Lundquist, "What is a Temple? A Preliminary Typology," in *The Quest for the Kingdom of God: Studies in Honor of George E. Mendenhall*, eds. H. B. Huffmon, F. A. Spina, and A. R. W. Green (Winona Lake, IN: Eisenbrauns, 1983); Lundquist, "The Legitimizing Role of the Temple in the Origin of the State," *Society of Biblical Literature Seminar Papers* 21 (Missoula, MT: Scholars Press, 1982): 271–297; Lundquist, "Temple, Covenant, and Law in the Ancient Near East and in the Old Testament," in *Israel's Apostasy and Restoration: Essays in Honor of Roland K. Harrison*, ed. Avraham Gileadi (Grand Rapids, MI: Baker, 1988), 293–305; Donald W. Parry, "Garden of Eden: Prototype Sanctuary," in *Temples of the Ancient World: Ritual and Symbolism* (Salt Lake City: Deseret, 1994), 126–151; Raphael Patai, *Man and Temple in Ancient Jewish Myth and Ritual* (New York: Ktav, 1967).

5   "The Temple was the embodiment of the covenant of David, in which the triple relationship between Yahweh, the House of David, and the people of Israel was established." Toomo Ishida, *The Royal Dynasties in Ancient Israel. A Study on the Formation and Development of Royal-Dynastic Ideology*, Beiheft zur Zeitschrift für die Alttestamentliche Wissenschaft 142 (New York: W. de Gruyter, 1977), 145; "Reinforcing the covenant with David, which formulated Yahweh's election of him, the Temple now testified to Yahweh's election of Mount Zion as his eternal dwelling-place" (Ishida, *Royal Dynasties*, 147). Besides the work of Ishida, we may mention the extensive research of John M. Lundquist (see n. 4 above), much of it collected in *Temples of the Ancient World*. Lundquist demonstrates the key position of the temple in the center of the ancient Near Eastern world-view or cosmology, not only for Israel's neighbors (Egyptian, Canaanite, Mesopotamian, or Hittite cultures) but for Israel herself, as reflected in the Old Testament.

one—that is, a "Messiah" (Hebrew) or "Christ" (Greek).[6] He also enjoyed the status of "son of God" according to the terms of the covenant.[7] In Solomon we have a "Christ," a Temple-builder, and the first *individual* in the canon of Scripture to be described as "son of God."

Second, the Temple was *the dwelling place* of God's "name,"[8] his "glory,"[9] and finally, God himself.[10] Third, the Temple was *the place of pilgrimage*. Three times a year, all the men of Israel were required to journey to the Temple to celebrate the feasts of Passover, Pentecost, and Tabernacles.[11] For Israelites, participating in these feasts meant undergoing water washings (ablutions) to enter a state of ritually purity.[12] Only then were Israelites able to offer sacrifice[13] and participate in the feast, which principally involved eating:[14] usually the meat of the sacrifice,[15] with bread[16] and wine,[17] the fruits of the Promised Land.[18] Through participation in these Temple sacrifices, Israelites made atonement for their sins.[19] The entire experience of the Temple—the ritual washings, the sacrifice, the eating and drinking, and the remission of sin—was only possible because of the work of the Temple ministers: the High Priest, his fellow priests, and the Levites.

Finally, a new Temple, often with divine properties, is a *central feature of the eschatology* of some of the prophets,[20] and at least an important feature in several

---

6   1 Kings 1:34, 39.

7   2 Sam. 7:14; Ps. 2:6–7.

8   Deut. 16:2; Ps. 74:7.

9   1 Kings 8:10–11; Ezek. 43:2–5.

10   Ps. 68:16; Ezek. 43:6.

11   Deut. 16:1–17.

12   Exod. 19:10–11; 2 Chron. 30:17–20; Lev. 11–15; esp. 15:31. The necessity of water washings is not explicit in the Pentateuch's descriptions of the feast, but it was required by the logic of the laws of cleanliness in Lev. 11–15 and elsewhere. The penalty for defiling the sanctuary with uncleanness was death (Lev. 15:31); therefore, worshipers had to be ritually clean. Moreover, there were a wide variety of causes of unseemliness (see Lev. 11–15); thus, the average Israelite would need to purify himself by ritual washing at some point before participating in one of the Temple festivals. Archeologists have found large numbers of *miqva'ot*—ritual baths—in Jerusalem and its environs, used for these ritual cleansings during the Second Temple period.

13   Deut. 16:2, 6; Lev. 23:8.

14   Deut. 16:3, 7–8; see also Lev. 7:11–17; 2 Chron. 30:22; Isa. 25:6.

15   Deut 16:4, 7.

16   Deut 16:3; Lev. 23:6.

17   Isa. 25:6; Luke 22:18, 20.

18   Deut. 16:13. Although the texts cited are largely for the feast of Passover, celebratory eating was an important part of all the feasts, even when not mentioned in the biblical descriptions. All three pilgrimage feasts (Passover, Pentecost, Tabernacles) marked important agricultural events (barley harvest, wheat harvest, and fruit harvest, respectively) and were natural times to enjoy the Creator's abundant gifts, similar to the American holiday, Thanksgiving.

19   See, for example, Lev. 4:20, 26, 35; 5:10, 13; 19:22; 15:25.

20   For example, Ezek. 40–48 and Joel 3:17–18.

others[21]—especially when one takes into account the relationship of the Temple, Zion, and Jerusalem.[22] It will be useful to bear in mind these points concerning the Temple as we proceed to explore John's deployment of Temple and Temple-festival motifs in his gospel, especially in relation to Jesus.

The First Passover and the Cleansing of the Temple

While the synoptic tradition describes the public ministry of Jesus as beginning in Galilee, John chooses instead to show Jesus revealing himself first in Judea, beginning in Jerusalem, at the Temple during the Passover (John 2:13–3:21).[23] Moreover, during these opening public scenes, John depicts Jesus proclaiming himself to be the new Temple (John 2:19–21). The account of Jesus' cleansing of the Temple thus announces themes that are unique to John and will continue to be emphasized throughout his Gospel—Jerusalem, the Temple, and the Temple feasts.[24]

Until the final week of his earthly life, Galilee forms the setting for most of Jesus' ministry as it is depicted in the synoptics. By contrast, the majority of John's Gospel is set in Jerusalem, and specifically in the Temple.[25] Moreover, most of the events in John take place during the Temple festivals, the succession of which serve to structure much of the narrative:[26] Passover;[27] an unnamed feast, possibly Pentecost;[28] Passover again;[29] Tabernacles;[30] Dedication;[31] and the final Passover.[32]

Jesus' teachings and "signs" during these liturgical festivals often correspond to the central themes of the festivals themselves; some scholars have gone so far as to argue that they relate specifically to the Jewish lectionary readings for those

---

21   Compare Zech. 6:12–15; 8:9–12; 14:16–21; Isa. 2:1–4; 56:3–6; 66:18–22; Jer. 33:10–11; Hag. 2:1–9, 15–19; Dan. 8:14; 9:17, 24–27; Mic. 1:1–4),

22   See Therath, *Jerusalem in the Gospel of John*, 64–65; Hoskins, *Jesus as Temple*, 69–89.

23   Therath, *Jerusalem in the Gospel of John*, xix.

24   Compare Therath, *Jerusalem in the Gospel of John*, 59.

25   See Correll, *Consummatum Est*, 44; Therath, *Jerusalem in the Gospel of John*, xiii–xix. For parts of the Gospel set in or near Jerusalem: see John 2:13–4:2; 5:1–47; 7:10–10:39; 12:12–20:31 (Jerusalem); 11:17–53; 12:1–11 (Bethany)—roughly three-quarters of the Gospel.

26   For a sustained treatment of the subject, see Gale A. Yee, *Jewish Feasts and the Gospel of John* (Wilmington, DE: Michael Glazier, 1989). Concerning the structure of the Fourth Gospel, the feasts are only one of several structuring elements. For a review of almost all the major structural proposals, see George Mlakushyil, *The Christocentric Literary Structure of the Fourth Gospel*, Analecta Biblica 117 (Rome: Pontifical Biblical Institute, 1987), 17–85.

27   John 2:13–3:21.

28   John 5:1–47.

29   John 6:1–71.

30   John 7:1–10:21.

31   John 10:22–39.

32   John 11:55–20:31.

feasts.[33] What is John's intent in emphasizing the Temple and the festivals? I would argue that it is to demonstrate that Christ is the fulfillment of the Temple and the worship performed there.[34]

The Passover was the greatest feast of Judaism in the period of the Second Temple, roughly 520 B.C. to 70 A.D. Its importance is reflected in the fact that John records three Passover celebrations during Jesus' public ministry. John may have known of Jewish traditions that anticipated the arrival of the Messiah at Passover.[35] Since Deuteronomy specified that the Passover lamb must be sacrificed at the central sanctuary (Deut. 16:2), the celebration of Passover was inextricably bound to the Temple. It was a national festival—again we think of the great national Passovers presided over by Hezekiah (2 Chron. 30) and Josiah (2 Chron. 35), those righteous sons of David and kings of Israel, who were solicitous for the care and maintenance of the Temple.

In John 2:13–25, we see Jesus, recently hailed as king of Israel (see John 1:49), showing his solicitude for the well-being of the Temple. Driving out the merchants and money changers, he rebukes them for making his "Father's house" (*oikon tou patros mou*) a "house of trade" (*oikon emporiou*). Jesus' actions and words here should be understood in light of Zechariah 14:21, which says of the eschatological Temple: "there shall no longer be a trader in the house of the LORD of hosts on that day."[36] The Judeans question Jesus, "What *sign* will you show us, since you do these things?" to which Jesus responds, "Destroy this Temple and in three days I will raise it up." They misunderstand, but the evangelist clarifies: "He spoke about the Temple of his body."

Although the literature on this passage is vast,[37] here we should summarize just some salient points. First, by beginning Jesus' public ministry with the Temple cleansing, John casts his whole ministry in light of the concept that he is the new Temple.[38] Second, by calling the destruction and raising of his Temple-body a

---

33   Aileen Guilding, *The Fourth Gospel and Jewish Worship: A Study in the Relation of St. John's Gospel to the Ancient Jewish Lectionary System* (Oxford: Clarendon, 1960). But see the cautions of Michael A. Daise, *Feasts in John: Jewish Festivals and Jesus' "Hour" in the Fourth Gospel*, Wissenschaftliche Untersuchungen zum Neuen Testament 2 Reihe 229 (Tübingen: Mohr Siebeck, 2007), 81–87.

34   See Hoskins, *Jesus as the Temple*, 2.

35   Therath, *Jerusalem in the Gospel of John*, 60–61.

36   Raymond E. Brown, *The Gospel according to John I–XII*, Anchor Bible 29 (Garden City, NY: Doubleday, 1966), 121.

37   Lucius Nereparampil has devoted a monograph to the pericope (*Destroy This Temple*, see n. 1), and every major work on the Temple-theme in John devotes extensive space to its exegesis.

38   Compare Coloe, *God Dwells With Us*, 84; Kerr, *The Temple of Jesus' Body*, 101; Therath, *Jerusalem in the Gospel of John*, 59. Also, see Rudolf Schnackenburg's summary: "The explanation given in [John] 2:21 gives the saying about the destruction and rebuilding of the Temple a similar, supremely christological significance. Further this explanation makes Jesus the 'place' where God is to be adored, the true 'house of God' (compare 1:51). With him and in him the time of

"sign," John establishes a strong link between this narrative and the account of Jesus' death and resurrection. This suggests that his death and resurrection should be interpreted as a Temple-(re)building account, while at the same time identifying in advance these events as the climactic "sign" in the sequence of "signs" that help to structure the narrative.[39] The "sign" of his death and resurrection—the "destruction" and "raising up" of his Temple-body— is the definitive "sign" toward which all the others are ordered: "In the context of the *definitive* sign that Jesus speaks about, all the other '*signs*' take on their *significance*."[40]

Finally, the proximity of Passover (John 2:13), the reference to Jesus' body, and to the consuming or "eating up" (*kataphago*) of Jesus (John 2:17), establish links between this episode and John 6, where, on another Passover, Jesus will speak of the necessity of eating (*phago*) his flesh and blood.[41]

The concept of Jesus as new Temple is, of course, not limited to this passage.[42] Already in John 1:14 (which reads, literally: "The Word became flesh and *tabernacled* among us") and in John 1:51 ("you shall see angels of God ascending and descending on the Son of Man"), Jesus has been compared to two precursors of the Temple: the Mosaic Tabernacle and Jacob's sanctuary at Bethel.[43] In John 4, the concept of Jesus as the "new sanctuary" is present during the discussion of the future irrelevance of both the Gerizim and Jerusalem temples.[44]

---

the worship of God 'in spirit and truth' (4:23) has dawned. His body is the source of the waters of life (19:34; so too 7:38), his person is the vine through whose vital force the disciples can work and bear fruit (15:4–8). ... [John's] ecclesiology is based entirely on christology, though he does not reflect further on the relationship between the glorified body of Christ and the 'body' of the Church. This Pauline thought is not found in John, though the evangelist in his own way gives equally strong expression to the doctrine of the unity of the risen Lord with his Church." *The Gospel according to John*, 3 vols. (New York: Seabury, 1980–82), 1:352; cited by Celestino G. Lingad, Jr., *The Problems of Jewish Christians in the Johannine Community*, Tesi Gregoriana Serie Teologia 73 (Rome: Editrice Pontificia Università Gregoriana, 2001), 257.

39 Nereparampil, *Destroy this Temple*, 92–98; Kerr, *The Temple of Jesus' Body*, 96–97.

40 Lingad, *The Problems of Jewish Christians*, 270;

41 Kerr, *The Temple of Jesus' Body*, 85–86. "Jesus will be consumed. The Hebrew word lying behind 'consume' commonly means 'to eat,' but it ... can be used of the fire that consumes the sacrifice offered to God. ... It is possible that here too there is an allusion to Jesus' death being a sacrifice." Kerr does not see the connection with John 6, where Jesus speaks of his "flesh" (*sarx*) and "blood" (*haima*) being "consumed" (*phago*). In John 6, too, there are strong sacrificial overtones and omens of the passion: "The bread which I shall give for the life of the world is my flesh" (6:51). Granted, in 2:21 Jesus speaks of his "body" (*soma*) and in 6:51–58 of his "flesh" (*sarx*) and "blood" (*haima*), but did the evangelist really expect his first-century readers to make *no connection* between Jesus' "body" and his "flesh" and "blood"? Kerr thinks that is the case (*The Temple of Jesus' Body*, 94), but this seems to me quite unreasonable.

42 On Jesus as the New Temple in John, see the concise summary of Beale, *The Temple and the Church's Mission*, 192–200.

43 Kerr, *The Temple of Jesus' Body*, 72, 133, 136–166; Coloe, *God Dwells With Us*, 23–27; Hoskins, *Jesus as Temple*, 116–135.

44 This is the major thesis of Um's monograph, *The Theme of Temple Christology in John's Gospel*

We also see a dramatic identification of Jesus and the Temple in John 7–10:21. There, the backdrop is the festival celebrating the building of the Temple (Tabernacles), during which the priests daily poured out water from the Pool of Siloam on the altar steps and kept the Temple courts illuminated twenty-four hours a day in anticipation of the eschatological prophesies.[45] In the midst of this, Jesus claims himself to be the true source of water and light, and brings light to a blind man through the waters of Siloam, thus supporting his claim to be the true Temple.[46]

In John 10:22–42, during the Feast of Dedication, which commemorates the re-consecration of the Temple by the Maccabees, Jesus describes himself as the one "consecrated" by the Father and sent into the world—that is, he calls himself the new sanctuary.[47] In John 14:2–3, Jesus again refers to his "Father's House," a Temple reference alluding to John 2:16 and supported by other Temple references—the house with many "rooms" is probably the many-chambered Temple of Ezekiel 41–43; and the "place" (Greek: *topos*; Hebrew: *mâqôm*) he goes to prepare connotes the "sacred place" of the Temple. In the final analysis, this passage describes Jesus' departure to be prepared as a Temple wherein his disciples will "dwell."[48]

Finally, in the climax of this Temple symbolism, in John 19:34, the evangelist records the flow of blood and water from the side of Christ, which is to be understood against the background of the river prophesied to flow from the eschatological Temple as well as the blood and water which flowed from the Temple altar in Jerusalem.[49]

(see note 1), which, despite its sweeping title, is actually an exegetical study limited to John 4:1–26. See also Coloe, *God Dwells With Us*, 85–113; Hoskins, *Jesus as Temple*, 135–145; Kerr, *The Temple of Jesus' Body*, 167–204; Therath, *Jerusalem in the Gospel of John*, 78–94.

45   See Ezek. 47:1–12; Joel 3:18; Zech. 14:8.

46   Coloe, *God Dwells With Us*, 115–143; Hoskins, *Jesus as Temple*, 160–170; Kerr, *The Temple of Jesus' Body*, 226–241.

47   See Coloe, *God Dwells With Us*, 145–155, esp. 153; Hoskins, *Jesus as Temple*, 170–175; Kerr, *The Temple of Jesus' Body*, 253–255.

48   This is the major thesis of James McCaffrey, *The House with Many Rooms: The Temple Theme of Jn. 14,2–3*, Analecta Biblica 114 (Rome: Pontifical Biblical Institute, 1998), 246–255.

49   "At the south-western corner [of the altar] there were two holes like two narrow nostrils by which *the blood that was poured* over the western base and the southern base *used to run down and mingle in the water-channel and flow out into the brook Kidron.*" (Mishnah *Middoth* [Measurements] 3:2). For other mentions of this drainage channel, see Mishnah tractates *Yoma* [Day of Atonement] 5:6; *Zebahim* [Sacrifices] 8:7; *Temurah* [Exchange] 7:6; *Tamid* [Always] 5:5. The same channel that was used to drain the blood into the river was also used for pouring out drink-offerings of wine. See Mishnah *Meliah* [Sacrilege] 3:3. Texts in *The Mishnah*, trans. Herbert Danby (Oxford: Oxford University, 1933); Jacob Neusner, *The Mishnah: A New Translation* (New Haven: Yale University, 1988). McCaffrey, Kerr, Hoskins, and many commentators link John 7:37–39 with 19:34. Coloe demurs (*God Dwells With Us*, 208–209).

Jesus' Baptismal Mystagogy

Thus, we can see that John introduces the theme of Jesus as new Temple in John 2:13–21 in order to pursue that theme at key points throughout the remainder of his gospel. As numerous scholars have noted from the strong literary connections, the Passover and new Temple contexts of John 2:13–25 are carried over to the next passage, Jesus' dialogue with Nicodemus (John 3:1–21).[50]

> Now when he was in Jerusalem at the Passover feast, many trusted in his name, seeing the signs (*semeia*) which he did. But Jesus did not trust himself to them, since he knew all (*pantas*), and he had no need that anyone should testify about a man (*anthropos*), for he himself knew what was in a man (*anthropos*).

> Now there was a man (*anthropos*) of the Pharisees, Nicodemus his name, ruler of the Judeans. This (man) came to him (at) night and said to him "Rabbi, we know that you have come from God as a teacher; for no one would be able to do these signs (*semeia*) which you do, unless God was with him."

The Temple cleansing culminated in a discussion of the "signs" (*semeia*) which Jesus performed, and how "men" (*anthropoi*) came to believe in his name because of the signs. This leads directly into Jesus' conversation with Nicodemus, who is presented in the very next verse (John 3:1) as a "man" (*anthropos*) who has come to believe because of the "signs" (*semeia*). Thus, the conversation with Nicodemus should be understood against the context of Jesus having indicated himself to be the new Temple during Passover.

Nicodemus comes to Jesus to discuss the "signs." The use of the term *semeia* ("signs") to describe Jesus' miracles is characteristic of John's Gospel. The synoptics typically use the term *dynameis* ("mighty deeds"), to describe the same phenomena. The difference in terminology seems intentional. John employs "signs" because he wishes to stress the role of the miracles, not as ends in themselves, but as indicators or pointers to a deeper reality—such as Jesus' identity as Messiah, Son of God, indeed, God himself.[51] The signs do point to Jesus' messianic and divine identity, to be sure; but, as I will argue, they also point to something greater than

---

50 See Mlakuzhyil, *Christocentric Literary Structure*, 105: "A good example of a few verses forming a 'bridge' between two adjacent pericopes is found in 2:23–25, which joins Jesus' cleansing of the Temple (2:13–22) to his dialogue-discourse with Nicodemus (3:1–21)"; also Lingad, *The Problems of Jewish Christians*, 263; Andrew T. Lincoln, *The Gospel According to Saint John*, Black's New Testament Commentary 4 (London: Continuum, 2005), 144; George F. Beasely-Murray, *John*, Word Biblical Commentary 36 (Waco, TX: Word, 1987), 45–46.

51 "The writer does not use our modern concept of incident, but that of a 'sign' (*semeion*) and thereby he means to point again to the double quality of an event at once visible and demanding a higher understanding in the context of faith." Cullmann, *Early Christian Worship*, 46.

themselves—the coming activity of the Spirit in the sacraments, which continues the presence and work of Christ himself.

The gospel, as scholars have suggested, is structured according to a succession of Jesus' signs which are all associated with Israel's liturgical feasts.[52] Usually, commentators point to seven signs performed by Jesus:[53] the changing of water into wine at Cana;[54] the healing of the royal official's son;[55] the healing of the paralytic at Bethesda;[56] the feeding of the 5000;[57] the walking on water;[58] the healing of the man born blind;[59] and the raising of Lazarus.[60] Although this is a popular reckoning of John's "signs," it should be noted that there is no textual indication that the walking on water is to be considered a "sign." At the same time, Jesus' death and resurrection is called a "sign" already in John 2:21. Therefore, I would suggest that the walking on water is not one of John's intended "signs," but rather that the death and resurrection of Christ is the seventh and climactic "sign" of his gospel.

The term "sign" (*semeion*) is deployed frequently (sixteen times) in John's first twelve chapters, but only once in the remaining chapters (see John 20:30). This is one of the reasons scholars generally see a two-fold division of John into a so-called "Book of Signs" (roughly John 1–12) and a "Book of Glory" (John 13–21). Arguably, John 2:18–19 already indicates—from the very start of Jesus' ministry—that the destruction and raising up of his body (which occurs in the "Book of Glory") is the ultimate "sign" confirming Jesus' authority. Therefore, the "Book of Glory" is related to the "Book of Signs" as its climax, bearing witness to the greatest of all Christ's "signs."

With this background and context, we return to the dialogue of Nicodemus and Jesus. Nicodemus wants to discuss Jesus' signs, which he understands as physical miracles indicating divine power at work through Jesus:

---

52 "The overall plan which John gave his Gospel flows immediately from his understanding of Jesus' ministry as one of 'signs.'" Dominic Crossan, *The Gospel of Eternal Life: Reflections on the Theology of St. John* (Milwaukee: Bruce, 1967), 41.

53 Many scholars (for example, recently Willis Hedley Salier, *The Rhetorical Impact of the Semeia in the Gospel of John*, Wissenschaftliche Untersuchungen zum Neuen Testament 2 Reihe 186 [Tübingen: Mohr Siebeck, 2004]) insert the walking on water (John 6:16–21) as the fifth sign, and omit the resurrection. However, the walking on water is never called a sign, it receives no further development or discussion, and was witnessed by no one but the disciples. The death and resurrection, on the other hand, is announced as a sign already in John 2:18–21. On this see Kerr, *The Temple of Jesus' Body*, 10–11.

54 John 2:1–11; compare John 2:11.

55 John 4:43–54; compare John 4:54.

56 John 5:1–15; compare John 6:2; 7:21–24, 31.

57 John 6:1–15; compare John 6:14.

58 John 6:16–21.

59 John 9:1–41; compare John 9:16.

60 John 11:1–54; compare John 12:18.

> This man came to Jesus by night and said to him, "Rabbi, we know that you are a teacher come from God; for no one can do these signs that you do, unless God is with him." Jesus answered him, "Truly, truly, I say to you, unless one is born anew (*anōthen*), he cannot see the Kingdom of God." Nicodemus said to him, "How can a man be born when he is old? Can he enter a second time into his mother's womb and be born?" Jesus answered, "Truly, truly, I say to you, unless one is born of water and the Spirit, he cannot enter the Kingdom of God."

Nicodemus understands enough to know that the *semeia* suggest that Jesus is a teacher of divine origin. While Nicodemus does not ask a question, the evangelist suggests that his remark implied a question about the nature of the signs; hence, Jesus is described as "answering" him. However, Jesus' "answer" (as is so often the case in John) initially seems unrelated to the stated or implied question. Jesus begins to speak to Nicodemus about a spiritual and divine birth, a birth "from above" (*anōthen*) necessary to "see the Kingdom of God." In this, he picks up on the royal theme announced in John 1:49 ("You are the King of Israel!") and perhaps implied by Jesus' exercise of king-like prerogatives over the function of the Temple in the narrative immediately preceding.

Nicodemus interprets Jesus' words in terms of *physical miracles*—this is as much as he has been able to comprehend about the "signs" to this point. His incomprehension is detected in his inquiry about how a man can return to his mother's womb. He is understandably baffled because—even granted that Jesus has miraculous powers over the physical world, the physical requirements for a rebirth in the natural sense seem not only supernatural but counter-natural and positively absurd. Jesus continues, "Unless a man is born of water and the Spirit, he cannot enter the Kingdom of God."

This statement clarifies his meaning and now the reader, if not Nicodemus, begins to understand that Jesus is talking about baptism.[61] John has prepared the reader to associate water, baptism, the Spirit, and divine sonship almost from the beginning of the gospel. In his prologue, he emphasized the need to become "children of God" by being "born of God"—as opposed to natural birth "of blood, of the will of the flesh or the will of a man."[62] In addition, John has already given the reader an account of Jesus' own baptism in water, in which the Spirit descends and marks Jesus out, not only as child, but as "Son of God."[63]

Here in his audience with Nicodemus, the motifs of water, baptism, Spirit, and divine sonship are all correlated. Jesus' words about being "born again (anew),"

---

61   See Cullmann, *Early Christian Worship*, 76; Lingad, *The Problems of Jewish Christians*, 280–282.

62   John 1:12–13.

63   John 1:31–34.

that is, becoming a child once more, and being "born of water and Spirit," pick up on those motifs of divine begetting associated with water and Spirit announced earlier in the gospel.[64] John's Christian readers would have understood the reference to rebirth by "water and Spirit" as a reference to Christian baptism, as the evangelist no doubt intended them to.[65] It is not accidental that the Nicodemus dialogue is followed immediately by references to Jesus and the disciples baptizing,[66] further description of John the Baptist's baptismal ministry, and a discussion of ritual washing leading to affirmation of Jesus' divine sonship,[67] and yet another account of Jesus' baptismal ministry.[68]

The dialogue between Nicodemus and Jesus continues:

> Nicodemus said to him, "How can this be?" Jesus answered him, "Are you a teacher of Israel, and yet you do not understand this? Truly, truly, I say to you, we speak of what we know, and bear witness to what we have seen; but you do not receive our testimony. If I have told you earthly things and you do not believe, how can you believe if I tell you heavenly things? No one has ascended into heaven but he who descended from heaven, the Son of Man."[69]

While a baptismal reference is certainly intended in John 3:5, Jesus' subsequent dialogue does not develop the water motif or deal with the specific actions of baptism; instead he focuses on the reality of the Spirit's action. The emphasis in John's gospel is always on the divine initiative; baptism, then, is not described as

---

64 Thus it is unnecessary to regard the mention of "water" in John 3:5 as intrusive in context and relegate it to a second hand, as Bultmann and others have done.

65 Some see in "water and Spirit" a reference to natural birth (water) followed by spiritual birth (Spirit). But Beasely-Murray points out that in context, "born of water and Spirit" is one event, an explication of what it means to be "born from above" (*John*, 47–49). Others suggest "water" simply means "Spirit" (Lincoln, *John*, 150), but this reduces Jesus' statement to a banal redundancy: "You must be born of Spirit and Spirit." See Matthew Vellanickal, *The Divine Sonship of Christians in the Johannine Writings*, Analecta Biblica 72 (Rome: Pontifical Biblical Institute, 1977), 181: "If the word 'Spirit' is to be taken in a real sense, and not figurative, the same should also be said of 'water', as both are put in the same way and coordinated with *kai*. It is worth noting that John 3:5 is in a context where John speaks often of baptism (compare John 1:25–33; 3:22, 23, 26; 4:1–2). Besides, the figurative understanding of 'water' is opposed to the whole tradition, which as we shall see, usually took it for granted, that 'water' here referred to Christian baptism."

66 John 3:22.

67 John 3:23–36.

68 John 4:1–3.

69 At some point after verse 13, the dialogue format is lost and the voice of the evangelist seems to take over. Some place the division between vv. 13 and 14, others between vv. 15 and 16, still others argue for understanding the quotation of Jesus' words as extending all the way to the end of v. 21.

a human action but as the human reception of divine action. One does not "birth oneself," rather one "is born" (*gennethenai*). The verb *gennao*, "to bear, beget" in John always appears in the passive, as the individual (*anthropos*) is always acted upon by the Spirit. As in John 1:13, where the evangelist stresses that the human will is not involved in the begetting of children of God, so in his conversation with Nicodemus Jesus emphasizes divine sovereignty in spiritual birth (John 3:8: "the wind blows where it wills ... you do not know ... where it goes," John 3:8).

Nicodemus has not understood Jesus' teaching on "birth from above" by means of "water and Spirit." His response ("How can this be?") is a rhetorical question implying: "This cannot be." As such, it is an expression of disbelief and therefore a rejection of the testimony of Jesus and John the Baptist. This reading is supported by Jesus' response ("You do not receive our testimony ... you do not believe").[70]

There is a discernible effort made by Jesus in this dialogue to lead Nicodemus from an "earthly" sphere of reference to a "heavenly" one.[71] Jesus' conversation implies a dualism between the "Spirit" (*pneuma*) and the "flesh" (*sarx*), between the "heavenly" (*epourania*) and the "earthly" (*epigeia*).[72] Clearly, his intent is to guide Nicodemus from the lower to the higher, from the earthly to the heavenly,[73] with the earthly regarded as precondition of the heavenly: "If I have told you earthly things and you do not believe, how can you believe if I tell you heavenly things?"[74]

---

70   Lingad takes Nicodemus as a representative of a type of Jewish Christian encountered by the "Johannine community": "This nonplused reaction [in 3:9] just shows their inability to move away from their own categories into the mysterious life in the Spirit that Jesus is offering. ... Nicodemus and the type of Jewish Christians he symbolizes can be [characterized by] their basic attitude of partial faith" (*The Problems of Jewish Christians*, 297).

71   "Jesus claims [in v. 12] that so far he has spoken to Nicodemus of earthly things, and that, since he has failed to believe, there is no point in going on to speak of heavenly things. Readers might well ask whether the topic of Jesus' conversation in vv. 3–8 was not already heavenly realities. It is likely, however, that 'earthly things' is a reference to Jesus' attempt to move from the earthly level of physical birth and the blowing of wind to the heavenly. Since such an attempt failed to evoke faith, it would be useless to try to speak directly of heavenly things without analogy to the earthly." Lincoln, *John*, 152.

72   Jesus' mode of instruction here is identical to the mode of instruction St. Irenaeus, circa 180 A.D., attributes to God in the Old Testament: "He instructed the people, who were prone to turn to idols, instructing them by repeated appeals to persevere and to serve God, calling them to the things of *primary* importance by means of those which were *secondary*; that is, to things that are *real* by means of those that are *typical*; and by things *temporal*, to *eternal*; and by the *carnal* to the *spiritual*; and by the *earthly* to the *heavenly*; as was also said to Moses, 'You shall make all things after the pattern of those things which thou saw in the mount.'" *Against the Heresies*, Bk. 4, Chap. 14, 3. Text in *Ante-Nicene Fathers*, vol. 1, eds. Alexander Roberts and James Donaldson (Grand Rapids, MI: Eerdmans, 1975), 479.

73   "The tactic of the Johannine discourse is always for the answer to transpose the topic to a higher level; the questioner is on the level of the sensible, but he must be raised to the level of the spiritual. An appreciation of the radical difference between the flesh and the Spirit is the true answer to Nicodemus." Brown, *John I–XII*, 128.

74   See Lingad, *The Problems of Jewish Christians*, 298–299.

This form of pedagogy from the "earthly" to "heavenly" may aptly be described by the Church's term "mystagogy."[75] In particular, in the Nicodemus dialogue there is a mystagogy that leads from the *signs* that Jesus performs to the activity of the Spirit in the *sacraments*—in this case, the sacrament of baptism.

At this point, we are in the position to step back and take in all of John 2:13–3:21 in one glance. During Passover, Jesus enters the Temple and cleanses it, fulfilling prophecies of the eschatological Temple (Zech. 14:21). Asked to produce a "sign," he speaks of his coming death and resurrection as a destruction and rebuilding of the Temple. During the Passover festival, he performs other *semeia* which elicit a superficial belief among the *anthropoi*. A paradigmatic example of the superficially-believing *anthropoi* is this *anthropos*, Nicodemus, who comes to talk with him about the *semeia*. Jesus wishes to move the conversation from the *semeia* to the deeper realities they are intended to signify—in this case the divine birth wrought by the Spirit in baptism. But Nicodemus is unable, at least at this point in his experience, to receive this mystagogical teaching.

Jesus' words and actions in this Passover narrative, then, point forward to a great "sign" yet to come—the destruction and raising of his body, also during the Passover. By this great sign, Jesus will replace the stone Temple (with his body, the new Temple[76]), and will fulfill the Passover (himself becoming the "Lamb of God"[77]). But the fulfillment of Temple and Passover is not the final *terminus* toward which this climactic finish to his "signs" points. This reading is supported by the mystagogical catechesis given to Nicodemus. All of this suggests that John envisions the fulfillment of the Temple and the Passover continuing in the sacramental signs of the Church, which themselves point to the work of the Spirit.[78]

---

75 Mystagogy (literally "revelation of the mysteries") is the theological explanation of the mysteries that are communicated in the Church's sacraments. In the original faith of the Church, everything in Jesus' life was a sign of the mystery, the plan of God (see Eph. 3:19), and, as Pope St. Leo the Great (d. 461) taught, "what was visible in our Savior has passed over into his mysteries," that is, his sacraments. Quoted in *The Catechism of the Catholic Church*, 2d. ed. (Vatican City: Libreria Editrice Vaticana, 1997), no. 1115. Traditional liturgical catechesis in the Church followed the example of Jesus in John, "proceeding from the visible to the invisible, from the sign to the thing signified, from the 'sacraments' to the 'mysteries.'" *Catechism*, no. 1075. See generally, Enrico Mazza, *Mystagogy: A Theology of Liturgy in the Patristic Age*, trans. Matthew J. O'Connell (New York: Pueblo, 1989).

76 Compare John 2:21.

77 Compare John 1:29, 36.

78 "We would insist here that the connection between these 'signs' and the later sacraments cannot be taken as simply the relation of past material action (cure of blindness) and present spiritual reality (gift of faith). Jesus' earthy activity attacked *all* the evils of human existence, including both sin and sickness. ... That the 'signs' reach consummation after the hour of glorification and retain power in the sacraments of the community is perfectly true, but the line between them is homogenous and not a jump from the material level to the spiritual." Crossan, *Gospel of Eternal Life*, 41.

The Second Passover and the Eucharist

The events of Jesus' second Passover as recorded in John take place in Galilee. Somewhat ironically, this section (John 6:1–71) constitutes the longest narrative in the gospel that is *not* set in or near Jerusalem. Obviously the entire chapter is too complex to interpret in detail.[79] I will confine myself, then, to making some observations about Jesus' feeding of the 5,000[80] and focusing on some key sections in his dialogue concerning the "bread of life."[81]

Jesus' feeding of the 5,000 is briefly narrated. Jesus sees the crowds and questions his disciples concerning how to feed them. A young boy is present with barley loaves and fish—appropriately so, since Passover fell at the barley harvest, and the Sea of Galilee was nearby. Jesus makes the crowd sit down on the abundant grass, and multiplies the loaves and fish so as to satisfy all. The references to the hills, the grass, the sitting down, and the plentiful food evoke Ezekiel's prophecy of God as a shepherd feeding his people with abundant pasture on the mountains of Israel.[82]

Probably a majority of commentators now recognize a eucharistic background to this narrative—certainly in the subsequent dialogue,[83] but even in the narration of the miracle itself. The arguments in favor of this are not confessional but exegetical. First, the diction of John 6:11 ("Jesus then took the loaves, and when he had given thanks, he distributed to them to those who were seated …") closely parallels, and seems intended to evoke, the narratives of the institution of the Eucharist in the synoptics and Paul.[84] Likewise, in John 6:23 the evangelist refers to the miracle as the eating of bread "after the Lord had given thanks (*eucharisteō*)," which is an odd description unless there is an intention to evoke the eucharistic practice of the early Church.[85]

Also arguing for a eucharistic interpretation is the constellation of motifs in John 6. These motifs strikingly parallel those of the eucharistic institution narra-

---

79   The narrative breaks into a clear threefold division: the feeding of 5,000 (John 6:1–15); the walking on water (John 6:16–21); and the bread of life discourse (John 6:22–71). Within this last division there are several subsections marked by transitions (for example, at vv. 41, 52, 60, 66), but the narrative progression and continuity is strong enough to consider the entire discourse John 6:22–71 as a literary unit.

80   John 6:1–15.

81   John 6:22–71.

82   Ezek. 34:13–15; compare John 6:3, 10–12.

83   See, especially, John 6:51–58.

84   Compare John 6:11; Mark 14:22, Luke 22:19; 1 Cor. 11:23–24, observing the correlation of terms, usually in sequence: "take" (*lambanō*), "bread" (*artos*), "give thanks" (*eucharisteō/eulogeō*), and "gave/distributed" (*didōmi/diadidōmi*). See also Brown, *John I–XII*, 247–248.

85   See Brown (*John I–XII*, 258) who recognizes the eucharistic allusion but doubts the originality of the phrase. While Brown expresses doubts, note that the Greek text UBS 4/NA 27 comes down on the side of its authenticity. See Eberhard Nestle, Erwin Nestle, and Kurt Aland, *Novum Testamentum Graece* [The Greek New Testament] (Stuttgart: Deutsche Bibelgesellschaft, 1979).

tives in the other gospels—the proximity of Passover; the body of Christ *given for* others (sacrificial terminology); the equation of Jesus' body with bread; the eating of his body and drinking of his blood, and even a reference to Judas' betrayal.[86] Moreover, the introduction of the "drink my blood" concept (John 6:53), when the dominant image and Old Testament background referent has been "bread" throughout, is inexplicable unless a eucharistic allusion is intended—all the more so since the drinking of blood was always viewed negatively in the Old Testament and Second Temple Judaism.[87]

Besides anticipating the Last Supper and the institution of the Eucharist, with which the evangelist presumes his readers are familiar,[88] the miracle of the loaves also relates to various prophecies of the abundant eschatological feast.[89]

This miraculous sign prepares for Jesus' long "bread of life" discourse. The main body of this discourse is composed of six interactions or dialogical units between the people and Jesus, each composed of a question or request from the people and a reply from Jesus. The following table gives a synopsis of the people's questions and Jesus' replies. In each case, the key words of Jesus that elicit the next question are marked:

People's Question/Request	Jesus' Response
Rabbi, when did you come here?	You seek me, not because you saw signs, but because you ate your fill. Do not *work* for food that perishes ... (John 6:26–27)

---

86   Compare John 6:51–71 with Matt 26:21–28; Mark 14:18–24; Luke 22:19–23; 1 Cor. 11:23–24. See also Brown, *John I–XII*, 284–285, 287, 291–293.

87   See Rodney A. Whitacre, *John*, IVP New Testament Commentary Series (Downer's Grove, IL: InterVarsity, 1999), 168; Brown, *John I–XII*, 284.

88   See Cullmann, *Early Christian Worship*, 93–102. As Cullmann points out, unless the obviously eucharistic verses of John 6:51–58 are excised—which is unjustified (see Peder Borgen, *Bread from Heaven: An Exegetical Study of the Concept of Manna in the Gospel of John and the Writings of Philo*, Supplements to Novum Testamentum 10 [Leiden: Brill, 1965])—one must presume that, during the entire writing down of John 6:1–50, the author *knew* he would eventually be making a strong eucharistic connection at the conclusion of the narrative.

89   See, for example, Isa. 25:6–8, 55:1–3, and Ezek. 34:13–15. This is perhaps why, upon witnessing the "sign," the people exclaim, "This is indeed the prophet who is to come into the world!" (John 6:14). They wish to make him king by force, but Jesus eludes him. As in John 3:2–3, so here, we observe a connection between the "signs" and the Kingdom of God. The people in Galilee are correct that Jesus' signs point to his kingly identity, but they are mistaken in their ideas about the form his kingdom will take.

What must we do, to *work* the *works* of God?	This is the work of God, that you *believe* in him whom he has sent. (John 6:28–29)
What sign do you do, that we may ... *believe* you?	My Father gives you the true *bread from heaven* ... (John 6:30, 32)
Lord, give us this *bread* always.	I am the bread of life. He who comes to me shall not hunger ... [or] thirst. ... *I have come down from heaven* ... (John 6:34–35, 38)
Is this not Jesus, the son of Joseph? ... How does he say, *I have come down from heaven?*	No one can come to me unless the Father ... draws him. ... *The bread which I shall give for the life of the world is my flesh.* (John 6:42, 44, 51)
How can this man *give us his flesh to eat?*	He who eats my flesh and drinks my blood has eternal life, and I will raise him up at the last day. (John 6:52, 54)

The people's understanding always remains on the level of "earthly" or natural-sensible reality. In the first four exchanges, their motivation is to get Jesus to repeat the miracle of the multiplication of the loaves. Though their words do not indicate it, Jesus perceives that is their motivation in initiating the exchange (see John 6:26). The people interpret Jesus' exhortation to "work for food that endures to eternal life" as a condition that he is requiring of them before he will multiply loaves again, so they ask for some clarification ("What must we do?"). When Jesus responds, "Believe in the one he has sent," the people ask for sign to justify their belief, and with no subtlety indicate the nature of the sign they wish—a repeat performance of the multiplication of bread. When Jesus explains that the true "bread from heaven" is "that which comes from heaven," they become most blunt: "Lord, give us this bread always."

From this point on in the conversation, Jesus becomes increasingly specific and direct. While the christological teaching in the first three responses was stated indirectly, beginning from John 6:35 his christological claims are open and explicit, and lead further to specifically eucharistic claims (beginning from John 6:51). Meanwhile, the questions from the people grow hostile. The fifth and sixth questions, in which the people are described for the first time as "Jews" (*Ioudaioi*), amount to statements of disbelief, similar to Nicodemus' final statement in John 3:9.

Thus, we observe this pattern: In his dialogue with the people, Jesus attempts a "mystagogy," trying to lead them to realize that the "earthly" miracle he has performed is a "sign" pointing to a "heavenly" reality.[90] Yet the people continue to understand Jesus' words in "earthly" terms. They persist in their desire that he repeat the miracle that gives them earthly food. As Jesus advances deeper into his mystagogy, explaining that the sign points to himself as the "Christ," and beyond that to his true and divine presence in the Eucharist, the crowd is left further and further behind and becomes increasingly unfriendly.

We sense a certain parallel with the Nicodemus episode. In both cases, some seek Jesus, approaching him on the basis of a certain "earthly" trust inspired by the signs he has worked. And in both cases, when Jesus attempts a mystagogical or sacramental instruction that explains the heavenly realities that these earthly signs point to, the seekers respond in confusion and disbelief. In both cases, it is Jesus' insistence on the reality of the sacramental miracle—baptismal rebirth by water and Spirit, and eternal life through eating the flesh of the Son of Man—that provokes disbelief.[91]

In the dialogue with the disciples that follows this confrontation (John 6:70–71), the parallel with the Nicodemus dialogue is again strong. With Nicodemus, after stressing the need of baptism, Jesus emphasized the divine initiative and sovereignty of the Spirit to bring about new life. Here, after stressing the role of eucharistic communion in the reception of eternal life, Jesus points to the Spirit as the sole and sovereign source of that life, rather than any human effort ("the flesh"). As baptism is portrayed primarily as an act of the Spirit received by humanity (anthropoi) rather than a human action, so to is the Eucharist.

We see then that in John's second Passover narrative the "sign" of the multiplication of the loaves is strongly connected to the celebration of the Passover in the Temple. The sign takes place in the context of the Passover and anticipates, in its very language (John 6:11, 23), the last Passover that Jesus will celebrate with his disciples. In the aftermath of this great sign, Jesus engages the crowd in a mystagogical dialogue attempting to lead them from the "fleshly" understanding of the

---

90 "The Johannine sign narrative, quite unlike in the synoptic accounts, is usually followed by a revelatory discourse that brings out the *significance* of the miracle wrought. ... Many of the Jews and the crowd(s) ... see Jesus' signs and are said to believe but do not really grasp their *significance*." Lingad, *The Problems of Jewish Christians*, 377.

91 Compare John 3:9; 6:52, 60. There are differences: in John 3, the dialogue begins with reference to a sacrament and then becomes pneumatological and christological. In John 6 there is a clear development of ever-more explicit christology and finally sacramentology. Moreover, in John 6 the final disbelief is more vehement than in John 3, and even becomes hostile.

physical miracle[92] to the "spiritual" realities of Jesus' identity,[93] and to how his presence is continued in the sacrament of the Church[94] through the power of the Spirit.[95] The move from *sign* to *sacrament* is even clearer here than in John 3:1–14. Here, the *nature of the sign itself* points to the sacramental content of Jesus' teaching in John 6:22–59.

The Eschatological River and the Man Born Blind

While the Passover is the dominant Jewish feast in the structure and theology of John's gospel, some treatment of John's narrative of the Feast of Tabernacles (John 7:1–10:21) is necessary[96] because it illustrates so clearly the relationship between the Temple, the signs, and the sacraments in John.

The Feast of Tabernacles celebrated God's dwelling with Israel—in the Tabernacle of Moses, the Jerusalem Temple, and ultimately in the eschatological Temple foretold by the prophets.[97] Two liturgical rites celebrated during this feast are of particular significance to understanding John—the water ceremony and the lighting of the Temple courts.[98]

Inspired by prophecies of an eschatological river from the Temple,[99] each day of the feast the Temple priests would fill a golden pitcher with water from the Pool of Siloam, carry it in liturgical procession to the Temple, and pour it out there at the base of the altar. Inspired by Zechariah 14:6–8 ("There shall be continuous day … "), it was the custom to light four menorahs of enormous scale within the Temple courts during the Feast of Tabernacles and to keep them lit continuously. Priests and Levites danced with torches while singing the "psalms of ascent."[100] According to tradition, the light from the Temple illuminated much of the city.[101]

---

92 John 6:26 ("you ate your fill of the loaves …").

93 John 6:35 ("I am the bread of life.").

94 John 6:56 ("He who eats my flesh and drinks my blood abides in me …").

95 See John 6:63.

96 In John 7:2 there is a note that "the Jews' Feast of Tabernacles was at hand," and the feast forms the backdrop for the narrative until John 10:22, when the temporal scene is changed to the Feast of Dedication.

97 See Therath, *Jerusalem in the Gospel of John*, 157–159. On the character of the Feast of Tabernacles, see Brown, *John I–XII*, 326–327; George W. MacRae, "The Meaning and Evolution of the Feast of Tabernacles," *Catholic Biblical Quarterly* 22 (1960): 251–276; Hermann L. Strack and Paul Billerbeck, *Kommentar zum Neuen Testament aus Talmud und Midrasch* [Commentary on the New Testament from Talmud and Midrash], 6 vols. (Munich: Beck, 1924), 2:774–812.

98 On the relevance of Tabernacles to Jesus' discourses in John 7–8, see Coloe, *God Dwells With Us*, 115–143; Hoskins, *Jesus as Temple*, 160–170; Kerr, *The Temple of Jesus' Body*, 226–250.

99 Ezek. 47:1–17; Joel 3:18; Zech. 14:8.

100 The "psalms of ascent" are Pss. 120–134, thought to have been sung when the Israelites journeyed to Jerusalem and the Temple to celebrate the festivals.

101 See the description in Craig R. Koester, *Symbolism in the Fourth Gospel: Meaning, Mystery, Community*, 2d. ed. (Minneapolis: Augsburg Fortress, 2003), 157–158. Raphael Patai points out

It is almost universally recognized that Jesus takes advantage of the symbolism of Tabernacles' liturgical rituals by applying them to himself in John 7:38–39 ("If anyone thirsts, let him come to me ...") and John 8:12 ("I am the light of the world."). To make these claims during the feast itself was tantamount to declaring himself to be the eschatological Temple.

Both these symbols of Temple fulfillment or replacement—water and light—converge in the "sign" that Jesus performs in healing the man born blind (John 9). Here, Jesus declares himself again to be the "light of the world," and validates that claim by bringing light to the eyes of a blind man by means of the Temple waters of the Pool of Siloam—the water source for the ceremonies of Tabernacles.

Already from the second century, the Church recognized the intentional baptismal symbolism in the way John relates this healing.[102] Jesus begins the healing by declaring himself to be the "light of the world" (John 9:5), evoking the early Christian understanding of baptism as "enlightenment."[103] Though Jesus could heal by uttering a word (John 4:53), he uses the Pool of Siloam in order to link his healing power with the baptismal washing in water.[104] To emphasize this point, John notes the etymology of Siloam ("which means sent": John 9:7), associating the pool with Jesus himself, the sent one (John 3:34).[105] The man's blindness *from birth* is ostentatiously reemphasized throughout because it seems to symbolize John's view of all mankind prior to the spiritual rebirth of baptism.[106]

In John 3 and John 6, we observed a post-sign mystagogical dialogue leading to a spiritual and sacramental comprehension. Likewise here, Jesus' final exchange with the Pharisees (John 9:39–41) makes clear that the real issue behind the entire

that in Jewish thought, the Temple was the mystical center of the universe and the source of cosmic water and cosmic light; furthermore, the furnishings and structure of the Temple were compared to features of a man's body: "The Temple corresponds to the whole world and to the creation of man who is a small world." Obviously, the Gospel of John resonates deeply with these concepts. See Patai, *Man and Temple*, 105–117, esp. 117.

102 This is demonstred in the art of the early Christian catacombs; see Brown, *John I–XII*, 380–381; Cullmann, *Christian Worship*, 102–103.

103 Heb. 6:4; 10:32. Brown, *John I–XII*, 381; Alf Correll, *Consumatum Est*, 67–68; Cullmann, *Christian Worship*, 103.

104 Compare Brown, *John I–XII*, 381: "the story in John 9 illustrates the healing power of water."

105 The early tradition of baptismal intepretation of this event is well expressed by St. Augustine: "He washes his eyes in that pool which is interpreted 'one who has been sent': he was baptized in Christ." Augustine, *Commentary on the Gospel of John*, 44:1–2, quoted in Brown, *John I–XII*, 381. See Brown's own comment in *The Gospel of St. John and the Johannine Epistles*, 2d. rev. ed., New Testament Reading Guide 13 (Collegeville, MN: Liturgical Press, 1965), 51: "This pool, bearing a name interpreted as "sent," stands, in John, for Christ, who is the one *sent* by the Father. It is John's emphasis on the symbolic meaning of the pool that suggested to Tertullian and St. Augustine a baptismal reference." See also Cullmann, *Early Christian Worship*, 104.

106 John 9:1, 2, 13, 18, 19, 20, 24, 32; Compare John 3:3: "Unless one is born from above, he cannot *see*." (compare John 1:4–5, 9); John 3:5: "Unless one is born of *water* and Spirit."

narrative has been spiritual, not physical blindness.[107] The enlightenment of the blind man by water points to the more profound "enlightenment" that Jesus offers in the waters of baptism—an enlightenment that many, like the Pharisees, reject.

Hearing these words in context, the astute in John's audience could discern once again that Jesus is the eschatological Temple from which we receive life-giving water and light, and that both the Temple and the Feast of Tabernacles are fulfilled in him. Moreover, John's original audience likewise would have understood from these words that the reality toward which the Feast of Tabernacles pointed is fulfilled in baptism, where believers receive spiritual light and wash in the water of rebirth. For those who hear these words today, the sacrament of baptism becomes all that the Feast of Tabernacles was meant to be. It remains the means by which the Christian experiences Jesus as the new Temple.

"The Holy Place" and the Temple of the Church

The account of the first Passover in John (2:13–3:21) has prepared the reader to interpret the death and resurrection of Jesus in the third Passover (John 11:55–20:31) as the destruction and rebuilding of the true Temple, and nothing less. The clearest references to the Temple motif in the last discourse is to be found in John 14:2–3:

> In my Father's house (*oikia tou patros mou*) are many rooms (*monē*); if it were not so, would I have told you that I go to prepare a place (*topos*) for you? And when I go and prepare a place (*topos*) for you, I will come again and will take you to myself, that where I am you may be also.

We have here several significant deployments of Temple terms and images.[108] First, the phrase, "Father's house," recalls the nearly identical description of the Temple in John 2:16 ("my Father's house"). The two expressions are certainly close enough for the connection to easily be made, yet there is a subtle, theologically significant alteration. In John 2:16 the phrase (*oikos tou patros mou*), employs the expected term, *oikos*, used in the Septuagint translation to describe the Temple, the palace, and other large buildings in the Temple complex. In John 14:2, however, the phrase is *oikia tou patros mou*, using *oikia*, which also means "house," but frequently tends toward a more personal and familial rather than architectural sense—"household," "home," or even "family." I concur with the detailed arguments of Mary Coloe and James McCaffrey that a shift is taking place in John

---

107 Brown, *John I–XII*, 377.

108 It what follows, we are dependent primarily on McCaffrey, *The House with Many Rooms*. See also Kerr, *The Temple of Jesus' Body*, 268–313. Kerr finds Temple allusions not only in 14:2–3, but in John 13 as well. He likens the footwashing of the disciples to the Old Testament requirement that both priests and sacrificial animals have their feet washed when entering the sanctuary. Thus, John 13 is a preparation for entering the new Temple.

14:2–3 as compared with John 2:16: the sense of the new Temple is being extended from Jesus' physical body to the community of God, that is, to God's "household" or "family."[109] The Temple concept is being applied to what the later Church tradition would call the Mystical Body of Christ.

The Temple reference in the phrase "Father's house" is confirmed by other Temple allusions in these verses. The reference to a "house" with "many rooms" could not fail to bring to mind the Jerusalem Temple, the largest and most multi-chambered edifice known to the Jewish reader. Indeed, the Temple's "many rooms" are immortalized in certain passages of the Old Testament (Ezek. 40–42).[110]

Jesus goes on to speak of preparing a "place" (topos; mâqôm) for the disciples. It is not coincidental that the last employment of "place" (topos) was in John 11:48, where Caiaphas, the High Priest, used it as shorthand for "holy place," a meaning it bears frequently throughout the Old Testament, especially in Deuteronomy and related texts.[111] Furthermore, the Septuagint translation employs the exact phrase John uses—"prepare a place" (etoimazō ton topon)—exclusively with respect to the tent-shrine of the Ark of the Covenant (1 Chron. 15:1, 3) or the Temple itself (2 Chron. 3:1).

Thus, Jesus is telling his disciples that his departure is necessary to prepare a Temple sanctuary for them in which they will dwell with him. Frequently this is understood in terms of a heavenly, eschatological fulfillment—the disciples will dwell with Jesus forever in the "Temple" of heaven. While an eschatological sense should not be excluded, one must also take into account that in the chapter that follows this, Jesus clearly speaks of the disciples "abiding" (menō) in Christ even now, in this life. The sense of "abiding" should not be isolated from the sense of the "abiding places" (monē) that Jesus will prepare for the disciples in John 14:2. One also must be cognizant of John 14:23: "If a man loves me ... my Father will love him, and we will come to him and make our dwelling (monē) with him."

Thus, Jesus goes to prepare a (holy) "place" for the disciples, with dwellings (monē) for them, but simultaneously the Father and Son will come to the faithful disciple and make their dwelling (monē) with him. Therefore, John 14 taken as a whole, describes a mutual indwelling of Father and Son with the disciples, a mutual indwelling which is treated at greater length and more explicitly in the (eucharistic) vine discourse of John 15:1–17, with its stress on "abiding" or "dwelling" (menō). All this suggests that Jesus' promise to prepare a Temple in which the disciples shall abide will be realized now, in this age, through the mutual indwelling

---

109 See McCaffrey, The House with Many Rooms,177–184; Coloe, God Dwells With Us, 160–162.

110 McCaffrey, The House with Many Rooms, 67–69, 73–75.

111 For example, Deut. 12:5, 11–14, 18, 21, 26; Jer. 7:12, 14, 20; 1 Kings 8:6–7, 21, 29–30, 35, 42. See McCaffrey, House with Many Rooms, 185; Coloe, God Dwells With Us, 164–167.

of the disciples, the Father, Son, and Spirit.[112] The disciples will be constituted a
Temple by the Spirit, whom the Father and the Son will send after Jesus departs.

The idea of the disciples as Temple—a concept also present in the scrolls
found at Qumran[113]—resonates on a deep level with other themes of the last
discourse, especially when these are understood in light of Old Testament Temple
traditions. As I noted above, the Temple was the dwelling place of the name
of God,[114] the glory of God,[115] and indeed, of God himself.[116] Compare these
characteristics of the Temple with what is said about the disciples during the last
discourse: they are the locus of the *name* of God: "I have manifested your name
to the men whom you gave me out of the world. ... I have made known to them
your name." They have received the *glory*: "The glory which you have given me I
have given them, that they may be one even as we are one" (John 17:22). They are
the dwelling of God: "the Spirit of Truth ... dwells with you, and will be in you"
(14:17); "If a man loves me. ... We will come to him and make our home with him"
(14:23). As Jesus spoke of the Father having "consecrated" (*hagiazō*) him as the new
Temple during the Feast of Dedication (10:36), so now Jesus prays for the Father to
"consecrate" the apostles (John 17:17, *hagiazō*) to continue the ministry of Jesus, the
new Temple in the world.[117]

While John does not develop the theme of the Mystical Body of Christ as
Temple as explicitly as Paul, a close reading of the last discourse does indicate that
the role of the Temple is being communicated from Jesus to the disciples. It follows
that they will continue to fulfill the function of the Temple after his departure.[118]

Signs and the "Greater Works" of the Disciples

A major theme in the last discourse is the commissioning of the disciples for ministry apart from the physical presence of Jesus. Jesus is "sending out" the disciples

---

112 "The divine indwelling in the midst of a believing community makes it appropriate to speak of
the community as a living Temple. The community is the house (household) of God. Aune goes
so far as to claim that this image is so all pervasive that it is the self-perception of the believing
community. 'It is possible that in John 14:2 (and also 8:35) the term *oikia* (*tou patros*) reflects the
self-designation of the Johannine community.'" Coloe, *God Dwells With Us*, 163; quoting Aune,
The Cultic Setting of Realized Eschatology, 130.

113 See the discussion in Margaret Daly-Denton, *David in the Fourth Gospel: The Johannine Reception
of the Psalms*, Arbeiten zur Geschichte des Antiken Judentums und des Urchristentums 47
(Leiden: Brill, 2000), 78–79.

114 See, for example, Deut. 16:2; Ps. 74:7.

115 See, for example, 1 Kings 8:1; Ezek. 43:2.

116 Ps. 68:16; Ezek. 43:6.

117 Coloe, *God With Us*, 154.

118 See Kerr, *The Temple of Jesus' Body*, 275–313.

just as he was sent from the Father.[119] This theme is reinforced by statements affirming that the experiences of Jesus will be replicated in those of his disciples.[120] One statement in particular deserves special attention:

> He who believes in me will also do the works that I do; and greater works than these will he do, because I go to the Father. (John 14:12)

The term "works" (*erga*) is used as a synonym for "signs," that is, referring to Jesus' miracles, in many places in the gospel.[121] What could it possibly mean that the disciples will do the same "works" and even greater "works" than Jesus? It could mean that the apostles would perform miracles, even more spectacular ones than those Jesus performed. There are two problems with this interpretation. First, a historical problem. While Acts does record the apostles, especially Peter and Paul, performing miracles similar to those of Jesus himself, one would be hard pressed to argue that they exceeded the "grandeur" of, say, the raising of Lazarus or the resurrection itself. Second, a theological problem. The "signs" and "works" Jesus performed were never ends in themselves. In fact, his comment, hinting at a kind of exasperation, in John 4:48 ("Unless you see signs and wonders, you will not believe"), suggests that the performance of miracles was a concession to a lack of faith among his contemporaries (compare John 20:29), but not a practice Jesus thought should be normative. Thus, the thesis that the "greater works" refers to miracles performed by the disciples that would "outdo" those of Jesus himself faces some formidable objections. But what other interpretive options are available?

One clue to the nature of the "greater works" is the explanation given at the end of Jesus' statement, "Because I go to the Father." Taken at face value, this is not much of an explanation: there seems to be no reason why Jesus' departure to the Father would result in the disciples accomplishing greater works than those of Jesus himself. The statement must be taken in conjunction with John 16:7: "It is to your advantage that I go away, for if I do not go away, the Counselor will not come to you; but if I go, I will send him to you." The reason the disciples will perform "greater works" is not because of the absence of Jesus, but because Jesus' departure will result in the *gift of the Spirit, through which the disciples will be empowered to perform these works.*

Another clue is the pattern we have observed—that, in the aftermath of performing signs, Jesus attempts to move those who have witnessed the sign from the "earthly" to the "heavenly"—from the physical miracle to that to which it points.

---

119 John 13:16, 20; 15:15; 17:18.

120 John 13:15; 15:20.

121 John 5:20, 36; 7:3, 21; 9:3; 10:25, 32, 38; 14:11; 15:24.

In John 3, Jesus tries to move Nicodemus from thinking of the "signs" in terms of "earthly things" (a physical re-birth) to "heavenly things"—rebirth by the Spirit, inseparably tied to baptism. In John 6, he urges the people not to seek earthly bread through another multiplication miracle, but heavenly bread—himself and his eucharistic presence, through which the Spirit gives life. And without doubt, in Jesus' hierarchy of significance, the eucharistic bread of his "flesh" is "greater" than the bread created by the multiplication of loaves.

Could the "greater works than these" that the disciples will perform include the divine works of baptism and Eucharist carried out by the power of the Spirit? This was noted long ago by Oscar Cullmann: "The "sacraments have this in common, that in the time after the resurrection they take the place of the miracles performed by the incarnate Christ."[122] At least the following conclusions may be warranted exegetically: whatever the "greater works" will be, they will not be performed apart from the power of the Paraclete sent by Jesus; and whatever they are, they will not be unrelated to the rebirth of baptism and the nourishment of the Eucharist, toward which Jesus' own "works" pointed.

That the "greater works" to be performed by the disciples do indeed relate in some way to baptism and Eucharist is supported by some of the imagery in the last discourse itself. Take, for example, the footwashing scene (John 13:1–20), where there is a strong emphasis on commissioning the disciples to continue the activity of Jesus himself: "You should do as I have done to you ... if you know these things, blessed are you if you do them ... he who receives any one whom I send receives me" (John 13:20). There is also reason to understand a baptismal motif throughout this scene.[123] Although the footwashing itself is unlikely to be a *direct* baptismal symbol, most commentators find it difficult to avoid a baptismal reference at least in John 13:9–10 ("He who has bathed does not need to wash, except for his feet; but he is clean all over.")[124] Whatever the footwashing symbolizes, it is related to the

---

122 See Cullmann, *Early Christian Worship*, 118. But Cullmann does not explain exactly how he arrives at this conclusion. Crossan comments: "Each of these works/words of Jesus were protosacraments, fragmented promises of the one great sacrament of the risen Lord who abides in the community of faith." *Gospel of Eternal Life*, 42.

123 See Francis J. Moloney, "A Sacramental Reading of John 13:1–38," *Catholic Biblical Quarterly* 53 (1991): 237–256. Moloney sees not only baptismal symbolism in the footwashing, but Eucharistic allusions in the account of the morsel given to Judas. He is convinced that John 13:9–10 would recall baptism for the early readers of the gospel. As for eucharistic references, in John 13:18 Jesus quotes Ps. 41:9, but John changes the Septuagint's verb *esthiō* ("eat") to the rarer *trōgō* ("munch") to make an allusion to John 6:51–58, where *trōgō* is used three times in a eucharistic context. Moloney is persuaded that the morsel to Judas is eucharistic, the point being that Jesus lays down his love for his disciples unconditionally, even for those, like Judas (and Peter!), who will fail him. Thus, in John 13 we have motifs of Jesus ministering to the disciples through baptism and the Eucharist—despite their sinfulness—as they in turn will minister to the early Church.

124 So Cullmann, *Early Christian Worship*, 108; Correll sees baptismal significance in John 13:10, and

cleansing accomplished in baptism. And the fullest meaning must be some form of continuation of the ministry of forgiveness of sins related to that which is achieved in baptism.

In addition to baptismal imagery, we also find eucharistic imagery in the last discourse. In Jesus' image of the vine and the branches there seems to be a strong Eucharistic theme.[125] The image of the vine itself is not distant from the "fruit of the vine," the wine of the Eucharist. The external attestation of an association of this passage with the eucharistic wine is, in fact, strong and ancient. As Cullman, Raymond Brown, and others have noted, the first-century Church manual, the *Didache*, records the following Eucharistic Prayer: "We thank you, our Father, for the holy vine of David your servant, that you have revealed to us through Jesus your servant."[126]

It should also be noted that the vine discussion takes place during the Last Supper. Although John does not recount the supper *per se*, his readers would have known of it and indeed, could scarcely have avoided understanding Chapters 13–17 in light of the synoptic accounts of the institution of the Eucharist.[127] Moreover, there is a strong connection between the theme of "abiding" in the vine discourse and the bread of life discourse in John 6.[128] The term "abide" (Greek *menō*), employed forty times in John, appears eleven times in John 15—by far the highest concentration of the term anywhere in the gospel. The theme of "abiding" is stated at the outset: "Abide in me, and I in you" (John 15:4). Outside of John 15, "abide" appears twenty-nine times, but *only once* when referring to the mutual abiding of Jesus in his followers and vice-versa; this one occurrence is in the bread of life discourse: "He who eats my flesh and drinks my blood *abides* in me, and I in him" (John 6:56). Thus, the idea of mutual abiding is only stated directly in John 6 and John 15.

To recap our findings thus far: the major block of teaching in John's third Passover narrative is the last discourse, which implies that the disciples will be formed into a new Temple through the work of Christ (John 14:2–3), and strongly emphasizes the commissioning of the disciples to continue the ministry of Christ after his departure. The disciples will, in fact, perform "greater works" than those

---

understands the footwashing itself as a symbol of the sacrament of penance (*Consummatum Est*, 69–73).

125 John 15:1–17; See Raymond Brown, *The Gospel according to John XIII–XXI*, Anchor Bible 29A (Garden City, NY: Doubleday, 1970), 672–674; Correll, *Consummatum Est*, 74.

126 See Cullmann, *Early Christian Worship*, 111–12. "Such an early connection of the vine and the Eucharist is impressive." Brown, "The Johannine Sacramentary," 72.

127 See Beasely-Murray, *John*, 222.

128 For a comparison of the true vine and bread of life discourses, see Cullmann, *Early Christian Worship*, 111–113.

Christ has displayed, once the Spirit is given to them. There is reason to think these "greater works" are related to the celebration of baptism and Eucharist, because in John 3 and 6 Jesus himself indicates that the reality of these two sacraments are of more value than the sensible "signs" he has performed. A possible sacramental sense of the "greater works" is supported by the fact that Jesus' commission to "wash feet" and to "abide in me" have baptismal and eucharistic connotations respectively. It is possible, then, that in the last discourse, we are to see that one of the ways the "works" or "signs" of Jesus will be continued is through the Spirit-empowered administration of baptism and Eucharist.

From His Pierced Side, a Stream of Blood and Water

There are several indications that John understands Jesus' death as the fulfillment of the Feast of Passover. First, he depicts the crucifixion beginning at noon on the day of preparation for the feast (John 19:14), at the time when the priests began to slaughter the Passover lambs in the Temple. In addition, the bystanders offer Jesus wine vinegar, the "blood of the grape," on a stalk of hyssop, the plant that was used to mark the lintels of houses with blood during the Passover ritual. John records the curious detail that not one of Christ's bones was broken (John 19:36), in fulfillment of the legal provisions concerning the Passover lamb (Exod. 12:46). Finally, Jesus' body was pierced, as the Passover lamb was pierced from end to end and placed over the roasting fire. Thus, at the crucifixion scene, the reader sees the culmination of the paschal lamb theme introduced at the beginning of the gospel: "Behold the Lamb of God, who takes away the sins of the world!" (John 1:29).

No less important are the indications of Temple fulfillment in John's passion narrative. That Jesus' death and resurrection should be understood as Temple destruction and rebuilding was, of course, forecast in John 2:21. A dramatic visual indication of Jesus as Temple at the cross is to be found in the "sudden flow of blood and water" from the side of the crucified Christ (19:34). This key, polyvalent image simultaneously evokes the themes of Temple, Spirit, and sacraments that have been running explicitly and implicitly throughout John.

Arguably, the first image that this bloody stream from Christ would evoke for a first-century Jew was the brook Kidron, which flowed along the base of the Temple Mount. The brook was connected to the Temple altar by a guttering system that channeled down the enormous amounts of blood from the thousands of Passover lambs being slaughtered, producing a torrent of bloody water.[129] At the cross, Jesus has become, in fulfillment of John 2:19–21, the new Temple from which flows this river of sacrifice.

---

129 See the Midrashic sources cited above, n. 49.

But the significance of the blood and water is not exhausted by the Temple reference. The magnetism between John 7:37–39 and John 19:34 has proved inexorable for most commentators. In the bloody flow from the side of the crucified Christ, we have a symbolic fulfillment of the promise of the river of the Spirit flowing from the "belly" of Jesus (compare John 7:37–39). It is not coincidental that only a few verses earlier (John 19:30), the evangelist speaks of Jesus "handing over his Spirit." While in one sense this speaks of his death, few commentators would deny the connection with the promise of the gift of the Spirit at Jesus' hour of "glorification," that is, the hour of his crucifixion. The Father is able to pour out the Spirit because of Christ's sacrificial death on the cross: this truth is visualized in the "river" flowing from Christ's body in John 19:34.

Of course, the Spirit has already been linked to the sacraments in earlier passages of John.[130] It is not surprising that many commentators have understood the dual flow as representative of baptism and Eucharist,[131] including mainstream critical scholars like Rudolf Bultmann, Raymond Brown and Andrew Lincoln.[132]

Addressing the symbolism of the blood first, we may note that the only mention of blood (*haima*) in its plain sense anywhere else in the gospel besides John 19:34 occurs in John 6:53–56, the eucharistic discussion of the necessity of "drinking the blood of the Son of Man."[133] Thus, within John, the association of these two passages is not only easy to make, it is difficult to avoid.[134] And if a sacramental symbolism is readily available for the blood, it is logical for the reader to expect

---

130   For example, John 3:3, 5; 6:51–59, 63.

131   So Coloe, *God Dwells With Us*, 200–201; Correll, *Consummatum Est*, 74–75; Cullmann, 114–116; John Paul Heil, *Blood and Water: The Death and Resurrection of Jesus in John 18–20*, Catholic Biblical Quarterly Monograph Series 27 (Washington, DC: Catholic Biblical Association, 1995) 105–109.

132   See Moloney, "When is John Talking about the Sacraments?" 130; Lincoln, *John*, 479: "Within the frame of reference of the gospel itself the significance of the blood and water is not hard to discover. The significance of the blood is set out in John 6:52–59, where there are clear eucharistic overtones." For Lincoln, sacramental symbolism is definitely secondary to what he calls "the theme of life," but he does recognize its presence. Bultmann is, ironically, the most emphatic about the sacramental symbolism: the flow of blood and water "can scarcely have any meaning other than that in the death of Jesus on the cross the sacraments of baptism and of the Lord's Supper have their origin" (*The Gospel of John: A Commentary*, trans. G. R. Beasely-Murray, ed. R. W. N. Hoare and J. K. Riches [Oxford: Blackwell, 1971], 525).

133   John 1:13, sometimes translated "blood" (so the Revised Standard Version), actually uses the plural *haimaton*, "of bloods," referring to generative bodily fluids generally, not Jesus' actual blood as in John 6:53–56 and 19:34.

134   "The mention of blood in John 19:34 creates the impression that 19:33–36 should be read alongside 6:51–58, which contains the only comparable mention of blood in the Fourth Gospel and occurs in a Passover context." Hoskins, *Jesus as Temple*, 178, following Donald Senior, *The Passion of Jesus in the Gospel of John* (Collegeville, MN: Michael Glazier, 1991), 125–126.

it for the water as well. Such symbolism, too, is close at hand: baptism has been associated with water since the beginning of the gospel, as we have noted.[135]

Furthermore, the most obvious parallel for the flow of water from Christ's side is his declaration concerning "living waters" flowing from his "belly" (*koilia*) in John 7:38, a passage that itself alludes to baptism, in the opinion of many.[136] But in John 7:38–39, the Spirit had not been given, because Jesus had not been glorified. In John 19, Jesus has experienced the "hour" of his "glorification" on the cross[137] and so hands over the Spirit in verse 30.[138] Now in John 19:34 the reader sees the flow of water that one has been lead to expect in association with the giving of the Spirit.[139] The connection with baptism—the rebirth by "water and Spirit"—would be natural for the first Christian readers to make. After all, the correlation of baptism, the reception of the Spirit, and the body of Christ was already traditional long before John's Gospel was written:

> For by one Spirit we were all baptized into one body—Jews or
> Greeks, slaves or free—and all were made to drink of one Spirit.
> (1 Cor. 12:13)

Notably, the last phrase of this quotation from St. Paul associates baptism with "drinking" the Spirit, even though the rite itself involved only washing. This suggests that *a "drinking" metaphor was also part of pre-Johannine baptismal symbolism*, and therefore the thirst-quenching water of the Spirit imagery in John 4:7–15 (the woman at the well) and John 7:38–39 may well allude to this sacrament.[140]

In this compressed, polyvalent image of Christ pouring forth blood and water on the cross (John 19:34), close on the release of his Spirit (John 19:30) we see a convergence of the themes we have been pursuing in this paper: Temple, sign, Spirit, and sacrament.[141] Jesus is the New Temple from which flows the bloody stream of sacrifice, dying as the true Passover lamb to fulfill that great feast, as part

---

135 John 1:26, 31, 33; 3:5. Brown, curiously, regards the baptismal symbolism of the water an easier exegetical conclusion to reach than eucharistic symbolism in the blood: Brown, *John XIII–XXI*, 951–52; compare *John I–XII*, 142, 179–180.

136 Brown, *The Gospel and Epistles of John: A Concise Commentary* (Collegeville, MN: Liturgical Press, 1988), 45; Correll, *Consumatum Est*, 60–62.

137 Compare John 12:23; 13:31–32; 17:1.

138 On the handing over of the Spirit, see Heil, *Blood and Water*, 102–103; Kerr, *The Temple of Jesus' Body*, 244–245.

139 John 3:5, 7:38–39.

140 For baptismal allusions in John 4:1–30, see Cullmann, *Early Christian Worshp*, 80–84.

141 "In a remarkable way John has brought together the prophecy of the waters flowing from the eschatological Temple (Ezek. 47:1–11) and the proclamation of Jesus at the Festival of Tabernacles (7:37–38) in the climactic moment on the cross. Here Jesus' body, soon to become

of the great "sign" of his death and resurrection (John 2:19–21). And now, at what may be considered the heart or climax of Jesus' final "sign," there flows forth water and blood, the river of the Spirit, baptism and Eucharist.[142]

The flow of blood and water appear to us in the context of the third and final Passover of the gospel. It should be recalled that at the first Passover, Jesus discoursed to Nicodemus on the necessity of birth "from above" through "water and Spirit," that is, through baptism. At the second Passover, he urged the crowds to "eat my flesh and drink my blood" in order to have "life" and be raised "on the last day." Now at the final Passover, we see both sacramental signs flowing together from the Temple-body of Christ. Coloe comments:

> The blood and water is the link between the events narrated and the community of believers of later generations. … When Jesus is no longer a physical presence with them, the community can still be drawn into his filial relationship with God and participate in the sacrificial gift of his life in their sacraments of baptism and Eucharist.[143]

the new Temple (2:21), becomes the source of living waters—the Spirit." Kerr, *The Temple of Jesus' Body*, 244–245.

142   Raymond Brown's comments on this passage, written near the end of his illustrious career and culminating a lifetime of study of this gospel, are apropos: "The Johannine references to these two sacraments [baptism and Eucharist], both the more explicit references and those that are symbolic, are scattered in scenes throughout the ministry. This seems to fit in with the gospel's intention to show how the institutions of the Christian life are rooted in what Jesus said and did during his life. Moreover, among the four gospels it is to John most of all that we owe the deep Christian understanding of the purpose of baptism and the eucharist. It is John who tells us that through baptismal water God begets children unto himself and pours forth upon them his Spirit (John 3:5; 7:37–39). Thus, baptism becomes a source of eternal life (John 4:13–14), and the Eucharist is the necessary food of that life (John 6:57). Finally, in a dramatic scene (John 19:34), John shows symbolically that both of these sacraments, baptismal water and eucharistic blood, have the source of their existence and power in the death of Jesus. This Johannine sacramentalism … reflects the essential connection between the sacramental way of receiving life within the Church at the end of the first century and the way in which life was offered to those who heard Jesus in Palestine." Brown, *An Introduction to the Gospel of John*, 234. Correll's sentiments are similar: "Why … is it that the Fourth Gospel mentions the sacraments at all in connection with the earthly life of Jesus? … The one aim is to link up in this way the earthly life of Jesus with the life of Christ who is alive and working in the Church; that is, to state the identity between the Jesus of history and the Christ who is present in the liturgy." *Consumatum Est*, 77.

143   Coloe, *God Dwells With Us*, 200.

Forgiveness of Sins and the New Temple

During the account of the suffering, death, and burial of Jesus, the themes treated in the last discourse remain in the background, until he is once again reunited with the disciples as a group in John 20:19–23, when he breathes on them the Spirit, bestowing the power to forgive sin. This brief but powerful scene should be understood as a conferral of those things promised to them when last he was with them, that is, during the last discourse.[144]

Jesus had promised his disciples peace[145] and the gift of the Holy Spirit.[146] Now he definitively confers both these gifts.[147] Particularly dramatic is the transmission of the Spirit to the disciples: this event has been anticipated since the beginning of the gospel both explicitly[148] and implicitly through the use of water as a symbol for the Spirit,[149] and it has just been "pre-enacted" at the cross.[150]

Remarkably, here in John 20:22–23, the gift of the Holy Spirit is associated with the power to forgive sins:

> He breathed on them and said to them, "Receive the Holy Spirit.
> If you forgive the sins of any, they are forgiven; if you retain the
> sins of any, they are retained."

This declaration to the disciples must be understood in relation to John 1:29, Jesus' first appearance in the gospel, where he is hailed by John the Baptist: "Behold, the Lamb of God, who takes away the sin of the world!" Although in this way the evangelist introduces Jesus to the reader as the one who "takes away sin," there is not a single instance of Jesus *explicitly* forgiving sin in the entire gospel. Now, to be sure, if one had time, a good case could be developed from the text of the gospel itself that the signs Jesus performs are symbolic of release from sin.

---

144 So Brown, *John XIII–XXI*, 1035–1036.

145 John 14:27; 16:33.

146 John 14:16, 26; 15:26; 16:7, 13.

147 John 20:19, 21, 22.

148 John 1:32; 3:5; 7:39.

149 John 4:10–15; 7:38; 9:7, 11; 19:34.

150 John 19:30. "For John this is the high point of the post-resurrectional activity of Jesus and ... in several ways the earlier part of this chapter has prepared us for this dramatic moment." Brown, *John XIII–XXI*, 1037.

The evangelist regards those in sin as spiritually sick,[151] blind,[152]and dead;[153] thus Jesus' miracles of healing may rightly be seen as *types* of liberation from sin.[154] Nonetheless, the fact remains that, although Jesus' mission is announced from the start as the "taking away of sin," this is never enacted personally by Jesus in the gospel (in contrast to the synoptics, compare Mark 2:5). Rather, the power to forgive is explicitly devolved upon the disciples through the power of the Spirit at the end of the gospel. The message to early Christians is clear: it is through the apostles that they will experience Jesus' ministry of "taking away sin." Significantly, *this was a function performed in the old covenant through sacrifices at the Temple.*[155]

Once again we recall Jesus' words to the disciples during the last discourse: "He who believes in me will also do the works that I do; and greater works than these will he do, because I go to the Father." Earlier I argued that this statement is elliptical—the complete thought is "greater works he will do, because I go to the Father, and thus the Spirit will be given [compare John 16:7]." Now in John 20:22–23, the Spirit is being given to the disciples, enabling them to forgive sins. Could the "forgiveness of sins" be at least an aspect of the "greater works" which the disciples will do? The plausibility is high: in the evangelist's hierarchy of value, what is greater, the curing of body or of soul? The removal of physical blindness or spiritual blindness? The restoration of physical life or spiritual life? To pose these questions is almost to answer them.

---

151 John 5:14.

152 John 9:40–41.

153 John 5:25.

154 With regard to the healings in John 5 and 9, for example, Cullmann argues: "The evangelist has undoubtedly in mind that other water in which forgiveness of sins is gained through Christ. In that act of baptism the miracle of forgiveness of sins takes place. *Christ's miracles of healing are continued in baptism.*" *Early Christian Worship*, 87. Emphasis added.

155 Beale's comments on this theme are apropos: "Jesus' various statements [in the synoptics] that he can forgive sin could also suggest that he is beginning to replace the Temple. ... [T]he Temple was the divinely instituted place where sacrifices were offered for the forgiveness of sins, but now Jesus has become the divinely instituted location where forgiveness is to be found." *Temple and Church's Mission*, 177. Beale's principle holds true in John 20:23 as well, only here Jesus is conferring the "templeness" on his disciples as the *locus* of forgiveness. The narrative of John began with a symbolic judgment on the ineffective Jerusalem Temple (John 2); it ends with the "building" of a new Temple, the body of disciples, later called the *ekklesia*. "If [the] link with John 7[:38–39] can be maintained, then Jesus' breathing the Spirit on the disciples could be considered a part of a commission of and an enablement for them to be part of the new Temple and to expand its borders, so that others in the world may be included (on which see John 17:18–23). The primary message they are to announce in their mission is the forgiveness of sins (v. 23), which, as we have seen in the synoptic gospels, became the function of Jesus instead of Jerusalem's Temple. ... Jesus' breathing into the disciples might well be considered to incorporate them into the new creation and Temple." *Temple and Church's Mission*, 199.

As we have seen, Jesus' "catecheses" following the performance of signs consistently attempted to lead the listener from the "earthly" to the "heavenly." He relativizes the importance of the signs understood as physical miracles, ("Do not work for food that perishes," John 6:27) while pointing to their ultimate significance ("I am the bread of life," John 6:35). Hence, we are justified in affirming that, for the evangelist, the "forgiveness of sins" administered by the apostles constitutes a "greater work" than a physical miracle of Jesus.

One may proceed further and ask, How will this forgiveness of sins be administered? The evangelist does not explain. Apparently his first readership knew how the apostles would dispense the forgiveness of sins and needed no further explanation. We, more distant from the sources of the apostolic tradition, are less certain of the evangelist's intent. One proposal is that the forgiveness of sins is to be mediated through the apostolic preaching, through which the apostles introduce people to the forgiveness of sin available in the gospel. While such an interpretation has appeal, especially since it fits the instinct among many that the early Church was non-sacramental and non-hierarchical, it is striking that *explicit* emphasis on the preaching role of the apostles is difficult to find in John's Gospel.[156] Thus, while the mediation of forgiveness of sins through preaching may be an aspect of the meaning of John 20:23, it is probably less central in the intent of the evangelist.

Can one say that one aspect of the "greater works" that involve forgiveness of sins through the power of the Spirit is, in fact, the administration of the sacraments, for example, baptism?[157] The evidence that this was within the intent of the evangelist is surprisingly strong. George Beasely-Murray summarizes the evidence:

> In the light of the missionary commission of Matt 28:19, the record of the mission of preaching in the Acts of the Apostles, and the association of the forgiveness of sins with baptism in the letters of the New Testament, it is likely that baptism is *assumed* here, as in Luke 24:46–47; compare Acts 2:38.[158]

---

156 Perhaps the strongest passage in this regard is John 17:20: "I pray ... for those who believe in me through their *word*," which assumes the preaching ministry of the apostles. But see Brown, *John XIII–XXI*, 1042, quoted below.

157 Interestingly, Brown allows that the power to admit to baptism may be an aspect of the authority to "forgive sins" conferred in this passage. See *John XIII–XXI*, 1041–1044. Brown does not note the fact that Jesus nowhere explicitly forgives sin in John. Perhaps thinking of the synoptics, he declares: "In his ministry Jesus forgave sin ..." *John XIII–XXI*, 1043.

158 Beasely-Murray, *John*, 384. Brown adds further support: "There is little internal support in Johannine theology for interpreting vs. 23 as a power to preach the forgiveness of sins. ... There is better internal Johannine support for relating the forgiveness of sins to admission to baptism, for some of the Johannine passages that have a secondary baptismal symbolism touch

Of course, the Catholic Church has long seen in John 20:23 a biblical basis not only for baptism but for the sacrament of penance as well. Is this ecclesiastical eisegesis? Significantly, Beasely-Murray, Brown, and other John scholars point out that the primary readership of John's Gospel was the Church itself, that is baptized persons; therefore, the evangelist's intent in emphasizing the apostolic power to remit sin in John 20:23 seems unlikely to be limited only to pre-baptismal sins.[159]

I believe that the disciples in John 20:22–23 are being commissioned to continue the ministry of reconciliation of Jesus, the "Lamb who takes away the sins of the world" (John 1:29). This completes what Jesus had initiated in the footwashing scene in John 13:1–20. Footwashing was part of the ritual cleansing prescribed for priests in Exodus (Exod. 29:4; 30:17–21; 40:30–32).[160] As scholars such as the Protestant, Ernst Lohmeyer, and the Catholic, André Feuillet, have noticed, Jesus' action in John 13 is a preparation of the apostles to share in his own priestly consecration, a consecration that he imparts to them through his "high priestly" prayer in John 17.[161] Now, in John 20, through the conferral of his Spirit, the apostles enter into the full share of Jesus' own ministry of priestly reconciliation.

on the question of sin. … It is important that the Church Fathers of the first three centuries understood John 20:23 in reference to the baptismal forgiveness of sins." *John XIII–XXI*, 1042.

159 Here the comments of Baptist scholar Beasely-Murray are pertinent: "[This] raises a further question, namely, whether the saying [20:23] is limited to entry into the Church or whether it applies also to life within the Church. … This gospel is directed to the Church, wherein believers stand continually in need of forgiveness of sins, and discipline at times has to be exercised regarding offending members. … When Church organization is sufficiently developed to ordain officers, it is inevitable that they play a role in such processes. … From this statement in v. 23 the Roman Catholic Church has evolved the sacrament of Penance. Protestants find this difficult to accept. … It is significant, however, that [in pastoral ministry, when] dealing with sin and guilt, an authoritative word of forgiveness is required from a representative of the Lord. … The churches have need to learn from one another." See Beasely-Murray, *John*, 384. Beasely-Murray's assertions about the development of "Church organization" and about the Church instituting the sacrament of penance as an exegetical development from John 20:23 are simply false historically. However, his comments are remarkable as an admission from a non-Catholic that the logic of John 20:23 involves a continuing exercise of the authority to forgive sins within the life of the Church, whose actual form would have to resemble what, in fact, the rite of penance has become within the Catholic Church. Brown's treatment of the passage (*John XIII–XXI*, 1042–45) is more complex, but affirms, albeit indirectly, that baptism and penance as practiced now by the Church are legitimate manifestations of the general grant of the power to forgive sins in 20:23. That is, these sacraments fall within the scope of the intent of the evangelist, although one cannot limit the meaning of 20:23 to these or the other sacraments. We should recall, too, the important conclusions of Oscar: "Baptism and Lord's Supper: here we have the once-for-all sacrament and the repeatable sacrament of forgiveness, but both in the same way anchored to Christ's death on the cross. The evangelist sees this meaning of both sacraments foreshadowed in the events of Jesus' life." Cullmann, *Early Christian Worship*, 71.

160 Compare Lev. 8:6; Num. 8:6–7.

161 "Through the washing of feet, Jesus makes his apostles the priests and leaders of the eschatological community and his own associates in the final kingdom." André Feuillet, *The Priesthood of*

Further, their works of administration of forgiveness may rightly be considered among the "greater works" that Jesus promised in the last discourse that his disciples would perform (John 14:12). In my treatment of the last discourse, I suggested that the "greater works" could have been, among other things, a reference to the Spirit-empowered administration of the sacraments. Now, in John 20:22–23, we see the bestowal of the Spirit and the power to forgive sins. Hence, I think we are correct, based on a careful consideration of the text, that John intends us to read this as conferring upon the apostles some form of sacramental ministry.[162]

Sign, Spirit, and Sacrament

John presents Jesus as the new Temple promised by Israel's prophetic Scriptures, and as the personal fulfillment of the all the feasts celebrated in the Temple. In fact, this is one theological idea: Jesus' fulfillment of the feasts is an aspect of his role as the Temple.[163]

Yet for Christian readers of John's Gospel—whether in the first century or the twenty-first—it is not satisfactory to stop at the affirmation that "Jesus is the new Temple." Christ has ascended; how is he still the Temple for us? How, where, and through what means is this fulfillment continued?

In Jesus' last discourse, we observed the theme of the commissioning of the disciples to continue the work of Christ after his departure. In John 14:2–3, the Temple imagery applied to Christ's body in John 2:19–21 transfers to Christ's Mystical Body, his disciples. Our exegesis showed how this community of disciples, the *ekklesia*, will now also be the Temple, since God dwells in them and they in God. Jesus promises the disciples that they will do the same "works" that he did, and indeed, "greater works than these," because the Holy Spirit will be given to them.

Christ and his Ministers, trans. Matthew J. O'Connell (Garden City, NY: Doubleday, 1975), 164, here concurring with the views of Ernst Lohmeyer, *Lord of the Temple: A Study of the Relation Between Cult and Gospel*, trans. Stewart Todd (Richmond, VA: John Knox, 1962). On Jesus' "high priestly prayer," see Feuillet, *The Priesthood of Christ*, 121–166. Compare Kerr, *The Temple of Jesus' Body*, 290–292.

162 As Cullmann comments, "Clearly the sacraments mean the same for the Church as the miracles of the historical Jesus for his contemporaries." *Early Christian Worship*, 70.

163 "Jesus' fulfillment of the Jewish feasts and the Temple are both connected with the nature and content of God's provision for all his people. Jesus is and gives the true food and true drink that deliver believers from thirst and hunger. He accomplishes this by offering his flesh and blood for the life of the world and sending the Spirit to enrich believers with the salvific benefits of his sacrificial death. Thus he simultaneously fulfills the Passover, Feast of Tabernacles, Feast of Dedication, and the Temple. Looking at the Temple in particular, he fulfills and replaces it as the place of sacrifice and the place from which God pours out his abundant provision upon his people." Hoskins, *Jesus as Temple*, 196. Remarkably, Hoskins sees no connection here with a sacramental fulfillment in baptism and Eucharist.

"Works" are a synonym of "signs" in the Gospel of John. The "signs" Jesus performs in the gospel are frequently manifestations of his fulfillment of the Temple and its feasts: the feeding of 5,000 represents a new Passover, for instance. Moreover, the "signs" of Jesus are not ends in themselves, they point to Jesus' identity, and further, they point forward to Jesus' presence in the sacraments. For example, in John 3 and 6, Jesus engages in a catechesis that seeks to lead his interlocutors from the "signs" to the reality they signify. In John 9, the sign itself is so closely analogous to the sacrament of baptism that the entire narrative is a kind of mystagogy, or sacramental catechesis. The climax of John's Gospel is the narrative of Jesus' final sign, his death and resurrection. And here all the signs of the gospel are fulfilled in a sacramental way—Jesus has departed, given up his Spirit, and from the new Temple of his body, the baptismal water and Eucharistic blood flow.

The post-resurrection narratives in John show us how Jesus' fulfillment of the Temple is to be extended in time by the "Temple" of his disciples. They, too, will perform signs and works, earthly signs that point to heavenly realities, the "greater works" of the sacraments that extend the light of Christ's forgiveness to those walking in darkness. They, too, will give his flesh and blood not for the nation only, but for the life of the world, to gather into one the children of God scattered abroad.[164] In these greater works of the sacraments we see Jesus' ultimate fulfillment of the Temple and its festivals and liturgy.[165] Indeed, it was through the Temple festivals and liturgy that the people of the old covenant experienced the Temple for what it really was—the site of reconciliation and communion with God; thus, they bear an analogy to the sacraments of the new covenant.[166] In the

---

164 Compare John 6:51; 12:52. Recall, too, Cullmann's argument that "the Gospel of John regards it as one of its chief concerns to set forth the connexion between contemporary Christian worship and the historical life of Jesus. ... It traces the line from the Christ of history to Christ the Lord of the community." *Early Christian Worship*, 37–38.

165 Compare our conclusion with the opinion of Schnackenburg: "They [the Johannine communities] were churches in which liturgical and sacramental life was flourishing. ... Their worship was the eschatological culmination of all worship practiced until then, transcending even the Jewish service of the Temple. Their pasch replaced and fulfilled the pasch of the Jews. ... In the sacraments they possessed testimonies and vehicles of the continuing redemptive acts of Jesus Christ (1 John 5:6), and obtained living and abiding union with the Son of God and through him perfect communion with God (John 6:56). ... It cannot be disputed that the Johannine Church experienced the word of Christ and the person of Christ as present in its solemn worship (comprising word and sacrament)." "Is There a Johannine Ecclesiology?" in *A Companion to John: Readings in Johannine Theology (John's Gospel and Epistles)*, ed. Michael J. Taylor (New York: Alba House, 1977), 247–256, at 254–255.

166 "Already in the Old Testament we find that the cult was the primary means of communion between God and his chosen people. The cult of the new covenant has its foundation and its centre in the Eucharist which Christ himself instituted." Correll, *Consummatum Est*, 4. "It was not Jesus' purpose to establish a new non-liturgical religion as a substitute for the old cult. Rather St. John saw the old cult as attaining its fulfillment and perfection in and through Christ. All

sacraments of the new covenant, we come to the new Temple, the Body of Christ, his Church.[167] And in the sacramental liturgy of the new Temple we experience the healing, life-giving, and reconciliatory reality of dwelling with God, receiving the promise he made to his people from of old.[168]

that the old Jewish cult had stood for and expressed was fulfilled in Jesus, who himself was the centre of the new Christian cult." Correll, *Consummatum Est*, 52.

167 "Although the Fourth Gospel does not refer to the Church as the Temple of God, it contains the theological bases for this Pauline title." Hoskins, *Jesus as Temple*, 198.

168 Cullmann expresses it this way: "Since Christ is the center of all worship, all the media of the past ... (purificatory rites, washings, baptism of John) are replaced by the media of grace, in which Christ ... communicates himself ... in the sacraments of baptism and Lord's Supper." *Early Christian Worship*, 118.

Letter & Spirit 4 (2008): 145–166

Temple, Holiness, and the Liturgy of Life in Corinthians

~: Raymond Corriveau, C.Ss.R :~

North American Redemptorist Novitiate

One persistent theme in the letters of St. Paul is his understanding of the Christian's daily life in cultic or liturgical terms—as the worship of God. In this, Paul anticipates one of the chief dilemmas of faith in the modern world—the rupture between religion and life, between liturgy and the ordinary, work-a-day world, between the "spiritual life" and "life in the world." Paul's presentation of daily life as a spiritual sacrifice and worship of God can offer to the modern believer a global vision that enables him to overcome this division.

In this article, I would like to take up this Pauline vision and to show how it is articulated in the Corinthian correspondence. Paul's letters to the Corinthians represent a unique application of his belief in the Christian life as liturgy. In these letters, Paul's understanding of the spiritualization of sacrifice, the cultic character of Christian being, and life and action as worship, are joined to a distinctive image of the Church as a new Temple and the baptized Christian as a temple of the Holy Spirit.

Through a close reading of the texts, I hope to shed light on this Temple imagery, which Paul seems to presume as part of the original Christian proclamation. I also hope to draw out those elements of the texts that highlight the Christian life as worship, which should be of particular relevance to the biblical renewal of moral theology.[1]

The idea that Christians are the Temple of God occurs three times in the course of Paul's two letters to the Corinthians.[2] I begin with its appearance in 2 Corinthians 6:16–7:1:

---

[1]   For a fuller treatment of these questions, see my *The Liturgy of Life: A Study of the Ethical Thought of St. Paul in his Letters to the Early Christian Communities* (Bruxelles: Desclée De Brouwer, 1970).

[2]   1 Cor. 3:16–17; 6:19; 2 Cor. 6:16. Among the studies on the Temple theme, see Bertil E. Gärtner, *The Temple and the Community in Qumran and the New Testament: A Comparative Study in the Temple Symbolism of the Qumran Texts and the New Testament*, Society for New Testament Studies Monograph Series 1 (Cambridge: Cambridge University, 1965); M. Fraeyman, *La Spiritualisation de l'Idée du Temple dans les Épitres Pauliniennes* [The Spiritualization of the Idea of the Temple in the Epistles of Paul], Analecta Louvaniensia Biblica et Orientalia 2:5 (Louvain: É. Nauwelaerts, 1948); Hans Wenschkewitz, *Die Spiritualisierung der Kultusbegriffe: Tempel, Priester und Opfer im Neuen Testament* [The Spiritualization of Cultic Notions: Temple, Priest, and the Sacrificial Victim in the New Testament] (Leipzig: E. Pfeiffer, 1932); Joseph Coppens, *De Spiritualisatie van de Cultus in Paulus' Brieven en in de Schriften van de Dode Zee* [The Spiritualization of Worship in Paul's Epistles and in the Dead Sea Scrolls], Analecta

146 Raymond Corriveau, C.Ss.R.

What agreement has the Temple of God with idols? For we are
the Temple of the living God; as God said,
"I will dwell among them, and move among them,
and I will be their God, and they shall be my people.
Therefore come out from them, and be separate from them,
says the Lord,
and touch nothing unclean; then I will welcome you,
and I will be a father to you, and you shall be my sons and
daughters,
says the Lord Almighty."
Since we have these promises, beloved, let us cleanse ourselves
from every defilement of body and spirit, and make holiness perfect in the fear of God.

This passage is the clearest statement in the Pauline epistles of the transition
from the notion of a material to a spiritual Temple in early Christianity. In the
context of 2 Corinthians, this passage appears in an integral section in which Paul
spells out the incompatibility of the Christian and pagan ways of life ("What has
a believer in common with an unbeliever?" see 2 Cor. 6:14–15). At the heart of this
incompatibility is the identity of the Church as the Temple of God. The dignity
of the Christian community as Temple is of such importance that he explains and
proves it by a series of Old Testament texts.

The Temple concept is one of unlimited richness, having its roots deep in the
Old Testament. We shall therefore note briefly, *first*, the terms used to convey the
reality, and *secondly*, the development of the Temple concept.

In classical Greek *naos* ("temple" or "shrine") is a cultic term designating the
dwelling of a god. It derives from *naiō*, meaning to dwell or inhabit. In a more
restricted sense it meant the shrine or sacred abode of the divinity, where the
sacred image was kept. In the Septuagint translation of the Old Testament, *naos*
corresponds either to *'ûlâm*, the portico of the Temple,[3] or to *hêkal*. *Hêkal* is a word
used for "the holies,"[4] but it can also signify the whole Temple proper[5]—that is, the
portico, "the holies," and the "Holy of Holies."[6] *Heiron* ("sanctuary," "temple") was
reserved by Ezekiel for pagan temples,[7] though it, too, came to be applied to the
Temple in Jerusalem.

Louvaniensia Biblica et Orientalia, 4:2 (Louvain: Publications Universitaires, 1962); C. F. D.
Moule, "Sanctuary and Sacrifice in the Church of the New Testament," *Journal of Theological
Studies* 1 (1950): 29–41.

3   Rarely: 1 Chron. 28:11; 2 Chron. 8:12; 15:8; 29:2, 17.

4   1 Kings 6:5, 17; 7:50; Ezek. 41:1.

5   Amos 8:3; Isa. 6:1.

6   Greek: *dabir*; Hebrew: *Dᵉbir*.

7   Ezek. 27:6; 28:18.

The "Habitation" of God

In the New Testament *naos, hieron, oikos,* and *hagion* are used regarding the Temple. *Heiron* generally designates the whole Temple complex or the outer courts. *Naos* is used for the Temple proper. It is used of the Temple in Jerusalem,[8] of heathen temples,[9] and above all, it appears in affirmations about the *pneumatic* or "spiritual" Temple.[10] In the New Testament as in the Old, *naos* has a pre-eminence over the other expressions and concepts for sanctuary as a richer expression more capable of development.[11]

The Jerusalem Temple (2 Sam. 7:1–3) was conceived by David to replace the portable tent used during Israel's sojourn in the desert as the dwelling of God among his people (1 Kings 8:18–29). The Temple was filled with the glory of God[12] and sheltered the Ark of the Covenant, the symbol of God's covenant and presence among his people.[13]

This "presence-habitation" of God[14] is the key reality expressed by the Temple concept throughout its evolution. All the laws of holiness and cult centered about this reality. The Temple was the focus of holiness[15] because the all-holy God[16] caused his presence to rest on the "Holy of Holies." From the Holy of Holies, holiness spread, as it were, in growing concentric circles with diminishing intensity.[17] Israel's land (Amos 7:17), the camp (Lev. 10:4–7), Jerusalem (Isa. 52:2), the Temple (Pss. 24:3; 2:6) were all made holy by God's presence. The vessels, various parts of the Temple (Num. 4:15), and especially the priests were holy. The lives of the

---

8   Matt. 23:16, 17, 21, 35.

9   Acts 17:25; 19:24.

10   John 2:19; 1 Cor. 3:16; 2 Cor. 6:16; Eph. 2:21.

11   Otto Michel, "Naos," in *Theologisches Wörterbuch zum Neuen Testament*, 10 vols., eds. Gerhard Kittel (Stuttgart: W. Kohlhammer, 1933–1979), 4:887; Eng. trans.: *Theological Dictionary of the New Testament*, 10 vols., trans. and ed. Geoffrey W. Bromiley (Grand Rapids, MI: Eerdmans, 1964–1985).

12   The *Kabod Yahweh*, the manifestation of his presence; compare 1 Kings 8:10–11; Exod. 33:7–11.

13   Exod. 25:22; compare 1 Sam. 4:4; 2 Sam. 6:2.

14   Conveyed by the Aramaic word, *Shekinah*, which was the visible dwelling of God among his people. The Hebrew verb *šakan* (to dwell), used of God's dwelling in the midst of Israel, and *miškan* derive from it as their root. Compare Yves Congar, *Le Mystère du Temple ou, L'économie de la Présence de Dieu à sa Créature de la Genèse à l'Apocalypse* (Paris: Cerf, 1958), 26–27; 33–34; 116–117. Eng. trans.: *The Mystery of the Temple or The Manner of God's Presence to his Creatures from Genesis to the Apocalypse* (Westminster, MD: Newman, 1962).

15   1 Kings 9:13; Num. 1:51; Holiness (Hebrew: *qōdeš*) is probably derived from *qādad,* to "cut" in the cultic sense of separation from the profane, destined for the service of God.

16   Lev. 11:44–45; 19:2; 20:7, 26; 21:8; 22:32; Isa. 6:3 in the sense of transcendent, inspiring religious fear. Compare also Exod. 33:20.

17   Gärtner, *The Temple and the Community in Qumran and the New Testament*, 23; Compare Joseph Bonsirven, *Le Judaîsme Palestinien au Temps de Jésus Christ,* 2: *La théologie Morale: Vie Morale et Religieuse* (Paris: Beauchesne, 1935), 111. English translation: *Palestinian Judaism in the Time of Jesus Christ* (New York: Holt, Rinehart and Winston, 1964).

priests were therefore subject to special prescriptions (Lev. 21:1–23).[18] It is in this context that the laws of ritual purity are understood (Lev. 17:26).

Throughout the history of Israel several currents of thought existed in regard to the Temple. These currents always involved a tension which was to be resolved only in the New Testament. The first current was to see the Temple perduring as the symbol of God's presence. In the messianic era all people would come to Zion (Isa. 2:1–3; Mic. 4:1–2) to pray in the Temple (Isa. 56:7). It is sometimes conceived as a Temple built by man for God.[19] But simultaneously texts might speak of a Temple coming down from heaven and built by God himself.[20]

Ezekiel speaks of the mobility of the glory of God,[21] of a new heart given to man (Ezek. 18:31; 36:26), and of an Israel purified by God himself dwelling among his people (Ezek. 37:24–28). This latter prophecy of Ezekiel 37 takes up Leviticus 26:11, which was of paramount importance for the Jews on the subject of the Temple of the future.[22] It is one of the texts used to support the affirmation of 2 Corinthians 6:16 that Christians are the Temple of the living God.

At the same time, a current of thought grew which saw the material Temple at Jerusalem as disappearing with the fulfillment of messianic prophecies (Isa. 66). The destruction of the Temple (Jer. 7:1; 21) brought to light the necessity of a more spiritual cult in accordance with the religion of the heart, when God would be present to his people in a new way (Jer. 31:31–33). It was not the building of a Temple which mattered, but a contrite heart sacrificing itself by obedience to the Word of God (Isa. 66:2).[23] The concept of holiness became gradually spiritualized. Separation from the profane became abstinence from sin and ritual purity was merged with purity of heart.

The existence of such currents explains how the Essenes at Qumran could break with the cult of the Temple, which they saw as having been defiled by the

---

18   Compare Gerhard Von Rad, *Old Testament Theology*, 2 vols., trans. D. M. G. Stalker (New York: Harper: 1962, 1965), 1:272–273.

19   Haggai saw the Temple of Zerubbabel as exceeding the former in glory (Hag. 2:6–9). Compare also Ezekiel's ideal description of the Temple, Ezek. 40–48. Herod's Temple was also part of this aspiration.

20   Ezek. 37:24. Even the prophecy of Nathan in 2 Sam. 7 conveys this ambivalence. God seems to reject David's plan by asserting that he himself will make his Temple by his dwelling, by his sovereignly active presence among his people (2 Sam. 7:14 is quoted in 2 Cor. 6:18). He then accepts the building of an earthly temple (2 Sam. 7:13). Compare Congar, *Le Mystère du Temple*, 46–47.

21   Ezek. 8:6; 9:3; 10:1, 18; 11:22.

22   Compare 1 *Enoch* 90:28; *Jubilees* 1:28, texts in *The Old Testament Pseudepigrapha*, 2 vols., ed. James Charlesworth (New York: Doubleday, 1983, 1985); Bonsirven, *Le Judaïsme Palestinien au Temps de Jésus Christ*, 1:431.

23   Compare François Amiot, "Temple," in *Vocabulaire de Théologie Biblique*, ed. Xavier Léon-Dufour (Paris: Éditions du Cerf, 1962), 1039–1043. Eng. trans.: *Dictionary of Biblical Theology*, 2d. ed., trans. P. Joseph Cahill (New York: Seabury, 1973), 594–597. Congar, *Le Mystère du Temple*, 72–101.

wicked High Priest and his people. The abandonment of Jerusalem led to the conviction that the presence of God, his Spirit, and his cult were no longer bound to the Temple there, but rather were allied now with the true Israel, represented by the community. And we see in the Dead Sea Scrolls evidence that the Essenes of Qumran believed that their community itself had become the new Temple of God:[24]

> At that time, the men of the community will constitute a true
> and distinctive Temple—a veritable Holy of Holies—wherein
> the priesthood may fitly foregather, and a true and distinctive
> synagogue made up of laymen who walk in integrity.[25]

At Qumran, we see developed a belief that it is God who builds a sanctuary for himself, a sanctuary constituted of the community in which he dwells.[26] This new Temple is now the center of cult, which is performed through the community's observance of the Law and through its liturgy. The true sacrifice is seen as being spiritual, offered in holy and pure lives, according to the Law, and in the prayer and praise of the community.[27] It is this conception of the Temple that brings us closest to the vision found in the epistles of St. Paul.[28]

---

24   Compare Gärtner, *The Temple and the Community in Qumran and the New Testament*, 16. The community, however, was not unfamiliar with the idea that God would once more dwell in the Jerusalem Temple. Compare Maurice Baillet, "Un Recueil Liturgique de Qumran, Grotte 4: 'Les Paroles des Luminaires,'" [A Liturgical Collection of Qumran, Cave 4: 'Words of the Luminaries'], *Revue Biblique* 68 (1961): 195–250, at 205.

25   1QRule of the Community [1QS] 9:5–7. Compare also 1QS 8:4–9; 5:6; 11:8. Text in *The Dead Sea Scriptures in English Translation*, rev. and enlarged ed., trans. with intro. Theodor Herzl Gaster (Garden City, NY: Anchor, 1964).

26   4QFlorilegium [4QFlor] 1:6.

27   Compare 1QS 8:9; 9:3; 4QFlor 1:6. Compare Gärtner, *The Temple and the Community in Qumran and the New Testament*, 18, 30, 44–46.

28   Even in comparing the Pauline conception to that of Qumran, we should not overlook some important differences which exist amid the resemblances. Jerome Murphy-O'Connor points out three of these fundamental differences: First, both Qumran and St. Paul attribute a sacrificial value to the lives of the members of the community (Rom. 12:1; Phil. 2:17; 1QS 9:3–5). However, for Paul it is the presence of God which is primary as constituting the Christians a Temple by his dwelling in them collectively and individually. This is why the Christian life has a liturgical value. By contrast, for the community at Qumran, the movement of thought was rather from sacrifice to the conception of the community as a Temple. Since they could no longer associate themselves with the meaningless worship (*Damascus Document* [CD] 6:17–20) offered in a profaned sanctuary (CD 5:6) by unclean ministers (CD 4:17; 5:6–11), the sectaries separated themselves to form a community where God could be truly worshipped by the sacrifice of a perfect life and the sacrifice of prayer (1QS, 9:3–6). It was thus that the community was conceived as the true spiritual Temple. Secondly, even though the spiritual sacrifices of Qumran were considered superior to the decadent Temple worship of the time, the sectaries never gave up hoping for the time when bloody sacrifices would again be offered in the Temple of the new Jerusalem in conformity with the prescriptions of the Law. Finally, while for Paul the Temple is holy because of God's presence (compare also Ezek. 42:13; 44:2; Ps. 5:7), at Qumran the

In Jesus the diverse currents of Old Testament thought and belief are resolved and fulfilled. Though respectful toward the Temple of Jerusalem,[29] Jesus predicted its imminent ruin (Matt. 23:38; 24:2) and the end of the old cultic regime—signified by the rending of the veil of the Temple at his crucifixion.[30] It is the body of Jesus which becomes the new sign of the divine presence among men (John 1:14). His resurrected body is the new definitive Temple "not made with hands."[31] His body, risen and filled with the plenitude of the divinity, has become the new cultic center of messianic times, characterized by the effusion of the Spirit.[32] In him the time is fulfilled for adoration "in spirit and in truth"[33]

The Temple in Primitive Christian Teaching

It is surprising, then, to find in Paul's epistles only vestiges of the affirmations regarding Christ as the Temple of messianic times.[34] What we do have, as very clearly expressed in 2 Corinthians 6:16, is the presumption that the Church, the community of the faithful, is the Temple of God. This suggests that this belief was a fundamental article of the primitive Christian catechesis.[35] This further suggests a development of belief in the primitive Church—the realization that Jesus was the new Temple, the new cultic center and dwelling of God, led to the understanding that Christian believers themselves were built up with him and by him into one and the same Temple.

The Christian community then became the convergence and fulfillment of the forces and elements which formed the Temple concept throughout its history. This is shown in the concatenation of Old Testament texts that Paul puts forward to explain and prove this idea to the Corinthians.

"For we are the Temple of the living God." By characterizing the Temple as belonging to the living God, Paul evokes an idea cherished by the Jews. Their God is always a living and active God as opposed to dead and inert idols.[36] He is

---

holiness of the Temple is attributed to the presence of the holy angels in the congregation (*IQS* 2:8–9). See Murphy-O'Connor, *Paul on Preaching* (London: Sheed & Ward, 1963), 292–293.

29   Luke 2:41–50; John 2:14; Matt. 5:23; 12:3–7; 21:12–17; 23:16–22.

30   Mark 15:38; Matt. 27:51; Luke 23:45.

31   Mark 14:58; John 2:19, 21; compare also 2 Cor. 5:1, where "not made with hands" means "risen." See also Congar, *Le Mystère du Temple*, 176, n. 1; Moule, "Sanctuary and Sacrifice in the Church of the New Testament," 33–34.

32   Zech. 12:9–10; 13:1; 14:8–9; Ezek. 47:1; John 7:38; 19:37; 4:14.

33   That is, in a true adoration in the Spirit of which one must be reborn in order to enter the Kingdom. Compare John 3:7–8; see also Heb. 9:11; 12:18.

34   Col. 2:9–10; Eph. 2:20–22; 1 Pet. 2:4–8.

35   Compare "Do you not know …" which prefaces the statements on the Temple in 1 Cor. 3:16 and 1 Cor. 6:19. Also Michel, "*Naos*," 4:810.

36   On the living God, compare Exod. 3:14; Num. 14:21, 28; Deut. 32:40; Josh. 3:10; Isa. 37:4, 14; 49:18; Jer. 4:2; 5:2. On dead idols compare Isa. 2:18; Jer. 2:27–28; 10:3–5; Bar. 6.

a God who has intervened in history, the God who brought the chosen people out of the land of Egypt (Exod. 20:2). He is the God of the prophets promising a new covenant (2 Cor. 6:16b), leading the way out of a hostile land (2 Cor. 6:17), and calling his people to adopted sonship (2 Cor. 6:18). In posing a living community as Temple in relation to a living God, Paul suggests a cultic relationship which at the same time is a call to a profound personal attitude of conversion and total renewal.

The network of texts that Paul puts forward in support of the Temple idea is a studied literary composition composed of three strophes. The first (verse 16b) is given as a justification for the assertion: "We are the Temple of the living God." The second strophe (v. 17) is put forward as a consequence: "You are obliged to keep the purity of priests." And finally, the third strophe (v. 18) returns by way of inclusion to the original idea of God's presence among his chosen people.

"As God said: 'I shall dwell (*enoikēsō*) among them and move among them, and I will be their God, and they shall be my people'" (2 Cor. 6:16). The first quotation sets the tone for the others. It is inspired by Ezekiel 37:27 and Leviticus 26:11–12, which were frequently used in relation to the Temple of messianic times. The context of the passage from Ezekiel is God's solemn promise that he will bring the Israelites back to their own land in a new Exodus. He will re-establish national unity, the Kingdom of David, and an everlasting covenant of peace.

> "I will set my sanctuary (*ta hagia mou*) in the midst of them for-
> evermore. My dwelling place (*kataskēnōsis*) shall be with them
> (*en autois*); and I will be their God, and they shall be my people."
> (Ezek. 37:26–27)

It will be noticed that Paul replaces *kataskēnōsis estai* by the verb *enoikēsō*. The verb is never used elsewhere in the Greek Bible for the dwelling of God among his people, or in the Temple. But it provides an excellent paraphrase of the idea in both the Ezekiel and Leviticus texts. In Ezekiel 37:27 *kataskēnōsis* corresponds to *miškān* (dwelling) in the Hebrew text. *Skēnēn* in Leviticus 26:11 also coincides with *miškān*.[37] All these words refer to the "presence" or the "dwelling," the *Shekinah* or glorious presence of God which was linked particularly to the meeting tent and the Temple. This is the "presence" that Paul refers when he writes: "I shall dwell among them," as a scriptural proof that Christians are now the new Temple.[38] The people of God[39] among whom he walks has become the Temple in which he dwells.

---

37   Lev. 26:11: "I will make my abode (*miškān* = *skēnēn*) among you, and my soul shall not abhor you. I will walk among you, and will be your God, and you shall be my people."

38   For God's dwelling among Christians see also John 14:23; Rev. 21:3.

39   Compare Lev. 26:12; Ezek. 37:27; 11:20; 36:38; Jer. 31:33; Zech. 8:8; 13:9.

"You Shall Be My Sons and Daughters"

"And I will be a father to you and you shall be my sons and daughters, says the Lord Almighty" (2 Cor. 6:18). This text makes us think of 2 Samuel 7:14,[40] which is part of the famous prophecy of Nathan to David. The prophecy speaks of the construction of the Temple and of a perpetual covenant which God makes with David. It also refers to the dwelling of God, who is always with his people by an active and saving presence.

In this context God promises through Nathan: "I will be a father to him, and he shall be my son" (2 Sam. 7:14). Again, Paul alters the phrase to accommodate the sense of the passage in 2 Corinthians. The phrase: "you shall be my sons and daughters" has probably been influenced also by such Old Testament passages as Isaiah 43:6, Jeremiah 31:9, and Hosea 2:1–2. Nathan's prophecy is fulfilled first of all in Christ.[41]

Before God, all sonship is concentrated in Christ, through whom Christians participate in Christ's own sonship so as to become sons and daughters of the Father.[42] Thus we see, woven into the notion of the Christian community as Temple, all the tenderness of the Father's presence and saving love for his children. In turn, the cult of this new Temple must become a loving response of sons and daughters in the service of the Father.

"Therefore come out from them and be separate from them, says the Lord, and touch nothing unclean; and I will welcome you" (2 Cor. 6:17). The middle of the three strophes is a free version of Isaiah 52:11.[43] In its original form it is an instruction to priests and Levites (those "who bear the vessels of the Lord"). And its context in Isaiah is the promised restoration of Israel, its return from exile in a new Exodus from out of Babylon. The Lord will return to Zion, going before his people. And he commands his people: "Depart, depart, go out thence, touch no unclean thing; go out from the midst of her, purify yourselves, you who bear the vessels of the Lord."

In the original text, *akathartou* referred to legal impurity,[44] as it does in so many of the Old Testament texts. It occurs most often in the holiness code of

---

40   Compare also 1 Chron. 17:13. "Says the Lord Almighty" is found in 2 Sam. 7:8.

41   Luke 1:32–33 and Heb. 1:5, where the exact words of the prophecy are applied to Christ.

42   Compare John 1:12; also Rom. 8:14–17; Gal. 4:5–7; This fact of sonship constitutes a notable difference in the notion of God's presence as conceived in the Old and New Testament. The Old Testament speaks more of a presence of action. God is considered to dwell where his action is most constant and favorable. In the New Testament, God dwells in the Christian by transforming him into the image of his Son through grace. See Murphy-O'Connor, *Paul on Preaching*, 290.

43   See also Jer. 51:45.

44   See John L. McKenzie, *Second Isaiah*, Anchor Bible 20 (Garden City, NY: Doubleday, 1968), 124. Albert-Marie Denis points out that the idea of purity in this context takes on an ideal messianic value, "L'Apôtre Paul, Prophète 'Messianique' des Gentiles," [The Apostle Paul, the 'Messianic' Prophet of the Gentiles], *Ephemerides Theologicae Lovanienses* 33 (1957): 245–318, at 280. For the

Leviticus.[45] It is true in these contexts that the reference is to taboos which cause ceremonial uncleanness. But the essential point about the ceremonial uncleanness is that the unclean person cannot approach God, enter his Temple, or share in his worship (Lev. 22:3). *Akathartou* is "that which makes it impossible for a person to come into the presence of God; it shuts him off from God."[46] In the Old Testament, the notion also underwent a process of moral spiritualization. It is used of sexual impurity (Hos. 2:10), of the moral uncleanness which destroys a nation (Mic. 2:10), and of sin generally (Ezek. 36:29).[47]

The theme of both cultic and moral purity was paramount in the Essene community at Qumran. Certain aspects of the priestly ideal were made general conditions for membership in the community—that is, the standards of purity originally applied only to the Levites, on certain occasions, were applied to all.[48] But the purity demanded did not stop at Levitical standards, but came to include inner purity from sin.

> Unclean, unclean he remains so long as he rejects the govern-
> ment of God and refuses the discipline of communion with him.
> … Only by the submission of his soul to all the ordinances of
> God can his flesh be made clean.[49]

For the Essenes, priestly purity and acceptance before God formed a unity. In the New Testament, both the noun and adjective are used in two senses—that is, of ritual uncleanness[50] and of ethical-religious impurity.[51] Paul's injunction to touch nothing unclean, then, is a call to a radical separation of the Christian, sanctified by God's presence, from the world of iniquity, ruled by the prince of darkness

---

idea of purity compare Lev. 11:15; see also Exod. 19:14, 22, where in the first Exodus, Levitical purity is demanded of priests and people.

45   Lev. 18:19; 20:25; 22:3; Judg. 13:7.

46   William Barclay, *Flesh and Spirit* (London: SCM, 1962), 29.

47   See Ezek. 39:24; Wis. 2:16.

48   The list of physical blemishes excluding a priest from the Temple was applied to membership in the community. Compare 1QS (Appendix) 2:3; also CD 6:17; 1QS 4:10; 1QWar Scroll [1QM] 7:5; 13:5; CD 7:3; 9:21; 10:10; 11:19; 12:19. Texts in *The Dead Sea Scrolls in English Translation*.

49   1QS 3:4–8; see also the obligation of holiness in 1QS 5:7–20; 6:23–7:9. Texts in *The Dead Sea Scrolls in English Translation*. Also Joseph A. Fitzmyer, "Qumran and the Interpolated Paragraph in 2 Cor. 6:14–7:1," *Catholic Biblical Quarterly* 23 (1961): 271–280, at 278; Joachim Gnilka, "2 Kor. 6:14–7:1 im Lichte der Qumranschriften und der Zwölf-Patriarchen-Testament," [2 Cor. 6:14–7:1 in Light of the Qumran Documents and the Testament of the Patriarchs] in *Neutestamentliche Aufsätze, Festschrift für Prof. Josef Schmid zum 70* [New Testament Essays for Prof. Joseph Schmid on his 70th Birthday], eds. Josef Blinzler, Otto Kuss, and Franz Mussner (Regensburg: F. Pustet, 1963), 86–99, at 92–93.

50   For example. Matt. 23:27. Unclean tombs, unclean spirits and demons are referred to often in the Gospels (Mark 1:23; Matt 10:1, etc.); people and things (Acts 10:14; 10:28).

51   2 Cor. 6:17; Eph. 5:5; Rev. 17:4.

(2 Cor. 6:14–15). It is a call to keep oneself untarnished from pagan aberration and depravity. We see the idea further developed in 2 Corinthians 7:1 as an obligation to cleanse oneself from every defilement of body and spirit, but more positively to perfect oneself in holiness and the fear of God.[52]

This quotation in 2 Corinthians 6:17 shows clearly the movement from the ritual-objective conception of purity[53] to a spiritual-religious conception. The call to separation is no longer a call to withdraw from a pagan land as in Isaiah 52:11, or from a defiled Israel as in Qumran. Certainly, it seems Paul has particular concrete dangers in mind which demand a certain distance in regard to the pagans. But the call has become essentially a call not to live as pagans—in unrighteousness, darkness, worshipping creatures in subjection to Belial.[54] He is asking them, as a consequence of God's presence among them as his spiritual Temple, to walk in a manner befitting their new status.[55]

The New Christian Holiness Code

In quoting from the closing chapter of the Levitical law of holiness (Lev. 26:12), Paul seems to be suggesting that the Church forms a kind "neo-Levitical" or priestly people.[56] In the refusal of any compromise with paganism and the world of sin, in the demands for purity, we have an ethical teaching conformed to this priestly ideal of the Church. These exigencies could well have formed part of the prescriptions of a new Christian holiness code,[57] developed as an aspect of the primitive Christian teaching.[58] The important point for us is that it underscores the cultic value of the moral life for this priestly community. Serving as priests in a community consecrated by the presence of the living God, Christians live their

---

52 We can find a similar use of the notion in Rom. 6:19. Paul in this text uses *akatharsia* and *anomia* to describe the situation of man under the dominion of sin, as opposed to the state of Christian righteousness and holiness.

53 Of the original ritual purity, see Isa. 52:11.

54 See Rom. 12:2; Eph. 5:7–11.

55 Compare Eph. 5:6 which demands a similar separation.

56 See Edward G. Selwyn, *The First Epistle of St. Peter: The Greek Text with Introduction, Notes, and Essays* (London: Macmilllan, 1947), 405; Jean Colson, *Ministre de Jésus-Christ ou le Sacerdoce de l'Évangile. Étude sur la Condition Sacerdotale des Ministres Chrétiens dans l'Église Primitive* [The Minister of Jesus Christ or the Priesthood of the Gospel: A Study of the Priestly Nature of Christian Ministers in the Early Church], Théologie Historique 4 (Paris: Beachesne, 1966), 62–63, 152.

57 It will be remembered that the constant refrain in the Levitical law of holiness was: "Be holy, for I the LORD, your God, am holy" (Lev. 19:2; 20:7, 26; 21:8). God demands of Israel that it adapt itself to his service—that is, that it be holy. Compare Albert Gelin, "La Sainteté de l'Homme Selon l'Ancien Testament" [The Holiness of the Human Person According to the Old Testament], *Bible et Vie Chrétienne* 9 (1957): 35–48. See also Gelin, *The Concept of Man in the Bible* (London: G. Chapman, 1968).

58 See also Rom. 13:12; Jas. 1:21; Col. 3:8; Eph. 4:25. Compare Selwyn, *First Epistle of St. Peter*, 373, 459.

lives as a worship "in spirit and in truth."[59] The last phrase recalls Ezekiel 20:34, again in the context of the new Exodus (compare also Ezek. 11:17).

We hear this same call to spiritual purification and holiness in the exhortation with which Paul concludes this passage. Believers are called to "make holiness perfect in fear of God (*epiteloutes hagiōsynē en phobō Theo*)." The word used for holiness (*hagiōsynē*) is rare[60] and signifies moral sanctity here as well as it does in 1 Thessalonians 3:13. The whole basis for this moral sanctity, of course, depends upon God who has redeemed and sanctified man in Christ.[61] Here this sanctifying action of God is expressed by the notion of God's presence, which constitutes the community as a consecrated Temple. Yet the divine action calls forth in the life and conduct of the believer a completion (*epitelein*) in moral dedication. This continual progress in moral sanctity is based on the fear of God (*en phobō Theo*).[62]

With the notion of fear we are confronted with one of the fundamental religious attitudes of the Old Testament. The notion is expressed usually by the two Hebrew roots *yr'* and *phd*. *Yr'* may mean fear of God and his punitive judgment,[63] but is the term normally used to convey the reverential fear of adoration.[64] This fear is the attitude of the chosen people confronted with the terrible[65] grandeur of God who makes a covenant with them. It is their reaction to the holiness and glory of the God of the covenant.[66] Before the all-holy God, they feel a fear which is at the same time terror, wonder, and confidence.[67] This fear permeates all religion and is the foundation of religious living.[68] Thus we see it within the whole covenant concept of joy and fellowship with a loving and gracious God.[69]

---

59 Compare the same theme in Jas. 1:26–27; see also Raymond Corriveau, "Genuine Religion," *Studia Moralia* 5 (1967): 113–125.

60 Found only in Rom. 1:4; 2 Cor. 7:1; 1 Thess. 3:13 in the New Testament.

61 1 Cor. 1:2.30; 6:11; 1 Thess. 5:23; 2 Thess. 2:13.

62 The idea of perfecting holiness is also found in Qumran: 1QS 8:20; CD 7:5.

63 See Gen. 3:10; Deut. 17:13; 19:2; 2 Sam. 6:9.

64 Compare Gen. 15:12–18; Exod. 3:2–6; 20:20; 1 King 18:11. Also John Murray, *Principles of Conduct: Aspects of Biblical Ethics* (Grand Rapids, MI: Eerdmans, 1957), 231 n. 1. *Phd* frequently has the meaning of terror but it can stand for reverential awe: Gen. 31:42; 42:53; Ps. 36:1; Jer. 2:19.

65 Expressed in Hebrew grammar by the Niphal participle of *yr'*. Compare Exod. 15:11; Deut. 2:21; 10:17; 1 Chron. 16:25; Pss. 47:2; 111:9.

66 Compare Exod. 19:1–20; 24:15–18.

67 See Paul Van Imschoot, "La Sainteté de Dieu dans l'Ancien Testament" [The Holiness of God in the Old Testament], *Verbum Salutis* 75 (1946): 35. In the words of William Barclay: "It describes the feeling of man 'lost in wonder, love, and praise.'" *New Testament Words* (London: SCM, 1964), 228.

68 Prov. 1:7; Sir. 1:14, 21; Ps. 111:1.

69 See Isa. 50:10; Pss. 22:23–24; 31:20; 33:18. See also Simon John De Vries, "Note Concerning the Fear of God in the Qumran Scrolls," *Revue de Qumrân* 5 (1965), 233–237, at 237.

In the New Testament, *phobos* and *phobeō* express the same notion of fear carrying on the tradition of the Old Testament.[70] It is no wonder, then, that we find the idea of "perfecting holiness in the fear of God" expressed in the context of the new covenant. In the presence of the all-holy God on Zion, Moses had ritually sanctified and consecrated the people, filled with the fear of God, in order that they might be prepared to approach God (Exod. 19:14–16). The Church lives in the presence of the God of the new covenant promised by the prophets.[71] In the face of this hallowed presence, the new people of God is seized in the same way by an overwhelming reverence and loving adoration. It is this "sense of God," this religious fear, which spurs the Christian on to the highest reaches of moral sanctity and dedication.

In 2 Corinthians 6:14–7:1 we see a more or less self contained unit in which the ideas of worship, chosen people, and Temple are closely woven together. The passage spells out a program of life which underscores the new life of the Christian as basically cultic or liturgical in character. The faithful have become members of Christ's Kingdom, beneficiaries of his revelation and justification. Even more—and this is the brunt of Paul's argument—they are the Temple of the living God, sanctified by his presence.

In the new Temple, the material symbol of the Old Testament gives way to the full reality which was foreshadowed by the Jerusalem Temple. All the longing of Judaism in regard to the new age and the new Temple are found fulfilled in the Christian community. God does dwell among his chosen people but with a dwelling so close, so intimate, and so real that it transcends even the wildest dreams of the Israelites. It is this presence which is the central reality of the new Temple and the new cult.

The old cult of the Temple had demanded a whole program of ritual purity of the servants of the Temple, which was God's consecrated "dwelling." So from the more intimate and personal "dwelling" in the Christian community there arises a new cult that comprises the whole moral life of the believer. It demands a separation from the godlessness and depravity of the pagan world. And positively it impels the believer, overpowered by wonder, love, and praise in the presence of God, to an ardent pursuit of holiness. Just as the priestly code of Leviticus had governed the lives of the Old Testament priests, so the priestly people of God also have a new code of worship. The whole community is to pursue a purity and holiness which corresponds to its priestly status. The mystery of the Christian community as Temple has brought us to the heart of the mystery of Christian life as a worship of the all-holy God.

---

70   Luke 1:50; Acts 9:31; Rom. 3:18; 11:20; 2 Cor. 7:1; Col. 3:22; Rev. 14:7; 15:4.

71   Compare Ezek. 37:27; Jer. 31:31; 2 Sam. 7:8. Also 2 Cor. 6:16–18.

God's Spirit Dwells in the Church

In 1 Corinthians we have two texts which treat of the Temple theme, 3:16–17 and 6:19–20. The text of 3:16–17 is primarily dogmatic in perspective but it does provide several elements for the liturgical character of Christian activity as it is rooted in the liturgical character of his existence:

> Do you not know that you are God's Temple, and that God's Spirit dwells in you? If anyone destroys God's Temple, God will destroy him. For God's Temple is holy, and that temple you are. (1 Cor. 3:16–17)

As in the other passages on the Temple we are presented with a doctrine which is presumed to be already known. "Do you not know that you are God's Temple." Paul explains what he means when he says "and that God's Spirit dwells in you." It is the presence of the Spirit which constitutes the Christian community as God's Temple.[72] The Spirit is the principal reality of Christian life, the characteristic feature of messianic times (Acts 2:47).

We notice that it is the community which is called a Temple. "The Spirit of God comes down on the community, and communicates himself to individuals through the community."[73] He is said to dwell (*oikei*) in the community as in a Temple, again recalling the whole Temple theology of Old Testament times.[74] It is this indwelling which constitutes the Christian Temple as holy, as it did in the Old Testament.[75] As a consequence, the Christian community is not profane but holy—a Temple of God's Spirit in which he dwells by charity and his gifts. Again we see in Paul's concept of holiness the idea of consecration to God and to cult.

In the broader context of his concerns in 1 Corinthians, Paul, by shifting to the image of the Temple, brings out the full gravity of any action which would seriously endanger the Christian community. He has especially in mind those members of the Corinthian community who are fostering division and schism in Corinth. In their foolish and dangerous quarrels over preachers (1 Cor. 3:4; 1:10), they are attacking the very foundation of the Temple by dividing Christ (1:12). In fact, all ministers or members of the community who falsify the Word of God and the faith to the extent of endangering the foundation of the Temple would also be included in his condemnation.

---

72 Compare also 1 Cor. 12:1–13.

73 Lucien Cerfaux, *The Church in the Theology of St. Paul*, trans. Geoffrey Webb and Adrian Walker (New York: Herder & Herder, 1959), 148, n. 8.

74 Gärtner, *The Temple and the Community in Qumran and the New Testament*, 58, 95, draws a comparison between the dwelling of the Holy Spirit among Christians and that of the holy angels in the midst of the Qumran community.

75 For this comparison with Qumran, see Gärtner, *The Temple and the Community in Qumran and the New Testament*, 59.

"If anyone destroys God's Temple, God will destroy him" (1 Cor. 3:17). The word which Paul uses for "destroy" (*phtheirein*),[76] is used in the Septuagint to translate *šḥt*, which has the double meaning of "destroy" and "judge," and is used both of man's evil work of destruction and of God's punishment. Occasionally, the word is used in eschatological contexts to signify damnation (2 Pet. 2:12; Gal. 6:8; Col. 2:22).[77]

Thus it would seem probable that in our context Paul sees damnation as the punishment for those who destroy or desecrate the Temple of the Church. The very idea of the desecration of the Temple has an eschatological association (Dan. 9:27; 12:11).[78] These schisms attack the very foundation of the faith preached by Paul and so cause the Temple to crumble. In removing Christ as the foundation, the schismatics cut off the vital relation between Christ and the community, causing the Temple to lose its quality of consecration, which is effected by Christ's Spirit in-dwelling in the community. We can thus understand the terrible punishments threatened upon the perpetrators of such a sacrilegious act.

Paul does not develop in 1 Corinthians 3:16–17 the thought of the Christian's activity as cultic in nature. Yet it remains implicit in the Temple image and in the holiness which that necessarily involves. What the apostle does develop is his own role in the construction of the Temple. As an apostle, he is in some way at the origin of the Christian life. The Christians are a consecrated Temple of which Paul has laid the foundation by his apostolic preaching and activity.

In this sense, this Temple text must be understood in light of Paul's meditation upon the "building" of the Church which immediately precedes it (1 Cor. 3:10–15). In combating the divisions that have cropped up at Corinth, Paul explains that the Christian community does not belong to any minister of the Gospel but to God (1 Cor. 3:1–9). To illustrate this he uses the image of the plantation. "Neither he who plants nor he who waters is anything, but only God who gives the growth" (1 Cor. 3:7). The apostles are only workers.[79] The plantation or building, however, belongs to God alone (1 Cor. 3:9).

---

76   1 Cor. 3:17; see also 1 Cor. 15:23; 2 Cor. 7:2; 11:3; Eph. 4:22; 2 Pet. 2:12; Rev. 19:2.

77   In Qumran there also are "men of destruction" who try to destroy the community, but fail and are themselves condemned to eternal destruction (1QS 4:12; 9:16; CD 6:15). Compare Gärtner, *The Temple and the Community in Qumran and the New Testament*, 59.

78   Paul may even be comparing the errors and schisms within the community to the profanations of Antiochus IV (see 1 Macc. 1; 2 Thess. 2:4–12). See Albert-Marie Denis, "La Fonction Apostolique et la Liturgie Nouvelle en Éspirit" [The Apostolic Office and the New Liturgy in the Spirit], *Revue Des Sciences Philosophiques et Théologiques* 42 (1958): 401–436; 617–656, at 423–424.

79   *Synergoi*: either "fellow workers in God's service" (so Victor P. Furnish, "'Fellow Workers in God's Service,' [*synergos* 1 Cor. 3:9]," *Journal of Biblical Literature* 80 [1961]: 364–370) or "fellow workers of God" (so Karl H. Schelkle, "Der Apostel als Priester" [The Apostle as Priest] *Theologische Quartalschrift* 136 [1956]: 257–283, at 272).

At this point Paul passes over to the image of the "building" (verses 9b–15). The Church at Corinth is God's building (v. 9). Paul is the skilled master builder who has laid the foundation of this spiritual edifice (v. 10; compare Rom. 15:20) through his missionary work.[80] The other workers must build on this foundation which he himself has laid. That foundation is Jesus Christ crucified (1 Cor. 3:11; 1:23).

The value of the work of each apostolic worker will be tested or verified by fire in the final judgment, Paul says. If the work survives the test because it was the result of solid doctrine and disinterested zeal, the worker will receive a reward (v. 14). However, if the work was the result of a doctrine which emptied the truth of its force, it will perish and the worker will forfeit his reward, though he himself may be saved "as through fire." Thus, it is that Paul points out the weighty responsibility of the worker who seeks to build up the Temple of the Church.

The model for that building up of the Church is, of course, Paul. By arousing faith in Christ crucified, which leads to baptism in him, Paul has laid the foundation of an edifice whose very existence is a liturgical offering. Other workers can also cooperate in the construction of the sanctuary, but only in continuity with the faith in Christ which he has preached. Any attempt to build on any other foundation, on a Christ of human whims and desires, can only result in the destruction of the Temple and its liturgical life. This constitutes a real profanation and will be punished with eternal punishment.

---

80   This work includes the whole process of *"Christum tradere,"* or handing on the Christian message. See Josef Pfammatter, *Die Kirche als Bau: Eine Exegetisch-Theologische Studie zur Ekklesiologie der Paulusbriefe* [The Church as Building: An Exegetical-Theological Study of the Ecclesiology of the Pauline Epistles], (Rome: Gregorian University, 1960), 27. Here the building activity is obviously that of the apostolate (see also 2 Cor. 10:8; 12:19; 13:10; Rom. 15:20; Eph. 4:11–12). Paul probably has in mind Jer. 1:9–10. But the whole Church, in its own way, also participates in the work of edification (1 Thess. 5:11; 1 Cor. 8:1; 10:23; 14:3–5, 12, 17, 26; Rom. 14:19; 15:2; Eph. 4:29. Compare also Eph. 2:21–22; 4:15–16, where the growth of the Temple-building is that of Christian life). Edification is a many-sided reality which can never be reduced to the purely ethical, even in such texts as 1 Thess. 5:11 (see Michel, *"Oikos,"* in *Theologisches Wörterbuch zum Neuen Testament,* 5:122–151, at 143). It is a communitarian notion, derived from the building-Temple metaphor, which is a symbol of God's presence through the Spirit of Christ. (See F. W. Young, "The Theological Context of New Testament Worship," *Worship in Scripture and Tradition: Essays by Members of the Theological Commission on Worship (North American Section) of the Commission on Faith and Order of the World Council of Churches,* ed. Massey H. Shepherd Jr. [New York: Oxford University, 1963], 86–87.) It conceals within itself teleological, pneumatical, cultic, and ethical facets (Michel, *"Oikos,"* 5:144, 147). Since almost every aspect of Christian life is referred to as unto edification, the whole of Christian life is ordered to the "building up" of the building-Temple and is thus ordered to the spiritual worship of the Temple community. In addition to the articles quoted we refer to G. W. MacRae, "Building the House of the Lord," *American Ecclesiastical Review,* 140 (1959): 361–376, with a bibliography on 362, to which we would add Congar, *Jalons Pour une Théologie du Laïcat* (Paris: Cerf, 1954), 467; Eng. trans.: *Lay People in the Church: A Study for a Theology of the Laity* (Westminster, MD: Newman, 1957).

The Body as Temple of the Holy Spirit

Our final text is 1 Corinthians 6:19–20:

> Do you not know that your body is a Temple of the Holy Spirit
> within you, which you have from God? You are not your own;
> you were bought with a price. Therefore glorify God in your
> body. (1 Cor. 6:19–20)

This text is part of a longer passage (1 Cor. 6:12–20) which is perhaps the most
developed moral exhortation of all the Pauline letters. Paul condemns fornication,
calling on theological motives of the highest order. He reacts against the attitudes of
the Corinthian libertines, a group that lived according to their own understanding
of nature, rejecting Christian chastity and treating of sexual behavior as essentially
the same as eating and drinking.[81] All was permitted to them.

Paul directs his principal arguments against the sophism of his opponents
expressed in verse 13: "Food is meant for the stomach and the stomach for food."
In answer, he shows that while food and the nutritive function are of the purely
physiological order and therefore of passing value, such is not the case with the
body. The body is not for immorality but for the Lord and the Lord for the body.
There is a mutual relation between the two realities.

We cannot help but see here the "belonging" of the Christian to Christ which
is effected by baptism[82] and by the Eucharist.[83] The dignity of the body is first
underscored by its future destiny. It is destined to rise in virtue of the resurrection
of Christ (v. 14) which will complete the lordship of Christ over the body. But in its
present reality there is also a community of life between the body of the Christian
and the risen Christ. "Do you not know that your bodies are members of Christ?"
(v. 15).

This belonging to Christ excludes, for instance, union with a prostitute. The
Christian who unites himself to a prostitute forms a corporeal unity with her
(compare Gen. 2:24; Eph. 5:28). He subjects himself and belongs so much to this

---

81   Jean Héring states that there must have existed a group of Gnostic libertines in Corinth. To
      this group he attributes the two basic tenets: First, everything which had to do with bodily life
      was unimportant for the spiritual life and the destiny of the spirit. This led some to extremes
      of asceticism and others to sexual debauchery. Second, they rejected the resurrection of the
      body since the body was created by an inferior divinity. See *La Première Épitre de Saint Paul aux
      Corinthiens*, Commentaire du Nouveau Testament 7 (Paris: Neuchatel, Delachaux & Niestlé,
      1949), 47; Eng. trans.: *The First Epistle of St. Paul to the Corinthians*, trans. A. W. Heathcote and
      P. J. Allcock (London: Epworth, 1962). However Robert M. Grant, while stating the probability
      of Gnostic tendencies in Corinth speaks more cautiously in constructing their doctrines. See *La
      Gnose et les Origines Chrétiennes* (Paris: Seuil, 1964), 137; Eng.: *Gnosticism and Early Christianity*,
      Lectures on the History of Religions New Series 5 (New York: Columbia University, 1959).

82   Compare Rom. 6:6; 1 Cor. 12:13; see also 1 Cor. 6:11.

83   Compare 1 Cor. 10:16, 24–27. Héring, *Corinthiens*, 47–48, sees the allusion to the Eucharist
      especially in the phrase "and the Lord for the body."

"mistress" that he withdraws his body from the lordship of Christ (v. 15). It is a rob-bery and a desacralization which has no equal in other sins which are "outside the body" (v. 18). In other words, a human being is defined religiously in terms of his Lord. To be united to a prostitute is to prostitute oneself. It is to become one flesh with this being of flesh (v. 16).[84] On the other hand, to remain faithful to Christ and incorporated with him is to become a spiritual unity with him (v. 17).[85]

The radical opposition is between two worlds—between the harlot and her heathen world with which the fornicator unites himself "in one flesh" and Christ and the new world of the *pneuma* with which the Christian is one spirit. We should also note that it is possible that Paul was confronting a situation of ritual prostitution in a pagan temple.[86]

It is in the context of this series of arguments that Paul passes on to a new reason, or rather the same reason under a new form: "Do you not know that your body is a Temple of the Holy Spirit within you, which you have from God?" (1 Cor. 6:19). The body of Christians is a temple. Many authors have pointed out a certain relation of this theme with the Hellenistic thought of the time. The Stoics, for instance, spoke of the divinity as dwelling in man.[87] The Jewish philosopher, Philo, likewise spoke of the soul as the house of God.[88] Yet, neither Philo nor the Stoics referred to the body (or the community) as a temple; indeed, both Stoicism and the doctrine of Philo are profoundly individualistic. And while certain affinities can be seen with Hellenistic thought, the direct source of Paul's doctrine is the Christ-event itself and the whole current of spiritualization at work in Judaism.[89]

---

84 Contrary to the use in Gen. 2:24 and Eph. 5:28, flesh here is used in the pejorative sense as opposed to the Spirit (Rom. 8:9, 22), in the sense of being opposed to life in Christ (Rom. 7:5; 8:5; Gal. 5:24). The biblical phrase is transposed from the conjugal union to the passing and lustful encounter which is its sinful degradation.

85 Compare Rudolf Schnackenburg, *The Moral Teaching of the New Testament*, trans. by J. Holland-Smith and W. J. O'Hara (Freiburg: Herder, 1965), 273–75; Ceslas Spicq, *Théologie Morale du Nouveau Testament* [The Moral Theology of the New Testament], 2 vols. (Paris: J. Gabalda, 1965), 1:557.

86 Héring draws attention to the fact that "the *pornai* were in general hierodules, that is, slaves attached to the service of a pagan temple (notably the temple of Venus Aphrodite) and were believed to put their adorers in relation with the divinity they served" *Corinthiens*, 48.

87 "Wretch, you are carrying God with you, and you know it not. Do you think I mean some God of silver or gold? You carry him within yourself, and perceive not that you are polluting him by impure thoughts and dirty deeds." Epictetus, *Discourses*, Bk. 2, Chap. 8, 13, in *The Philosophy of Epictetus*, ed. John Bonforte (New York: Philosophical Library, 1955); see also *Discourses*, Bk. 1, Chap. 14, 14; Bk. 1, Chap. 8, 11.

88 "Be zealous therefore, O soul, to become a house of God, a holy temple (*hieron hagion*), a most beauteous abiding-place; for perchance, perchance the Master of the whole world's household shall be thine too and keep thee under his care as his special house, to preserve thee evermore strongly guarded and unharmed." *On Dreams*, Bk. 1, 149, in *Philo*, trans. F. H. Colson, and F. H. Whitaker, Loeb Classical Library, (London: Wm. Heinemann, 1934).

89 See Congar, *Le Mystère du Temple*, 186.

What is important here is the application of the identity of the Church as Temple to the body of the individual member of the Church. The message is that we cannot separate the community and its members.[90]

In 1 Corinthians 6:19–20 it seems that Paul is aware he is repeating what he said three chapters earlier. In fact he begins in exactly the same way ("Do you not know … " Compare 1 Cor. 3:16; 6:16). Again he seems to presume an established teaching and is drawing from a general principle to make a particular application. The community and the body are made a temple by the Holy Spirit who dwells in Christians to make them participate in the new world of grace and of life.[91] While he is speaking of the individual believers, there remains on the horizon the idea of the community insofar as all Christians are members of the body of Christ (1 Cor. 6:15).

Throughout the passage it is the body which Paul wishes to vindicate as hallowed ground, not to be desecrated by *porneia,* which means unlawful sexual intercourse or fornication. To make his case, the apostle insists on the relation of the Spirit with the body of flesh. The Spirit dwells in the bodies of Christians (v. 19) and begets the life of Christ in them. The Spirit of Christ[92] has transformed his risen body to become a "life-giving Spirit" (1 Cor. 15:45). The risen body of Christ is now "the focal point of a spiritual power which acts on men to bring about their resurrection and to give them life."[93] For this reason, the Christian "who clings to the Lord becomes one spirit with him" (1 Cor. 6:17). It is through baptism and the Eucharist that this union with the body of Christ (v. 15) in the Spirit (v. 17) is effected. Baptism is in one Spirit (1 Cor. 12:13) and through the Eucharist we come into real and spiritual union with Christ (1 Cor. 10:4, 17).

In the Temple theology of the Old Testament, the divine presence made up the essential reality of the Temple. So too here as Paul teaches that the Spirit of Christ makes the body of Christians "the Temple of the Holy Spirit." As the Temple of the old covenant was consecrated by the glory of God, so the bodies of Christians are consecrated as temples by the Holy Spirit.

---

90   "The religious character of the community identifies itself with that of its members. … The texts suggest now the idea of the community, now that of the individual lives. The same theme can be applied to the body." Lucien Cerfaux, *Le Chrétien dans la Théologie Paulinienne* (Paris: Cerf, 1962), 256; Eng. trans.: *The Christian in the Theology of St. Paul,* trans. Liliam Soiron (London: G. Chapman, 1967). For a brief presentation of the notion of body in St. Paul, see John L. McKenzie, *Dictionary of the Bible* (Milwaukee: Bruce, 1965), 100–102. He shows how the biblical notion of "corporate personality" is involved. Also J. de Fraine, *Adam et son Lignage: Études sur la Notion de "Personnalité Corporative" dans la Bible,* Museum Lessianum, Section Biblique 2:195 (Paris: Desclée de Brouwer, 1959), 207–208; Eng. trans: *Adam and the Family of Man* (Staten Island, NY: Alba House, 1965).

91   Compare Rom. 8:4, 9–11; Cerfaux, *Le Chrétien dans la Théologie Paulinienne,* 256–257; Congar, *Le Mystère du Temple,* 184.

92   Rom. 8:9; 2 Cor. 3:17; 1 Cor. 6:11.

93   Cerfaux, *Le Chrétien dans la Théologie Paulinienne,* 276.

The Consecration of the Christian

Consecration and the holiness that it demands was one of the principle themes associated with the old Temple. In the new Temple, it is union with Christ and the gift of the Holy Spirit which puts man in contact with the holiness of God. He who adheres to the Lord receives his Spirit (1 Cor. 6:17). The words *ho kollōmenos* ("he who clings or adheres") express the idea of connaturality between the Spirit and the *pneumatic* man. The connaturality, effected by baptism, [94] affects man in his nature and substance.[95] Our bodies, united with Christ and destined for resurrection, already take on a higher mode of life that is divine.

> They have something of a holiness that belongs to buildings consecrated for worship. A Christian can be thought of as the priest in the Temple of his own body, in which sanctuary he serves God and keeps out whatever might profane it.[96]

It is in this context that 1 Corinthians 6:18 is to be understood. The gravity of fornication, which is the one sin which is against one's own body, is that it totally falsifies the religious destiny and meaning of the body. Fornication thus becomes a complete alienation of the body from its true master and an abominable desecration of a sanctuary consecrated by the Holy Spirit himself. Even more, as has already been mentioned, the prostitution which is envisaged was possibly sacred prostitution. In this case, resort to the prostitute became the most terrible abomination of the Old Testament—the introduction of strange gods into the Temple of the all holy God.

---

94 In 1 Cor. 6:11 the process of sanctification is united with baptism: "But you had yourselves washed, you were sanctified, you were justified in the name of the Lord Jesus Christ and in the Spirit of our God."

95 "The adherence of which Paul speaks confers on man a quality of sanctity. It is a reality which posits a special reference to God, which gives rise to rights and duties, and which, in Pauline thought, is of its nature intrinsic, just as it was in the thought of the ancients." Cerfaux, *Le Chrétien dans la Théologie Paulinienne*, 276, n. 2.

96 Cerfaux, *The Church in the Theology of St. Paul*, 148–149. In this light it is no wonder that when Paul speaks of the life of celibacy and virginity in 1 Cor. 7, he again stresses holiness. "The unmarried woman, and the virgin, is anxious about the affairs of the Lord, how to be holy in body and spirit" (1 Cor. 7:34). "Body and spirit" in this verse express the totality of the human being. Compare Spicq, *Théologie Morale due Nouveau Testament*, 564, n. 3. The virgin or celibate is totally consecrated to the Lord. Consecrated virginity becomes a privileged mode of living one's baptismal consecration, a drawing out of its ultimate consequences. Compare F. X. Durrwell, *In the Redeeming Christ*, trans. Rosemary Sheed (London: Sheed and Ward, 1963), 214. Set apart and dedicated to the Lord and the things of the Lord, virgins are thus called to live a life conformed to this holy state. Their virginal lives are a most active form of participation in the spiritual cult of the new Temple. It is in this way that Lucien Legrand speaks of "cultic continence." *The Biblical Doctrine of Virginity* (London: G. Chapman, 1963), 78–86. See also, Xavier Léon-Dufour: "L'Appel au Célibat Consacré" [The Call to Consecrated Celibacy], *Assemblées du Seigneu* 95 (1966): 17–23.

Paul's final argument takes up the christological-redemption theme of our belonging to the Lord because he has redeemed us at the cost of his own life—"You are not your own; you were bought with a price" (1 Cor. 6:19–20). It is a theme closely connected with the theme of the habitation of the Holy Spirit. The presence of the Spirit brings about a consecration, while Christ wins our redemption.[97] Lucien Cerfaux in speaking of this says:

> Paul passes without effort from one notion to the other, doubt-lessly because they are bound together in his thought. The Spirit dwells in the Temple. It is his house by the will of God who makes him dwell in Christians (*ou exete apo Theou*). Thus Christians are in some way the property of the Spirit, as they are the property of Christ by right of purchase (the purchase of redemption).[98]

The main point of the verse (as also of 1 Cor. 7:23) is that Christians have no rights of their own (Acts 20:28; 1 Pet. 1:19). They are the property of Christ, redeemed by his precious blood (compare Rev. 5:9; 1 Pet. 1:19). Because Christians belong not to themselves but to God, Paul urges them to reverence their bodies (1 Cor. 6:20b). For in reverencing their bodies they glorify (*doxazein*) God himself. *Doxazein* is certainly a cultic term and is used in the Septaugint to designate the act of cult.[99] And Paul takes up that meaning in his use of the term,[100] as he also presupposes the whole of the Old Testament understanding of the *doxa* of God.

In the Old Testament, the *doxa* of God appears in the living creative power of creation and in the historical revelation of God to Israel (Exod. 19:16). God's glory dwells in "the holies" and will reveal itself in all its fullness in the eschatological future. We could translate *doxa* as the powerful splendor or the splendorous power of God. Wherever God manifests his glory, his glory reaches out to transform into God's dwelling place everything that is receptive to this power. In so doing it arouses from creatures the response of *doxazein*—of worship, honor, and praise.

---

97   Compare Cerfaux, *Christ in the Theology of St. Paul*, 312. The same close association of themes is taken up in Rom. 8:9: "But you are not in the flesh, you are in the Spirit, if the Spirit of God really dwells in you. Any one who does not have the Spirit of Christ does not belong to him."

98   Cerfaux, *Le Chrétien dans la Théologie Paulinienne*, 256, n. 2. Also *Christ in the Theology of St. Paul*, 312–13.

99   Compare Lev. 10:3; Ps. 4:23; Isa. 6:7, 13. Two of the better studies on *doxazō* and *doxa* are those by Gerhard Kittel and Gerhard von Rad in *Theologisches Wörterbuch zum Neuen Testament*, 2:235–258.

100   In the Pauline epistles *doxazein* occurs twelve times. Rom. 1:21; 8:30; 11:13; 15:6, 9; 1 Cor. 6:20; 12:26; 2 Cor. 3:10; 9:13; Gal. 1:24; 2 Thess. 3:1. As Heinrich Schlier points out, in Paul *doxa* and *doxazein* occur most often in a salvation-historical context. "Doxa bei Paulus als Heilsgeschichtlicher Begriff" [Glory as a Salvation-Historical Term in Paul], *Studiorum Paulinorum Congressus Internationalis Catholicus 1961* [International Catholic Congress of Pauline Studies], vol. 1 Analecta Biblica 17 (Rome: Pontifical Biblical Institute, 1963), 45–56.

This conception of *doxa-doxazein* is further developed by Paul. "The Father of glory" (Eph. 1:17), destined man from the beginning to "glory" (Rom. 9:23).[101] The glory of the "immortal God" (Rom 1:23) in creation was already directed to our eternal destiny. For God made creation the place and the medium of his presence (Rom. 1:19–21). And the glory of God radiating from creation called for its acknowledgment in *doxazein*, in worship, on the part of those who saw themselves indebted to the Creator. In so doing the glory of God would reflect back to their praise.

However, the glory of God radiating from creation was lost for man by sin (Rom. 3:23; 1 Cor. 1:21). And so God again caused men to experience his powerful splendor in Jesus Christ (2 Cor. 3:8; 4:4, 6; Phil. 4:9) and his Gospel (2 Cor. 4:4.6; 3:9) "for our glorification" (1 Cor. 2:7). The *doxa*, disclosed in Jesus Christ and the Gospel, becomes our *doxa* through baptism (Rom. 8:30; Eph. 5:26–27) and faith (Eph. 3:16–19). God thus gives his *doxa* to the believer, who grasps it in faith and gives himself to it in worship and praise. All aspects of Christian living become, consequently, ways of testifying to the glory of God.

"Glorify God in Your Body"

We are thus in a position to better understand Paul's urgent admonition: "Glorify God in your body (1 Cor. 6:20b)." Christian existence, which is a response to the glory of God in Christ, further radiates the *doxa* of God in *doxazein*. In glorifying God (*doxazein*) one gives back the *doxa* to God, so to speak. And it allows the glory of God to reflect further and to dwell upon earth.

Already in 1 Corinthians 6:19 with the mention of the Temple of the Holy Spirit there was associated an image of the glory of God, which filled the Jerusalem Temple in the form of a cloud. Now, in 6:20, we are told that we must make a cultic response to the glory of God offered to us in Christ and his gift of redemption. That cultic response is a chaste life, unsullied by fornication. Drawn into the ambit of God's glory, the Christian is consecrated as his Temple and shares in the splendor and sanctity of God himself. Through a life lived in conformity with that holiness and that splendor, man's body becomes a further reflection of God's glory in the world about him. It becomes a continuous worship and praise of God.

In the Corinthian correspondence, as throughout the Pauline corpus, the Christian life is shown to have a liturgical character, a character that flows from the identity of Christians as "temples" of God and members of the Church, which is the new Temple of God, sharing in the spiritual edifice of Christ crucified and risen.

The Spirit that dwells in this new Temple dwells in the believer by baptism. And it is this divine presence which constitutes the whole Church and individual Christians as a consecrated Temple. It is the special mark of Christians that they

---

101 See also Rom. 8:29; 1 Cor. 2:7; Eph. 1:4.

worship and serve by the Spirit of God (Phil. 3:3). This service is the priestly service of the new spiritual Temple in a life shaped and penetrated by the Spirit.

Paul in his exhortation to chaste living touches on the very heart of one's being as a Christian. *First*, as a person redeemed by Christ and destined to resurrection and eternal union with the Lord of glory, one shares, even now, in a community of life with Christ. One is "consecrated" as a member of Christ's body through baptism and the Eucharist. He pulsates with his Spirit and already radiates with his glory. It is therefore not a thing of indifference to subject this body to a prostitute, to become "one flesh" with her and her heathen world of sin and vice. For by this union he puts himself in complete contradiction with that which he is as "one spirit" with the Lord.

Secondly, the Christian is a Temple of the Holy Spirit, who has become such precisely in virtue of the redemption of Christ. Transformed by Christ, the Christian participates in Christ's life-giving Spirit. The "presence" of the Holy Spirit makes of the body of Christians a consecrated temple with all that that implies—a special sanctity and separation for the service of God. This divine presence is a dynamic presence. It is the moving force of the moral life of Christians, which gives to their whole life a cultic value. The sanctity and service demanded of the believer are no longer essentially ritual. It is the whole existence of the Christian, united to Christ in the Holy Spirit, which becomes the worship of the new Temple. The Christian, in the living out of one's moral life, becomes a priest in the temple of his own body, dedicated to the service of God. The person's life, lived in moral purity and holiness, becomes an extension of God's glory in the world and a constant worship and praise of God.

Letter & Spirit 4 (2008): 167–188

THE INDWELLING OF DIVINE LOVE:
The Revelation of God's Abiding Presence in the Human Heart

~: Thomas Dubay, S. M. :~

Marist Center

The indwelling of the Trinity is easy to understand and it is difficult to understand. It is so patent that a child can appreciate its splendor, so mysterious that theologians have disagreed for centuries in explaining its details. Yet there is no truth more central to the Christian mystery than man's union with his God, a truth mentioned repeatedly in both the Old and New Testaments, a truth prominent in the ecclesiology of the Second Vatican Council, a truth basic to liturgical and contemplative prayer, a truth that many find irresistibly attractive when it is taught in a fresh, scriptural manner.

The indwelling mystery is crucial to the supernatural economy established by an incredibly loving God. It is the teaching of the Catholic Church, based on the manifest testimony of Scripture, that the divine inhabitation is the end or goal of the divine economy.

> The ultimate end of the whole divine economy is the entry of God's creatures into the perfect unity of the Blessed Trinity (John 17:21–23). But even now we are called to be a dwelling for the Most Holy Trinity: "If a man loves me," says the Lord, "he will keep my word, and my Father will love him, and we will come to him, and make our home with him" (John 14:23).[1]

It is in view of the inbeing of the Trinity—imperfectly grasped through faith, perfectly through vision—that all else in the Christian order of things has been structured. When man sinned, he lost the Trinity and his orientation toward seeing the Trinity. Fortunately, God so loved the world that he sent the way that men might repossess the truth and the life that was to abide in their hearts. The beatific vision is the end of the supernatural economy for every man not only temporally but also ontologically; and the beatific vision implies the indwelling presence—the perfect, fully blossomed indwelling presence of our blessed God in his human habitation.

The incarnation and crucifixion, as well as the Eucharist and the other sacraments, are all themselves directed to the ultimate glorification of the Trinity

---

1   *The Catechism of the Catholic Church*, 2d. ed. (Vatican City: Libreria Editrice Vaticana, 1997), no. 260.

achieved in men through the marvelous intimacy of visional presence. When we proclaim in the Creed at Mass that the Son descended from heaven and became incarnate "for us men and for our salvation," it is declaring that the hypostatic union itself, together with its redemptive results, is oriented toward this same visional presence, since what is salvation if not the face to face fruition of the Trinity in our risen body?

In this article, I propose to trace out some scriptural themes dealing with the inabiding Father, his Son, and their Holy Spirit. In returning to these themes we hope to better understand the foundations of this profound doctrine of the divine indwelling. These themes, in turn, furnish some of the solid theological bases of a profound prayer life, in addition to offering us deeper insights into the meaning of the incarnation and the divine economy.[2]

God did not reveal the divine indwelling in an unprepared suddenness. He first laid the foundation centuries before the Word appeared in visible form. He proceeded slowly, methodically, thoroughly. Thus, in this article I propose to follow the divine pedagogy from the preparation of this revelation in the Old Testament to its completion in the New Testament.

Being a part of the supernatural plan for man, divine revelation follows the pattern of a gentle unfolding, like the bud of a rose. This is why the loving kindness of God lifts the curtain before the redemptive plan in the surprisingly general terms of an opposition between two offspring. Slowly he sharpens the message to a Messiah born of a people, then a tribe, finally a maiden. Divine wisdom gradually prepares a people for an exquisite reality—the incarnation of the Word. And the Word, too, once he has appeared, exercises an impressive restraint in letting even his intimates know who he is. God's workings with men are smooth.

So it is with our indwelling mystery. Were we to imagine that the astonishing declarations of the New Testament on the divine inhabitation through love struck the Jews as entirely strange, we would be gravely mistaken. Yet at the same time there must be no mistake about the fact that this revelation *is* astonishing. There is the promise of Christ quoted above in the *Catechism*: "If anyone love me ... we will come to him and make our abode with him" (John 14:23). There is again St. Paul's declaration: "Do you not know that you are the Temple of God and that the Spirit of God dwells in you" (1 Cor. 3:16).

When the Jews first heard of this sublime and touching familiarity with the Lord God, they may have been mystified, but we doubt that they were shocked.

2   In this article I am drawing on material originally published in *The Review for Religious*, which has graciously granted me permission to use it here. See "The Indwelling of God: Old Testament Preparation," *Review for Religious* 26 (1967): 203–230; "Interindwelling: New Testament Completion," *Review for Religious* 26 (1967): 441–460; "Indwelling Dynamism," *Review for Religious* 26 (1967): 685–702; "Eucharist, Indwelling, Mystical Body," *Review for Religious* 26 (1967): 910–938; and "Indwelling Summit," *Review for Religious* 26 (1967): 1094–1112. See also my *God Dwells Within Us* (Denville, NJ: Dimension Books, 1971), 196–221.

They had been gradually prepared to accept this new man-to-God intimacy by a whole series of instructions in the Pentateuch, the prophets, the Psalter, and the wisdom literature. By these teachings the Hebrews had been conditioned to thinking of God as nearby, as warmly dwelling with his people, as taking up a habitation in their midst. It is this conditioning that we will investigate first.

Scripture's Invitation to Intimacy

A common misconception notwithstanding, one of the traits of the Old Testament, at once remarkable and comforting, is the degree of intimacy—and yes, we may say tenderness—that the infinite God encourages between himself and his creatures. This we must appreciate fully as a preparation for our understanding of the indwelling mystery of evangelical revelation. Indeed, the Old Testament is invaluable as a prelude and introduction to the mystery of the Trinity abiding in man's heart.

The ancient Hebrew looked upon the Lord God as being near to some men and afar off from others, as shining upon some and hiding from others. Yet he knew that this God of his was everywhere. Even though the Lord declared himself especially present in some places, he was nonetheless in every place when one really got down to asking the question.

To say that God is in heaven (1 Kings 8:30), is to say that he is everywhere in his exalted majesty. He is repeatedly asked to hear from heaven the prayers of his people (2 Chron. 6:21, 23, 25, 27, 30, 35, 39), and he is so immense that the heavens cannot contain him (1 Kings 8:27; 2 Chron. 6:18). No matter where the evil go they cannot escape the punishing presence of this God (Amos 9:2). Nothing is secret to him who is both close at hand and afar off (Jer. 23:23–25).

In a graphic manner the psalmist well sums up the inescapability of the Lord God:

> Where can I go from your spirit?
> From your presence where can I flee?
> If I go up to the heavens, you are there.
> If I take the wings of the dawn,
> if I settle at the farthest limits of the sea,
> even there your hand shall guide me,
> and your right hand hold me fast. (Ps. 139:7–10)

As we might expect, the fullest Old Testament revelation of the divine immensity was given toward the end of the ancient dispensation. Written about a century before Christ, the Book of Wisdom speaks not only of God's presence *to* all things, but also of his *filling* the world and *being in* all that he has made.

> The spirit of the LORD fills the world, is all-embracing, and knows man's utterance. Therefore, no one who speaks wickedly can go unnoticed. (Wis. 1:7–8)

> You spare all things because they are yours, O LORD and lover of souls, for your imperishable spirit is in all things. (Wis. 11:26–12:1)

God has a personal, dynamic contact with man in the Old Testament. God not only *is* in all things, he has a personalized knowledge and contact with everything that issues from his creating fingers, but especially with his human creations fashioned after his own image. Job lays down that all things lie open to the divine eye. "He beholds the ends of the earth and sees all that is under the heavens. ... He splits channels in the rocks; his eyes behold all that is precious. He probes the wellsprings of the streams, and brings hidden things to light" (Job 28:10–11, 24). Susanna calls on the omniscience of her God as a witness to her innocence under accusation. "O eternal God, you know what is hidden and are aware of all things before they come to be: you know that they have testified falsely against me" (Dan. 13:42).

God's Tender Stooping to Humanity

More important still was the ancient Hebrew's conviction that his Lord God was interested in him, that he saw his every action, that every action had an importance before him. This Lord searched the very heart of man. The first word of the Lord to come to the prophet Jeremiah was a word of personal divine interest shown through knowledge that preceded the prophet's conception and consecrated him while he was yet unborn (Jer. 1:5). But this provident God looks upon all men, not only his select messengers. He witnesses their inner thoughts, observes their hearts, understands their every deed and watches their every step. The Spirit of this Lord fills the world and embraces all things. He can be named the searcher of hearts and souls (Jer. 1:4–5; Prov. 15:3; Wis. 1:6–7; Sir. 15:18–19; 17:15; 23:19–20).

We can already begin to see why the Hebrew felt so near to his God. God was not an omnipotent Creator who was disinterested in his creation. We think rather that the vivid sense of the divine reality so impressive in the Old Testament was partially due to the Israelite's conviction of the divine closeness consequent on the divine omniscience. Psalm 139 beautifully illustrates our point by combining in several masterly strokes the Lord's immensity, his omniscience, his tender care, and his awesome skill.

> O LORD, you have probed me and you know me;
> you know when I sit down and when I stand;
> you understand my thoughts from afar.
> My journeys and my rest you scrutinize,
> with all my ways you are familiar.
> Even before a word is on my tongue,
> behold, O LORD, you know the whole of it.

> Behind me and before, you hem me in
> and rest your hand upon me.
> Such knowledge is too wonderful for me;
> too lofty for me to attain. (Ps. 139:1–6)

This passage obviously merits careful meditation by anyone who wishes to drink in the spirit of God's tender stooping to man, as we shall finally see it revealed in the fullness and beauty of the Gospel indwelling mystery. The psalmist continues by developing the omnipresence of God and its never ceasing providential implications (Ps. 139:7–10). Finally, he reflects on the divine artisan fearfully and wonderfully fashioning his limbs within the very womb of his mother.

We should notice in this section of Psalm 139 that God is especially present in the mother's womb *because he is producing an effect*. This concept of the divine presence explained by effects produced is prominent in theologians' explanations of the indwelling. For our purposes now it is helpful for us to notice that one of the special characteristics indicating the divine presence among the chosen people was a peculiar manifestation or effect. Thus God indicated his presence in the sanctuary by the *Shekinah*, a white cloud. Elsewhere he is present by producing with a strong arm the marvelous works, the *mirabilia Dei*: the fiery bush (Exod. 3:1–4), the ten plagues (Exod. 7:14–11:10), the division of the Red Sea (Exod. 14:10–31), the quail and the manna (Exod. 16:4–36), the water from the rock (Exod. 17:1–7), and especially the awesome theophany on Mount Sinai (Exod. 19:16–20:21).

In Psalm 139 this same God is fearfully, wonderfully, but quietly present within the maternal womb, fashioning the psalmist's body and thus showing personal interest and love.

> Truly you have formed my inmost being;
> you knit me in my mother's womb.
> I give you thanks that I am fearfully, wonderfully made;
> wonderful are your works.
> My soul also you knew full well;
> nor was my frame unknown to you
> When I was made in secret,
> when I was fashioned in the depths of the earth.
> Your eyes have seen my actions;
> in your book they are all written;
> my days were limited before one of them existed.
> How weighty are your designs, O God;
> how vast the sum of them!
> Were I to recount them, they would outnumber the sands;
> did I read the end of them, I should still be with you.
> (Ps. 139:13–18)

The God whom the very heavens could not contain chose to reveal to an insignificant nation that he would somehow dwell in their midst—not only on rare and special occasions. He proposed a permanent and calm abiding in the very midst of his people. "I will set my dwelling among you and will not disdain you. Ever present in your midst, I will be your God, and you will be my people" (Lev. 26:11–12; 22:32). Because this nearby God is so sacred, the Israelites must be at special pains to keep their camps becomingly clean during their travels simply for his sake and his presence in their very midst (Deut. 23:15).

Ark, Temple, and the Habitation of God

In a special manner the Lord of hosts dwells in Jerusalem, the faithful city and the holy mountain. "Thus says the LORD: I will return to Zion, and I will dwell within Jerusalem" (Zech. 8:2–3). This special presence of the Lord among his people is to be a reason for their singing and rejoicing (Zech. 2:14–17). Within the chosen nation itself, the Lord God had a sacred abode in his Temple at Zion. Whether his presence in the sanctuary was viewed as distinct from that peculiar to the nation as a whole is not clear, but the mere fact of it is clear and, moreover, indicated in several ways.

Quite simply, God is said to be in the Temple built for him (1 Kings 8:12–13). So he is sought there and prayers reach him in it. "When my soul fainted within me, I remembered the LORD; my prayer reached you in your holy Temple" (Jon. 1:5, 8). The priests who serve in the Temple are close to their Lord. The unfaithful Levites "shall no longer draw near me to serve as my priests, nor shall they touch any of my sacred things," whereas the faithful who cared for the sanctuary during the time of Israel's infidelity "shall draw near to me to minister to men, and they shall stand before me to offer me fat and blood" (Ezek. 44:13, 15; 2 Sam. 7:6; Exod. 28:35).

Within the Temple itself the Lord is somehow especially found in the holy place, and there he is enthroned (Ps. 22:3; Lev. 16:1–2). Even more specifically, he is on the Ark of the Covenant itself and on occasion he will speak from this sacred spot (Ps. 99:1; 1 Chron. 13:6; Ps. 80:1; Exod. 25:22; Num. 7:89). Here also David sits before the Lord (1 Chron. 17:16).

This divine dwelling is singular enough that the Israelites are to take up a collection of precious materials and then construct a fit habitation for their Lord. "They shall make a sanctuary for me, that I may dwell in their midst. This dwelling and all its furnishings you shall make exactly according to the pattern that I will now show you" (Exod. 25:8–9). Then, in a concrete manner, the Lord God teaches the sacredness of this special presence by prescribing in detail the richness of his habitation (Exod. 25–27).

Over and above the peculiar presence of the Lord to his chosen people in their Temple, it seems that he gave himself intimately to some men and withdrew himself from others. For instance, while God is close to the humble, he is far from the proud and the wicked (Ps. 137:6; Prov. 15:29). In an exquisite passage we are told of the gentle, kindly, good-giving presence of the Lord to those who love him.

> The eyes of the LORD are upon those who love him;
> he is their mighty shield and strong support,
> a shelter from the heat, a shade from the noonday sun,
> a guard against stumbling, a help against falling.
> He buoys up the spirits, brings a sparkle to the eyes,
> gives health and life and blessing. (Sir. 34:16–17)

It was natural, therefore, to seek the Lord when he was near and to ask for the divine presence.

> Seek the LORD while he may be found, call him while he is near.
> (Isa. 55:6)

> But you, O LORD, be not far from me;
> O my help, hasten to aid me. (Ps. 22:20)

Perhaps at once the most homely and the most touching illustration of what we are saying is the account of Moses' familiarity with God. We are told that the Lord would speak to his servant face to face, as familiarly as one man speaking to another. In one of these conversations Moses dares to remind this mighty Lord that he has already called him an intimate friend who had found the divine favor.

So intimate are these two that the puny man dares to bargain with God. "If you are not going yourself (with us), do not make us go up from here," Moses argues. "For how can it be known that we, your people and I, have found favor with you, except by your going with us?" Rather than crush the Israelite as a brash upstart laying down conditions for the Almighty, the Lord gently responds that "this request, too, which you have just made, I will carry out, because you have found favor with me and you are my intimate friend" (Exod. 33:7–19).

Even though Moses was a special intimate with the Lord God, this loving protector wished an astonishing familiarity with each individual among his chosen people. He desired to be personally close to them. He wanted their love, confidence, yearning, delight. He was preparing them for the disclosure of the indwelling presence of the yet unrevealed Trinity.

The most basic of the biblical God-and-man relationships is love, mutual love. The loving kindness characteristic of God in his merciful dealing with his human children occurs in the Old Testament many more times than we should care to count. And the occurrences are strongly worded. Because the skies seem limitless in expanse, the Hebrew sees in them an image of the gentleness of his

God: "O LORD, your kindness reaches to heaven; your faithfulness to the clouds. ... How precious is your kindness, O God" (Ps. 36:6, 8). His goodness shows itself in many ways, but one of the most touching is his fatherly forgiveness. The psalmist confides:

> Guide me in your truth and teach me,
> for you are God my savior,
> and for you I wait all the day.
> Remember that your compassion, O LORD,
> and your kindness are from old.
> The sins of my youth and my frailties remember not;
> in your kindness remember me, because of your goodness,
> O LORD. (Ps. 25:5–7)

This gentle God wanted the Hebrews to know of his desire to be intimate with them and of the great love he bore toward them, and so he plainly opened his heart and told them so. So close is this familiarity with Israel, too, that he uses the metaphor of marital love to illustrate it.

> For he who has become your husband is your Maker. ... For a brief moment I abandoned you, but with great tenderness I will take you back. ... With enduring love I take pity on you, says the LORD, your redeemer. (Isa. 54:5, 7)

So touching is this divine love for man, and the consequent closeness of God to man, that he takes man in his arms, draws him on with a kind of human affection, fondles him like a child at his cheeks.

> It was I who taught Ephraim to walk, who took them in my arms; I drew them with human cords, with bands of love; I fostered them like one who raises an infant to his cheeks. Yet, though I stooped to feed my child, they did not know that I was their healer. ... How could I give you up, O Ephraim? ... My heart is overwhelmed, my pity is stirred. (Hos. 11:3–4, 8)

Rightly may this tender God who stoops to man declare "with age-old love I have loved you" (Jer. 31:3). Rightly, too, does the Book of Wisdom ascribe love as the reason for the divine activity of creation and conservation, as it speaks of God's Spirit being in all things.

> You love all things that are and loathe nothing that you have made; for what you hated, you would not have fashioned. And how could a thing remain, unless you willed it; or be preserved had it not been called forth by you? But you spare all things,

because they are yours, O Lord and lover of souls, for your imperishable Spirit is in all things. (Wis. 11:24–12:1)

While there is in these texts no clear affirmation of God's special indwelling in those he loves, there is an unmistakable revelation of a love whose consequence is an intimacy and closeness indicated by the images and expressions used—finding favor; intimate friend; taking back with great tenderness; enduring love; embracing man in the divine arms and fondling him at the divine cheeks; the divine heart overwhelmed; age-old love; lover of souls who is in all things. This divine love theme is surely only one step removed from the New Testament's revelation that this God dwells in man's soul as in a temple.

Love and Longing in the Psalms

Not only does God, as revealed in the Old Testament, overflow with an amazing love for his human children, they in turn are to love him in an entire surrender. In the Gospel, Jesus Christ makes this love of man for God a condition for the indwelling presence of the Trinity; thus, we may not omit to notice how the Old Testament prepares for this aspect of the indwelling mystery.

Early in the Hebrew revelation the love-command was given. And it was given with an unusual solemnity, a total wholeness, a remarkable insistence.

> Hear, O Israel! The Lord is our God, the Lord alone! Therefore, you shall love the Lord your God with all your heart, and with all your soul, and with all your strength. Take to heart these words which I enjoin on you today. Drill them into your children. Speak of them at home and abroad, whether you are busy or at rest. Bind them at your wrist as a sign and let them be as a pendant on your forehead. Write them on the doorposts of your houses and on your gates. (Deut. 6:4–9)

Although Deuteronomy does not tell us, as Jesus will later explain, that this is the greatest of all commandments, the author does make clear its centrality by the expressions he uses—take to heart; I enjoin on you; drill into your children; write on the doorposts, and the like. Man's love for God is indeed crucial for his spiritual life.

We would expect, then, a proliferation of love protestations throughout the Old Testament. But we do not find them. This is strange only on first sight. Indeed, a man declares his love for his wife and a mother for her children in many ways besides the plain expression: "I love you." So also the Jew protests his love for God in his countless expressions of wonder and praise for the divine goodness, kindness, mercy, power, and wisdom scattered especially throughout the Psalter.

Yet simple acts of explicit love are not lacking either. The psalmist exclaims and wonders at the goodness of God and then commands the love man should have for him:

> How great is the goodness, O Lord,
> which you have in store for those who fear you. ...
> Love the Lord, all you his faithful ones. (Ps. 31:19, 23).

And the faithful Hebrew does use the simple "I love you" expression toward his Lord:

> I love you, O Lord, my strength,
> O Lord, my rock, my fortress, my deliverer. (Ps. 18:1–2).

The psalmist loves so much that he weeps when he sees men neglect the divine law (Ps. 119:136). He loves the very house of God (Ps. 26:8). The love of man for God in the Old Testament is also expressed in the persistent themes of man's yearning for God. Throughout the sacred pages the Hebrew is admonished to seek, to desire, to yearn after the Lord God, for it is in so longing that he can attain fulfillment and the very divine presence. When the Lord is to scatter his people among the nations he leaves them with the precept: "Yet there too you shall seek the Lord, your God; and you shall indeed find him when you search after him with your whole heart and your whole soul" (Deut. 4:29). This same message the Holy Spirit transmits to Jeremiah for his exiled people: "When you call me, when you pray to me, I will listen to you. When you look for me, you will find me. Yes, when you seek me with all your heart, you will find me with you, says the Lord" (Jer. 29:12–14).

The Lord wants his people to desire him, to open their mouths that he might feed them (Ps. 81:10). The psalmist invites us to give thanks for the wondrous kindness of the Lord, "because he satisfied the longing soul and filled the hungry soul with good things" (Ps. 107:8–9).

If, then, those who seek the Lord with their whole heart will find him present, as Jeremiah promised, and if this Lord wants the seekers to yearn with an open mouth and ten times more vehemently than their straying (Bar. 4:28–29), then we may conclude that the deeper the longing on man's part, the more intimate the coming on God's part. And it would seem that the Hebrews learned this lesson, that they burned in yearning for the Lord their God.

We feel that ardor in the extraordinary claim of the psalmist:

> One thing I ask of the Lord, this I seek:
> to dwell in the house of the Lord all the days of my life,
> that I may gaze on the loveliness of the Lord and
> contemplate his Temple. (Ps. 27:4)

Dwelling with God is the vehement longing of the psalmist:

> How lovely is your dwelling place, O Lord of hosts!
> My soul yearns and pines for the courts of the Lord.
> My heart and my flesh cry out for the living God. ...
> I had rather one day in your courts than a thousand elsewhere.
> I had rather lie at the threshold of the house of God
> than dwell in the tents of the wicked. (Ps. 84:1–2, 10)

The extraordinary character of this desire for God and his presence is brought out by the strong words used to translate it, such words as yearn, pine, and cry out. The beauty of the passages in which these longings are expressed merit careful meditation. To quote just two:

> As the hind longs for the running waters,
> so my soul longs for you, O God.
> Athirst is my soul for God, the living God.
> When shall I go and behold the face of God? (Ps. 42:1–2)

> O God, you are my God whom I seek;
> for you my flesh pines and my soul thirsts liked the earth,
> parched, lifeless, and without water.
> Thus have I gazed toward you in the sanctuary
> to see your power and glory,
> for your kindness is greater than life. (Ps. 63:1–3)

"Only In God is My Soul at Rest"

The longing of the Hebrew is to rest and delight in the divine presence. This is another persistent theme of the Old Testament's preparation for the revelation of the divine indwelling. Man is present, intimately present, to that in which he fully rests. He is present, too, in a vital way to that in which he fully delights. Thus the psalmist invites all to take refuge in the Lord that they might be glad and exult in him, for he is joy to those who love him (Ps. 5:11).

Even a man who has sinned grievously can regain the presence of God and enjoy his Savior:

> Cast me not out from your presence,
> and your holy spirit take not from me.
> Give me back the joy of your salvation
> and a willing spirit sustain in me. (Ps. 51:11–12)

We may be tempted to see an implicit recognition of the divine presence in the soul contained in the last phrase, since to sustain man's spirit within him God must be there. Yet, while this inference is valid, we cannot conclude for certain that the psalmist was thinking of it.

The communication between God and the soul is brought out in all of its rich personal relationships under the images of the well spread banquet, exultation, night watching, winged protection, a clinging fast (Ps. 63:5–8). And this delightful rest in God, this joyful closeness to him is to be man's lot forever:

> You will show me the path to life,
> fullness of joys in your presence,
> the delights at your right hand forever. (Ps. 16:11)

We are surely now less than a step away from the indwelling presence and its beatifying consequences:

> The just live forever, and in the LORD is their recompense,
> and the thought of them is with the Most High.
> Therefore shall they receive the splendid crown,
> the beauteous diadem, from the hand of the LORD—
> for he shall shelter them with his right hand. (Wis. 5:15–16)

If man's joy is in the Lord God, if he is destined to possess a life of delights in the divine presence, if his reward is to live in the Lord and thus have his crown forever, it follows that man's heart has only one goal, one destination, one resting place—"Only in God is my soul at rest; from him comes my salvation" (Ps. 62:1). The absoluteness of this statement is striking. Even shocking. To say *in God only* is man's rest is to say that the human heart is weary and disturbed and discontent until it dwells somehow in its Creator. Nothing on earth can satisfy or calm it. Nothing. Perhaps this is why St. Paul will later admonish us to "rejoice *in the Lord* always" (Phil. 4:4) and the Master himself will say "these things I have spoken to you that *my* joy may be *in you*, and that your joy may be *full*" (John 15:11).

We are then, in this yearning of the soul for rest in the divine presence, at the threshold of the new dispensation and its revelation of God's familiarity with man. We cannot say that the Old Testament indicates an appreciation of an indwelling presence. But we can say that the themes we have looked at—the omnipresence of God, his love and abiding presence with his people, his fatherly closeness to men and women, his call to a relationship of intimate mutual love, and their longing for his presence—prepared the Hebrew mind and heart to accept this revelation and to expect that the next step in the divine condescension would be some more intimate union.

The New Revelation: In Him We Have Our Being

Yet the new revelation of the Gospel tells of an intimacy deeper than anyone could have imagined. God is still near, to be sure, but so near that he is within. He now is given to the human person. He abides, dwells, inhabits the temple that man and the Church have become.

As we saw in our study of the Old Testament, the ancient Hebrew was keenly aware of the divine immensity pervading all things from the very heights of heaven to the inner workings within his mother's life-giving womb. In a masterful discourse directed to men of another cultural world, the Athenians, St. Paul presents this same truth:

> So Paul, standing in the middle of the Areopagus, said: "Men of Athens, I perceive that in every way you are very religious. For as I passed along, and observed the objects of your worship, I found also an altar with this inscription, 'To an unknown god.' What therefore you worship as unknown, this I proclaim to you. The God who made the world and everything in it, being Lord of heaven and earth, does not live in shrines made by man, nor is he served by human hands, as though he needed anything, since he himself gives to all men life and breath and everything. And he made from one every nation of men to live on all the face of the earth, having determined allotted periods and the boundaries of their habitation, that they should seek God, in the hope that they might feel after him and find him. Yet he is not far from each one of us, for 'In him we live and move and have our being'; as even some of your poets have said, 'For we are indeed his offspring.'"

This last remark of the apostle, "in him we live and move and have our being," bespeaks the natural divine presence to creation—God's natural presence in all things. By his divine activity he is closer to us than the very air we breathe. This truth was well expressed by Pope St. Gregory the Great (d. 604) over thirteen centuries ago. God, he said, is

> within all things, outside of all things, above them all, below them all. He is above by power, below by sustenance, exterior by magnitude, interior by penetration. On high ruling, below containing, externally surrounding, internally penetrating. He is not above by one part of his substance, below by another, or outside by one part and inside by another. But wholly one and the same, everywhere sustaining by presiding and presiding by sustaining just as he penetrates by surrounding and surrounds by penetrating. … Within he penetrates without being diminished,

without he surrounds without being extended. He is therefore, both above and below without being confined in a place. He is rich without breadth. He is fine without loss.[3]

From all this, then, it follows that if a speck of dust lies on the desk before me, God must be wholly within it pouring out its entire "to be" at every moment. If there is a tree on the lawn outside my window, he must at every moment utterly penetrate its every cell or it would immediately vanish into its native nothingness. If there is a star a billion light years from my office—and there are billions of them—the divine power must constantly pervade and pour out its flowing existence. If there is a sinner down the street blaspheming his Maker, that Maker must be in the sinner providing his being and life and breath.

The relation of creation to Creator is quite unlike that of watch to watchmaker. In the latter case the craftsman can make his watch, wind it up, and then die—the watch will continue to be and to run. In the former case, the Creator must at every moment conserve his creature with a continuing creation and provide for its activity with a primal concurrence. God must be utterly everywhere.

Now, if this be so, how can Jesus say that if a man fulfills certain conditions, God will come to that man, as he does in John 14:23? Ordinarily, we do not come to where we are. Yet Jesus says that he and his Father come to a lover but not to a sinner. How do they come? What is this abode they promise to make in the lover? What is new in this presence of God?

We must first grasp the deep differences between a local, spatial, material presence of one body to another on the one hand and a know-loving-enjoying presence of person-friends on the other. There is an intimacy and closeness in the latter that is completely lacking in the former and cannot be supplied by it. Now it so happens, interestingly enough, that the New Testament revelation repeatedly links the interpersonal relationships of loving, knowing, and delighting to the new and special abiding of the Trinity in the hearts of certain men.

If anything is obvious in Jesus' revelation of the divine inhabitation, if anything is crucial to the whole mystery, it is love—love for God primarily, but even love for neighbor. The revelation of Jesus is striking: "If you love me, keep my commandments. And I will ask the Father and he will give you another Advocate to dwell with you forever, the Spirit of truth" (John 14:15–17). Consider what is being said: *If* you love Jesus, he will ask the Father to send the Spirit to *dwell* with you forever. This Advocate has always been in a man, but now he will *dwell*, with all the interpersonal overtones the word carries with it. Moreover, this love is mutual: "If anyone love me ... my Father will love him." And the result is the same—the Father, Son, and Spirit, "will come to him *and make our abode with him*" (John 14:23).

---

3   *Morals on the Book of Job*, Bk. 2, Chap. 12, in *Morals on the Book of Job*, 3 vols., trans. and ed. James Bliss (Oxford: J. H. Parker, 1844–1850).

To Abide in Love

When St. John comes to write his first letter, he does not forget the condition of the divine inhabitation he learned from his Master's lips. The doctrine is the same:

And we have come to know, and have believed, the love that God has in our behalf. God is love, and he who abides in love abides in God, and God in him. (1 John 4:16)

Now the mystery is seen to be so wrapped up in love that the beloved disciple introduces it with a charming yet profound one-word definition of the dweller: God is love. He tells us, too, that so marvelous, so intimate is this abiding that not only is God in man but man is also in God. He who abides in love abides in God, and God in him. The mystery is not only an indwelling, it is an *inter-indwelling*, a mutual indwelling. But what, then, does it mean to speak of the dwelling, abiding, coming of God? How do Father and Son come to a place in which they already are? In answering this question we must remember the context in which Jesus and the apostles were speaking. Distance or nearness to God for the Jews was not so much a spatial matter as it was a question of moral worthiness. For the Hebrew, God looked at the sinner from afar but he came close to the just. Hence, "distance" from God's presence is not a question of feet or miles, since God is absolutely everywhere; rather, that distance was measured in the personal relationship between God and man. When God leaves, it is a withdrawal of friendship. When he comes, it is an arrival of love, the personal intimacy of knowing affection. He is present in the sinner by omnipotence, but in the just he comes as supernatural lover.

The love is mutual, both ways: God for man and man for God. It is this two-way affection that makes the relationship a matter of supernatural friendship. Love is a condition that only a person can fulfill. Because the Spirit is given under the conditions of love and obedience, our texts suggest that this new presence includes a *personal love relationship*. Already, then, we have an element that far transcends a natural omnipresence due to power and knowledge. God is in a tree, but he has no personal love relationship with that tree. Hence, with St. John of the Cross (d. 1591) we can observe:

The soul lives where it loves rather than in the body which it animates, because it has not its life in the body, but rather gives it to the body, and lives through love in that which it loves.[4]

The new love of inter-indwelling intimacy between God and man includes a new supernatural divine disclosure.

---

4   *Spiritual Canticle*, Stan. 8, 3. Text in *The Collected Works of St. John of the Cross*, trans. Kieran Kavanaugh and Otilio Rodriguez (Washington, DC: Institute of Carmelite Studies, 1979)

> I will ask the Father and he will give you another Advocate ...
> whom the world cannot receive because *it neither sees him nor
> knows him.* But *you shall know him, because he will dwell with you,*
> and be in you. (John 14:16–17)

> In that day *you will know that I am in my Father, and you in me,
> and I in you.* ... He who loves me will be loved by my Father, and
> *I will love him and manifest myself to him.* (John 14:20–21)

The just man, through the indwelling presence, possesses a special knowledge of God. By this mysterious presence of God within we know of the inter-indwelling with Christ and his Father. And we know of our sharing in that communion. The abiding guests somehow make their presence known to their living Temple, in which by the Spirit they have come to abide. "You shall know him *because* he will dwell with you and be in you" (John 14:17). This is a loving, tasting, intimate knowledge by what we may term a supernatural empathy.

Abiding in His Flesh and Blood

This mutual abiding of God and man is central, too, to the mystery of the Eucharist presented in the Scriptures. Here we see the intimate connection between the abiding presence of God promised by the incarnation and the mission given by Christ to his apostles at the Last Supper. In John's Gospel, notice the striking similarities between Christ's words about the divine indwelling and his description of the sacramental communion with his body and blood.

> Amen, amen, I say to you, unless you eat the flesh of the Son of
> Man and drink his blood, you shall not have *life in you.* ... He
> who eats my flesh and drinks my blood, *abides in me and I in him.*
> (John 6:54, 57)

What is this "life in you," if it is not the knowing, loving, and enjoying of the Trinity attained by the gift of the Spirit? Jesus is saying that a man cannot live a trinitarian life unless he is nourished by the Eucharist. But how are we to understand this? How does the Eucharist cause the indwelling life?

God could have set up a divine economy of salvation in which the conferring of divine gifts would depend on the divine will alone. In this case an eternal fiat would have been sufficient to account for all that is. But the New Testament makes it clear that in our present order of salvation, supernatural gifts are dispensed through the human nature of Christ.

When Jesus enters Peter's house and finds his mother-in-law lying ill with a fever, he does not merely will to cure with an inner act of volition. He chooses, rather, to show outwardly how this miraculous gift is somehow dependent, not only on his human will but also on his human body: "He *touched* her hand, and the fever left her and she rose" (Matt. 8:15). The crowds soon learned the lesson of the divine plan. Luke summarizes their realization that the eternal Word chose to use his human nature as an instrument in effecting supernatural effects: "All the crowd were trying to touch him, for power went forth from him and healed all" (Luke 6:19).

A human nature of itself could not cure Peter's mother-in-law; but joined to the divine in the person of the Word, it can and does produce supernatural effects—miracles, charisms, grace. The fathers were aware of this causality and among the examples they used to illustrate it was the vivid image of burning coal. Just as the fire in a red-hot piece of coal diffuses its heat through the coal, so does the divine nature of the Word diffuse its miraculous and grace-giving power through his human body and soul.

If, then, all graces in our supernatural economy come through the God-man, it follows that the indwelling grace also comes through him. And if we receive this same God-man, human nature as well as divine, in the Eucharist, it further follows that this Eucharist nourishes the indwelling. Such seems to be the very thought of Jesus himself. "He who eats my flesh and drinks my blood, *abides in me and I in him.*"

The abiding he is talking about is more than sacramental. It is indwelling. We have two reasons for this interpretation. First, the word "abiding" indicates some sort of permanent duration, and yet the sacramental presence is transitory, lasting as long as the sacramental species of bread and wine remain. The sense of Jesus seems instead to be: "If you eat my flesh and drink my blood, I will be in you not only at that moment, but more. I will dwell in you abidingly—that is, I will live permanently in you as a result of your sacramental nourishment.

Our second reason for this interpretation is the very wording of the verse. It is a description of indwelling. The same St. John who reports the indwelling mystery in his Gospel and in his first epistle uses here the same expression:

> Abide in me and I in you. ... He who *abides in me, and I in him,*
> he bears much fruit. (John 15:4-5)

> He who abides in love *abides in God and God in him.* (1 John 4:16)

> He who eats my flesh and drinks my blood, *abides in me and I in him.* (John 6:54)

It looks very much as though Christ is speaking of the indwelling presence in each case. Further, Christ says that a man cannot live the indwelling mystery if he culpably neglects the Eucharist: "Unless you eat the flesh of the Son of Man and drink his blood, you shall not have life in you" (John 6:57). And again, what is this life? Nothing other than knowing, loving, and enjoying the Trinity. Without the Eucharist, the sacrament of his body and blood given to his Church, the indwelling trinitarian life cannot be otherwise sustained and nourished.

The Joy in the Temple-Soul

Christ gives as the reason for the revelation of the indwelling mystery our mutual delight in God. "These things I have spoken to you that my joy may be in you, and that your joy may be made in full" (John 15:11). We are perhaps not straining the text to see the expression, "that *my* joy may be *in you*," as probably meaning that the very joy of Jesus also indwells—for God is joy just as he is love. In any event, the verse plainly teaches that to have Jesus abiding in the soul through love is a completely delightful situation: "that your joy may be *full*."

St. Peter, too, relates the experience of God within to our mystery:

> Crave as newborn babes, pure spiritual milk, that by it you may grow to salvation; if, indeed, you have tasted that the Lord is sweet. Draw near to him, a living stone, rejected indeed by men but chosen and honored by God. Be yourselves as living stones, built thereon into a spiritual house. (1 Pet. 2:2–5)

According to Peter, neophytes in the faith are to crave for spiritual milk—that is, suitable food for their souls, a reference to both the Word of God and the Eucharist. The Greek word for "if" (*ei*) can mean not only "if" but also "since" or "because." The causal meaning is preferable here, for Peter is saying that since these new Christians have tasted how sweet the Lord is, they are all the more to yearn after him and his truth.

Tasting the goodness of a thing can be done only by the experience of it through some sort of contact, the kind of contact that brings the thing tasted within the taster. Hence, when Peter speaks of the just man as tasting the sweetness of the Lord, he is implying an indwelling experience, a delight found in the Lord within. St. Paul likewise speaks of a similar thought often, drawing on the language of the psalms: "Rejoice *in the Lord* always" (Phil. 4:4; Pss. 33:1; 97:12).

Peter likewise refers directly to the indwelling mystery itself when he speaks of the faithful as "a spiritual house," a clear image of the Temple, the privileged habitation of God in the Old Testament. This concept is closely akin to that of Paul when he refers to the faithful collectively as a Temple: "Do you not know that you are the Temple of God and that the Spirit of God dwells in you?" (1 Cor. 6:19; 2 Cor. 6:16).

So intimate are the interpersonal relations of knowing, loving, and enjoying in the new revelation that the temple-soul belongs to the abiding Trinity in such a way that it no longer belongs to itself.

> Or do you not know that your members are the Temple of the
> Holy Spirit, who is in you, who you have from God, and that
> you are not your own? For you have been bought at a great price.
> Glorify God and bear him in your body. (1 Cor. 6:19–20)

God has purchased this temple-soul by his own blood; it belongs to him
alone as his own delightful dwelling. His love for this soul must be inconceivable
for he has paid an almost incredible price for it. It is his. Yet at the same time, and
even more inconceivably, he is *its* possession. God belongs to man.

Over and over in the New Testament, words are used to describe the divine
inhabitation that imply a bestowal of possession rights. Through the *giving* of the
Spirit, man somehow owns the Spirit and can enjoy the Spirit.

> Therefore, he who rejects these things rejects not man but God,
> who has also *given* his Holy Spirit to us. (1 Thess. 4:8)

> And hope does not disappoint, because the charity of God is
> poured forth in our hearts by the Holy Spirit who has been
> *given* to us. (Rom. 5:5)

> And what agreement has the Temple of God with idols? For you
> are the Temple of the living God, as God says, "I will dwell and
> move among them, I will be their God and they shall be my
> people." (2 Cor. 6:16)

Redemption and Divine Possession

In our third text, St. Paul explicitly connects dwelling with possession. To appreciate fully Paul's idea we should recall the two Old Testament texts he is citing. He
draws on texts from both the Law and the prophets. He cites first Ezekiel, where
God is telling his people that he will make an everlasting covenant of peace with
them, that he will multiply them, and place his sanctuary among them forever.
God then declares through the prophet: "My dwelling shall be with them; I will be
their God and they shall be my people" (Ezek. 37:27). Paul also refers to a text from
Leviticus, in which God is likewise speaking of his covenant, of making his people
numerous, and of establishing his dwelling among them. He continues: "Ever present in your midst, I will be your God and you will be my people" (Lev. 26:12).

Paul sees a connection in each of these texts between God's dwelling among
his people and the mutual possession one of the other. Because God will dwell
with them, he will be theirs and they will be his. Paul amplifies and clarifies the
meaning of the Old Testament revelation. God not only dwells among his people.
He is in them. They are a Temple, a Temple of a God who is not inert, static, weak,
but rather living, dynamic, powerful. They are, therefore, sacred and possessed of
a great dignity.

Moreover, for Paul the soul is sealed with the Spirit, indicating that the possessive union is so close that the divine somehow impresses itself into the human:

> And in him you too, when you had heard the word of truth, the good news of your salvation, and believed in it, were sealed with the Holy Spirit of the promise, who is the pledge of our inheritance, for a *redemption of possession* (*apolytrōsin tēs peripoiēseōs*), for the praise of his glory. (Eph. 1:13–14)

The "redemption of possession" may refer, I believe, to the mutual possession resulting from the donation of the Spirit. God possesses man, as Paul indicates ("You are not your own" 1 Cor. 6:19), as a result of the redemption and divine indwelling. Man, in turn possesses God because the Spirit is given to him (Rom. 5:5). This interpretation fits well with John's description of the result of love: God is in man and man is in God (1 John 4:16).

"For the praise of his glory" indicates the final cause, the motive of the redemption and the mission of the Spirit into the hearts of men. God must be the end of all things, and so the divine habitation is a fact in order that the great goodness and good greatness of God may be honored and loved forever. Such should be the purpose, too, of man's every act, a mandate that flows from the believer's identity as a Temple of God. "Whether you eat or drink or do anything else, do all for the glory of God" (1 Cor. 10:31).

The mutuality of interpersonal intimacy—knowing, loving, enjoying, possessing—leads understandably and beautifully to the concept of inter-indwelling. This doctrine is indeed beautiful, since the interpersonal relationships so implicated in our mystery are mutual—God knows, loves, and enjoys us and we, in turn, know, love, and enjoy him.

Transfiguring Consummation

What we see in the pages of sacred Scripture is the final development or fulfillment of a pattern of an astonishing divine-human intimacy. Though shrouded still in deep mystery, the divine indwelling means interpersonal familiarity and intimacy based on a real inabiding.

And what we have seen is that the new revelation of Jesus Christ must be understood and tasted in the light and savor of the old. If anything at all clearly emerges from our Old Testament study of the Lord God's intentions toward his people, it is precisely this same interpersonal familiarity and intimacy—just a step short, however, of the inter-indwelling made possible by Christ. With the new revelation comes new love, new knowledge, new delight, inter-abiding, familial adoption and mutual possession.

And the New Testament suggests, however briefly, something of the glorious final outcome of divine inhabitation, when the abiding guests shall be seen face to face. We shall rise in glorious bodies patterned after that of Christ himself because of the Spirit abiding within (Rom. 8:11). We are destined to be forever in the presence of the Father and to share in the very trinitarian life. There are many mansions in this house of the Father, and the Son has gone to prepare places for his own, so that where he is they also may be. This Son has already prayed, "Father I want those you have given me to be with me where I am, so that they may always see the glory you have given me." And he has promised that the good and faithful servants will enter into the very joy of their master (John 14:2–3; 17:24; Matt. 25:21).

But this is no ordinary joy. This is an immersion in Beauty, an enthrallment with the Father seen face to face. "Eternal life is this: to know you the only true God, and Jesus Christ whom you have sent" (John 17:3). For the Hebrew, "to know" was no mere intellectual matter. It was a meeting with a person, an encounter. A man "knew" his wife in sexual intercourse. Eternal life is a deep drinking of the beauty of the Lord. But this is, of course, through a knowing, even an intellectual knowing.

> Now we are seeing a dim reflection in a mirror, but then we shall be seeing face to face. The knowledge that I have now is imperfect, but then I shall know as fully as I am known. (1 Cor. 13:12)

> What we are to be in the future has not yet been revealed; all we know is that when it is revealed we shall be like him because we shall see him as he really is. (1 John 3:2)

> The throne of God and the Lamb will be in its place in the city; his servants will worship him; they will see him face to face, and his name will be written on their foreheads. It will never be night again and they will not need lamplight or sunlight, because the Lord God will be shining on them. They will reign forever and ever. (Rev. 22:3–5)

There is no victory like the victory over death, no triumph like the triumph of the resurrection. "Death is swallowed up in victory," shouts St. Paul. "Death, where is your victory? Death where is your sting? ... Let us thank God for giving us the victory through our Lord Jesus Christ" (1 Cor. 15:54–57).

The Temple that we are is to be transfigured in body as well as in soul, that it might become at last a worthy habitation for the divine fire within. The transfiguration of the Temple is modeled after the very pattern of the risen Lord. The risen Lord remains the cornerstone of the spiritual house. This Jesus "will transfigure these wretched bodies of ours into copies of his glorious body" (Phil. 3:21). The transformation of the Temple is a resurrection patterned after that of Christ Jesus.

It is a glorification of our bodies sharing in that of the Lord who, on the mount and in the presence of his disciples was transfigured.

By some mysterious power the abiding Spirit will so transfigure our mortal Temple that it will shed the imperfections of its earthly state and become a worthy eternal habitation of the most sacred God. In the fullest sense we can apply to the transformed elect the praise of the Lord God directed to his people.

> You grew more and more beautiful. ... The fame of your beauty
> spread through the nations, since it was perfect, because I had
> clothed you with my own splendor. (Ezek. 16:13–14).

So marvelous is this final glorification of God's sons that St. Paul presents the material universe as yearning for its completion as we groan in our bodies, waiting to be set free (Rom. 8:19–23).

If the glorification of the earth is the result of its orientation to man, and if the transfiguration of man is due to his immersion in the beauty of indwelling Father, Son, and Holy Spirit, it follows that the final splendor of the whole universe is a consequence of the trinitarian dwelling in man, the pinnacle of visible creation.

Letter & Spirit 4 (2008): 189–207

NOTES

~:~

LIVING STONES IN THE HOUSE OF GOD:
The Temple and the Renewal of Church Architecture

~: Denis R. McNamara :~

The Liturgical Institute, University of Saint Mary of the Lake

Two fundamental biblical concepts still inform our understanding of Catholic liturgical art and architecture: *synagogue* and *temple*.[1] Many recent interpretations of the notion of active participation in the sacred liturgy, however, emphasize the external and communitarian aspects of liturgical participation. Consequently, today's liturgical and architectural establishments are far more comfortable thinking of the church building as synagogue than temple. Liturgical specialists, who have at times even secularized the concept of synagogue and redefined Catholic church buildings as "meeting houses," remain suspicious of the use of Temple language for liturgy and its allied arts.[2] For this reason, the notion of the church building as *domus Dei*, or "house of God," derived from the Temple, has taken a distant back seat to the notion of the building as *domus ecclesiae*, the "house of the Church" or "house of the people of the Church."

The results of this theological imbalance have appeared clearly in much recent liturgical architecture. The formal, polyvalent, public and cultic aspects of liturgical architecture have been diminished in recent years, replaced instead by designs emphasizing the casual, domestic, and intimate. The "real" Church, some claim, is the members of the congregation in whom God now dwells, because the New Testament speaks of God's presence no longer dwelling in a Temple but in the "living stones" of the *ekklesia*.

Some Catholics have interpreted this theology of living stones to mean that church buildings need no longer be sacramental or have any relation to the Temple. At first glance their questions seems reasonable: if God no longer needs animal

---

1 The ideas developed in this essay are are drawn from my forthcoming book *Shadow, Image and Reality: Beauty, the Bible and Catholic Liturgical Architecture* (Chicago: Hillenbrand, 2009).

2 See for instance, Marchita Mauck, *Shaping A House for the Church* (Chicago: Liturgical Training Publications, 1990) and Richard Vosko, *God's House is Our House: Re-imagining the Environment for Worship* (Collegeville, MN: Liturgical Press, 2006). One publisher even named its line of short books on Catholic liturgical architecture the "Meeting House Essays."

sacrifices or desires a temple building limiting his presence to a small room visited once per year, and his presence is found in his people, then what is the need for an elaborate church building? A good Catholic understanding of the topic gives us an answer by bringing us back again to the "both/and" approach to these terms. Simply put, a Catholic church building finds its theological underpinnings in both the synagogue and the Temple, yet ultimately transcends them both to become an image of the heavenly Jerusalem.

A church depends on at least three theological foundations. First, it is a memory and fulfillment of the Temple. Second, it stands as a transformed syna-gogue, a witness to the Christians who gather in a particular place which speaks of the newly-reordered relationship between God and humanity. Lastly, and most · importantly, the art and architecture of a church building are sacraments of a glori-fied heavenly future, revealing to us the beauty of our heavenly destiny, thereby enthusing us for the work of being conformed to Christ. This essay serves as an introduction to the first of these three theological sources, bringing the evidence of God's revelation found in the shadows of the typology to light in order that we might better understand how the Temple theology operative in Scripture and the liturgy can give intellectual roots to the current task of the church architect.

Between Synagogue and Temple

In his classic, *Liturgy and Architecture*, Louis Bouyer argued that the synagogue almost exclusively provided the immediate architectural precedent for the church building. He gave the synagogue a high dignity, arguing that Jews of the late Second Temple era and the early Christians understood the synagogue as more than a classroom; they saw it as a place for the prayerful hearing of Scripture, where its revelations were proclaimed, discussed, and understood. Bouyer argued that the synagogue was always associated with ritual celebration and was "closely connected with the acknowledgement and the cult of a special presence of God" and therefore linked with the Temple of Solomon.[3] Its "seat of Moses," which he argued would eventually be adopted in early Church architecture for the bishop's throne, formed a natural focus of the teaching authority of rabbis who carried on the living tradition.

The synagogue then, Bouyer claimed, provided the obvious model for many early Christian churches; that the word "temple" does not even appear in the index of the original 1967 edition tells us something of Bouyer's interest in the Temple as conceptual model for the church building. The Temple, after all, so closely tied to the old Law, was a place where God's presence was exclusive and limited, and involved the offering of animal sacrifices, which, as the author of the Letter to the Hebrews explicitly stated, were no longer necessary.

---

3   Louis Bouyer, *Liturgy and Architecture* (Notre Dame, IN: University of Notre Dame, 1967), 8–24.

It should not be surprising that we have similar difficulties understanding the Temple in our own day. One could even argue that most Christian denominational divisions about liturgy break on how the continuing role of the Temple is understood. The Old Testament says much more about the Temple than the synagogue, since the latter finds its great period of growth after the destruction of the Temple in the first century. But at first glance, Scripture does seem to set up a certain paradox between the major uses of each building: ritual animal sacrifice and offerings of vocal prayer.

Books like Exodus, Leviticus, and Kings are heavy with minute details of the bloody ritual sacrifices of the Tabernacle and Temple. Yet Psalm 50, Isaiah 1:11, and 1 Samuel 15:22 tell us that God has no need for bullocks and the flesh of animals. Instead, what pleases him are obedience and an upright heart. This tension was evident between the different groups within Judaism that opposed and promoted the Temple worship, and no clear resolution is evident in the Old Testament.

However, as Cardinal Joseph Ratzinger wrote in *The Spirit of the Liturgy*, the solution to this seeming contradiction is found in the person of Jesus Christ, who reconciles the differing strands of Judaism by being the *Logos incarnatus*, the Word made flesh. [4] In Christ, the Word and the sacrificial victim are brought together into one, and so the Eucharistic Prayer spoken at every Mass is in fact a sacrifice of praise, the praise of God by people with upright hearts offering the one sacrifice of Christ to the Father.

"Here at last is right worship," according to Ratzinger, a real sacrifice offered in spirit and truth. He laments that modern theological discussion has made the synagogue the "exclusive model for the liturgy of the new covenant ... in strict opposition to the Temple which is regarded as an expression of the Law and therefore as an utterly obsolete 'stage' in religion." The result, he argues, has been "disastrous," because the notions of priesthood and sacrifice "are no longer intelligible" therefore making the "comprehensive 'fulfillment' of pre-Christian salvation history and the inner unity of the two testaments disappear from view."[5]

History in the Ages of Shadow, Image, and Reality

Ratzinger brings the various strands of Old Testament, New Testament and eschatological thought together by using the patristic concept of *shadow, image,* and *reality,* a trio of words which serves as a handy interpretive guide for the large meta-narrative of salvation history.[6] The term "shadow" applies to the Old Testament's preparation through typological precursors, while "reality" speaks of the time when God's restoration of his creation will be complete and all will enjoy heavenly glory. By contrast, our earthly sacramental worship happens in a time of

---

4   Cardinal Joseph Ratzinger, *Spirit of the Liturgy* (San Francisco: Ignatius, 2000), 47.

5   Ratzinger, *The Spirit of the Liturgy,* 49.

6   Ratzinger, *The Spirit of the Liturgy,* 54.

the *image*, a sacramental participation in reality which is something between the Old Testament shadow and unmediated participation in the things of heaven.

In the Jerusalem Temple, God gave the chosen people a shadow of the Christ who was to come. Our time, the time of the New Testament, is a time of dawn. The rising sun proves to us that the darkness is vanquished but has not yet reached its zenith, just as creation still awaits full divinization.[7] In this understanding, Christ's victory over sin and death is real and operative— the veil separating heaven and earth is torn, and grace flows freely even as the pilgrim Church journeys toward full attainment of its goal. Today, in the sacramental worship of the Church, humanity is given the image of a glorious heavenly future as an efficacious means of full, conscious, active, and fruitful participation in the earthly liturgy's foretaste of the reality of heaven.

The image like the shadow "is only mediated through the signs of salvation," Ratzinger claims, and therefore "we need mediation," because as yet, "we do not see the Lord 'as he is.'"[8] So here we find the essence of the "already but not yet" nature of the time of image and its architectural theology.[9] Mediating signs and symbols provide the means by which "we learn to see" heaven's openness. These signs and symbols are the vehicle through which we "know the mystery of God in the pierced heart of the crucified."

In other words, we participate in the heavenly liturgy, not in shadow as in the Old Testament, nor fully as we will the end of time, but in a sort of "in-between" pilgrimage in which heavenly things are mediated in the very material of this earth. Christ's "once for all" is accomplished, but the heavenly Jerusalem is still under construction as salvation history continues to unfold toward completion.

"Christ is being brought to fulfillment in his Church ... and all of us contribute to its fulfillment ... which will reach completion only on judgment day."[10] Here the ministerial role of the liturgical artist and architect finds it greatest dignity. The work of the liturgical architect becomes *a part of the process in making God "all in all" by showing us what our glorified future looks like.*[11] The Temple, whose characteristics in size, proportion, and ornament are revealed in Scripture by God himself, form an essential part of this understanding.

This rich layering of meanings in liturgical architecture has found rather little consideration since the Second Vatican Council, which grew out of the twen-

---

7   Ratzinger, *The Spirit of the Liturgy*, 54.

8   Ratzinger, *The Spirit of the Liturgy*, 60.

9   Jean Corbon, *Wellspring of Worship* (San Francisco: Ignatius, 2005), 77–78.

10   St. John Eudes, *Treatise on the Kingdom of Jesus*, 3–4, in *The Liturgy of the Hours According to the Roman Rite*, The Divine Office, 4 vols., (New York: Catholic Book Publishing, 1975). 4:559–560. In order to preserve the living connection between Scripture, liturgy and scholarship, I am citing patristic readings found in the Church's official prayer, the Divine Office, also known as the Liturgy of the Hours.

11   Compare 1 Cor. 15:28.

tieth-century liturgical movement's desire to rebalance the relationship between Word and Eucharist, synagogue and Temple, and between priest, rite and people. However, as often happens, certain exaggerations arose which tended to see the church as a de-sacralized synagogue which was commonly called a "meeting house" or the "skin for liturgical action." A faulty antiquarian mindset often lead to the substitution of a domestic model of architecture for the notion of church building as an evocation of the synagogue, the Temple, and the Heavenly Jerusalem. Glory was replaced by earthiness and anticipated eschatology by a supposed sincerity and commonness.

A crucial notion to understanding the relationship between the Temple and today's church building remains: we do not imitate the Temple today because the Temple in itself was glorious. To do so would be like returning to animal sacrifice because it was dramatic. We look to the lessons of the Temple because it gave us a foreshadowing knowledge of heavenly glory. Today's church building shows us the Temple fulfilled and transfigured as the heavenly Jerusalem, and is as different from the Temple as the Mass is from the sacrifice of bulls. Nonetheless, understanding biblical typologies gives us an insight into the very reality we celebrate now, so unveiling the mysteries of the Temple can help us recover new aspects of a theology of liturgical architecture which is deep, rich, and rooted in biblical promises.

Salvation History and the Preparation for Divine Friendship

The Temple, of course, rightly finds its place in salvation history. Though the Fall brought about a rupture in God's relationship with creation, in his mercy and love he desired to restore all to himself. The Old Testament chronicles God's free and gracious attempts to call his people back to himself, making covenants and promises so that God might be once again "all in all" (1 Cor. 15:28).

In the well-known narrative, God intervenes with Abraham, Moses, and Jacob. In a high point of the salvation story, God gives Moses the Ten Commandments, revealing how he wants his people to live. More than the stern dictates of a tyrannical God, the commandments were a merciful revelation, a loving disclosure of his own inner logic about how to restore divine order to the world. A world without false gods, theft, adultery, covetousness, false witness, and so on is a world which more closely resembles its original state and is therefore more like what God intends it to be. In this light, St. Irenaeus could rightly say that the Ten Commandments "prepared man for friendship" with God and harmony with his neighbor, and thereby "raised man to glory because it gave man friendship with God."[12]

But after teaching man how to act, God teaches him how to worship, telling Moses to build his desert Tabernacle (Exod. 25–39), and David and Solomon how

---

12   St. Irenaeus, *Treatise Against Heresies*, Bk. 4, Chap. 14, 2–3, in *The Liturgy of the Hours*, Office of Readings, Wednesday in the Second Week of Lent, 2:177–178.

to build the great Temple in Jerusalem (1 Kings 5; 2 Sam. 7). In each case, God's presence with his people moves more and more toward inwardness: from things such as burning bushes to persons such as Moses; from fleeting moments in the desert to sustained presence in the Temple; from simple presence of action to the joy and peace of communion.[13] Even in the time of shadow, the process of undoing the Fall is begun as God leads Israel back to himself. Despite the disobedience and chastisements of the chosen people, God's self-revelation continues in preparation for a high point of salvation history: the incarnation. In the incarnation, a God who was distant and veiled becomes yet more imminent and legible by taking human form. In Christ, God speaks in a language humans understand from a human-divine mouth to humanity's natural ears. In making God present in his very body, Christ becomes the new Temple, and in sharing his presence through the sending of the Spirit, the Church becomes incorporated into this same Temple as a Mystical Body with Christ as its head.

Christ promises a glorious heavenly future where God is all in all, later revealed in apocalyptic terms to St. John in the Book of Revelation. Art and architecture feature prominently in this divine project of salvation history—not as a human adjunct to some gossamer spiritual plan, but with hard and fast architectural directions given by God himself. After the Fall, Scripture reveals a three-part narrative. First, in the Old Testament, the Temple and city of Jerusalem establish an image of God's presence with humanity that prepares the world for the coming of Christ. Second, Christ comes at the incarnation to form the Christian community into a Temple of "living stones." This "Temple," in the age of the Church, is made in the image of Christ's Mystical Body. Though it remains bound to the fallen world, it works with and reveals God's grace, slowly restoring the world to the fullness of what God wants it to be. Third, at the end of earthly time, the new heaven and new earth show God's complete indwelling and reunification of himself with his creation. In each case, the notions of sacrifice and presence remain. Yves Congar called the mystery of the Temple an episode in the story of God's "ever more generous, ever deeper presence among his creatures."[14] This story continues today, and therefore the Temple still has lessons to teach.

Enthroned on the Mercy Seat

In the beginning, God met Adam and Eve in the garden, which was the place of God's presence and therefore the primordial Temple. After the Fall, God's presence manifests itself in different ways, from the burning bush (Exod. 3:2) to the fire, cloud, and thunder of Mount Sinai (Exod. 19:16). But these appearances would eventually become more frequent and of greater intimacy, and to allow for this,

---

13   See Yves Congar, *Mystery of the Temple: The Manner of God's Presence to his Creatures from Genesis to the Apocalypse* (Westminster, MD: Newman, 1962), xi.

14   Congar, *The Mystery of the Temple*, x.

God instructs Moses to build the Tabernacle in the desert. This Tabernacle was a semi-permanent tent-like structure which could be taken down and moved, and formed the first of the shadowy revelations of Temple theology.

Much of the Book of Exodus is filled with painstaking detail as to how it should be built. Different materials for the tent-like fabric were specified for different sections, with special mixtures of colored wool and linen, acacia wood, gems, and clasps of bronze, silver and gold. The three segments of the building's design were directed by God to have specific proportions, with the last two separated by an elaborately woven veil which included images of cherubim.

The rarest and most precious materials were reserved for the cube-shaped inner room called the most holy place or Holy of Holies, the home of the Ark of the Covenant atop of which God's presence, the *Shekinah*, settled down in the form of a cloud. A cedar box covered in gold, the Ark served as a container for a jar with manna from the desert (Exod. 16:33), Aaron's staff which had miraculously flowered into almond blossoms (Num. 17:8), and the tablets of the Ten Commandments. Guarding the Ark were gold-covered statues of cherubim.

Though Jewish traditions differ as to some of the details of the Ark and its ornamentation (one calls it God's footstool while another calls it God's throne, for example), it marked the place of God's dwelling and presence, and gives us one of God's names: "the one enthroned between the cherubim" (Isa. 37:16). Later called by Luther the "mercy seat," this area atop the Ark is known as the *kapporeth*, a Hebrew word with a double meaning; it is both a literal cover, as it was for the physical Ark, but also something which covered, in the sense of "cleansing" or "wiping out." For this reason, the *kapporeth* is sometimes called the propitiatory or place of atonement, because the presence of God is holy and wipes out the guilt of sin. In the time of shadow, the area atop the Ark was the throne of God on earth. All of this finds it completion in the reality of the eschaton, prefiguring the Book of Revelation's description of the throne in heaven upon which the one was seated and surrounded by angels (Rev. 4:2).

In Moses' Tabernacle, God directed that the High Priest wear an *ephod*, a colorful embroidered vestment. Moreover, the High Priest was directed to wear a breastplate in which were set twelve gemstones in four rows of three: sard, topaz, emerald; garnet, sapphire, diamond; hyacinth, ruby, amethyst; beryl, carnelian, jasper. These stones represented the twelve tribes of Israel—that is, all of humanity—being brought into the presence of God for transformation.

In the time of shadow, these mute stones were simply minerals of exceptional light and color, but would eventually be understood as prefiguring the "living stones" of the Christian era of grace. Later, the reality of heaven itself would be described in similar terms; the walls of the heavenly Jerusalem are described symbolically in the Book of Revelation as being composed of these twelve gemstones, meaning that the city is composed of God's redeemed and fulfilled creation. In the time of reality, God has filled all with his presence, bringing everything together in radiant ordered harmony. The heavenly city, then, is the completion and perfection of the shadowy Temple typology, and it is precisely this glorious heavenly future that today's liturgical art and architecture are called upon to make present. The texts of Vatican II remind us that liturgical art and architecture should be "worthy, becoming and beautiful, signs and symbols of *heavenly realities*."[15]

A Theology of the Covenant in "Built Form"

The Tabernacle can be understood as a precursor for the permanent Temple built by Solomon in the tenth century B.C. After a period of relative peace and stability in Jerusalem, the construction of Solomon's Temple grew from the sudden realization by King David of a breach in architectural decorum. After building himself a house of stone and cedar (2 Sam. 5:11), David suddenly realized that the Ark of the Covenant where God dwelled was still housed in a tent like that in the time of Moses.

David says to the prophet Nathan: "I am living in a house of cedar, but the ark of God stays in a tent" (2 Sam. 7:1). Later, the Lord visits David and encourages him in this thinking, saying: "Are you the one to build me a house to live in? … I have been moving about in a tent and a tabernacle" (2 Sam. 7:5–6). This problem of decorum occurs later in Scripture with the rebuilding of the second Temple under the auspices of the Persian King Darius. When facing resistance to the reconstruction of the Temple after its destruction by the Babylonians in 586 B.C., the Lord spoke through the prophet Haggai saying: "Is it a time for you yourselves to be living in your paneled houses, while this house remains a ruin?" (Hag. 1:3). This lesson in architectural hierarchy remains potent throughout salvation history and becomes a formative notion in our own day for the building of churches.

Though David collected money and materials for the Temple, it fell to his son Solomon to actually build it.[16] Despite the differing takes on the building of the Temple in 1 Kings and 2 Chronicles, the directions for building the Temple are quite specific, and the Scriptures describe these instructions as coming directly from God. The Temple of Solomon bears a formal similarity to the Tabernacle of Moses, being made up of three parts. The porch or *ulam*, opened to the *hekal* or holy place, a large rectangular interior room decorated with gold, palm trees, and flowers. The most sacred precinct was the Holy of Holies (the *debir* or most holy place), a cube-shaped room of 20 cubits on each side paneled in gold-covered cedar in which was placed the Ark of the Covenant and its attendant cherubim.

---

15 Second Vatican Council, *Sacrosanctum Concilium*, Constitution on the Sacred Liturgy (December 4, 1963), 122, in *The Documents of Vatican II*, ed. Walter M. Abbot (Chicago: Follett, 1966), 174. Emphasis added.

16 Solomon himself would later be seen as a type of Christ, since Christ, the "Son of David," builds the Temple of his body, the Church.

The *hekal* and the *debir* prove most important for the study of contemporary church architecture because, along with Noah's Ark, they represent the earliest use of architectural typologies in salvation history; hence they provide the theological foundation for buildings which would follow. They can also help today's architects understand that church buildings come with a revealed and developed intellectual pre-history that can determine the theological ideas that should go into designing a new church. The Temple is not simply a now-defunct building of the Old Testament, but a window into how a loving God desired—and we might even say required—a theology of the covenant in built form.

Israel and the Temple in the Divine Plan

After centuries of theological and historical preparation, Solomon's Temple became the preeminent place of contact with God and surety of his presence. Though there had been many smaller Temples in the region, under King Solomon these buildings were ordered to be destroyed, and the Temple of Jerusalem increased greatly in importance. What had been one Temple among many became central and now also royal. Here the twelve tribes of Israel, divided and scattered, found the possibility of a natural focus. The process of unification which runs through God's mission of salvation here finds it precursors in location, liturgy, government, and architecture.

Once per year in the well-known ritual for the Feast of the Atonement, the Jewish High Priest passed through the Temple porch and larger interior room, and then entered the Holy of Holies. He brought the blood of animals to sprinkle and atone for his own sins, thereby making him worthy to act as intercessor for the people. Bringing the prayers of praise and petitions of the people to God, he entered into God's presence in the Holy of Holies amidst dense clouds of incense, then returned with the animal blood, pouring and sprinkling it and thereby bringing God's blessing. Because it had been brought into God's presence in the Holy of Holies, it was considered transformed because "the presence of God is holy and confers holiness."[17]

David had placed the Temple atop Mount Moriah in Jerusalem, now more often called the Temple Mount. Though much of the information about the historical setting of the Temple remains obscured by the lack of archaeological work on its site, the symbolic importance of the location would not have been lost on Jewish and early Christian thinkers. Every aspect of God's intervention in the life of his people was considered part of the divine plan to return his lost people to himself by revealing himself in symbolic form.

The location of the Temple in the heart of David's city was already charged with meaning based on important events believed to have occurred there. Scripture tells us that the Lord was displeased with David's plan, incited by Satan, to count

---

17   Congar, *The Mystery of the Temple*, 16.

the people of Israel while leaving out the tribes of Levi and Benjamin in the numbering (1 Chron. 21). David was standing by the threshing floor of Ornan the Jebusite when he suddenly saw a vision of an angel threatening to destroy the city. Because David and the elders repented, the Lord ultimately relented and destruction was averted. Averting the judgment of God would become a critical Christian motif, where Christ becomes the victim offered in humanity's place. The stone on the threshing floor is said to have become the location for the construction of an altar and eventually the Holy of Holies of the Temple itself.

But the stone of the threshing floor was already layered with meaning. It was understood as the site of Abraham's offering of his son Isaac, the place from where the waters of Noah's flood welled up, and the spot where Jacob's dream and vision of heaven took place.[18] The Temple's location was therefore overlaid with symbolic meaning useful to Israel and later to Christianity: each was a precursor of the Messiah. On this spot Abraham prefigured Christ by offering his own beloved son. Jacob's dream showed the ladder by which angels traveled between heaven and earth, making the things of heaven knowable to humanity. The floodwaters of Noah represented chaos and evil, and the rock which capped them revealed God's power to keep evil in check, as evidenced by the repeated mention in the psalms of the Lord as rock of salvation, controlling the waters. As such, the Lord could control the chaos of sin brought about by the Fall and initiate his plan of salvation.

It goes without saying that building the Temple was a large and costly operation. It meant coordinating the movements of people and gathering materials from all around the known world. It required everything that the earth and humanity could offer: stone, timber, gold, silver, bronze, copper, iron, linen, dyes, and wool. It also required human effort and cooperation: quarrying, log-cutting, mining, linen making, dyeing, weaving, carving, transport and so on. It also made necessary international cooperation: cedar from Lebanon, architects and bronze founders from Tyre, and Phoenician transport ships.

The directions for the plan, fittings and furnishings of the Temple were quite specific, and Margaret Barker reminds us that "Israel herself remembered that the Temple in all its detail was part of the divine plan, revealed, along with the commandments, on Sinai."[19] The specific attributes of the Temple, then, were not to be changed arbitrarily. They revealed something specific about God and his plan for salvation. In a symbolic reading, building the Temple meant taking inert matter from around the earth and shaping it through the use of intellect, will and God's revelation to join an almost unimaginable number of individual parts into an ordered whole in which God would dwell. Here again is the typology of the

---

18   Margaret Barker, *The Gate of Heaven: The History and Symbolism of the Temple in Jerusalem* (London: SPCK, 1991), 19.

19   Barker, *The Gate of Heaven*, 17.

later Mystical Body of Christ or "God's building" (1 Cor. 3:9) and the heavenly city of Jerusalem. At the heart of the Christian revelation is the notion that many will become one, formed into the image of Christ who is the image of the Father and where He dwells. Since many nations were called upon to build the Temple and all of Israel was called to worship there, the Temple prefigured that time when all nations would be called back to God.

The Heavenly Garden and the Mountain of the Lord

One of the great Temple images is that of the garden. Quite simply, the *hekal* of "the Temple interior was a garden representing the heavenly garden on the mountain of God, the original Garden of Eden."[20] Genesis tells that the original garden contained the Tree of Life, the Tree of the Knowledge of Good and Evil, as well as other trees which were "pleasant to the sight and good for food," revealing that there once existed an original state of order, peace, fertility, and right relationship with God.

When our first parents defied the wishes of God and ate of the Tree of the Knowledge of Good and Evil, this right order was disrupted, and the Lord ordered Adam and Eve forth from the garden. He sent the aforementioned cherubim to place a flaming sword to guard the gate to prevent their return. This sword became a potent image of the separation of man from full union with God, and St. Gregory the Great would later write that the "sacred blood of Christ has quenched the flaming sword that barred access to the Tree of Life. The Christian people are invited to share the riches of Paradise."[21] This new access to Paradise occurred fully in Christ, but even in the Temple the typological preparation for this reality was already at work.

The understanding of the Temple as garden is not hard to fathom; the biblical description of the Temple's interior is full of vegetal forms. The cedar within the *hekal* "was carved in the form of gourds and open flowers" (1 Kings 6:18), and received "carved figures of cherubim and palm trees and open flowers, in the inner and outer rooms" covered in gold (1 Kings 6:29). Since the instruction for building the Temple is to be understood as revelation and not merely as some sort of arbitrary interior decoration, the precision of the detail given in the Scriptures meant that this architecture would reveal something specific which could not be changed without damage to God's disclosure. In this way, it was more than a neutral skin for cultic action merely intended to keep out the weather. As God's "house," it prefigured where God would dwell, becoming a revelation of his heavenly dwelling and how it would be opened to humanity once again. It also became an image

---

20 Barker, *The Gate of Heaven*, 27.

21 St. Leo the Great, *Sermon* 15:3–4, in *The Liturgy of the Hours*, Thursday of the Fourth Week of Lent, 2:313–314.

with a multiplicity of meaning that the word "house" implies: family dynasty, royal lineage, and kingdom.

A symbolic reading of this garden-like ornament provides the key to understanding this artistic command of God: in his desire to reunite himself with his creation, God has here invited humanity back into a glorified Garden of Eden. This time, the creature goes past the cherubim carved in the doors, recalling the same cherubim which had formerly prevented Adam and Eve's return to the Tree of Life. Now humanity, represented by the Jewish priests, walked around with the angels in the garden as an image of a restored earth, making things appear to "be" again what they once were.

In one sense, then, the *hekal* or Holy Place serves as a memory of the original Garden of Eden in which God "walked" with our first parents without the necessity of a Temple. The Temple's *hekal* is a recall, but a "shadowy" preparation for the time when the restoration brought about in Christ would be real and effective. That time is now in the age of the Church. The garden room of the Temple, the holy place, finds its fulfillment in the nave of today's church, a place of invitation back into right relationship with God.

Passing Beyond the Veil

In Solomon's Temple, the Ark of the Covenant found a permanent home. It rested in the *debir* or Holy of Holies, a cube-shaped room in the rear of the Temple. Separating the *debir* from the *hekal* was the great veil. This extravagantly rendered tapestry literally obscured the view between the two rooms, but was understood symbolically to represent all that separated heaven and earth. In order to enter the Holy of Holies and be in God's presence on the Feast of the Atonement, the earthly High Priest literally had to *pass beyond the veil*, giving us to this day the allegorical phrase used to describe a person leaving this world at death. As Barker has written:

> [The] *hekal* represented the earth and the *debir* the heavens; between them was the veil which separated the holy place from the most holy (Exod. 26:33). The veil represented the boundary between the visible world and the invisible, between time and eternity. Actions performed within the veil were not of this world but were part of the heavenly liturgy. Those who passed through the veil were the mediators, divine and human, who functioned in both worlds bringing the prayers and penitence of the people to God and the blessing and presence of God to his people.[22]

---

22   Barker, *The Gate of Heaven*, 105.

Composed of wool and linen, it was woven from blue, purple and crimson threads in a description quite similar to those given to Moses for his desert tabernacle (2 Chron. 3:14; Exod. 26:31–33). Presumably, like at the Tabernacle of Moses, the veil also had images of the cherubim woven into it, again suggesting those angelic guards of the garden.

The veil was immense, estimated to have been composed of 200 square meters of wool and linen. Because it was sprinkled with blood, it needed to be washed frequently and it was reported that 300 priests were needed to immerse it. The Mishnah tells that 82 young women were necessary to weave each of the two veils made every year.[23] The need for observant Jewish women to be constantly busy weaving new veils has given us the iconic tradition of the Virgin Mary doing needlework when Gabriel appeared to her at the Annunciation.[24] The weaving the veil signifies the Virgin's role as *Theotokos*, the God-bearer who "wove" the presence of God in her own womb. Like the actual veil in the Temple, the Christ woven in her body both revealed and concealed the presence of God.

The first-century Jewish historian Josephus, who lived at the time of King Herod's Temple, believed the veil served as a symbol of the cosmos. The scarlet color suggested fire, he said, the linen represented the earth, blue the air, and purple the sea (as the blood of fish joined to the blue of the waters).[25] Moreover, Josephus tells that the veil "had also embroidered on it all that was mystical in the heavens."[26] Elsewhere, Josephus wrote that the veil of Moses' desert Tabernacle, which would likely have served as a carefully respected model for the Temple veil, was "made in way of imitation and representation of the universe."[27]

Writing in the first century, the Greek-speaking Jewish philosopher, Philo of Alexandria, described the veil as "woven of such and so many things as the world was made of, [being] the universal Temple which [existed] before the holy Temple."[28] Like the garden of the holy place which presented a new earth, the veil symbolized that all of creation had been brought to divine worship, including the

---

23 Barker, *The Gate of Heaven*, 106.

24 *The Book of James*, Chap. 9. An apocryphal gospel probably written in the second century, *The Book of James* is sometimes also known as the *Protoevangelion*, and was mentioned by Origen. Though not given the weight of Scripture, this document has proven greatly influential over the centuries. It relates that the Virgin Mary, who had been educated at the Temple, was chosen by the High Priest to work the scarlet and purple threads when the angel Gabriel appeared to her to announce that she was to bear Christ. See *The Ante-Nicene Fathers*, vol. 8, eds. Alexander Roberts and James Donaldson (Peabody, MA: Hendrickson, 2004), 361–367.

25 Barker, 109. See also Josephus, *Antiquities of the Jews*, Bk. 3, Chap. 6; Bk. 3, Chap. 7, in *The Works of Josephus*, trans. William Whiston, (Peabody, MA: Hendrickson Publishers, 1994), 85–88; 88–91.

26 Josephus, *The Wars of the Jews*, Bk. 5, Chap. 5, in *The Works of Josephus*, 705–709.

27 Josephus, *The Antiquities of the Jews*, Bk. 3, Chap. 7, in *The Works of Josephus*, 88–91.

28 Barker, *The Gate of Heaven*, 109, citing Philo of Alexandria, *Questions and Answers on Exodus*, 2:85.

sea and the heavens. Similarly, Josephus writes that the seven branched candlestick in the Temple represented the 7 known planets.[29]

Interestingly, when entering the garden-like *hekal*, the High Priest wore a garment of materials similar to the veil, symbolically enrobing himself in all of creation and bringing it into the presence of God. Exodus 28 describes these priestly garments of the desert Tabernacle made of blue, purple and scarlet threads. Josephus described the robes of the priests in Moses' tabernacle as being symbolically composed of all creation as well. The vestment was also described as "being like lightning in its pomegranates," with bells sewn on that were said to represent thunder.

Semi-precious stones called sardonyxes were attached to the shoulders of the High Priest's *ephod*, which Josephus tells us were emblematic of the sun and the moon.[30] Each of the twelve gems of the High Priest's breastplate were carved with the name of one of the sons of Israel, described in Exodus as being "like a signet" and each engraved "for the twelve tribes" (Exod. 28:17–21). Josephus' commentary on the priestly garments in the Temple of Solomon reveals that they were similar to those of the Tabernacle.[31] In the time of shadow, the earthly High Priest obediently followed the Law in this ritual, but as is evident in the Letter to the Hebrews, Christians would later see Christ as the true (or better yet, the "real") High Priest who took on human nature, entering the real Holy of Holies in heaven, tearing the veil and bringing heaven and earth together.

In the time of image, we see all of this Temple symbolism as the bringing of creation back to God to be made complete once again in the process of the "undoing" of the Fall. The twelve stones symbolized the twelve tribes of Israel (and therefore all of humanity), the fabrics the four basic elements of the world, the power of lightning and thunder the majesty of God, and even the sardonyxes as the sun and the moon. Writing in the late second century, St. Clement of Alexandria saw a mystic meaning in the Tabernacle and its furniture, echoing Josephus's explanation of the four colors of the woven threads. He called the garment of the High Priest the "symbol of the world of sense," which prophesied Christ's "ministry in the flesh" in which he took on the matter of the universe in order to return it to God for transformation.[32] Bringing creation to God meant that God could therefore offer it back divinized and ordered, blessed by his presence.

Interestingly, though, the High Priest removed his outer garment and wore only white linen robes into the heavenly *debir*. "In the *debir* he no longer represented the created world, but was deemed one of the heavenly entourage. The white linen garment was the dress of the angels, given to favored human beings upon their as-

---

29   Josephus, *The Antiquities of the Jews*, Bk. 3, Chap. 7, in *The Works of Josephus*, 88–91.

30   Josephus, *Antiquities of the Jews*, Bk. 3, Chap. 7, in *The Works of Josephus*, 88–91.

31   Josephus, *Wars of the Jews*, Bk. 5, Chap. 5, in *The Works of Josephus*, 705–709.

32   Clement of Alexandria, *Stromata*, Bk. 5, Chap. 6, in *The Ante-Nicene Fathers*, vol. 2, eds. Alexander Roberts and James Donaldson (Peabody, MA: Hendrickson, 2004), 452–453.

cent to heaven."[33] Clement of Alexandria deciphers this linen garment as evidence of the High Priest's purified ascent to a more heavenly state, a precursor of the "bright array of glory" of the "ineffable inheritance of that spiritual and perfect man" after becoming "son and friend" of God once again.[34]

Like today's altar servers who wear white albs because they enter into the sanctuary of a church building, the High Priest joined the white-robed heavenly beings by crossing the veil and entering the Holy of Holies, into the presence of God. Just as the Jewish High Priest brought all of creation and all of humanity to God, so today's priest, who acts as Christ, brings all of creation to the Father, wearing above his white alb the vestments of color, gold, embroidered flowers and saints, speaking on behalf of all present and the entire world. He does this by walking through the modern-day *hekal* which we call the nave, and then enters into our sacramental image of the *debir*, the sanctuary.

The High Priest in the Holy of Holies

The Holy of Holies, or the *debir*, was the innermost region of the Temple building, a cube-shaped room in which God chose to dwell and which made present in earthly time and space the timelessness and spacelessness of heaven. Here was placed the Ark of the Covenant which had been carried around with the desert Tabernacle since the time of Moses, though by the time of Christ, the Second Temple enlarged by Herod no longer contained the Ark, since it had disappeared after the time of the Babylonian captivity.

God's directions for building the Holy of Holies in both the desert Tabernacle and Solomon's Temple insisted that the proportion of the twenty cubits on each side be maintained. In the Book of Revelation, heaven itself would be described to St. John as cubic in shape as well, revealing something of the "shape" or nature of God. This understanding of the cube as a heavenly shape again comes through in the writings of Josephus, who says that the area within the cubic Holy of Holies in Moses' tabernacle was "a heaven peculiar to God."[35]

Medieval theoreticians of numbers sometimes described the Son as the square of the Father, since as the perfect image of the Father, Christ could be understood as a multiplication of him.[36] Taking this idea further and continuing the process with the Holy Spirit, one might see the nature of God as having simi-

---

33 Barker, *The Gate of Heaven*, 113.

34 Clement, *Stromata*, Bk. 5, Chap. 6, in *The Ante-Nicene Fathers*, 2:452–53.

35 Josephus, *Antiquities of the Jews*, Bk. 3, Chap. 6, in *Works of Josephus*, 85–88.

36 See Otto von Simson, *The Gothic Cathedral* (New York: Harper and Row, 1962), 27, citing Thierry of Chartres' quest to explain the Trinity through geometrical hypotheses: "Thierry recalls that Plato, 'like his master Pythagoras,' identified the metaphysical principles of monad and dyad with God and matter, respectively. God is the supreme unity, and the Son the unity begotten by unity, as the square results from a multiplication of a magnitude with itself. Rightly, Thierry concludes, is the Second Person of the Trinity therefore called the first square."

larities with the cube as a qualitative ratio. The number of persons of the Trinity total three when added, thereby maintaining threeness, yet, when cubed (1 x 1 x 1 or 1³), the number "one" still remains one. Though it would take the Christian revelation to make this Trinitarian numerology more fully understood, the shape of heaven was clearly associated with the cube, which was itself associated with God, and this typology served for later interpretation in the Book of Revelation.

But in ancient Jerusalem, to enter this cubic room in the Temple and step into the presence of God was *to be made holy*. Here the High Priest entered to perform the atonement rites, sprinkling blood from a slaughtered animal and then exiting the Holy of Holies to pour the blood on the altar in the *hekal*. This atonement ritual signaled God's pledge of fidelity to his covenants with his people and the spreading of his divine life from his heavenly throne to earthly reality. This bloody ritual seems so foreign to modern sensibilities, but it was a typological precursor of the coming of Christ, the true High Priest. As Robert Barron has written, the earthly High Priest "was acting as the mediator between divinity and humanity, a priest offering sacrifice on behalf of the people and, strangely enough, on behalf of Yahweh himself. In the process, he was making symbolically real the restoration of creation according to God's intentions."[37]

This role of earthly High Priest as mediator who passes beyond the veil into heaven, pleads for his people, and returns with the blessings and divine life of God was understood by the earliest Christians as a preparation for the coming of the true High Priest, Jesus Christ. Christ bridged the great divide between heaven and earth, tearing the veil which separated them, and allowing the sacramental flow of divine life to gush to his creation, causing it to become divinized and restored to full unity with its creator. When Christ came as the true High Priest, he did not enter into a mere shadowy copy of heaven as did the human High Priest. He entered into the reality of heaven itself in the supreme atonement, returning with the blessings of God's presence in a more efficacious form. The author of the Letter to the Hebrews understood this symbolic reality:

> … when Christ came as a High Priest of the good things that have come, then through the greater and perfect tent … he entered once and for all into the holy place, not with the blood of goats and calves, but with his own blood, thus obtaining eternal redemption. … For Christ did not enter a sanctuary made by human hands, a mere copy of the true one, but he entered into heaven itself, now to appear in the presence on our behalf. (Heb. 9:11–12, 24)

This reality is made present again in Catholic liturgy today as it recalls the Temple liturgy. The priest reenacts, or more accurately, reveals by making present,

---

37   Robert E. Barron, *The Eucharist* (New York: Orbis, forthcoming 2008).

the actions of Christ himself, making the eternal reality of Christ's intercession at the right hand of the Father knowable to our senses. In a great continuity with the Jewish tradition, today's Catholic priest sacramentally re-presents the reality of Christ as heavenly intercessor, and only secondarily serves as the recall of the Jewish High Priest. Since Christ did not come to abolish the Law, but to fulfill it, the old Law of the Temple is not erased, but continues in a way entirely transformed by Christ for our own day. Similarly, the church building fulfills the Temple typologies as well, not as a shadowy copy of the true Holy of Holies, but as an image of the reality of heaven in true participation.

In the Book of Revelation, the angel shows John an image of the Church, saying "Come, I will show you the bride, the wife of the Lamb" (Rev. 21:9). This fully divinized Church is then described as being cubic in shape and now *composed of* twelve gems similar to those found on the breastplate of the high priest (Rev. 21:16). The living stones of the earthly Church, then, become completely transformed to be the radiant gems of the heavenly city, God's building completely restored and filled with divine life. Our earthly church building is intended to show this reality now by way of foretaste.

In symbolic language, this bride, the Church, is a *polis* made up of the twelve tribes—now all of humanity—having been fully conformed to the "shape" or image of God, joyfully and peacefully taking their places as destined for them. When speaking of heaven, the seventh- or eight-century hymn, *Urbs Beata Jerusalem* ("Blessed City of Jerusalem"), still used in the Church's liturgy at the dedication of a church, says that "its stones are fashioned by many a stroke and blow of the Savior-mason's hammer and chisel. Thus shaped they go to the making of this mighty structure, each being fitly joined to each and finding its appointed place in the whole building."[38]

Read in this light, Josephus' description of the Temple stands pregnant with theological content waiting for Christian fulfillment: "[T]he whole structure of the Temple was made, with great skill, of polished stones, and those laid together so very harmoniously and smoothly ... that the agreement of one part with another seemed rather to have been natural."[39] This imagery of the many coming together as one, undoing the divisions of the Fall, becoming again "as it was in the beginning," is symbolized to this day in our church buildings, where many stones come together to form the place not only where God's presence dwells, but to show what the heavenly reality might be like.

In a similar way, the churches we build and the images we put in them are not an unnecessary clinging to the things of worship before Christ. Because architecture is the built form of ideas, it recalls the buildings and events of the Old

---

38   Translation taken from *The Hours of the Divine Office in English and Latin*, vol. 2 (Collegeville, MN: Liturgical Press, 1964), 922.

39   Josephus, *The Antiquities of the Jews*, Bk. 8, Chap. 3, in *The Works of Josephus*, 216–218.

Testament. However, it presents them to us today in a completely transformed manner. This is fitting for us, as beings who acquire knowledge through our senses. It is also fitting for God, who made us to be so. Some limited written evidence indicates that the early Christians imitated the Temple of Solomon in their buildings, suggesting that the basilican church form composed of a porch, nave, and sanctuary bore resonance for those who understood Temple worship. Eusebius would make this comparison explicit by calling a bishop who built a great church the new Solomon, Zerubbabel and Bezalel. He also called the altar in the church the "Holy of Holies."[40]

The Earthly Priest "in Persona Christi"

The Temple and its art and architecture can make us look with new eyes at what our priest is doing at every Mass: acting *in persona Christi*, making present to us again the very action of Christ, the true High Priest.[41] When an earthly priest enters through the front door of a church, past the porch, processing in white alb and circular embroidered vestment through the nave as an image of restored creation, he does what the High Priest of the Temple did. More importantly, he does what Christ did in coming to earth in the incarnation, taking on the matter of the universe and walking again with his creation as he once did in the Garden of Eden, then proceeding into God's presence in the sanctuary.

This gives a whole new meaning to the vegetal ornamentation found in churches throughout the centuries, be it the leafy capitals of columns or floral patterns in stone, paint or stained glass. It also informs us as to the nature of a church sanctuary and its iconography as a point of destination filled with images of the heavenly realm. Throughout history, the Temple as revealed building and prefiguration of heavenly realities is never far away from the minds of the Church's great builders.[42]

---

40 Eusebius, *The Church History*, Bk. 10, Chap. 4, in *A Select Library of Nicene and Post-Nicene Fathers*, Second Series, vol. 1, eds. Philip Schaff and Henry Wace (Grand Rapids, MI: Eerdmans, 1997), 375. Solomon, of course, was the "builder" of the first Temple, Bezalel was the builder of Moses' Tabernacle, and Zerubbabel served as architect for the building of the second Temple after its destruction by the Babylonians.

41 Pope Pius XII stated the theology of the priesthood beautifully in his 1947 encyclical on the liturgy, *Mediator Dei*: "The priest is the same, Jesus Christ, whose sacred person his minister represents. Now the minister, by reason of the sacerdotal consecration which he has received, is made like to the High Priest and possesses the power of performing actions in virtue of Christ's very person. Wherefore in his priestly activity he in a certain manner 'lends his tongue, and gives his hand' to Christ." Text in Pamela E. Jackson, *An Abundance of Graces: Reflections on Sacrosanctum Concilium* (Chicago: Hillenbrand, 2004), 141.

42 For a seminal exposition on the medieval understanding of the role of the Temple in Gothic architecture, see Otto Georg von Simson *The Gothic Cathedral: Origins of Gothic Architecture and the Medieval Concept of Order*, Bollingen Series, 48 (New York: Harper & Row 1957), esp. 37–38; 95–96. See also Wayne Dynes, "The Medieval Cloister as Portico of Solomon," *Gesta* 12 (1973): 61–69.

When the earthly priest steps from the nave to the sanctuary, he enters again into our sacramental presentation of the heavenly Holy of Holies. He goes to the altar bringing the prayers and petitions of the people to the Father as well as offerings of grain and wine. In an echo of Melchizedek as well as the Passover rituals of the Last Supper, the Catholic priest of today brings bread and wine, offers a sacrifice of praise in the sanctuary, and then returns with the gifts transformed as bearers of the divine life in the Eucharist. In many Orthodox and Eastern Catholic traditions, the altar is not only understood as a heavenly table, but also the throne of God like the Ark, where his presence remains and where heaven and earth meet. The walls are enriched with images of the angels and saints of heaven. Since the faithful are members of the Mystical Body by virtue of their baptism, they share in the common priesthood as well, offering Christ to the Father with the priest in real participation.

While in the Temple the Ark contained the old Law of the Ten Commandments and God's fleeting presence rested atop it, the fulfillment of the new law is found in the Eucharistic presence. This abiding presence in the reserved Blessed Sacrament links directly back to the Temple without limiting God's presence to a single place or building. In the time of image, Cardinal Ratzinger writes, our tabernacle with the reserved Blessed Sacrament serves as the new and fulfilled version of this abiding presence, where "his presence (*Shekinah*) really does now dwell among us."[43] His active presence gushes beyond the veil and out to the world in the people of his Church, yet they continually return to his altar for nourishment and restoration.

The centrality of the idea of Christ's body as the new Temple demands a certain investigation into the nature of the old Temple. To see the Temple as something foreign to Christianity is to deny God's loving prepration in the time of shadow. The Temple indeed served as a touchstone for the earliest Christians, who came to understand how God would redeem them by looking at the Old Testament typologies that relate to the Temple.

As Orthodox theologian Leonid Ouspensky has written, after the apostles were denied access to the synagogues and the Temple, "they built Christian sanctuaries, and they did so in strict accord with the revealed character of the place of worship, with the very principle according to which the tabernacle and the Jerusalem Temple has been built."[44] The New Testament is full of references to the Temple, and many of the activities of the earliest Church occurred in its courts. The words *Temple, priest* and *offering* permeate the christological and ecclesiological language of the New Testament as well as the Book of Revelation. In understanding the Temple, then, we come to better understand the Church.

---

43   Ratzinger, *The Spirit of the Liturgy*, 89.

44   Leonid Ouspensky, *The Theology of the Icon* (Crestwood, NY: St. Vladimir's Seminary, 1978), 23.

Letter & Spirit 4 (2008): 209–224

"The Mystery of His Will":
Contemplating the Divine Plan in Ephesians

~: William A. Bales :~

Mount Saint Mary's Seminary

The text of Ephesians 1:8b–10 reads:

> In all wisdom and insight, he [the Father] has made known to us
> the mystery of his will in accord with his favor that he set forth
> in him [Christ] as a plan for the fullness of times, to sum up all
> things in Christ, in heaven and on earth.[1]

This is one of the passages that compounds the feeling that Paul's letter to the Ephesians is so "mysterious" that one despairs of ever coming to a clear understanding of its meaning. What does the phrase *mystery of his will* mean? If it has been made known, as Paul plainly says it has, then what is it? What is this *plan* that Paul speaks of? In what way does the plan *sum up* all things in Christ? And what specifically is the referent of *all things*—apparently a reference to things that encompass not only earth but also heaven?

Scholars have shown that the word "mystery" (Greek: *mysterion*), as it is used both in Ephesians and in the rest of the New Testament, is best understood against a Semitic background attested in both the Septuagint and in the Qumran documents.[2] In general terms, *mysterion* is used simply to indicate a secret.[3] Here are two examples from the Septuagint:

> He who betrays a secret [*mysterion*] cannot be trusted, he will
> never find an intimate friend. (Sir. 27:16)

---

1   Unless otherwise noted, the translation I am using throughout is that of the New American Bible; hereafter NAB.

2   See, for example, Raymond E. Brown, "The Semitic Background of the New Testament *Mysterion* (II)," *Biblica* 40 (1959): 70–87, especially at 74–84; Raymond E. Brown, *The Semitic Background of the Term "Mystery" in the New Testament* (Philadelphia: Fortress, 1968); Chrys C. Caragounis, *The Ephesian Mysterion: Meaning and Content*, Coniectanea Biblica, New Testament Series 8 (Lund: Gleerup, 1977), 117–135; Franz Mussner, "Contributions Made by Qumran to the Understanding of the Epistle to the Ephesians," in *Paul and the Dead Sea Scrolls*, eds. Jerome Murphy-O'Connor and James H. Charlesworth (London: Geoffrey Chapman, 1968), 159–178.

3   In the Septuagint, the word *mysterion* occurs in Jth 2:2; Tob. 12:7, 11; 2 Macc. 13:21; Wis. 2:22; 6:22; 14:15, 23; Sir. 22:22; 27:16, 17, 21; Dan. 2:18, 19, 27, 28, 29, 30, 47. In the Septuagint version of Daniel, *mysterion* is used to translate the original Aramaic *raz*, which is also used in the documents found at Qumran.

I will not conceal anything from you. I have said, "It is good to
guard the secret [*mysterion*] of a king, but gloriously to reveal the
works of God."[4] (Tob. 12:11)

In these two examples, *mysterion* simply refers to commonplace, everyday
confidences.[5] In the second example, the archangel Raphael uses a proverb about
"guarding the *mysterion* of a king" as a lead-in to the "secret" that he, God's angel,
had been with Tobias all along.

The word *mysterion* is also used in the Septuagint to indicate a secret *plan* of
some sort:

[B]ut Rhodocus, of the Jewish army, betrayed military secrets
[*mysterion*] to the enemy. He was found out, arrested, and im-
prisoned. (2 Macc. 13:21)

He summoned all his ministers and nobles, laid before them his
secret [*mysterion*] plan, and urged the total destruction of those
countries. (Jth. 2:2)

The "military secrets" mentioned in 2 Maccabees probably involve secret *plans*
that a certain Rhodocus leaked to the Greek enemies. The passage in Judith speaks
of the King of Assyria's "secret plan" about how he was going to exact revenge on
the "whole region" (Jth. 2:1).

"During the Night, the Mystery Was Revealed"

Related to the notion of a secret plan in general, *mysterion* in the Septuagint of
Daniel is used to indicate a secret plan of *God*—that is, how God is going to
order future events in some special and important way. The Babylonian King
Nebuchadnezzar has a dream about a large and terrifying multi-tiered metallic
statue that finally gets pulverized by a stone cut from a mountain. Wary of his
sycophantic court wise men, the king demands, on pain of death, that they tell
him both the dream and its interpretation. At this point, Daniel, along with his
three Hebrew friends, prays to God that the *mysterion*—meaning here both the
details of the dream itself *and* its interpretation—be revealed to them. And so it
happens:

Daniel went home and informed his companions Hananiah,
Mishael, and Azariah, that they might implore the mercy of
the God of heaven in regard to this mystery [*mysterion*], so that
Daniel and his companions might not perish with the rest of the

---

4   The translation here is the Revised Standard Version.

5   So also in Sir. 22:22; 27:17, 21.

wise men of Babylon. During the night the mystery [*mysterion*] was revealed to Daniel in a vision. (Dan. 2:17–19a)

As Daniel relates the *mysterion* to the king, it becomes apparent that it has to do with future events, fixed by God, concerning the rise and fall of successive kingdoms. These kingdoms will subjugate God's people until they themselves are ultimately destroyed at the coming of God's kingdom, a kingdom that will exercise universal and unending dominion over the whole earth:

> In the lifetime of those kings the God of heaven will set up a kingdom that shall never be destroyed or delivered up to another people; rather, it shall break in pieces all these kingdoms and put an end to them, and it shall stand forever. That is the meaning of the stone you saw hewn from the mountain without a hand being put to it, which broke in pieces the tile, iron, bronze, silver, and gold. The great God has revealed to the king what shall be in the future; this is exactly what you dreamed, and its meaning is sure. (Dan. 2:44–45)

Some observations about the Danielic use of *mysterion* are needed at this point. First, the basic idea of *mysterion* as a "secret" still applies; however, now the secret is seen to be God's secret. Second, the secret constitutes a knowledge of future events, events of great significance—the rise and fall of tyrannical kingdoms and the defeat of these kingdoms with the rise of God's kingdom. Third, the *mysterion*, though given in unintelligible symbols to King Nebuchadnezzar in his dream, is revealed truly and accurately only through God's chosen prophet, Daniel. Fourth, (and rather obvious) the *mysterion*, having been revealed, is no longer a secret. Daniel's *public* narration of the dream and its authoritative interpretation indicates that God wants not only the king, but the whole world to know what he is going to bring about in due time—namely, the end of all opposing dominions and the establishment of his everlasting Kingdom.

Having said this much, one must concede that Daniel's "revelation" of the *mysterion* still leaves many questions unanswered, many further "secrets" we might wish to know. For instance, how specifically is God going to bring about this everlasting kingdom? What will the kingdom be like? Who or what is symbolized by the destroying "stone"? Is it the long hoped-for Davidic Messiah or is it someone or something else? Is the kingdom to be understood as the restored and revived Davidic Kingdom? What will be the privileges and blessings for those who become a part of this kingdom? How will one be able to partake of the blessings of this coming kingdom?

Even with all these unanswered questions, it is clear that the Danielic use of *mysterion* moves us into the realm of the divine plan for saving humanity. With the Fall in Genesis 3 had come alienation from God and estrangement from one another.

Our fallen nature became prey to the forces of Satan and the other evil spirits, and to the ultimate evil, death—not just physical death—but to the bleak prospect of enduring for endless ages cut off from the source of all goodness and happiness; an infinite, hopeless, ashen existence, a life that cannot be called life, but death eternal. The divine plan, as understood in Daniel and throughout the Old Testament, has to do with God undoing and overthrowing the effects and consequences of the Fall by restoring the glory and dignity of humanity as well as reconciling humanity to communion and union with God Himself. If the pre-lapsarian world was a kind of "temple" in which God and humanity dwelt together in harmony and love (which it was), then the restored world would likewise be such a place, only on a far grander and more glorious—we Catholics would say "divinized"—level.[6] God raised up Israel to be a light to the nations, to prepare the way for the restoration of all things and to begin the process of overthrowing Satan's work. But Israel, too, "falls" repeatedly, failing to accomplish the vocation God placed upon it. For a brief, shining moment, during the reign of King Solomon, the oaths God swore to Abraham and David found some degree of realization.[7] Yet, because of sin, not only had this ascendency taken centuries longer than it should have, but it all fell to ashes, ruin, and disgrace in the subsequent decades and centuries. The fall of the Northern Kingdom, the exile of the Southern Kingdom with its inglorious return and subservient status—these catastrophes raised questions about how the story would ever work out for the good. The revelation of the *mysterion* in the book of Daniel is a marvelous promise that the divine plan for history *would be realized*, despite the human weakness and sin that had filled human history with so much misery and disaster.

The Mystery of the Kingdom

As we will see, the Danielic use of *mysterion* will prove very helpful as we seek to understand the use of the word in the New Testament and specifically in Ephesians.[8] In the Pauline usage, the Old Testament trajectory of the word is confirmed and comes to full flower. We find *mysterion* used to indicate the formerly-secret-but-

---

6   For scriptural intimations of this plan, see for instance, 2 Cor. 6:16b–18; Isa. 43:6–7; Ezek. 37:24–28.

7   See Gen. 17:6-8; 22:15-18; 2 Sam. 12-16.

8   Franz Mussner ("Contributions Made by Qumran," 163) has traced points of contact between the use of "mystery" in Ephesians and its use in the Dead Sea scrolls (which, like the Aramaic of Daniel, uses the word *raz*). In particular, he has noted that the Qumran documents speak of secret knowledge designated as "mystery," "insight," "wisdom" hitherto hidden by God but now revealed to the Teacher of Righteousness and through him, to the Qumran community. As in Daniel, the revealed *raz / mysterion* is connected with a hoped-for salvation in the last days where God and his people defeat the forces of evil in a glorious reversal of fortunes. Any proposed interdependence, however, between the Qumran documents and Ephesians would be quite speculative (so also Caragounis, *Mysterion*, 117–135). Daniel is the more likely background for both Qumran and Paul, as well as the rest of the New Testament.

now-revealed-plan of how the whole story of salvation history will be worked out in all of its cosmic, glorious dimensions. This will certainly include the datum about God's coming kingdom revealed to Daniel via Nebuchadnezzar's dream. But it will encompass much more.

As with Daniel, in the New Testament the *mysterion* is revealed through God's chosen instruments:

> When you read this you can understand my insight into the mystery [*mysterion*] of Christ, which was not made known to human beings in other generations as it has now been revealed to his holy apostles and prophets. (Eph. 3:4–5)

God's first chosen instrument is Christ himself. Jesus uses the word *mysterion* when explaining to his disciples the great privileges they had come to receive as his chosen followers:

> He answered them, "The mystery [*mysterion*] of the kingdom of God has been granted to you. But to those outside everything comes in parables, so that they may look and see but not perceive, and hear and listen but not understand, in order that they may not be converted and be forgiven." (Mark 4:11–12)[9]

Jesus uses *mysterion* here to refer to the insight he has given the disciples to interpret the confusing parable he had just spoken to the crowds. The "global" tenor of Jesus' statement, however, could easily be understood to mean that the disciples had already been given some measure of insight into other "secrets" of the Kingdom of God, the kingdom Jesus had come to proclaim and, in his person, inaugurate. Yet, it is likely that Jesus' statement also has a proleptic element to it—that is, the disciples' must await Jesus' death, resurrection, and ascension in order to grasp the deeper understanding of the kingdom's mysteries.

The notion of *mysterion* in Paul exhibits greater depth and clarity. On a number of occasions, Paul uses *mysterion* as a virtual synonym of the Gospel itself:

> Now to him who can strengthen you, according to my Gospel and the proclamation of Jesus Christ, according to the revelation of the mystery [*mysterion*] kept secret for long ages but is now disclosed and through the prophetic writings is made known to all nations, according to the command of the eternal God, to bring about the obedience of faith, to the only wise God, through Jesus Christ be glory forever and ever. Amen. (Rom. 16:25–27)

---

9   The parallel passages in Matt. 13:11 and Luke 8:10 also use *mysterion*.

The phrase "according to the revelation of the mystery [*mysterion*] kept secret for long ages but is now disclosed" is essentially in apposition[10] to Paul's preceding statement "according to my Gospel and the proclamation of Jesus Christ." Other examples of this near synonymous usage of *mysterion* and Gospel can be observed in several other texts in Paul:

> When I came to you, brothers, proclaiming the mystery [*mysterion*] of God, I did not come with sublimity of words or of wisdom ... and my message and my proclamation were not with persuasive (words of) wisdom, but with a demonstration of spirit and power. (1 Cor. 2:1, 4)

Thus should one regard us: as servants of Christ and stewards of the mysteries [mysterion] of God." (1 Cor. 4:1)

> [B]e watchful with all perseverance and supplication for all the holy ones
>
> and also for me, that speech may be given me to open my mouth, to make known with boldness the mystery [*mysterion*] of the Gospel. (Eph. 6:18–19)

> [A]t the same time, pray for us, too, that God may open a door to us for the word, to speak of the mystery [*mysterion*] of Christ, for which I am in prison. (Col. 4:3)

> Similarly, deacons must be dignified, not deceitful, not addicted to drink, not greedy for sordid gain, holding fast to the mystery [*mysterion*] of the faith with a clear conscience. (1 Tim. 3:8–9)

> Undeniably great is the mystery [*mysterion*] of our religion: He was manifested in the flesh, vindicated in the spirit, seen by angels, proclaimed to the Gentiles, believed in throughout the world, taken up in glory.[11] (1 Tim. 3:16)

The text from Ephesians 6:19 is especially telling, for the Greek construction underlying the translation makes explicit that the *mysterion* is the Gospel.[12] The

---

10   A grammatical construction where what follows virtually restates the preceding statement, word, or phrase.

11   Slightly modified NAB.

12   The Greek reads *to mysterion tou euaggeliou* ("the mystery of the Gospel). The noun *tou euaggeliou*

Gospel, of course, is the story of God's redemptive work in and through Christ. The Gospel is neatly summarized in texts like Acts 10:36–43 and 1 Corinthians 15:3–5, 22–26, which tell of Jesus being anointed with power, proclaiming the Kingdom, working miracles which liberate people from Satan and his tyranny, then dying, rising from the dead, and finally being enthroned on high as sovereign Lord, King, Judge, and giver of heavenly gifts. Other Pauline texts also use equivalent terms for "the Gospel" in apposition with the word *mysterion*:

+ Colossians 4:3: *to mysterion tou christou*[13] (the *mysterion* of Christ);

+ 1 Timothy 3:9: *to mysterion tēs pisteōs* (the *mysterion* of the faith); and

+ 1 Timothy 3:16: *to tēs eusebeias mysterion* ("the *mysterion* of [our] religion").

To proclaim Christ is to proclaim the *mysterion*; to proclaim the faith is to proclaim the *mysterion*; to proclaim our religion is to proclaim the *mysterion*. The material immediately following the genitive in 1 Timothy 3:16 (see quote above) strikingly demonstrates how Paul can use the word *mysterion* to summarize the Gospel message: "He was manifested in the flesh, vindicated in the spirit, seen by angels, proclaimed to the Gentiles, believed in throughout the world, taken up in glory."

Ephesians and the Meaning of Salvation History

Our understanding of the *mysterion* is taking shape. To repeat, what we are talking about when we speak of the New Testament *mysterion* is the working out of the story of salvation history. To speak of the *mysterion* is to speak of how the biblical story moves forward and comes to its dénouement. More precisely, the *mysterion* is about how the many catastrophes we hear of in the Old Testament are rectified and reversed, and how renewal, restoration, and transformation come to humanity through the coming of Christ and his Kingdom into the world. The *mysterion* constitutes the story of how God brings to fruition the many and wonderful promises

---

("the Gospel") is a genitive of apposition, which is to say that it refers to the same thing as the noun just prior, *to mysterion* ("the mystery"). A more "wooden" translation would be, "the mystery, that is, the Gospel." For more on this common grammatical construction, see Daniel B. Wallace, *Basics of New Testament Syntax: An Intermediate Greek Grammar* (Grand Rapids, MI: Zondervan, 2000), 52–54.

13   The genitives *tou christou*, *tēs pisteōs*, and *tēs eusebeias* could also be categorized as genitives of definition, description, or even content (see Wallace, *Basics*, 45–55). Whatever classification one uses, it is clear that the words in the genitive closely describe or identify with the word *mysterion*.

he had made throughout the Old Testament, promises that he had made concerning this reversal, restoration, and transformation of all things.

It is especially in Ephesians that we see how the *mysterion* constitutes, so to speak, the "rest of the story" of salvation history. The impossible, tangled mess that humanity (in general) and Israel (in particular) have made of things is all impossibly, stunningly, overthrown. Through Jesus' life, death, resurrection, ascension, enthronement, and bestowal of heavenly gifts, all is restored, renewed, and transformed.

To understand the idea of the *mysterion* in Ephesians, one must travel somewhat methodically through the letter, beginning with the word's first occurrence and then following not only later usage of the word but related themes as well. While a truly thorough journey is the stuff of books, not short articles, we will look at several key texts and note key themes connected to the Ephesian *mysterion*. We will observe that Paul reveals the *mysterion* in layers—analogous to how those anatomical drawings in certain encyclopedias are revealed in greater and greater detail as the successive layers of printed transparencies are folded on top of one another.

The most important use of *mysterion* is also its first occurrence, in Ephesians 1:9–10. This verse provides important clues for helping us open the trove of understanding to be found in Ephesians' use of *mysterion*. We begin with the Greek word *anakephalaiōsasthai*,[14] one of the most important words in the New Testament.

The meaning of *anakephalaiōsasthai* (Eph. 1:10b) is important to the discussion of the Ephesian *mysterion* because of its syntactical relation to the word *mysterion* in Ephesians 1:9. This syntactical relation can be seen by setting aside the digressions within 1:8b–10. The train of thought can then be easily traced. In the following quotation, the digressions have been set off in brackets:

> [In all wisdom and insight,] He has made known [to us] the mystery (*mysterion*) of his will, [in accord with his favor] that he set forth [in him] as a plan [for the fullness of times,] to "sum up" [?] (*anakephalaiōsasthai*) all things in Christ, [things in heaven and things on earth.] (Eph 1:8b–10)

Without the digressions, the passage reads: "He has made known the mystery (*mysterion*) of his will, that he set forth as a plan to 'sum up' (*anakephalaiōsasthai*) all things in Christ." And so it becomes clear: the *mysterion* is the Father's *plan* to "sum up"[15] all things in Christ. The importance of the meaning of *anakephalaiōsasthai*

---

14   In Greek grammar, *anakephalaiōsasthai* is an aorist middle infinitive form of the verb *anakephalaioō*.

15   We use "sum up" here, but this will be modified as we proceed, for the whole point of the following discussion is to determine with as much precision as possible the meaning of *anakephalaiōsasthai*.

becomes apparent—*anakephalaiōsasthai* defines the plan. The *mysterion* is the plan, therefore, *anakephalaiōsasthai* defines or describes the "content" of the *mysterion*.

Mysterion and Anakephalaiōsasthai

The verb *anakephalaioō* occurs only three times in Scriptures.[16] In Romans 13:9 *anakephalaioō* means to "sum up" or to "gather together under a general idea":

> The commandments, "You shall not commit adultery; you shall not kill; you shall not steal; you shall not covet," and whatever other commandment there may be, are summed up [*anakephalaioutai*] in this saying, [namely] "You shall love your neighbor as yourself." (Rom 13:9)

A similar meaning for *anakephalaioō* can be observed in ancient writers such as Aristotle, Dionysius of Halicarnassus, and Quintilian.[17]

The Greek of LXX (Theodotian) Psalm 71:20 reads: *anakephalaioōthēsan proseuchai dayid* ("the prayers of David are [?]"). It is unclear whether the verb indicates that David's prayers are "gathered together"[18] or "brought to a conclusion."[19] The word *anakephalaioō* is perhaps used in the second sense in the *Epistle of Barnabas*,[20] which speaks of how Christ "brought about an end" to sin, though this passage is open to other interpretations.

The word *anakephalaioō* derives immediately from the noun *kephalaion*, which has several meanings.[21] In rhetorical contexts, *kephalaion* can mean "the main point" as in "the gist" or "the summary" of what is under discussion (Heb. 8:11).[22] It can also mean a "sum" in the sense of a "cumulative total" of something—for instance,

---

16 In Eph. 1:10, Rom. 13:9, and LXX (Theodotion) Ps. 71:20. Theodotion was a second century Jewish scholar who produced a Greek version of the Old Testament. Whether or not, at any given point in his version, he was revising an existing Greek translation or was working from actual Hebrew manuscripts, is debated. It appears to have became a popular version among some early churches.

17 See Henry Liddell and Robert Scott, *A Greek-English Lexicon* (Oxford: Clarendon, 1996), sub verbum *anakephalaioomai*.

18 So Heinrich Schlier, "Anakephalaioomai," in *Theological Dictionary of the New Testament*, 10 vols., ed. Gerhard Kittel, trans. and ed. Geoffrey W. Bromiley (Grand Rapids, MI: Eerdmans, 1964–1985), 3:682.

19 So Martin Kitchen, *Ephesians* (New York: Routledge, 1994), 37.

20 *Barnabas* 5:11, text in *Ancient Christian Writers: The Works of the Fathers in Translation*, vol. 6, trans. James A. Kleist (New York: Newman, 1948), 53.

21 See Walter Bauer, Frederick Danker, William Arndt, and F. Wilbur Gingrich, *A Greek-English Lexicon of the New Testament and other Early Christian Literature* (Chicago: The University of Chicago Press, 2000), sub verbum *kephalaion*; Liddell and Scott, *Greek-English Lexicon*, sub verbum *kephalaios, a, on*.

22 See Liddell and Scott, *Greek-English Lexicon*, sub verbum *kephalaios, a, on*, II.2.

of money (Acts 22:8), of people (Num. 4:2; 31:20,49), or of words (Dan. 7:1).[23] The word *kephalaion* can also mean "chief" in the sense of "ruler" or "director."[24] It can also indicate some prominent event or "crowning act" that brings something to completion.[25]

Both *anakephalaioō* and *kephalaion* are related to the noun *kephalē*, which has the basic meaning of "head." The meaning of *kephalē* in the Pauline corpus is disputed, as is its meaning in Ephesians.[26] Scholars have argued that in Ephesians *kephalē* could indicate "authority over," "source," or both of these meanings.[27]

Without the prefix "*ana-*," the verb *kephalaioō* can mean "to sum up," "to bring under a head" (that is, "to bring under the rule of"). Alternately, in a more passive sense, it can mean "to be summed up," "to amount to," or "to be combined."[28] These meanings are very similar to the attested meanings for *anakephalaioō* itself.

When used in compound verbs, the prefix "*ana-*" can add a directional "upward" sense, as in *anabainō* ("to go up") or *anablepō* ("to look up").[29] It can also add a sense of repetitiveness as in *anagennaō* ("to be born again"), or it can indicate a return to a former condition (*anablepō* ["to see again"], *anakainizō* ["to restore"]). This prefix can also intensify a verb, as in *anastenazō* ("to groan deeply") or *anaphoneō* ("to cry out loudly").[30]

In light of these grammatical considerations and precedents, there are at least several possible interpretations of the word *anakephalaiōsasthai* in Ephesians 1:10. It could mean "to sum up," or "to gather under a general heading." It could mean "to bring to a conclusion." It could also be a way of saying, "to bring to a *kephalaion*" ("summation" or "head").[31] In this latter reading, *anakephalaiōsasthai* could mean "to summarize." This meaning, when used of people or things and not of ideas,

---

23   Liddell and Scott, *Greek-English Lexicon*, sub verbum *kephalaios, a, on*, II.5.

24   Liddell and Scott, *Greek-English Lexicon*, sub verbum *kephalaios, a, on*, II.3.

25   Liddell and Scott, *Greek-English Lexicon*, sub verbum *kephalaios, a, on*, II.6.

26   For the occurrences of *kephalē*, see Eph. 1:22; 4:15; 5:23. The disputed occurrences in the Pauline corpus (besides those in Ephesians) are 1 Cor. 11:3; Col. 1:18; 2:10, 19.

27   For recent discussions of the meaning of *kephalē* in Ephesians and in the Pauline corpus, see Gregory Dawes, *The Body in Question: Metaphor and Meaning in the Interpretation of Ephesians 5:21–23* (Leiden: Brill, 1998), 12–49; Wayne Grudem, "The Meaning of *Kephalē* ("Head"): A Response to Recent Studies," *Trinity Journal* 11 (1990): 42–71; Stephen Miletic, *"One Flesh": Eph. 5.22–24, 31. Marriage and the New Creation*, Analecta Biblica 115 (Rome: Pontifical Biblical Institute, 1988), 67–87.

28   See Liddell and Scott, *Greek-English Lexicon*, sub verbum *kephalaioō*.

29   Other examples include: *anabibazō* ["to go up, ascend"], *anakuptō* ["to stand up"]). If the prefix occurs with a verb in a context that has to do with teleology (purpose) rather than something physical, the sense can be that of "fulfillment," "completion," or "perfection."

30   In some cases, *ana-* appears to be simply a stylistic addition with little denotative implication whatever (*anaggellō* ["to announce" = *aggellō*]).

31   So Schlier, "*Anakephalaioomai*," 681.

comes close to the meaning of "to gather together." It is also possible that it means "to bring under the rule of" as in "to bring under the authority of." [32]

Several contextual considerations help bring more precision to our inquiry. First, in Ephesians 1:10 *anakephalaiōsasthai* is associated with a realized eschatological perspective. That is to say, the *anakephalaiōsasthai* is taking place in "the fullness of times" (Eph. 1:9). The association of *anakephalaiōsasthai* with eschatology strongly suggests that the word may indicate "restoration"[33] or "bringing to a culmination."

Second, in its immediate context in Ephesians, *anakephalaiōsasthai* has a cosmic and spatial perspective. It affects "all things, things in heaven and things on earth."[34] In this sense, the meaning might be related to the statement in Colossians 1:20 about God reconciling "things in heaven and things on earth" through Christ. Indeed, *anakephalaiōsasthai* in Ephesians 1:10 probably suggests a similar "bringing together" of these two once-separate spheres, heaven and earth. Hence, we can suggest that the word is meant to also indicate an idea of "unification."[35]

Third, the *anakephalaiōsasthai* of "all things" takes place "in Christ" (*en tō Christō*). The preposition *en* may have an instrumental force ("through Christ's agency") or a local, corporate sense ("in Christ").[36] Understood either instrumentally or locally, it is clear that Christ is the power behind the activity of the *anakephalaiōsasthai* of all things.

There is no evidence to suggest that the word *anakephalaioō* had acquired any special meaning either for Paul or his audience. As we have noted, use of the word in the New Testament is rare, and elsewhere in ancient writing the word conveys a range of meanings. Therefore, as the audience hears or reads the word *anakephalaiōsasthai* in Ephesians 1:10, they would not have any pre-understanding or assumptions about what Paul might have meant.

In other words, the *mysterion* is introduced in a somewhat mysterious fashion. Based on the possible meanings for *anakephalaioō* with which they were familiar, the audience might have supposed that the eschatological *plan* has to do with "all

---

32   It is also possible that *anakephalaiōsasthai* may preserve the sense of "source" or "authority over" attested for the related noun *kephalē*. Also, the prefix *ana-* might add the sense of restoration or intensification to *anakephalaiōsasthai*.

33   As was seen above, the prefix *ana-* can add this nuance.

34   The phrase "all things, things in heaven and things on earth" most likely refers to the totality of the cosmos, meaning especially all human beings (both good and evil) and all angels (both good and evil). So Ernest Best, *A Critical and Exegetical Commentary on Ephesians*, International Critical Commentary (Edinburgh: T. & T. Clark, 1998), 140; Rudolf Schnackenburg, *Ephesians: A Commentary*, trans. Helen Heron (Edinburgh: T. & T. Clark, 1991), 60; Andrew Lincoln, *Ephesians*, Word Biblical Commentary 42 (Dallas: Word, 1990), 34.

35   So Schnackenburg, *Ephesians*, 60.

36   The interpretation of these *en-* phrases is a problem throughout Ephesians. See John A. Allen, "The 'In Christ' Formula in Ephesians," *New Testament Studies* 5 (1958–59): 54–62; Best, *Ephesians*, 153–154; Lincoln, *Ephesians*, 21–22.

things" now being "gathered together" or "brought under authority" or "united" or "brought to a culmination" or "restored" by Christ. That is about all that could be guessed at this point in the letter.

One could go further and posit that at Ephesians 1:10 Paul does not *intend* or *expect* his audience to understand fully what the *anakephalaiōsasthai* of "all things" means. Although the lengthy *berakah*, or prayer of blessing that begins the epistle (Eph. 1:3–14) is probably not meant to be understood as a thematic introduction to the letter,[37] and although Paul did not write Ephesians specifically as an exposition of the *mysterion*, nonetheless, the *mysterion* and ideas latent in the *anakephalaiōsasthai* "of all things in Christ" are opened up as the letter progresses. What has been brought under, restored, and brought to a culmination in and through Christ will be developed and clarified later. Paul's introduction and development of the *mysterion* in this fashion is possibly an example of *insinuatio*, a rhetorical technique where ambiguous or subtle phraseology is used at the beginning of a work not only to catch the attention of the audience, but to entice the audience to discover the hidden meaning or meanings as the work moves forward.[38]

The Church in the Mystery of "Mysterion"

Ephesians 1:20–23 is connected to and flows from the prayer requests that precede it. Paul prays first that his audience might "understand the hope that belongs to God's call" (1:18a). Next he prays that they might understand "what are the riches of the glory of God's inheritance that belong to the saints" (1:18b).[39] In Ephesians 1:19a Paul then prays that the audience might understand "the surpassing greatness of God's power" available to them (1:19a).

This power available to Christians is said to be "in accord (*kata*) with the exercise of his great might" (1:19b). The word *kata* is usually understood rather nebulously as "in accord with" or "according to." In this instance, as is the case with several other occurrences of the word in Ephesians, *kata* is best understood as indicating that what has just preceded *has come about as a result of* what follows.[40]

---

37   So Best, *Ephesians*, 111–12. For opposing views, see Peter O'Brien, "Ephesians 1: An Unusual Introduction to a New Testament Letter," *New Testament Studies* 25 (1979): 510–512; Peter O'Brien, *The Letter to the Ephesians* (Grand Rapids, MI: Eerdmans, 1999), 93; Nils A. Dahl, "Addresse und Pröomium des Epheserbriefes" [The Address and Introduction of the Letter to the Ephesians] *Theologische Zeitschrift* 7 (1951): 241–264; Lincoln, *Ephesians*, 18–19.

38   See Richard A. Lanham, *A Handbook of Rhetorical Terms*, 2d. ed. (Los Angeles: University of California, 1991), 91.

39   This is a disputed translation. Many scholars understand the possessor of the "inheritance" as God himself, and therefore the inheritance as the saints, God's "inheritance." I think it much more plausible, and in keeping with the spirit of the *berakah* in chapter one, that all three of Paul's prayer requests have to do with blessings that now belong to his Christian audience by virtue of their faith.

40   See, for example, Eph. 1:11 (first occurrence); 3:7 (both occurrences). See Bauer, *Greek-English Lexicon*, sub verbum *kata*, B.5.a.δ.

The surpassing greatness of God's power for Christians has come about as a result of "the work of his (God's) great might" (1:19b).

This work of God's great might is then specified in 1:20–23. What God has "worked in Christ"[41] can be described concisely as Christ's exaltation, whereby the Father:

+ raised Christ from the dead (1:20b);

+ made him to sit at his right hand[42] in the heavens (1:20c), far above every principality, authority, power, and dominion[43] (1:21);

+ put all things beneath his feet (1:22a);

+ gave him as head over all things (1:22b);[44] and

+ made him the "life-giver" and "filler" of all things (1:23).

In 1:22b–23 Paul returns to his point (from v. 19b) that Christ's exaltation is for the sake of the Church (1:22b). From his position of exalted glory, Christ completely fills "all things." The Church is singled out as the locus of Christ's "filling" in a special way, being described as his "fullness" (1:23).[45]

---

41 Which is to say, perhaps, worked "with respect to" Christ. See *en* in 1 Cor. 4:2.

42 The notion of being seated at God's right hand is drawn from the Old Testament and would appear to indicate the enthronement of an individual to a position of favor, honor, and power (see Ps. 110:1). The right hand of God, particularly as seen in the psalms, signifies God's power exercised against Israel's enemies (see Pss. 20:6; 21:8; 44:3; 60:5; 98:1; 118:15). Most commentators see in Eph. 1:20 an allusion to Ps. 110:1.

43 These categories of beings are most likely the evil angelic forces mentioned elsewhere in the letter (3:10; 6:12). So, for example, Clinton E. Arnold, *Power and Magic: The Concept of Power in Ephesians* (Grand Rapids, MI: Baker, 1992), 41–56; Thurston Moritz, *A Profound Mystery: The Use of The Old Testament in Ephesians*, Supplements to Novum Testamentum 85 (Leiden: Brill, 1996), 19; Lincoln, *Ephesians*, 62–65; Peter T. O'Brien, "Principalities and Powers: Opponents of the Church," in *Biblical Interpretation and the Church*, ed. D. A. Carson (Exeter: Paternoster, 1984), 110–150, especially 125–128, 133–136.

44 The phrase "and he gave him as head over all things" in verse 22b connects with and rephrases "and he put all things beneath his feet" in v. 22a, immediately preceding. Thus, the thought is, "and he put all things beneath his feet and gave him as head over all things—for the sake of the Church." Two considerations suggest this interpretation: (1) the word for "all things" (*panta*) occurs in both halves of the verse; and (2) the word for "head" (*kephalē*, v. 22b) and "put under" (*hypotassō*, v. 22a) occur in close connection later in Eph. 5:21 and 5:24 where wives and the Church are spoken of as being subject to (*hypotassō*) their husbands and to Christ, their respective heads (*kephalē*). See the concurring view of Dawes, *The Body in Question*, 139.

45 There has been considerable scholarly discussion regarding the meaning of the word *plērōma* ("fullness") as well as the phrase *to plērōma tou ta panta en pasin plēroumenou* ("the fullness of the one who fills all things in every way") in Eph. 1:23. Bringing together clues found in 1:23, 2:20–22, and 3:16–19 results in the notion that what Paul has in mind is the "filling" of the Church (the

With respect to the "mystery" in Ephesians, two things are particularly important. First, Ephesians 1:22 is reminiscent of the *anakephalaiōsasthai* of all things (*ta panta*) in Christ from Ephesians 1:10. The word *kephalē* ("head") in 1:22 reminds one of the word ana*kephalaiōsasthai* in 1:10. The *panta* ("all things") in 1:22 (used twice) evokes the *panta* in 1:10. The notice that all things have been subjected "under" (*hypo*) Christ's feet (1:22a) and that he has been given as head "over" (*hyper*) all things (1:22b) recalls the general meaning of the verb *anakephalaiōō* as "gathering under."

As was suggested earlier, by using the word *anakephalaiōsasthai* Paul probably was introducing a word targeted to entice the audience to discover its meaning as the letter progressed. Ephesians 1:22 is the first and most important explication of the *anakephalaiōsasthai* of all things in Christ. At this point in our study, we can say that it is very likely that a major aspect of the "*mysterion*" is that all things have been subjugated under the exalted Christ.[46]

Second, Ephesians 1:20–23 indicate that the riches, power, and fullness that the Church has received have come about as a result of the exaltation of Christ.[47] All blessings flow to the Church and humanity from the exalted Christ. Paul thus makes it clear that the *mysterion* was inaugurated at the event of Christ's exaltation. In Ephesians 2:6 Paul states that the audience itself has already come to participate in the glory and power of Christ's exaltation.

Further on in the letter, Paul will make a remarkable assertion concerning the *mysterion*—that because of its participation in the power of Christ, it is actually through the Church that the evil demonic forces experience defeat and humiliation:

> [A]nd to bring to light (for all) what is the plan of the mystery
> [*mysterion*] hidden from ages past in God who created all things,
> so that the manifold wisdom of God might now be made known
> through the Church to the principalities and authorities in the

---

new Temple) with the presence of God's glory, a New Testament fulfillment and analog of how Solomon's Temple was filled with God's glory at its dedication (2 Chron. 7:1).

46   Many scholars share this general approach to how Eph. 1:22 relates to 1:10. See, for example, Herbert A. Meyer, *A Critical and Exegetical Handbook to the Epistle to the Ephesians*, trans. from the 4th German ed. by M. J. Evans, rev. and ed. by W. P. Dickson (New York: Funk & Wagnals, 1884), 322–323; Schnackenburg, *Ephesians*, 60; O'Brien, *Ephesians*, 114; Lincoln, *Ephesians*, 35. See especially Schlier ("Anakephalaiooomai," 682), who comments: "The *anakephalaiooomai ta panta en tō christō* ['unifying dominion' (?) of all things in Christ] obviously consists in the *auton edōken kephalēn hyper panta tē ekklēsia* [... He gave him as head over all things for the Church] (1:22). The summing up of the totality takes place in its subjection to the head. ... To be sure, *anakephalaiousthai* is to be derived from *kephalaion* [a summation] rather than *kephalē* [head]. But it is most likely that what is meant by the designation of Christ as *kephalē* led Paul in Ephesians to choose this relatively infrequent but rich and varied term which agrees so well with his intention."

47   Compare Eph. 1:18, 19, 23.

heavens. This was according to the eternal purpose that he accomplished in Christ Jesus our Lord. (Eph. 3:9-11)

The "manifold wisdom" that is now being made known to the evil demonic forces (principalities and powers) is that the power of the exalted Christ is working through the Church to bring about their downfall and defeat. This is God's plan—the *mysterion*—now revealed. Rudolf Schnackenburg has aptly commented:

> To the extent that the Church, through the Gospel, inwardly wins back humanity alienated from God and formerly enslaved by the "powers," she reveals to the ungodly powers God's manifold wisdom (compare Eph. 3:10) and the deprivation of their own power. Hence the Church is the representative of the nonviolent and yet powerful rule of Christ, but still more: she is a power which pervades and transforms the world—if she convincingly communicates to the world the effective healing-power of Christ within her—that is, convinces by her own unity and love (compare Eph. 4:12–14).[48]

As the letter moves forward, other aspects of the *mysterion* are revealed, all finding their source in the exalted Christ. The audience will discover that the *anakephalaiōsasthai* of all things in Christ means the following:

+ That though once far off and cut off from God and his promises, Christians are now brought near (having been made the very dwelling place of God), and are the beneficiaries of the fulfillment of his promises (Eph. 2:12–13; 19–22);

+ though the audience was once divided and scattered (particularly with respect to their ethnicity), they are now as believers united and gathered together by and in Christ (Eph. 2:11–22; 3:6);

+ though once dead, they are now renewed or restored in him (2:5);

+ though once poor, they are now made rich (1:18; 2:7);

+ though once weak, they are now made strong (1:19,22; 3:10; 6:11–18);

---

48 Schnackenburg, *Ephesians*, 84. The interpretation of the phrase "the manifold wisdom of God" is debated. In context, however, it is best understood as the functional equivalent of the Ephesian "mystery" (so Lincoln, *Ephesians*, 185–195; Best, *Ephesians*, 323–324; O'Brien, *Ephesians*, 245–246; Caragounis, *Mysterion*, 108).

- though once darkness, they are renewed as light (5:8);

- though once spiritually "deformed" and "stunted," so to speak, they now find their perfection and culmination in him as they grow into his glorious likeness (4:13); and

- though once little more than puppets of the "ruler of the power of the air," they are now ruled by Christ (1:20–22) and rule with Christ (2:6), dominating the vile "powers" that formerly dominated them (3:9–11).

In sum, by the end of the letter, Paul will have made clear to his audience that the allusive plan of the *"mysterion,"* explicated in the phrase *"anakephalaiōsasthai* of all things in Christ," has to do with events now being realized in the age inaugurated by Christ. Theirs is an age that anticipates and even participates in the age to come. The scope is universal. For Christians, the emphasis is on participating in the power, rule, and glory of Christ. To the Church belongs victory, unification, and restoration.

That part of the cosmos that rejects Christ (both angels and human beings) remains outside of these blessings. They must acknowledge the sovereignty of Christ and his Church, but not willingly. With respect to this second group, the *anakephalaiōsasthai / mysterion* involves subjugation, humiliation, and ultimate defeat (see 1:21–23; 3:10; 6:11–18).

As the letter unfolds, Paul intends that the members of the Church at Ephesus begin to understand the plan of the *"mysterion"* and their place in that plan. They are to be uplifted and given a sense of the dignity and privilege that is now theirs. The eschatological plan whereby all things, particularly evil powers, are subjugated under Christ's rule has begun. God's people are being united in an invincible, everlasting kingdom that will fill the earth. The promises to Israel, especially to Abraham and David, are being fulfilled. This entire process began with the exaltation of Christ. All of history had been moving toward this time when all things would be brought under his dominion and lordship. The secret is now revealed; the realization of the plan has begun.

The audience begins to see for themselves what they have now become: empowered, transformed children of Almighty God, called by Christ to bring the Gospel—the *mysterion*—to the world; to reign with Him, to battle and conquer the forces of darkness, and to dwell in the peace, joy, and glory of the Church—the new Temple, the new Jerusalem.

Letter & Spirit 4 (2008): 225–243

"You Are Gods, Sons of the Most High":
Deification and Divine Filiation in St. Cyril of Alexandria and the Early Fathers

~: Daniel A. Keating :~

Sacred Heart Major Seminary

I wish to pursue in this article the topic of baptism and its relation to our "sonship"—that is, to our becoming sons and daughters of God in Christ. I then want to take up the related topic of Christian deification, asking the question: Is deification properly a Christian doctrine? But I have chosen to follow the path of my own discovery, rather than simply present my conclusions in systematic form.

Sometimes it is more helpful to present, as it were, the final architectural drawing in its finished form. But at other times it is useful to show how one arrived at this final form, revealing the sketches along the way that led to the finished product. I am adopting the latter procedure in this case, because I think it will help give this topic a certain freshness and offer new insights that might not be as apparent if only the final form were presented.

I began my studies on St. Cyril of Alexandria (378–444 A.D.) some years ago with the rather vague notion of investigating his doctrine of the Holy Spirit. As I read through his writings with this aim in view, what I found was different from—and rather more than—what I had expected. I found myself needing to grapple, not just with Cyril's pneumatology, but with his panoramic understanding of our salvation, following up various leads and seeking to put together in a coherent whole what he said about our share in the divine life of God.

Eventually this led me to the subject of deification. But the avenues that brought me to the subject of deification are crucial to how I understand and evaluate the controversial subject of deification. And so to begin, I will offer an abbreviated account of St. Cyril's understanding of our salvation in Christ through the Spirit, and then move to consider deification and its value for Christian theology and practice.

One of the first things to strike the reader of Cyril's New Testament biblical commentaries is the importance he places on Jesus' baptism by John the Baptist in the Jordan River.[1] By the time Cyril comes to comment on it, the baptism of Jesus

---

1   For a full treatment of the baptism of Jesus in Cyril, see Daniel A. Keating, "The Baptism of Jesus in Cyril of Alexandria: The Re-Creation of the Human Race," *Pro Ecclesia* 8 (1999): 201–222.

already possessed a long and varied interpretative history in patristic theology. Cyril draws upon and develops this tradition in his own characteristic manner.[2]

The particular theological problem surrounding the baptism, especially for Church Fathers coming after the First Council of Nicea (325 A.D.), was a reading of this event that led to "adoptionism." According to the adoptionist account, Jesus' anointing by the Spirit was the event in which he *came to be* the Son of God. This, by implication, denied his eternal divine sonship.[3] Given the potential problems that the baptism of Jesus raised in the post-Nicene climate, it is all the more remarkable that Cyril emphasizes the central importance of the baptism, even as he defends it against adoptionist readings.

In his *Commentary on John*,[4] Cyril immediately draws our attention to the witness of the Baptist who says: "I saw the Spirit descend as a dove from heaven and it *remained* on him" (John 1:32). It is this word, "remain," that catches Cyril's eye. Cyril admits of course that the Spirit came upon many people in the Old Testament before the time of Christ. But it is only upon Christ, the New Adam, that the Spirit descends and *remains*. The abiding of the Spirit upon Christ at his baptism is qualitatively different from all other anointings of the Spirit that we see in the Scriptures before Christ. For Cyril, the baptism of Jesus is nothing less than the decisive return of the Holy Spirit to the human race for the sanctification of our nature.

Cyril reads the text of the baptism in the light of Paul's Adam-Christ typology (Rom. 5:12–21; 1 Cor. 15:20–22, 44–49), enabling him to accomplish two ends at once. First, by viewing Christ as the representative man, Cyril resolves the exegetical *crux* of why Christ submitted to baptism. He did so not for himself—being the eternal Son of God he required nothing—but for our sake, as the first fruits of the new human race. Secondly, the Adam-Christ typology also enables Cyril to unfold the overall scope of the plan of redemption from this one event.

By viewing the baptism of Jesus in this light, Cyril transfers the significance of the text from Jesus' own career *per se* to a revelation of the redemption of the

---

2   For the baptism of Jesus in patristic thought, see Robert Wilken, "The Interpretation of the Baptism of Jesus in the Later Fathers," *Studia Patristica* 11 (1967): 268–277; Kilian McDonnell, *The Baptism of Jesus in the Jordan: The Trinitarian and Cosmic Order of Salvation* (Collegeville, MN: Michael Glazier, 1997); and Sebastian P. Brock, "Clothing Metaphors as a Means of Theological Expression in Syriac Tradition," in his *Studies in Syriac Christianity: History, Literature and Theology* (Brookfield, VT: Variorum, 1992), 15–23.

3   Gabriele Winkler, "A Remarkable Shift in the Fourth-Century Creeds: An Analysis of the Armenian, Syriac and Greek Evidence," *Studia Patristica* 17 (1982): 1396–1401, demonstrates how Jesus's baptism was progressively dropped from the creeds precisely in order to eliminate subordinationist readings of Jesus's relationship to the Father.

4   All quotations from Cyril, unless otherwise noted, are made by the author from *Sancti patris nostri Cyrilli Archiepiscopi Alexandrini in d. Joannis Evangelium* [Our Holy Father Archbishop Cyril of Alexandria's Commentary on the Gospel of John] (hereafter, *In Jo.*), 3 vols., ed. P. E. Pusey, (Oxford: Clarendon, 1872). For Cyril's exegesis of the baptism of Jesus in John, see *In Jo.* 1:32–33, vol. I, 174–190.

human race. Cyril envisages the Adam-Christ typology in such a way that Christ becomes, in his capacity as the Second Adam, not only the *agent* but also the *recipient* of redemption. On this view, the incarnation is more than an instrumental means whereby God has access to the human race and can accomplish a work of salvation upon us. By becoming a man, the eternal Word also carries out the work of redemption and recreation in himself, as representing in himself the new humanity.

Baptism and the New Temple of the Spirit

At his baptism, Christ is revealed as the new Temple in which the Holy Spirit dwells effectively, so that the Church, which is his body, can also become the Temple of the Holy Spirit, enabling each of us as well to become personal dwelling places of God in the Spirit. For Cyril, *the* true temple is the Word incarnate himself. Because it is the eternal Word—one who is truly God—who has become flesh, his very body is now the true Temple of God on earth (John 2:21). Cyril underlines that nowhere in the Scriptures previous to Christ is anyone called a "temple" of God—this is only true of Christ because he is God incarnate.[5] But the Word has obviously taken our humanity as his temple, not for his own sake but for ours, so that we might become temples of the Holy Spirit within us (1 Cor. 6:19) and "become partakers of the divine nature."[6]

The characteristic feature of Cyril's exposition of Jesus' baptism is the prominence he accords to the Holy Spirit in the narrative of salvation. He renarrates the opening chapters of Genesis in terms of the imparting of the indwelling Spirit to Adam and the subsequent flight of the Spirit due to the sin of Adam, or "the Fall." He describes redemption, then, in terms of the reacquisition of the Spirit, signified by the dove descending on Jesus, finding in him a reliable and secure dwelling place, free from all sin. In turn, Jesus secures the Spirit for our sake, sanctifying the whole of our nature in himself.[7]

If the baptism of Jesus displays in a particularly poignant way the divine plan of salvation in Cyril, other mysteries in the life of Christ are essential for illuminating the completion of that plan. The crucial hinge text for Cyril is John 7:39, "For as yet the Spirit had not yet been given, because Jesus was not yet glorified."[8] Cyril

---

5　See *In Jo.* 2:21–22, vol. 1, 212–13; 7:39, vol. 1, 696.

6　*In Jo.* 17:18–19, vol. 2, 722. For Cyril, Christ's humanity itself remains pre-eminently the "Temple of God." He is the Temple in the fullest sense, because his flesh becomes life-giving in the Eucharist, while our flesh does not give life in the same way (see *In Jo.* 6:57, vol. 1, 537). But because of our participation in Christ through the Holy Spirit received in baptism, we too are rightly called "temples of God" because God makes his effective abode in us.

7　Not all of this is new with Cyril, for discrete aspects of his exposition can be found in Irenaeus, Origen, and Athanasius before him. Yet the strikingly prominent place he accords to the gift, loss, and reacquisition of the Spirit surpasses what we find in their accounts.

8　For Cyril's exegesis of John 7:39, see *In Jo.* 7:39, vol. 1, 690–698.

begins his explanation of John 7:39 by admitting first of all (as Augustine does) that the Spirit was plainly at work in the prophets and others before the glorification of Christ, and then asking in what possible sense the Spirit was "not yet given" until after Christ's resurrection. In answer, he recounts the creation of Adam and traces the entire narrative of salvation in broad strokes, leading to the incarnation, death, and resurrection of Christ, the new Adam.

Cyril offers what can be described as a "narrative of the Holy Spirit" in the economy of salvation. According to this narrative, the breathing of life into Adam (Gen. 2:7) is nothing other than the gift of the indwelling Spirit. Adam and his descendants drove away and lost this same Spirit through the progressive sin of the human race.[9] And though the Spirit was plainly active throughout the history recorded in the Old Testament, it was only in Christ himself, the New Adam, that the Spirit came once again to dwell effectively in the human race. Christ received the Holy Spirit as man for our sake, Cyril tells us, so that the Spirit might once again inhabit our humanity and cause us to become "partakers of the divine nature" (2 Pet. 1:4).

But why, for Cyril, is the Holy Spirit not given in this full sense until Christ's glorification? First, since Christ became the first fruits of our renewed nature only at the time of his resurrection, it would be impossible for us, as "the plant," to be seen springing forth before "the root," the resurrected Christ. In Cyril's view, our human nature is only fully renewed in Christ's resurrection, thus marking out the boundary line for our reception of the Spirit. Our humanity needed to be fully renewed in Christ in order to provide a proper dwelling place for the Spirit.

Second, the gift of the Spirit, dependent on Christ's resurrection, is genuinely new, different *in kind* from the activity of the Spirit in the Old Testament. To show this, Cyril points us to Matthew 11:11, where Jesus calls the least in the Kingdom of Heaven greater than John the Baptist. For the prophets, the Spirit was a light and illumination, but among those in the Kingdom of Heaven, the Spirit "himself dwells and has his habitation."

Cyril draws the distinction between the old and the new covenants precisely in terms of the abiding gift of the Holy Spirit. Notably, he says that our new birth into the Kingdom of God occurs not by "grace alone," but by "God indwelling and taking up his abode within us" through the Holy Spirit.[10] And this, he concludes, is the meaning of John's statement that "the Spirit had not yet been given, because Jesus was not yet glorified." The evangelist is signifying nothing less than "the complete and entire dwelling of the Holy Spirit in human beings."[11]

To complete Cyril's narrative of salvation, we need to look briefly at how he handles the gift of the Spirit breathed upon the disciples in John 20:22 and how he

---

9   Here Cyril cites Gen. 6:3 in support.

10   *In Jo.* 1:12–14a, vol. 1, 137.

11   *In Jo.* 7:39, vol. 1, 696–698.

understands the purpose of the ascension of Christ referred to in John 16:17. Why, Cyril asks, does Christ "breathe" the Spirit on the apostles on Easter Day? He does so in order to reveal that the recreation of the human race follows the pattern of the original creation, and also to show that Christ as the New Adam is also the one who gives the Spirit. This is how Cyril puts it:

> Therefore, in order that we might learn that it is *this* one who was the Creator of our nature in the beginning, and who sealed us by the Holy Spirit, the Savior again bestows the Spirit for us through a visible inbreathing on the holy disciples, as on the first fruits of our renewed nature. For Moses writes concerning our creation of old, that he breathed into his face the breath of life (Gen. 2:7). As therefore from the beginning he was fashioned and came to be, so too is he renewed. And just as then he was formed in the image of his creator, so too now, through participation in the Spirit, he is refashioned to the likeness of his maker.[12]

The same one (Christ Jesus) featured as the *recipient* of the Spirit at his baptism is now prominently displayed as the *giver* of the Spirit. The two-fold reality of Christ as the Second Adam appears here. As the Spirit was breathed into Adam, so the Spirit returns upon the Second Adam at the Jordan, Christ receiving it as a first fruits for us. But Christ as the Second Adam is also a "life-giving Spirit" (1 Cor. 15:49), and so is the one who imparts the Spirit to his apostles, as the first fruits of his Church.

For Cyril, however, the endpoint of Christ's representative role does not end here. It is completed only with his ascension and enthronement to the right hand of the Father.

> [Christ] places us in the presence of the Father, having departed into heaven as the first fruits of humanity. For just as, being himself Life by nature, he is said to have died and risen again for our sake, so too, ever beholding his own Father, and in turn also being seen by his own Father, he is said to be manifested now (that is, when he became man, not for his own sake but for us) as man. And therefore this one thing was seen to be lacking in his dispensation towards us, our ascension into heaven itself, as in Christ, the first fruits and the first [of all].[13]

The significance of the mystery of the ascension for Cyril resides in Christ ascending, interceding, and reigning *as man*, as the first fruits of our ascension to

---

12   *In Jo.* 20:22, vol. 3, 135.

13   *In Jo.* 16:17, vol. 2, 619.

come. In Christ's fully restored human nature now in the presence of the Father the divine purpose for the whole human race is revealed and perfected in the first fruits.

This, in highly abbreviated form, is the outline of Cyril's account of our salvation in Christ as the first fruits. The mystery of the baptism of Jesus plays a pivotal role here, but only in concert with all the mysteries linked together.

Salvation and Filial Adoption

What I do not have the time to develop here is how Cyril unfolds from this narrative of salvation his account of how we are adopted as "sons and daughters" of God through the Spirit.[14] He offers a very rich account of our filial adoption as sons and daughters, primarily through the coordinated means of baptism and the Eucharist, and then unfolds a vision of the moral life and the virtues grounded in the example of Christ himself. In lieu of the fuller development, let me offer three conclusions regarding Cyril's account of our adoptive sonship in Christ.

The principal and foundational conclusion is this: for Cyril a full and comprehensive account of the appropriation of divine life must include the human reception of, and progress in, this divine life. Human response and the moral life are not merely tacked on to a theological account that begins and ends with divine action through the Word. Divine initiative possesses both temporal and theological priority, but human response is essential for the effective reception of what the Father has accomplished in Christ through the Spirit.

Second, Cyril's account of the human reception of divine life is exceptionally well christologically grounded and centered. Christ is the agent of divine life and salvation, being Life himself, and accomplishes the restoration of human nature in himself. But he is also the pattern for *our* human reception of the divine life as man, first for our reception of the Spirit, and also for our response of love and obedience to the Father, and for a way of life conformed to the Father through himself. In other words, Christ is both the agent of our redemption and the primary exemplar for how we as human beings are made new and refashioned into the image and likeness of God.

The third and final conclusion concerns the dynamic outworking of the divine life in us: the gift of divine life, in cooperation with our own free response, yields a divine way of life and ushers in a progressive sanctification aimed at the perfection of the divine image in us. Cyril conceives of our growth into the image of God as rooted in the life-giving sap of the Spirit that flows from our union with Christ through faith and love. This union is productive of a variety of fruits: good works, manifold virtue, a life of godliness, and a share in the mission of Christ to the world. Cyril does not offer a technically drafted account of the spiritual life, or

---

14   For a thorough discussion, see Daniel A. Keating, *The Appropriation of Divine Life in Cyril of Alexandria* (Oxford: Oxford University, 2003).

a theory of spiritual growth.[15] But building upon biblical metaphors and examples in the life of Christ, he displays a high degree of confidence in the spiritual fruitfulness available to us in this life as sons and daughters of God.

This study of Cyril's understanding of salvation led me (and in fact required me) to address the issue of the doctrine of deification in Cyril. Cyril does in fact employ the characteristic vocabulary of divinization,[16] but I have been able to locate only about twenty instances of the terms in his massive corpus, many of them appearing in one early work on the Trinity (the *Thesaurus*). For someone often hailed as the theologian of deification *par excellence*, it is instructive that he used the technical vocabulary rather sparingly. Why was he so cautious about using the terminology he inherited from Athanasius and Gregory of Nazianzus? I believe that under the press of anthropormorphite teaching about God in the early fifth century, and due to the polemics of the Nestorian controversy, Cyril largely refrained from using the characteristic terminology of deification, and instead more commonly employed the classic text from 2 Pet. 1:4 (that we have become "partakers of the divine nature") as his summary statement of deification.[17]

Cyril's teaching on deification may be understood in two senses, the first a strict and narrower sense, the second a broad and more comprehensive one. In the strict sense, deification is the impartation of divine life effected in us through the agency of the indwelling Spirit in baptism and through Christ's life-giving flesh in the Eucharist. Properly speaking, *Christ in us*—through his Spirit and his life-giving flesh—is the source and ground of our deification, accomplishing our justification, our sanctification, our divine filiation, and our participation in the divine nature. In the broad and more comprehensive sense, deification includes our progressive growth into the divine image. If for Cyril our deification is preeminently God's life implanted in us, bringing about the full spiritualization of human nature, it cannot be dissociated from our free and faith-filled response to God and our growth in virtue through obedience to the divine commands, yielding a way

---

15 Perhaps Cyril's most programmatic account of growth in the divine life appears in his *Letter to the Monks of Egypt*, where he comments on the stepwise path to holiness drawn from 2 Pet. 1:5–8: "And on my part I say that those who have chosen to tread that illustrious path of the spiritual life in Christ, that path we ought to love so much, must first of all be adorned with a simple and pristine faith, and then add to it virtue, and when this is done, try to gather the riches of the knowledge of the mystery of Christ, and strive vigorously for perfect understanding. For this, I think, is what it means to 'arrive at the perfect man, and reach the measure of the state of the fullness of Christ' (Eph. 4:13). Text in John Anthony McGuckin, *St. Cyril of Alexandria and the Christological Controversy: Its History, Theology, and Texts*, Supplements to Vigiliae Christianae 23 (Crestwood, NY: St. Vladimir's, 2004), 246.

16 For the development of the technical vocabulary of deification in Christian sources, see Norman Russell, *The Doctrine of Deification in the Greek Patristic Tradition* (Oxford: Oxford University, 2004), 333–344.

17 As far as I can determine, Cyril cites or alludes to 2 Pet. 1:4 far more frequently than any other Christian author in antiquity.

of life pleasing to God. Without our free adherence of faith and progress in virtue through obedience it is no longer human life in its entirety that is divinized.

It is fitting to offer the following selection in order to conclude and sum up Cyril's magnificent understanding of our share in the divine life of the Trinity as sons and daughters of God. In it we find a densely constructed account of the Trinity, of creation, of the incarnation of the Word, and of the sanctifying work of the Spirit, all put at the service of the gift of divine life and sonship to the human race:

> It was not otherwise possible for man, being of a nature which perishes, to escape death, unless he recovered that ancient grace, and partook once more of God who holds all things together in being and preserves them in life through the Son in the Spirit. Therefore his only-begotten Word has become a partaker of flesh and blood (Heb. 2:14), that is, he has become man, though being Life by nature, and begotten of the Life that is by nature, that is, of God the Father, so that, having united himself with the flesh which perishes according to the law of its own nature ... he might restore it to his own life and render it through himself a partaker of God the Father. ... And he wears our nature, refashioning it to his own life. And he himself is also in us, for we have all become partakers of him, and have him in ourselves through the Spirit. For this reason we have become "partakers of the divine nature" (2 Pet. 1: 4), and are reckoned as sons, and so too have in ourselves the Father himself through the Son.[18]

The "Doctrine" of Deification: Is it Christian?

At a certain point in my study of Cyril, I began to ask how this impressive account of our divine filiation through Christ in the Spirit compared with other accounts by significant patristic authors, especially those in the Western tradition. This led me eventually to compare Cyril's account with that of Theodore of Mopsuestia (350–428 A.D.), St. Augustine (350–430), and Pope St. Leo the Great (d. 451), respectively. Subsequent to this, I began to read and study St. Thomas Aquinas (1225–1274) more fully (both his *Summa Theologiae* and his biblical commentaries), and ask whether aspects of this account of deified life in Christ can be found in his thought.

What I found (with the single exception of Theodore) are striking similarities on the basic outline and understanding of our salvation, amidst of course many smaller differences and individual features. What I hope to do now is to offer an outline of the doctrine of deification as I have found it in the Tradition, handling

---

18   *In Jo.* 14:20, vol. 2, 485–486.

certain recurring objections along the way, and conclude with the need for a more thorough and accurate presentation of the doctrine of deification today.

There is no better place to begin an investigation of deification than with what is commonly termed the "formula of exchange" (often designated in the Christian tradition as the *admirabile commercium* [literally, "the wonderful exchange"]). In essence, this formula states that the eternal Son of God became what we are so that we could become what he is. There is no single established formula—each author who employs this paradoxical expression devises his own version. The earliest examples come from St. Irenaeus about 175–185 A.D. Irenaeus is considered the originator of this way of summarizing our redemption.

> For it was for this end that the Word of God was made man, and he who was the Son of God became the Son of man, that man, having been taken into the Word, and receiving the adoption, might become the son of God.[19]

> But (we follow) the only true and steadfast Teacher, the Word of God, our Lord Jesus Christ, who did, through his transcendent love, become what we are, that he might bring us to be even what he is himself.[20]

Norman Russell identifies this Irenaean principle as the "fundamental tenet" of the Christian doctrine of deification.[21] Hans Urs von Balthasar describes the formula of exchange as the "fundamental approach" to the doctrine of salvation found in the Church Fathers.[22]

Following Irenaeus—and probably dependent upon him—we find wide attestation to this formula throughout the patristic period. It is noteworthy that some form of this expression can be found in writers from Alexandria, Constantinople, Antioch, Syria, North Africa, and Rome. A selection of these witnesses, varying widely in expression, will show just how widespread was this manner of summing up the content of Christian faith.

St. Clement of Alexandria, in the third century, writes that "the Word of God became man, that you may learn from man how man may become God."[23] St. Athanasius of Alexandria, writing in the fourth century, made the formula of

---

19   Irenaeus, *Against the Heresies* Bk. 3, Chap. 19, 1, in *Ante-Nicene Fathers*, vol. 1, eds. Alexander Roberts and James Donaldson (Grand Rapids, MI: Eerdmans, 1975), 448.

20   Irenaeus, *Against the Heresies*, Bk. 5, Preface, in *Ante-Nicene Fathers*, vol. 1, 526.

21   Russell, *The Doctrine of Deification*, 321.

22   Hans Urs von Balthasar, *Theo-Drama: Theological Dramatic Theory*, vol. 4, trans. Graham Harrison (San Francisco: Ignatius, 1994), 244.

23   Clement of Alexandria, *Exhortation*, Bk. 1, Chap. 1, in *Ante-Nicene Fathers*, vol. 2, eds. Alexander Roberts and James Donaldson (Grand Rapids, MI: Eerdmans, 1975), 174.

exchange of key part of his anti-Arian theology: "For he was made man that we might be made God," and "he himself has made us sons of the Father, and deified men by becoming himself man."[24]

From the Cappadocian fathers of the fourth century we hear the same message. St. Gregory of Nazianzus exhorts his hearers: "Let us become as Christ is, since Christ became as we are; let us become gods for his sake, since he became man for our sake."[25] St. Gregory of Nyssa argues that the Word became incarnate "so that by becoming as we are, he might make us as he is."[26] In the late fourth century, the Antiochene St. John Chrysostom teaches that "he became Son of man, who was God's own Son, in order that he might make the sons of men to be children of God."[27] And St. Ephrem the Syrian, also writing in the fourth century, adds his own terse formulation of this truth: "He gave us divinity, we gave him humanity."[28]

The formula of exchange is widely attested also in the West. In the fourth century, St. Hilary of Poitiers offers his own twist on this expression: "For when God was born to be man the purpose was not that the Godhead should be lost, but that, the Godhead remaining, man should be born to be god."[29] St. Ambrose of Milan, also in the fourth century utilizes the exchange formula to show how the eternal Son became what he was not in order to bring us to what he was:

> For [the Son] took on him that which he was not that he might
> hide that which he was; he hid that which he was that he might
> be tempted in it, and that which he was not might be redeemed,
> in order that he might call us by means of that which he was not
> to that which he was.[30]

Augustine employs some form of this expression on numerous occasions.

---

24   Athanasius, *On the Incarnation of the Word*, 54, in *A Select Library of the Nicene and Post-Nicene Fathers of the Christian Church*, Second Series, vol. 4, eds. Philip Schaff and Henry Wace (Grand Rapids: Eerdmans, 1975), 65; *Four Discourses Against the Arians*, Dis. 1, 38, in *Nicene and Post-Nicene Fathers*, vol. 4, 329.

25   Gregory of Nazianzus, *Oration* 1, 5, quoted in Russell, *The Doctrine of Deification*, 215.

26   Gregory of Nyssa, *Against Apollinaris*, 11, quoted in Russell, *The Doctrine of Deification*, 229.

27   John Chrysostom, *Homilies on the Gospel of John*, Hom. 11, 1, in *A Select Library of the Nicene and Post-Nicene Fathers of the Christian Church*, First Series, vol. 14, eds. Philip Schaff and Henry Wace (Grand Rapids: Eerdmans, 1975), 38.

28   Ephrem of Syria, *Hymns on Faith*, Hymn 5, 7, quoted in Russell, *The Doctrine of Deification*, 322.

29   Hilary of Poitiers, *On the Trinity*, Book 10, 7, in *Nicene and Post-Nicene*, Second Series, vol. 9, 183–184.

30   Ambrose of Milan, *On the Holy Spirit* Bk. 1, Chap. 9, 107, in *Nicene and Post-Nicene*, Second Series, vol. 10, 107.

God wanted to be the Son of Man and he wanted men to be the sons of God.

The Son of God [became] the Son of man that he might make the sons of men the sons of God.

For this thing God does, out of sons of men he makes sons of God: because out of Son of God he has made Son of Man. ... For the Son of God has been made partaker of mortality, in order that mortal man may be made partaker of divinity.[31]

In the fifth century, Pope St. Leo adds the testimony of Rome:

[The Savior] was made the son of man, so that we could be the sons of God.

He united humanity to himself in such a way that he remained God, unchangeable. He imparted divinity to human beings in such a way that he did not destroy, but enriched them, by glorification.[32]

Witness to this formula appears also in the writings of major theologians, both East and West, of later centuries. In the East we find some version of this formula in St. Maximus the Confessor (seventh century), St. John of Damascus (seventh-eighth centuries), and Symeon the New Theologian (tenth and eleventh centuries). Thomas Aquinas shows that this formula was alive and well in the Latin Middle Ages:

The only-begotten Son of God, wishing to make us sharers in his divine nature, assumed our nature, so that made man he might make men gods.[33]

---

31 Augustine, *Tractates in John*, Trac. 12, 8, in St. Augustine, *Tractates on the Gospel of John 11–27*, trans. John W. Rettig, The Fathers of the Church 79 (Washington: Catholic University of America, 1988), 36; *Tractates in John*, Trac. 21, 1, in *Tractates on John 11–27*, 179; *Expositions on the Psalms*, Ps. 52, 5, in *Nicene and Post-Nicene*, First Series, vol. 8, 204 (translation slightly adjusted).

32 Pope St. Leo, *Sermon 26*, 2 (my translation); *Sermon 91*, 2, in *St. Leo the Great: Sermons*, trans. Jane P. Freeland and Agnes J. Conway, The Fathers of the Church 93 (Washington: Catholic University of America, 1996), 384.

33 Thomas Aquinas, *Opuscula* [Minor Work] 57, cited in Andrew Louth, "Manhood into God: The Oxford Movement, the Fathers and the Deification of Man," in *Essays Catholic and Radical*, eds. Kenneth Leech and Rowan Williams (London: Bowerdean, 1983), 74.

For the human mind and will could never imagine, understand or ask that God become man, and that man become God and a sharer in the divine nature. But he has done this in us by his power, and it was accomplished in the Incarnation of his Son: "That you may become partakers of the divine nature" (2 Pet. 1:4).[34]

To note just one example in the modern period, Joseph Ratzinger (now Pope Benedict XVI) provides us with a contemporary restatement of this exchange at the heart of the Gospel: "This exchange consists of God taking our human existence on himself in order to bestow his divine existence on us, of his choosing our nothingness in order to give his plenitude."[35]

"You Are Gods, Sons of the Most High"

When studied in context, it is clear that the formula of exchange in the Fathers is directly dependent upon the scriptural witness. Paul's statement in 2 Corinthians 8:9—"For you know the grace of our Lord Jesus Christ, that for your sake he became poor, though being rich, so that by his poverty you may become rich"—provides the logic for the idea of exchange.[36]

The key texts on sonship (Gal. 4:4–6; Rom. 8:14-17, 29; 1 John 3:1–2), in conjunction with the texts on Christ as the New Adam and our transformation into his image (Rom. 5:12–21; 1 Cor. 15:44–49; 2 Cor. 3:18; Eph. 1:10) supply the primary biblical foundation and framework for the formula that the Son of God became as we are, so that we might become as he is. By asserting that "the Son of God became the Son of Man, so that the sons of men might become the sons of God," the Fathers were attempting to sum up the scriptural testimony concerning our redemption.

Christ, by virtue of his divine-human constitution and by means of his saving actions, is the center and locus of that redemption. He is the Second Adam who renews our nature in himself, thus inaugurating a new humanity, and breathes his Spirit into us, causing us to be adopted as sons of the Father. By means of the indwelling of God, we are set on a course in which we freely cooperate, to be conformed to the image of the Son (Rom. 8:29). It is only in the life of the age to come that this transformation will be completed, and we shall see him as he is (1 John 3:2).

This account of our redemption embraces the full expanse of the biblical narrative, from Adam to Christ and the glory that awaits us in the new creation. It

---

34 Aquinas, *Commentary on Ephesians* 3:19 [182], in Thomas Aquinas, *Commentary on Saint Paul's Epistle to the Ephesians*, trans. and intro. Matthew L. Lamb (Albany, NY: Magi, 1966), 147.

35 Joseph Ratzinger, *Dogma and Preaching*, trans. Matthew J. O'Connell (Chicago: Franciscan Herald, 1985), 84.

36 My translation.

incorporates the victory of Christ over the enemies and ills that beset the human race: the power of indwelling sin, the slavery of the devil, and the curse of death on our nature. And it is both christocentric and trinitarian: the Father sends his Son in our fallen humanity, to redeem the human race and to win for us adoptive sonship through the Spirit.

At this point the question may reasonably be asked: How did we move from this account of the redemption of our nature in Christ to the language of deification? Why was this language employed, and how was it warranted? There has been a longstanding judgment by critics that both the language and concept of deification were foreign intrusions into the Christian faith from the world of Greek philosophy and the mystery religions of the ancient world. This was famously argued by Adolf von Harnack and others continue to revisit this case against the notion of Christian deification.[37] The early Christians certainly were aware of—and normally quite critical of—the various religious and philosophical currents of their day. In defense of the Fathers against this charge, Norman Russell and other scholars of the history of deification argue that the Christian teaching on deification was quite distinct, both in content and vocabulary, from other varieties.[38] It was a counter-proposal to Greco-Roman views rather than a capitulation to them.[39]

On close inspection, one finds that the early Christians who used the terminology of deification, far from being simple enthusiasts for ideas and concepts drawn from Greek thought and religion, were attempting to describe a biblical account of our filiation in Christ through the Holy Spirit. In fact the specifically Jewish context may be even more significant than the Greco-Roman environment for the emergence of the notion of deification in Christianity.[40] And surprisingly, a short text from the Old Testament, Psalm 82:6, turns out to be the primary spur and warrant for the development of the technical terminology of deification.

In the Greek text of Psalm 82, the Lord God stands in the assembly "of the gods" and gives judgment against them (verse 1). In verses 6–7, he addresses his auditors as both "gods" and "sons of the Most High," who will nevertheless die like (mere) men because of their failure to judge in righteousness. The specific warrant

---

37   See Adolf von Harnack, *History of Dogma*, vol. 2, trans. Neil Buchanan (Gloucester, MA: Peter Smith, 1976), 10–11, 317–18. For a more contemporary version of this critique, see Benjamin Drewery, "Deification," in *Christian Spirituality: Essays in Honour of Gordon Rupp*, ed. Peter Brooks (London: SCM, 1975), 33–62.

38   Russell, *The Doctrine of Deification*, 52; see also Jules Gross, *The Divinization of the Christian According to the Greek Fathers*, trans. Paul A. Onica (Anaheim: A & C, 2002), 2.

39   Balthasar concludes that the exchange formula "is not due to some irruption of Greek thought into the biblical milieu: it results from the effort made to secure the full soteriological meaning of the New Testament's *pro nobis.*" *Theo-Drama*, 4:245.

40   Gross, *The Divinization of the Christian*, 7–79; Russell, *The Doctrine of Deification*, 53–78.

for applying the terms "gods" in Psalm 82:6 to human beings is the testimony of Jesus himself in John 10:34–35.

There, Jesus reasons that if Scripture calls "gods" those to whom the word of God came, then he (Jesus, the one sent directly from the Father) should not be condemned for calling himself "the Son of God." What is important in both the psalm and in Jesus' citation of it is the coincidence of the terms "gods" and "sons". It is precisely because of this coincidence that the early Fathers saw in this psalm a shorthand account of our destiny in Christ, and hence believed themselves warranted to identify as "gods" those who are "the sons of God" through Christ.

This is just how the second-century Christian apologist, St. Justin Martyr, interprets Psalm 82:6 in his *Dialogue with Trypho*. He cites these verses to show that Christians are truly children of God, and he reads the psalm in its entirety as a prophecy of what is proclaimed in John 1:12–13—that through Christ we have been given the power to become children of God.[41] In the same way, Irenaeus cites Psalm 82 as designating our graced adoptive sonship in Christ:

> And again: "God stood in the congregation of the gods, he judges among the gods." He [here] refers to the Father and the Son, and those who have received the adoption; but these are the Church. For she is the synagogue of God, which God—that is, the Son himself—has gathered by himself. ... But of what gods [does he speak]? [Of those] to whom he says, "I have said, you are gods, and all sons of the Most High." To those, no doubt, who have received the grace of the "adoption, by which we cry, *Abba*, Father" (Rom. 8:15).[42]

The same application of this psalm can be found in Clement of Alexandria, who is importantly the first Christian author to employ the language of deification.[43] It is noteworthy for our subject here that in all these early instances, Psalm 82 is linked to our becoming "gods" (that is, "sons and daughters of God") through the agency of Christian baptism.

What conclusions can we draw from these early Christian testimonies to the interpretation of Psalm 82:6? First, the application of the psalm to our filial adoption in Christ predates—and is also concurrent with—the appearance of

---

41   Justin Martyr, *Dialogue with Trypho*, Chap. 124, in *Ante-Nicene Fathers*, vol. 1, 261–262. For this reading of Justin, see Carl Mosser, "The Earliest Patristic Interpretation of Psalm 82, Jewish Antecedents, and the Origins of Christian Deification," *Journal of Theological Studies*, New Series 56 (2005): 35–41.

42   Irenaeus, *Against the Heresies* Bk. 3, Chap. 6, 1, in *Ante-Nicene Fathers*, vol. 1, 419. For other citations of Ps. 82:6 in Irenaeus, see *Against the Heresies*, Bk. 3, Chap. 19, 1; Bk. 4, Chap. 38, 4.

43   Clement of Alexandria, *The Instructor*, Bk. 1, Chap. 6, in *Ante-Nicene Fathers*, vol. 2, 215. For Clement's use of Ps. 82:6, see Mosser, "The Earliest Patristic Interpretation of Psalm 82," 54–58.

the technical terminology of deification in Christian writers. It was precisely the Christian adaptation of this psalm, very probably building on an earlier Jewish exegesis, that ushered in the practice of identifying Christians as "gods."

Secondly, the pairing of "gods" and "sons of the Most High" in Psalm 82:6 supplied the early Church with a biblical bridge between our adoptive sonship and our being called "gods" in a clearly defined and delimited way. What does it mean that Christians are called "gods"? It means exactly what the New Testament teaches about our being "sons of God" through Christ and in the Holy Spirit. And how did all this come to pass? "The Son of God became the son of man, in order to enable the sons of men to become sons of God." In a majority of cases, the technical terminology of deification in the early Church describes just this: our becoming "sons of God" by grace. The formula of exchange and the language of deification are two ways of expressing the same reality.

Deification in the Tradition: Some Conclusions and Consequences

In the light of this overview of the origins of the doctrine of deification in the fathers, I would like to offer three conclusions that can guide our efforts to speak and teach about deification. The first is that the doctrine of deification is (and must be) grounded in and closely aligned with the Scripture. Deification in its fundamental form emerged, not primarily as a speculative exercise aimed at harmonizing Greek thought with Christian faith, but as the expression of Christian belief in the face of various unorthodox accounts that threatened that faith. It was the Gnostic challenge of the second and third centuries, and the Arian crisis of the fourth, that gave rise to the classic concepts and language of deification. In other words, the doctrine of deification arose from the Church's hard-fought efforts to interpret the Scriptures rightly in the face of alternative interpretations of those same Scriptures. It is important when teaching on deification to show how it derives from and synthesizes the scriptural testimony to our "sonship" in Christ.

A second conclusion, closely related to the first, is that the doctrine of deification is not the patrimony of the Eastern Church alone, or an eccentricity of certain schools of Western theology. Rather, deification concerns the basic economy of God in Christ through the Spirit that is at the patristic root of both the Eastern and Western theological traditions. Despite real differences between schools of thought and individual writers, there is a remarkable convergence on the substance of the doctrine of deification between the Eastern and Western traditions. Though the doctrine of deification has occupied a much larger role in the language and piety of the East than of the West, it is also a teaching solidly rooted in the Western tradition.

The third conclusion is that a theological account of Christian deification must be firmly embedded within classical Christian doctrine and the creedal confession of the Church. Deification is not something unto itself, and does not stand alone. It needs to be understood and taught in close correlation with justification, sanctification, filial adoption, regeneration, grace-filled union, transformation, and so forth. Deification is a kind of summary term that expresses all that God intends for us in Christ through the Spirit.

There is, it must be acknowledged, a persistent and recurring objection to the idea of deification in Christian theology. This concern arises principally within Protestant circles, but Catholic theologians and philosophers also worry about this potential implication of some versions of the doctrine of deification. Here is a strong form of the objection: Does the doctrine of deification, by means of its elevated and potentially exaggerated rhetoric, effectively compromise the fundamental distinction between God and the created order, and so lead explicitly or implicitly to a form of pantheism?

To restate the question against the backdrop of contemporary religious movements: Doesn't the notion of deification play into the hands of those religious movements that claim, "you yourself are God," and so refuse to recognize any sovereign and transcendent God deserving of our worship and obedience? The answer given by the Christian tradition is a resounding "No." These concerns are not new—they were present from the very beginning of discussion of deification in the Church. Clear distinctions were set in place to ensure that talk of deification would not fall prey to pantheism or fail to uphold the transcendence of the divine nature. Properly understood, the Christian doctrine of deification not only maintains the distinction between God and the created order, but is premised on it. Christian deification dissolves if the fundamental difference between what is divine and what is human is compromised.[44]

The primary statement in the Christian tradition that upholds this difference takes some form of the saying, "we become gods, not by nature, but by grace." A few examples from the chorus of voices that attest to this position will suffice. In the East, Athanasius has this to say: "Wherefore [the Word] is very God, existing one in essence with the very Father; while other beings, to whom he said, 'I said you are gods' (Ps. 82:6), had this grace from the Father, only by participation in the Word, through the Spirit."[45] From the West, Augustine is particularly eloquent on this point. He consistently states that our share in the divine life—by grace and not by nature—is distinct from Christ's natural divinity.

---

44   To fully defend and explain this claim, an understanding of the concept of "participation" in the Fathers and in Aquinas is necessary. For a brief account of the concept of participation, see Daniel A. Keating, *Deification and Grace* (Naples, FL: Sapientia Press, 2007), 97–104.

45   Athanasius, *Four Discourses Against the Arians*, Dis. 1, 9, in *Nicene and Post-Nicene Fathers, Second Series*, vol. 4, 311.

It is evident, then, as he has called men gods, that they are deified by his grace, not born of his substance. ... If we have been
made sons of God, we have also been made gods: but this is the
effect of grace adopting, not of nature generating.[46]

But let no one believe about the only-begotten Son what he believes about those who were called the children of God according
to grace, not nature, as the evangelist said, "He gave them power
to be made children of God" (John 1:12). On this same point, the
Lord himself recalled what was said in the Law: "I have said, 'you
are gods, and all of you sons of the Most High'" (Ps. 82:6).[47]

And finally this from Aquinas, when he is explaining how and in what sense Christ
loved his disciples as the Father loved him (John 15:9):

For [Christ] did not love them to the point of their being gods
by nature, nor to the point that they would be united to God
so as to form one person with him. But he did love them up to
a similar point: he loved them to the extent that they would be
gods by their participation in grace—"I say you are gods" (Ps.
82:6); "He has granted to us precious and very great promises,
that through these you may become partakers of the divine
nature" (2 Pet. 1:4).[48]

Divinization and Deification in Catholic Teaching

It is quite notable that the *Catechism of the Catholic Church* uses the language of
deification and cites some of the very texts that we have been looking at here. The
article on the incarnation, while not using the term "deification" explicitly, cites
2 Peter 1:4 (an important text for deification), and makes reference to the classic
patristic "formula of exchange" that lies at the root of the doctrine of deification:

The Word became flesh to make us *"partakers of the divine nature"*
(2 Pet. 1:4): "For this is why the Word became man, and the Son
of God became the Son of man: so that man, by entering into
communion with the Word and thus receiving divine sonship,

---

46   Augustine, *Expositions on the Psalms*, Ps. 49, 2, cited in Russell, *The Doctrine of Deification*, 331.

47   Augustine, *Tractates in John*, Trac. 54, 2, in St. Augustine, *Tractates on the Gospel of John 28–54*,
     trans. John W. Rettig, Fathers of the Church 88 (Washington DC: Catholic University of
     America, 1993), 302.

48   Aquinas, *Commentary on John* 15:9–13 [1999], in Thomas Aquinas, *Commentary on the Gospel of
     St. John*, vol. 2, trans. and intro. James A. Weisheipl and Fabian R. Larcher (Petersham, MA: St.
     Bede's, 1999), 397.

242 Daniel A. Keating

might become a son of God" [Irenaeus]. "For the Son of God became man so that we might become God" [Athanasius]. "The only-begotten Son of God, wanting to make us sharers in his divinity, assumed our nature, so that he, made man, might make men gods" [Thomas Aquinas].[49]

But it is also quite noteworthy that the *Catechism* does not explain what all this means—it relies largely on simple citation. And when it does use the term "divinize," it supplies little description of what the term means. Man in original innocence is said to be in a state of holiness and "destined to be fully 'divinized' by God in glory," but we are not told what this divinization (either partial or full) entails.[50] On three occasions, the term "divinize" is found in citations of the Greek fathers, without further explanation.[51] The fullest sense of deification appears in a paragraph where the grace of Christ is identified as "the *sanctifying* or *deifying* grace received in Baptism" (emphasis in original).[52] Here deification is placed in parallel with sanctification, and located at the point of baptism. As we have seen, this is just how the fathers locate and understand deification.

One day in class a student approached me with a copy of the *Catechism* open in her hands. She pointed to the article on the "formula of exchange,"[53] and asked in a somewhat exasperated voice, "What does this mean?" The *Catechism* itself does not provide a direct answer. Given this situation, I believe there is need for a sound catechesis on the meaning of "deification" or "divinization" today—first among those trained in theology, and then something simpler for all readers of the *Catechism*. If this is done with care, it can open our eyes to see more deeply into the riches of what is ours from the Father in Christ through the Spirit.

Deification, rightly understood, ensures that our understanding of "sanctification" does not stop short at cleansing and purification from sin; that sanctification has as its end and goal communion with God himself brought about by his direct agency. It ensures that our understanding of salvation is nothing short of the union with God that we were created for, and that our creaturely destiny is found in direct relationship with the eternal God—Father, Son and Holy Spirit.

A proper Christian account of deification also undercuts the tendency of our age towards idolatry, towards making ourselves gods or identifying ourselves

---

49   *The Catechism of the Catholic Church*, 2d. ed. (Vatican City: Libreria Editrice Vaticana, 1997), no. 460.

50   *Catechism*, no. 398.

51   In *Catechism*, no. 1589, Gregory of Nazianzus states that the priest of Christ is "divinized and divinizes." In *Catechism*, no. 1988, Athanasius links our divinization with the gift of the indwelling Spirit; and in *Catechism*, no. 2670, Gregory of Nazianzus claims that we are divinized by the Spirit in baptism.

52   *Catechism*, no. 1999.

53   *Catechism*, no. 460.

as God. Unlike Adam and Eve who succumbed to the temptation to become "like God" on their own terms, we become "sons of God" and "gods" only in Jesus Christ, the true Son and image of God. Through deification, we are not enabled to become "gods" on our own and to achieve equal status with God. Rather, we are called to be gods by *participating* in God himself, by being joined to the incarnate Word through the Spirit. Accurately presented, deification reminds us that in Christ we remain the creatures that we are, yet find our joy and delight in being elevated by grace to communion with God and participation in his life and power.

The doctrine of deification enhances the doctrine of the incarnation, and consequently of the Trinity and the divine economy of the Father in Christ through the Spirit. It reminds us that there is no bypassing the incarnation or making it a temporary stage on the way to things higher. The incarnate Word remains the central locus of our salvation and deification—and our creaturely participation in the divine life is always mediated by being in Christ and members of his body.

We are "sons and daughters in the Son" and are deified to the degree that we are found in, and transformed into the image of, Christ himself. The primary warrant, then, for Christian deification is that it ensures and enhances the full biblical revelation of our call: to become sons and daughters formed in the image of Christ; to be temples of the Holy Spirit and members of the household of God; to live in direct and eternal communion with the Father through the Son and in the Holy Spirit.

Scripture, Doctrine, and Proclamation:
The Catechism of the Catholic Church and the Renewal of Homiletics

❧ John C. Cavadini ☙
University of Notre Dame

One of the most striking features of the *Catechism of the Catholic Church* is the way that it uses Scripture. It does not use Scripture primarily to back up or to corroborate doctrinal statements, but rather it incorporates Scripture into the very articulation of the doctrine. Scripture is not only cited as a way of authorizing the doctrinal statements, but is woven into the text of the *Catechism*, so that Catholic doctrine is actually articulated in scriptural terms and language.

Like the *Confessions* of St. Augustine, the *Rule* of St. Benedict, or *Lumen Gentium* and the other documents of the Second Vatican Council, the *Catechism* is a Scripture-infused text, where scriptural passages, words, phrases, and sentences simply make up part of the text itself. "I think it would be fair to style this as a *scriptural catechesis*, a catechesis carried out not simply with the support of the words of Scripture but *in* the words of Scripture. It is a catechetical narrative that *relies* on the words of Scripture to speak its main points, so that it almost becomes a kind of glossed scriptural proclamation rather than a scripturally corroborated dogmatic statement."[1]

I believe this practice of the *Catechism* is inspired by *Dei Verbum*, Vatican II's declaration on divine revelation. In *Dei Verbum* we read that "Sacred Tradition and Sacred Scripture … are bound closely together and communicate one with the other. For both of them, flowing out from the same divine wellspring, come together in some fashion to form one thing and move towards the same goal."[2] You could say that the *Catechsim* "performs" this "coming together" of Scripture and Tradition in a textual tapestry whose threads are drawn on the one hand from Scripture and, on the other, from various traditional sources—from the creeds, the writings of the Fathers, and from formulas and teachings of the Church councils. The teaching authority of the Church, or magisterium, is the "servant" of the Word of God, according to *Dei Verbum*; and the magisterium is present

---

1 John C. Cavadini, "The Use of Scripture in the *Catechism of the Catholic Church*," *Letter and Spirit* 2 (2006): 25–26, at 28.

2 Second Vatican Council, *Dei Verbum*, Dogmatic Constitution on Divine Revelation (November 18, 1965), 9, in *The Scripture Documents: An Anthology of Official Catholic Teachings*, ed. Dean P. Béchard (Collegeville, MN: Liturgical Press, 2002), 19–31.

in the *Catechism* as the authorial voice, "arranging and organizing the texts from Scripture and Tradition."[3]

The Church's teaching authority "serves" these two streams of transmission of the one Word of God by contextualizing Scripture in the Tradition's rule of faith, and by contextualizing the rule of faith in its original primary character—as a summary of scriptural teaching. This means that the exposition of Catholic doctrine is enlivened by the appeal to the imagination that scriptural texts carry in their images and stories, prophecies, and proclamations.

The scriptural texts and images have a kind of "overplus" of meaning that can never be fully reduced to doctrinal formulas. That "overplus," as part of the exposition of doctrine itself, keeps the exposition of doctrine from closing in on itself, as though its formulas could ever fully express the lofty mysteries they state. At the same time, unless scriptural texts and images are contextualized or contoured in doctrinal exposition, the "overplus" of meaning in the scriptural text can turn into a kind of indeterminacy of meaning that could not be summarized and "handed on" in any normative way to future generations of Christians.[4]

The *Catechism's* incorporation of Scripture into the actual exposition of doctrine, then, enacts and implies a kind of pedagogy—a manner and a spirit of teaching. It is that which I would like to characterize more fully in this article.

For various reasons, in recent times there has grown up a gap in the minds of Catholics between "Scripture" on the one hand, and "doctrine" or "dogma" on the other. Doctrine or teaching is seen as a kind of overlay on the scriptural text, in some fundamental way foreign to it. It is as though Catholics had internalized a Protestant critique of Catholic doctrine as "unscriptural," or as though the dominant academic mode of interpreting the Scriptures—the historico-critical—has engendered the reflex that the only proper way of interpreting Scripture is by reading each book, and each segment of each book, in its own individual historical context. It is interesting to me that both a certain strain of evangelical Christianity and historico-critical scholarship both share the presupposition that doctrine is a foreign overlay on the text of Scripture and cannot be used to discover or illuminate its meaning.

I am not here interested in polemicizing against historico-critical scholarship and its method of contextualizing Scripture. *Dei Verbum* makes clear that historical and literary study of the texts is one of the ways of approaching the meaning of Scripture, and the *Catechism* often reflects an acceptance of the results of historico-critical scholarship.[5] But interpreting Scripture as the Word of God also involves

---

3   Cavadini, "Use of Scripture in the *Catechism*," 30.

4   See the illuminating discussion on the relation between the formulas of doctrine and the realities they express in *The Catechism of the Catholic Church*, 2d. ed. (Vatican City: Libreria Editrice Vaticana, 1997), no. 170. See also Cavadini, "The Use of Scripture in the *Catechism*," 28, 31.

5   This acceptance of historical findings can be seen, for instance, in the *Catechism's* treatment of

contextualizing it within the rule of faith, as I have noted above. If for no other reason, this reflects the fact that the books of Scripture as we know it would not even have been preserved or handed down to us unless the Fathers thought they were united by a common witness to the rule of raith and the creeds that emerged from the rule of faith. Scripture as such, in other words, has a "traditional" form.[6]

However, one of the fruits of an imbalanced reliance on historico-critical scholarship as the only proper way to contextualize Scripture has been an odd convergence with the anti-Catholic view that doctrine is an obscuring overlay upon the pure truth and meaning of the scriptural text, a second order addition or even distortion of its truth. It is as though Lessing's "ugly ditch" has re-constituted itself in new territory, with Scripture on one side, and doctrine on the other.[7]

This in turn has generated a kind of dichotomy in the way we think about the teaching ministries of the Church, and, in particular, preaching. Those charged with preaching the Word of God feel especially constrained by this dichotomy. The homily is supposed to illuminate the scriptural readings from the lectionary, to "break open the Word" just proclaimed. And who would argue with that? But this aim is too often *contrasted* with preaching doctrinally, as though doctrine had nothing to do with the scriptural text.

The pedagogy exemplified in the *Catechism* recovers the ancient, patristic balance between proclamation of the Word in Scripture and handing on the teachings of the faith in doctrine. This exemplification is at the same time a call to a renewed scriptural and doctrinal pedagogy. I would argue that failing to "hear" this call or to appropriate the example of the *Catechism* results not only in undercatechized Catholics, but in Catholics who are ripe either for proselytizing by the evangelical megachurches or Pentecostal sects on the one hand, or for the agnostic secular *status quo* on the other.

Once you split "Scripture" from "doctrine" and preach on the basis of such a split, you are actually teaching and propagating that very split. In this process, Catholics "learn" that the exposition of Scripture has little to do with doctrine—so why not, then, go to the churches where this split is prosecuted in a much more thoroughgoing and unencumbered way? For Catholic doctrine is embodied in Catholic liturgical action and prayer; and, if Catholic doctrine is held to be essentially unscriptural, then the rest of the liturgy will come to seem also as resting on indefensible doctrinal additions that simply encumber the full expression of Scripture. On the other hand, if people have already begun to doubt the truth of

---

the relationship between Jesus and the Judaism of his time, *Catechism*, nos. 574–594. See the discussion in Cavadini, "The Use of Scripture in the *Catechism*," 31–34.

6   This is argued more fully in a paper by Charles Kannengeisser, as yet unpublished.

7   G. E. Lessing, the eighteenth-century philosopher, proposed that there is an "ugly broad ditch" (*der garstige breite Graben*) between historical truths and the religious claims of Christianity. See his "On the Proof of the Spirit and of Power," in *Lessing's Theological Writings* (Stamford, CA: Stanford University, 1956), 51–55.

the Scriptures because of popularized versions of historico-critical worries that the real Jesus is buried irrecoverably in the sedimented overlay of the Church's proclamation, they will not get any help from a homiletic practice that essentially accepts the very dichotomy between Scripture and Tradition that is pushing them away.

It is important, then, to cultivate and expand the scriptural pedagogy of the *Catechism*—not only so that Catholics can be better catechized, but also so we stop forming Catholics into the false dichotomy between Scripture and doctrine which is so foreign to authentic Catholic tradition and which actually militates against it.[8] I would like to spend the rest of this article trying to illustrate what a Scripture-infused doctrinal preaching, or a doctrinally shaped scriptural preaching, would look like.

Preaching About the Birth and Nature of the Church

This new kind of preaching would *not* look like the old fashioned apologetics, that is, a project of how to prove or defend Catholic doctrine from Scripture. Such a method would be a step backwards from the *Catechism*, which, as I have already pointed out, does not use Scripture in this way. Trying to "prove" Catholic doctrine from Scripture only serves to feature the dichotomy between them, as though Scripture itself were not doctrinally shaped in its origin and conception, and as though doctrine were a body of interesting information about the cosmos with no intrinsic connection to scriptural proclamation.

In following the example of the *Catechism*, we are looking at a new kind of apologetics—one that does not try so much to prove Catholic teaching from the Scriptures, but rather tries to articulate doctrine in a scriptural way, and to shape the exposition of Scripture in a doctrinal way. Such a renewed homiletics[9] would be more trusting of the scriptural images and narratives as suggestive and fruitful in their own right. The *Catechism* trusts them; why shouldn't the preacher? Such a homiletics will also be more trusting of Catholic doctrine as essentially a summation and continuation of the same proclamation we find in Scripture.

But how to help the preacher recover a scripturally infused eloquence of teaching? The project I have in mind is a homiletic commentary on the *Catechism*. This would not be conceived as a line-by-line commentary, but rather would seize on a small number of central passages in the *Catechism*, each of which would head up a small cluster of passages with supplementary import. We could feature especially those elements of Catholic teaching that have a markedly "Catholic"

---

8   One reason I was disappointed to see the official publication of the shortened version of the *Catechism*, the *Compendium*, was that, just as I suspected, all the Scripture had been removed, thus backing away from the pedagogical challenge and invitation proposed by the *Catechism* itself. See *Compendium, Catechism of the Catholic Church* (Washington, DC: United States Conference of Catholic Bishops, 2006).

9   The same would apply to hymns.

distinctiveness, that is, the very doctrines that are notoriously difficult to "prove" from Scripture though they are all profoundly scriptural. In turn, these are all mostly doctrines connected in some way to the distinctive Catholic doctrine of the Church—the doctrine of the Church itself, the doctrine of the sacraments and especially of the Eucharist and holy orders, the Marian doctrines, and the doctrine of the saints and eschatology more generally.

For example, what does it mean to say that Christ Jesus "instituted" the Church? I think that hidden in the minds of many Catholics is the idea that the Church is something like the United States of America or the Elks' Club. These are voluntary associations of individuals created by the decision of each one to come together in order to pursue certain common objects of interest, and defined essentially by that joint decision to come together. Their relationship is well expressed in the initial language of the U. S. Constitution: "We the people, in order to form a more perfect union, provide for the common defense ... "

The person who "institutes" this kind of association is the one who writes or approves a charter, a constitution, or a set of rules defining the structure of the association, perhaps the one who had the idea for this association in the first place. In the minds of most Americans, including many Catholics, a "church" is very much like this. They see "church" as an association of people who come together freely to share certain common beliefs, to reinforce those beliefs, and to pray to God together just like they do at home, only doing it together offers mutual encouragement. According to this way of thinking, Jesus is the one who had the idea for this association, and set up the twelve apostles as its structure, and so "instituted" the Church.

Now, it is true that Jesus chose the Twelve with Peter as their head, and, as the *Catechism* says, thus "endowed his community with a structure that will remain until the Kingdom is fully achieved."[10] But to emphasize this *in isolation* as the meaning of the Church's institution, and to cite such passages as Mark 3:14–15 and Matthew 16:18 as "proofs" of it, only serves to reinforce the idea of the Church as a voluntary club which Jesus invented and structured as he saw fit. Scripture, under this model, becomes the historical record of this institution, and very little more; the rest of Catholic doctrine is an overlay on this bare historical account.

The homiletic commentary I have in mind would make this paragraph from the *Catechism* as the place to start:

> The Church is born primarily of Christ's total self-giving for our salvation, anticipated in the institution of the Eucharist and fulfilled on the cross. "The origin and growth of the Church are symbolized by the blood and water which flowed from the open side of the crucified Jesus" (*Lumen Gentium*, 3; John 19:34). "For

---

10   *Catechism*, no. 765.

it was from the side of Christ as he slept the sleep of death upon the cross that there came forth the 'wondrous sacrament of the whole Church'" (*Sacramentum Concilium*, 5). As Eve was formed from the sleeping Adam's side, so the Church was born from the pierced heart of Christ hanging dead on the cross (St. Ambrose, *Commentary on the Gospel of Luke*, Bk. 2, 85–89).[11]

This passage invites us to reflect on three scriptural images as a way of learning about the constitution of the Church—namely, Christ hanging dead on the cross, the blood and water flowing from the pierced side or heart of Jesus (John 19:34), and Eve formed from the side of Adam (Gen. 2:21–23). The *Catechism* suggests that if you ponder these images and preach in such a way that you help others to ponder them, you will come to an image of the Church that allows one to see what it means, most fully, to say that Christ Jesus instituted the Church. The image of Christ hanging dead on the cross is an image of his "total self-giving," and the image of the blood and water flowing from his side is an image of the Church and its sacraments proceeding from that total self-gift. The image of Eve coming forth from the side of Adam provides a kind of theology in pictures: the Church, born of Christ's total self-giving, is created in that very love and is as intimately united to Christ as "bone of my bone and flesh of my flesh," to use another image from the Genesis narrative.

These texts don't "prove" the Catholic doctrine of the Church from Scripture, rather they offer images which the preacher can use to send home the idea that if the Church has a constitution or definition, it is nothing other than the "total self-giving" of Christ on the cross, and the Church is therefore the enduring presence of that total self-giving in time and space, in history. No merely voluntary association could claim that. Far from being essentially defined as a "club" or voluntary association, the Church is here able to be portrayed as what it truly is, Christ's spouse, something as close to him as his own Body.

It could be objected that this passage refers to Scripture passages relatively infrequently read in the liturgy, for example, the passion according to St. John. But that is where the "cluster" idea comes in. This passage could be at the head of a cluster of *Catechism* passages that speak about Christ's total self-gift. This self-gift is covered in a series of stunningly beautiful passages in the *Catechism*,[12] which comprise a rich tissue of scriptural phrases, allusions, and citations woven together with traditional sources and magisterial statements. Any one of these scriptural passages, amply represented in the lectionary, can be the beginning of a catechetical homily on the Church as born out of the total self-gift of Christ, anticipated in the institution of the Eucharist and fulfilled on the cross.

---

11   *Catechism*, no. 766.

12   *Catechism*, nos. 606–618.

A preacher could decide that during the course of a given lectionary cycle, he was going to preach on the character of the Church, each time drawing the assembly's attention to Christ's total self-giving as that which creates and defines the Church. In one of these homilies, he can even tie in Christ's selection of the Twelve as a structure, because the sequence permits one to tie this easily into the idea of Christ's self-gift.

> The Eucharist that Christ institutes at that moment will be the memorial of his sacrifice (1 Cor. 11:25). Jesus includes the apostles in his own offering and bids them perpetuate it (Luke 22:19). By doing so, the Lord institutes his apostles as priests of the new covenant: "For their sakes I sanctify myself, so that they also may be sanctified in truth" (John 17:19).[13]

A homily on Mark 3:14–15 or Matthew 16:18 (accounts of the election of the Twelve and of Peter), when joined to the ideas in no. 622 of the *Catechism*, show that the Twelve are not simply an organizational rubric for something like the Elk's Club only holier, but are instead themselves defined by their participation in Jesus's total self-giving and by their role in perpetuating it. Someone could preach once a month, on the average, on Scriptures from (or closely related to) this cluster of passages from the *Catechism*. It would fill people's imaginations with the true and full Catholic idea of the Church, and at the same time fill them with images of the total self-gift that is the constitution of the Church.

It is easy to see how you could also have a cluster of similar *Catechism* passages starting with no. 766 of the *Catechism* at the head, and connecting it through the idea of Christ's total self-gift— his sacrifice on the cross—to the later sections on the Eucharist. One could move, for example, from no. 766 to no. 616: "It is love 'to the end' (John 13:1) that confers on Christ's sacrifice its value." This passage could easily be connected to the sections on the Eucharist as a sacrifice (nos. 1362–1372). In turn, these easily connect to the sections on the real presence, via reference to no. 1380 (one of the most beautiful sections of the *Catechism*) and then full circle to no. 1396, which states, "The Eucharist makes the Church," citing in the process 1 Corinthians 12:13, 10:16–17, and *Sermon* 272 of St. Augustine (which itself is full of scriptural references).

What does it mean to say that the Eucharist "makes" the Church? That the Church, in the words at the head of the cluster, is "born primarily of Christ's total self-giving for our salvation, anticipated in the institution of the Eucharist and fulfilled on the cross."[14] Further, we know that "he wanted us to have the memorial of the love with which he loved us 'to the end' (John 13:1) even to the giving of his life," and that "in his eucharistic presence he remains mysteriously in our midst as

---

13 *Catechism*, no. 611.

14 *Catechism*, no. 766.

the one who loved us and gave himself up for us (Gal. 2:20), and he remains under signs that express and communicate this love."[15]

Then it makes sense that the Eucharist makes the Church because, as the *Catechism* explains, "those who receive the Eucharist are united more closely to Christ."[16] In other words, we are formed into one Body by his total self-giving on the cross, the same one here present in the Eucharist. That is a far cry from the anti-Catholic stereotype of the Church, and the beauty is that it is all tied, in persuasive scriptural images, to the love of Christ poured out for us on the cross, something intrinsically appealing that needs no apology or defense.

But my main point is that this cluster of short sections from the *Catechism* cites so many different Scripture passages that one would have multiple opportunities during the course of a lectionary cycle to use one of these scriptural passages to draw any of the others or all of the others into play in an exposition of the Catholic doctrine of the Eucharist. One would have a fully orthodox and precise exposition of the doctrine, filled with scriptural images that appeal to the heart as well as to the mind, something that could be used, with variation of course, four or five Sundays out of a year. That would provide effective catechesis that was both doctrinally precise and moving—and therefore persuasive.

Proclaiming Mary as "Eschatological Icon of the Church"

I would like to provide one more (not unrelated) example, and that is the case of Mary. Catholics almost never hear homilies about Mary anymore, except perhaps those delivered somewhat awkwardly on the feast days of the Assumption and the Immaculate Conception. I say "awkwardly" because nowhere does the dichotomy between Catholic doctrine and Scripture seem so glaring as in the case of Mary, and especially these two dogmas of the faith. That is because one has in one's mind the mistaken idea that for these doctrines to be properly scriptural, they must be "proven" from passages that explicitly mention them.

However, Scripture works with images, and the homilest has to be able to feel comfortable with images and preaching based on these images. For example, John 19:26–27 presents the poignant image of Jesus giving Mary to his beloved disciple as his mother. The passage is not included so that we can realize from the historical record what a good boy Jesus was, model son that he is, thinking about providing for his mother even while he was dying on the cross.

The beloved disciple is imaged here as the new son of a new mother, Jesus's mother, who is now the mother of Christ's faithful, herself an image or icon of the Church. Mary in this passage is both herself and, precisely as such, an image of the Church, spiritual mother to all of us. Her motherhood of Jesus is a completely integrated act, both physical and spiritual, perfectly conformed to the will

---

15   *Catechism*, no. 1380.

16   *Catechism*, no. 1396.

of the Father and thus perfectly configured to her Son's total self-gift that is the constitution of the Church. Her very being, as Jesus' mother, is defined by the love revealed and enacted in Jesus's self-giving, and so she is at once an *icon* or image of the Church as it will be when it is itself perfectly configured to this love, and the mother of the Church, our spiritual mother.

This is why, as the *Catechism* says, devotion to Mary is "intrinsic to Christian worship."[17] One would never know this from the low mariology that presents the historical Mary, insofar as we can know her, as a kind of special role model, reducing the scriptural contribution to simple historical reporting, and replicating the old divide between Scripture (here as an historical record) and doctrine (as a later overlay). The image of the woman clothed with the sun in Revelation 12:1–17 is then interpreted as an image of the Church. But the image is multivalent. There is nothing wrong with its representing both Mary *and* the Church, and the Church *because* it also represents Mary. The Son to whom she gives birth in Revelation 12:13 is then Jesus, and "the rest of her children" in 12:17, the members of the Church.

It could be objected that these two passages with their two powerful images, John 19:26–27 and Revelation 12:1–17, are just two passages and come up rarely in the liturgical cycle, and so offer only limited opportunity to preach on Mary. But that is true only if you have a "low" mariology (Mary as "role model" for disciples) in mind. A cluster of *Catechism* sections with no. 972 at the head would easily provide or suggest enough passages that one could include Mary in one's preaching many times in a lectionary cycle.

According to the *Catechism*, Mary is an "eschatological icon of the Church."[18] Especially in alliance with no. 963, "Mary, Mother of Christ, Mother of the Church," and no. 726, "Mary, the new Eve, ("mother of the living"), mother of the 'whole Christ'," one can find legitimate license to preach on Mary when preaching on any relevant Scripture passage on the Church. In addition, the sections of the *Catechism* on Mary[19] are full of references to Scriptures both in the New and Old Testatments, as well as references to patristic and magisterial documents that themselves contain links to Scripture passages.

A homiletic commentary on the *Catechism* would help preachers to exploit all of these links. Mary is a "wholly unique member of the Church. ... The exemplary realization (*typus*) of the Church."[20] She is this, not as a mythological creature or goddess, but as a true human mother in history as we know it, the presence to us in maternal form of the most burning love of the crucified, the total self-gift of Christ that forms us and begets us as his members. How would that not be a moving and

17　*Catechism*, no. 971.

18　*Catechism*, no. 972.

19　*Catechism*, nos. 487–511; 721–726; 963–975.

20　*Catechism*, no. 967.

orthodox homiletic catechesis on Mary, available from many scriptural texts in the lectionary, even if Mary is only part of the homily?

In addition to the example of the *Catechism*, I would like to point to one more salient example of the kind of catechetical preaching I am talking about. That is found in Pope Benedict XVI's first encyclical, *Deus Caritas Est* ("God is Love").[21] This is essentially a homiletical catechesis on Christian love in the form of a meditative elaboration on certain key Scripture passages, certainly 1 John 4:8, reflected in the title, but even more centrally, the focal image of the pierced heart of Christ, from John 19:34–37.

All of the scriptural texts used in this encyclical radiate out from this latter image as hubs from the center of a wheel. Ultimately, as Hans Urs von Balthasar famously said, "Love alone is credible."[22] Benedict, with this encyclical has proposed what we might call an "apologetics of love." If "love alone is credible," that is, if love is the only reality that is its own apology and needs no further defense, it would be easy to create a persuasive apologetics for Catholic doctrine ultimately based on the truth that "God is Love"—a love we see in the pierced heart of Christ on the cross.

I have tried to illustrate how that can be done for catechesis on the doctrine of the Church and on the doctrine of the Eucharist. But all of the major mysteries of the Christian faith go back to the over-arching mystery of the love of God revealed in Christ. Creation, the Trinity, the incarnation—all of the great catechetical themes can be propounded in the moving scriptural vocabulary of God's infinite Love. A homiletic commentary on the *Catechism* would set up "clusters" of passages in the *Catechism* that would guide the reader to key passages in this apologetic of love (such as no. 766), and show the path linking them to the expositions of each major doctrine. Each cluster would also generate a cluster of scriptural passages from which the homilist could authentically preach on any of these doctrines, in a way formed by the eloquence of God's love itself.

---

21   Pope Benedict XVI, *Deus Caritas Est*, Encyclical Letter on Christian Love (December 25, 2005) (Washington, DC: United States Conference of Catholic Bishops, 2006).

22   Hans Urs von Balthasar, *Love Alone Is Credible* (San Francisco: Ignatius, 2004 [1968]).

Letter & Spirit 4 (2008): 255–288

Tradition & Traditions

~:~

The Sign of the Temple:
A Meditation

~: Jean Cardinal Daniélou, S.J. :~

On the lowest level, which is not essentially Christian, but is part of the historical heritage of Christianity, though generally separated from it, the Christian mystery is the mystery of creation. I mean by this not only an original dependence of the universe in relation to a personal and transcendent God, but also the actual dependence of all things in his sight, and consequently a divine presence which confers upon the whole cosmos a sacramental value.

At the birth of mankind, the whole creation, issuing from the hands of God, is holy; the earthly Paradise is nature in a state of grace. The house of God is the whole cosmos. Heaven is his tent, his tabernacle; the earth is his "footstool." There is a whole cosmic liturgy, that of the source of the flowers and birds.

> Multiplied blessings made an overflow,
> The silence of the soul was a still pond.
> The rising sun became a monstrance now,
> Filling the heavens with a shining sound.
>
> Smoke was a censer, and the cedar-trees
> Composed an ever-mounting barricade.
> Days of delight were as a colonnade
> Fanned by the calmness of the twilight breeze.[1]

The time of the patriarchs still retains something of this paradisal grace. The Spirit of God still broods upon the waters. God is not yet the hidden God, dwelling apart within the Tabernacle. He talks with Noah on familiar terms. His relationship with Abraham is that of a friend: "And the Lord appeared unto him in the plains of Mamre; and he sat in the tent door in the heat of the day; and he lifted up his eyes and, lo, three men stood by him; and when he saw them, he ran to meet them from the tent door, and bowed himself toward the ground, and said, My Lord, if I now have found favor in thy sight, pass not away, I pray thee, from

---

1   Charles Péguy, "Eve," in *Oeuvres Poétiques Complètes* (Paris: Gallimard, 1941), 710.

Thy servant: let a little water, I pray you, be fetched, and wash your feet."[2] Abraham has that *parrhesia* with God, that freedom of speech which, in the days of ancient Greece, was the right of a free citizen, and by which St. Paul and the brethren symbolized the liberty of the children of God with their Father. The whole of nature is still a temple consecrated to him. A group of trees, a spring of fresh water, these are fragments of Paradise in which he offers his sacrifices; a rough stone is an altar dedicated to him.

This is the primitive level, common to all men, whose traces are still to be found, twisted, soiled, perverted, in every religion. So in Greek religion we have the sacred wood, the *alsos*, with its fountain; but polytheism has corrupted the primitive gesture. God "in times past has suffered all nations to walk in their own ways. Nevertheless he left not himself without witness, in that he did good, and gave us rain from heaven, and fruitful seasons, filling our hearts with food and gladness"[3]. Only the wise men continued to seek for signs in the heavenly Temple, contemplating, explaining, and defining, according to the positions of the stars, the sites of towns and altars. The shepherds and the Magi are, as it were, the flowering in the Gospel of this underlying, primary stratum, which corruption has not altogether spoiled, nor Mosaic revelation destroyed.

For us today, it still constitutes the holy in its rudimentary form, which darkly hints at the divine presence in the silence of night, in the shadows of the forest, in the vastness of the desert, in the lightening-flash of genius, in the purity of love. It is this basic level that was recognized by that Boer farmer to whom Otto refers, who in the solitude of the desert, where the sun poured forth its rays upon the plain, was aware of a voice speaking to him. It is this level that explains the religious awe with which the earth deserves to be surrounded. But this sacramental element has no meaning except in relation to a personal presence. "Awe," writes Péguy, "stretches forth indeed to encompass the whole universe. We too easily forget that the universe is creation; and awe, like charity, is due to every creature." It is this personal presence, at once hidden and revealed by signs, that awakens in us this holy dread.

In the Cosmic Temple

In the cosmic Temple, man is not living primarily in his own house, but in the house of God. This is why he knows that he should revere those creatures who do not belong to him, that he can lay hands on nothing without permission. All is holy; the trees are heavy with sacramental mysteries. Primitive sacrifice is simply the recognition of the sovereign realm of God. He takes the first-fruits, and leaves the rest to man. But at the same time, man is part of creation and has his role to play in it. God has in some way left creation unfinished, and man's mission is to bring it to

---

2   Gen. 18:1–4.

3   Acts 14:16–17.

fulfillment. Through his work he exploits unknown material resources, and thus work is sacred, being cooperation in the task of creation. Through knowledge and art he removes it from its ephemeral condition to enable it to subsist spiritually.[4]

Indeed, by sacramental use man confers on visible things their supreme dignity, not merely as signs and symbols, but as effective means of grace in the soul. So water effects purification, oil communicates power and unction, salt gives the savor of heavenly things. Man is thus the mediator through whom the visible universe is gathered together and offered up, the priest of that virginal creation over which God lovingly watches. Through man the silent litany of things becomes an explicit act of worship.

> Nature without me is vain, it is I who give it a meaning;
> All things become in me eternal, are laid on my altar.
> Water now washes the soul, not only the travel-worn body;
> My bread becomes for me the very substance of God.[5]

Thus the whole of nature, as St. Paul says, expects that man will lead it to its end. The sacred character of love, in particular, is not derived from the shadowy presence of the race using individuals for its own ends, but from the presence of God in the handiwork that love causes men to share. "When I was close to him I nearly always had the sense of God's actual presence," wrote Alice Ollé-Laprune of her husband.

Such is the innocence of creation. Creatures are holy, expecting that man will lead them to their goal. But man has the power to violate this order. When he turns away from God, when he profanes himself by ceasing to be a consecrated creature, he also profanes the world on which he imposes sacrilegious uses. The material inventions that are meant to help men to free themselves from matter and bring to realization the community of mankind, we transform into instruments of hatred. The beauty of the body, which is the lovely reflection of the beauty of the soul, its visible "glory" which should awaken in us loving awe, we transform into an instrument of selfish pleasure. The blessings of culture, intended to help men to become more truly human by developing the powers of their minds, we transform into an instrument of perverted specialization and highbrow aestheticism.

But creation itself is free from all these faults, wherever she may "suffer violence." She, too, rebels in her holiness and purity against such profanation by sacrilegious rites; and she expresses her rebellion by the resistance that she makes

---

4   This is well expressed by Paul-Jean Toulet (1867–1920): "Whispering woods, if I should die, / Perish without my artistry."

5   Paul Claudel, *Cinq Grandes Odes, Suivies d'un Processional pour Saluer le Siècle Nouveau* [Five Great Odes: Followed by a Processional to Greet the New Century], 4th ed. (Paris: Éditions de la Nouvelle Revue Française, 1913), 174. Eng. trans.: *Five Great Odes; [Poetry]*, trans. Edward Lucie-Smith (Chester Springs, PA: Dufour Editions, 1970).

when we turn her aside from her goal. Between her and us there is a battle waged, which is the result of sin.

> You know nothing in the vast universe
> That may not be a means of unhappiness.[6]

This is the hostile world that we know so well, where everything is threatening; and the more sensitive we are, the more it is so. No one has felt this more acutely than Ranier Maria Rilke:

> The terrible in every breath of air,
> You breathe it all too clearly.

The rebellion of creatures is the cause of our suffering, which is the resistance of matter to our will. It was unknown in Paradise, it will be unknown in Paradise regained, and Jesus already restores this Paradise, mastering the winds and waves, healing the sick. It is the cloudiness of the world that, far from showing us God, hides him from us and confines us to earth. So we become slaves, we that are called to be kings. What are the fires of hell but the rebellion of the creature, defined all too clearly?

How are we to rediscover the lost harmony, how are we to be reconciled with things? Here is the nostalgia that lies perhaps at the center of poetry, which is a quest for the cosmic privileges of Paradise lost, a glorification of the body without using the conversion of the heart as intermediary. But everything depends on this conversion. Things themselves have never changed. They remain what they always were; they await us in brotherly innocence. It is we that are "underlings." If I seek to rediscover the joys of Paradise, to move at ease amid created things, I must give them back their proper meaning, I must restore their honorable mission as servants of humanity. Then they will cease to burden me with silent reproaches, they will begin once again to chant before me:

> None but the pure heart knows
> The perfume of the rose.[7]

I must recover the purity of my glance. Then only will creatures once more become bearers of light from heaven.

It is this paradisal reconciliation that we find in St. Francis of Assisi, in St. John of the Cross: "Yes, the heavens are mine and the earth is mine and the peoples are mine. ... What more can you desire? What do you seek, my soul?" Nothing remains of our prostration before the powers of the cosmos and history, those swords of Damocles hanging over mankind. Cosmic fear is vanquished, the

---

6   Péguy, "Eve."

7   Paul Claudel, *Figures et Paraboles* [Figures and Parables] (Paris: Gallimard, 1936), 28.

universe has become once more a Temple where we are at home with God in the cool of the evening, where man comes forward, silent and composed, absorbed in his task as in a perpetual liturgy, attentive to that presence which fills him with awe and tenderness.

In the Tabernacle of Moses

The establishment of the Tabernacle, whose ultimate form is the Temple, is the fundamental mission entrusted by God to Moses. The Temple is his concern, as the covenant is Abraham's. This mission is described in the Book of Exodus. Its object is the building of a sanctuary that will be the dwelling of God alone. This sanctuary is to consist of a threefold enclosure; first of all, an outer court, the *temenos*, the *templum*; then a tent, the tabernacle proper; and finally, within the tent, the sanctuary, divided off by a veil, in which are to be found the Ark, the Mercy Seat, the cherubim. It is here that God was to be present.

The completed forms of this ideal pattern, revealed to Moses on Sinai, passed through many vicissitudes. At first it was to be a portable sanctuary, borne by the Hebrews through the wilderness, consisting of a tent of cloth covered by a tent of leather. It is a long way from this to the Temple of Herod which was known to Jesus, and which was an elaborate stone structure. In this interval the sanctuary had been at Shiloh, and not greatly honored there. Then David had solemnly brought the Ark to Jerusalem, and left a plan of the Temple which Solomon carried out. This Temple, destroyed by Nebuchadnezzar, was roughly rebuilt by Nehemiah and the Jews who returned from exile.

But the external form matters little. The essential religious fact is that of the presence of God in the Temple, which endured from the time of Moses till the death of Christ. The destruction of the Temple in 70 A.D. only gave sanction to its discontinuance. The Temple is the dwelling, the *Shekinah*, in which the glory of God abides. "A cloud covered the tent of the congregation, and the glory of the LORD filled the tabernacle. And Moses was not able to enter into the tent of the congregation, because the cloud abode thereon, and the glory of the LORD filled the tabernacle."[8] It is here that God meets his representatives.

Thus Ezekiel: "So the spirit took me up, and brought me into the inner court; and, behold, the glory of the LORD filled the house."[9] It is here that on the threshold of the New Testament Zechariah, the father of John the Baptist, is to receive the news of the birth of his son. "And there appeared unto him an angel of the LORD standing on the right side of the altar of incense."[10] Here is the center of the religious life of Israel. In the wilderness the Tabernacle is the center of the nomads' camp; after the return from exile, the little "remnant" of those who had

---

8   Exod. 40:34–35.

9   Ezek. 43:5.

10   Luke 1:11.

escaped forms a veritable monastic community in the restored Temple; and the "dispersed" come to worship there from every quarter of the *oecumene*.

This love of the Temple finds an echo in the psalms. Nowadays we chant the verses—and rightly—in praise of the Church. And indeed it is ultimately to her that they refer in prophetic terms, but it was in relation to the Temple that they were first uttered:

> LORD, I have loved the habitation of your house:
>   and the place where your honor dwells. ...
>
> O how amiable are your dwellings: O LORD of hosts!
>   My soul has a desire and longing
>   to enter into the courts of the LORD. ...
>   One day in your courts is better than a thousand. ...
>
> One thing I have desired of the LORD, which I will require:
>   even that I may dwell in the house of the LORD
>   all the days of my life,
>   to behold the fair beauty of the LORD,
>   and to visit his Temple.[11]

What difference is there between the Mosaic Temple and the cosmic Temple? What stage does the revelation on Sinai mark in the economy of the presence of God? At first sight it seems that a step back has been made. Up to the time of Moses, sacrifices could be offered anywhere. Henceforward, none are pleasing to God but those that are offered in the Tabernacle. There are no longer many sanctuaries, but only one: "You shall utterly destroy all the places, wherein the nations which you shall possess served their gods, upon the high mountains, and upon the hills, and under every green tree."[12]

This seemed so harsh a decree that for centuries the priesthood had to resist the determination of the Hebrews to raise altars, even when it was not a question of idolatry. The cult is concentrated in a single place. In the divine plan this was in reality a necessary stage, for the great danger was polytheism; the singleness of the sanctuary was, as it were, the sign of the oneness of God. It was this that Josephus understood when he wrote: "There is only one Temple for one God, for like always attracts like, and the Temple is common to all, as God is common to all."[13] And indeed it was for this reason that Judaism, alone in the ancient world, remained monotheistic.

---

11   Pss. 26:8; 84:1, 2, 10; 27:4.

12   Deut. 12:2.

13   Josephus, *The Antiquities of the Jews*, Bk. 3, Chap. 6. Eng. trans. in: *The Works of Josephus*, trans. William Whiston (Peabody, MA: Hendrickson, 1994).

The second feature which seems to have been characteristic of the religion of Sinai is the gulf that it fixes between God and man. Happy were the days, it might be said, when God talked on easy terms with the patriarchs. Henceforth he dwells in the secrecy of the Holy of Holies, guarded by the threefold enclosure. Only the Jews can enter the first of these enclosures—and only after purifying themselves; the second enclosure is confined to the priesthood; and as for the Holy of Holies, only the High Priest can enter it, once a year, with feelings of sacred awe and reverence. Let no profane person dare to cross the forbidden threshold, lest, as Heliodorus[14] says, he be struck down by the angels. Formerly the whole of nature was the house of God, filled with the divine presence. Now there is a barrier between the sacred and the profane—that which is *pro fanum*, outside the Temple. The priests, we read in Ezekiel, "shall teach my people the difference between the holy and the profane."[15]

This may inspire us with regret, with nostalgia for primeval Eden. Nevertheless the revelation on Sinai marks an advance, for by thus separating man from God, it draws attention to two things. First, it demonstrates the greatness, the holiness of God; he is indeed the altogether other. We know how the easy-going anthropomorphism of the Greeks brought them to the worship of idols; by contrast with this, the God of Israel is a transcendent God, hidden in the darkness of the Tabernacle which symbolizes his essential mystery, his incomprehensibility. This is a great advance in the knowledge of God.

As Gregory of Nyssa says, "The true understanding of that which Moses was seeking consists in realizing that the object of the quest transcends all knowledge and remains entirely separated by his incomprehensibility, as by darkness. This is why John the mystic, who explored that shining darkness, said that no man has seen God, making it clear by this denial that the knowledge of the divine essence is inaccessible not only to man, but to the whole world of the intellect."[16]

This separation between God and man draws attention, therefore, to a second reality—the sinfulness of man. It unfolds the meaning of that basic impurity which is called original sin. On account of this, as St. Paul well showed, the Law, which does not save but rather condemns, emphasizes the necessity of the Redeemer, prevents man from becoming sufficient to himself, compels him to recognize his fundamental lack, and thus, as Blaise Pascal says, makes him "hold out his arms to his deliverer." To pass from the ignorance of the child to the holiness of the saint, there is no short cut; the way lies through the humility of the sinner. The path from Eden to the Promised Land must needs pass through Sinai—that is, through the region of humility and purification.

---

14   See the account in 2 Macc. 3.

15   Ezek. 44:23.

16   Gregory of Nyssa (d. 386), *Life of Moses*. Eng. trans.: *The Life of Moses*, Classics of Western Spirituality (New York: Paulist, 1978).

However, if the Mosaic Temple marks an advance upon the cosmic Temple, it does not destroy it, but rather carries it forward. It is the property of these successive economies that each at the same time surpasses and preserves its predecessor. So Jesus says in his turn: "I am not come to destroy [the Temple of Moses], but to fulfill." So the Temple retains a clearly defined cosmic meaning. The cosmic Temple comprised three realms—heaven, earth, and the water. The Mosaic Temple continues them. The Holy of Holies, the abode of God, represents heaven, where God dwells in darkness; the Tabernacle signifies earth, and it is there that the symbols of the permanent cultus are to be found, the elements of the liturgy—the altar of incense, which carries forward the sweetness of flowers; the table of the show-bread, which represents the offering of the first-fruits; the candlestick, where holy oil continually burns; and finally the *atrium* which contains the "sea of brass," which was used for burnt offerings, and corresponds to the waters. Thus the whole cosmos is, as it were, mirrored in the Temple, which is its microcosm, like the cathedral which sums up all the fauna and flora carved in its various chapels.

The Glory of the Angels

The Temple of Moses was only a passing stage. A new order appears with Christ, who is the reality of which the Temple was only a symbol. Henceforth the abode of God, the *Shekinah*, is no longer the Temple, but the manhood of Jesus. "In this place is one greater than the Temple."[17]

The Temple must soon disappear, its veil must be rent after the "*Consummatum est*." It has ceased to correspond to anything whatever. It represents a world that no longer exists. The glory of the Lord, the *doxa*, has deserted it. This glory, which indicates the presence of God, is the visible radiance that surrounded the Tabernacle, but it was a radiance which was only a debased form of that radiance in the intellectual realm, in the angelic creation, which everywhere surrounds the three divine persons, creating around them a sacred region. The angelic creation was symbolized in the cosmic Tabernacle by the armies of heaven, in the Mosaic Tabernacle by the cherubim. Their mission is to hide from profane eyes the glory of the Lord. Such also are the seraphim of Isaiah:

> "Above [the Temple] stood the seraphims: each one had six wings; with twain he covered his face, and with twain he covered his feet, and with twain he did fly. And one cried to another, and said, Holy, holy, holy, is the Lord of hosts: the whole earth is full of his glory."[18]

The glory of the Lord dwelt in the Temple until the coming of the incarnation. But from that day it began to dwell in Jesus. The very word that St. John

---

17   Matt. 12:6.

18   Isa. 6:2–3.

uses to describe the incarnation—"dwelt among us"—is that which indicates the dwelling of God in the Temple. And the presence of God which overshadows the Virgin is the same cloud whose presence showed that God dwelt in the Tabernacle. Here we see that, with the divine indwelling and the visible glory, henceforth also the invisible glory is to surround the manhood of him in whom God dwells in corporeal form.

Here we witness the appearance of the archangels who, with Gabriel, are henceforth to surround the manhood of Jesus, to hover in the background, but always to be present, and not so much to praise as to be themselves that glory in the highest heavens which already surrounds the child conceived in the virgin's womb. Here is the very mystery of the man-God, whom the angels worship, and who annihilates himself in the flesh; here, side by side with the earthly appearances, is the celestial, hypercosmic event of the incarnation.

Henceforth we shall find Jesus everywhere surrounded by this twofold presence. There is the procession of angels that everywhere accompanies the Word, of which they are the radiance, the fringe of the intellectual realm; there is also the nakedness of the cradle. We shall find the same contrast in the agony, where twelve legions of angels are present at the very moment of the kiss of Judas and the smiting of Malchus—the utmost human nakedness and the utmost heavenly radiance, Bethlehem and the Mount of Olives on the one hand, and on the other the chorus of *"Gloria in excelsis"*[19] and the warring angels of Michael. *"Salutarem saeculorum, ipsum regem angelorum, sola Virgo lactabat."*[20]

This magical verse from one of the responses for the liturgical vigil of the Epiphany throws the whole contrast into dramatic relief. The humble virgin gives her breast to the child, and in the background, suggested by these angels, the aeons manifest themselves,[21] the heavens with their cosmic dimensions, a vast shadow losing itself in the Milky Way; the virgin with her diadem of stars feeds with celestial milk the Savior of the aeons. This is the virgin of the *"ab initio et ante saecula creata sum"*—"from the beginning and before all ages, I was created"—who hovers behind Mary of Nazareth. It is true of her, as of the Son of Man, of heavenly Man, that her cosmic image represents a state of pre-existence in the thought of God. She is present in the primeval garden, as she was present on the first morning of

---

19　"Glory to God in the highest."

20　"The virgin alone nursed the very king of angels, the Savior of ages." Compare the hymn by Jean Mouton (d. 1522), "Nesciens Mater Virgo Virum" [The Virgin Mother Gave Birth].

21　I have retained the word "aeon," which is a Greek term, in preference to the word "age," because the latter merely evokes a temporal idea, while "aeon" expresses rather the idea not of a time, however long, but of a period qualitatively of a different order, of a definite spiritual world, which may be considered either as a realm of duration (the biosphere is an aeon), or as a personal reality (every angel is a spiritual world).

creation—"*Necdum fontes aquarum eruperant*"[22]—as part of the hidden mystery in God before all aeons.

Thus the archangels are associated with all the mysteries in the life of Jesus. Gabriel presides over the annunciation, over all annunciations, over Mary, over Zechariah, over Joseph, over the shepherds, over the procession of which he is the supreme figure. Raphael presides over divine acts, miracles, healings; he is the angel of Bethesda, who troubles the waters of healing, and he is also the comforter, the protector. It is the angels who minister to Jesus in the wilderness at his temptation and comfort him at his agony. Finally it is Michael whose legions hover in the background at the passion, charged with the wrath of the Almighty, a dazzling radiance that drives back the advancing hosts and casts Saul upon the ground, for no man can see the glory of the Lord and live.

This glory is above all the Word, the ray of eternal light, the Word of silence; but it is also the angels, radiations of the ray, harmonic powers of the Word. They inspire with holy dread all who without due permission approach the Son of God. They keep watch over the gate of the primeval garden; they forbid the threshold of heaven to those who are not clothed with a wedding garment. They establish around the Word a sacred region, the Temple of the intellectual realm.

Everywhere they precede and follow the Word. They prepare the way before him and complete his handiwork. They surround him not only at the throne of glory, but also in his various missions. They go up with him into the presence of the Father, bearing in their hands that incense which is the prayer of the righteous. They pass through the spaces of charity with a swiftness that is denied to our fleshy hearts. They are indeed the heaven of heavens, of which Scripture speaks, for heaven is not visible space, but the invisible depths of the intellectual rays of the Word, the splendor of his imagery reflected in innumerable mirrors.

Rilke glimpsed their splendor when he described them as "lines of height, summits tinged with the purple dawn of all that was created ... passages, stairs, thrones—mirrors of glittering splendor."[23] But he misunderstood their ministry, making himself equal to the angel, as the angel made himself equal to God and sought to penetrate by effraction into the divine darkness.[24] So he arrived in

---

22   "When there were no springs abounding with water" Prov. 8:24.

23   *Duino Elegies*, 2. Eng. trans.: *Duino Elegies*, trans. J. B. Leishman, and Stephen Spender (New York: W. W. Norton, 1939).

24   "Ah, mighty angel, tell the universe / The wondrous deeds that we ourselves have done." St. Bernard of Clairvaux (*The Word of Isaiah*, 3) notes that the two wings that forbid the eyes of the wicked to gaze upon the divine mysteries are admiration and veneration. Yet Lucifer knew admiration, but not veneration, which is adoration and submission, and which he replaced with emulation—the despairing attempt to make oneself equal to the angels through one's own efforts. This, too, was Rilke's idea, and his attempts—he who had so exalted a sense of the sacred—was to conquer it by his own efforts, by penetrating in solitary pride the realms of death. But charity is the only way that leads to God, and jealousy is rather the wing that sets a barrier, an insurmountable threshold, between our gaze and the light of heaven.

the end at nothing but a desert, a desolate solitude that recalls the landscape of William Blake, in that cosmic silence that terrified Pascal and caused Gérad de Nerval to despair.[25]

In the New Temple of Christ

Thus the manhood of Jesus became the new Temple and "the place where thine honor dwelleth." It is this that Christ proclaimed to the Samaritan women when he told her: "The hour cometh, when ye shall neither in this mountain, nor yet at Jerusalem, worship the Father ... when the true worshippers shall worship the Father in spirit and in truth."[26] That is to say, not that they will not worship in any temple, but that they will worship in the true Temple of the Spirit, as opposed to the figurative Temple of the flesh. This is why Christ was able to reply to the Pharisees who accused him of misunderstanding the Temple: "In this place is one greater than the Temple." From that time, the Temple of stone might be destroyed; it would be of no importance, since after three days the true Temple was to be finally established. And indeed, three days after the veil of the Temple was rent, the Temple of the new Law, the glorified manhood of Jesus, was raised up forevermore.

But between these two moments, between the appearance of the new Temple at the incarnation and the end of the old Temple at the passion, there was a unique period during which the two temples existed side by side, and the mystery of their connection, of their joint construction, was shown in a marvelous light. This encounter between the reality and the figure, a living and historical encounter, took place for the first time at the presentation.

This was truly a unique moment in the sequence of periods. Up till then, there had been only a figurative Temple, an image of that which was to come, a sign also of the promise to David. But here we see at once the figure and the reality, the promise and the gift. This is the wondering cry of the psalmist: "We have thought of thy loving-kindness, O God, in the midst of thy temple."[27] It is in the very heart of the figure that the reality was manifested, in the heart of the promise that the gift was conveyed.

To carnal eyes, there is a child in the Temple; to the eyes of Simeon, unsealed by the Holy Spirit, this child is more than the Temple. He is the one for whom the Temple has kept ceaseless vigil. The Temple is now rendered useless. The blossom bursts forth, the sealed Ark that held the secret of the king flies open, and the mystery is revealed, the veil is rent, all peoples are bidden to enter. This is what is to shine forth at Pentecost. But it is already virtually accomplished for Simeon: *"Lumen ad revelationem Gentium"*—"a light to lighten the Gentiles." The

---

25   "He answered: All is dead. I have surveyed / The worlds, and lost my light in milky ways."

26   John 4:21, 23.

27   Ps. 48:9.

Temple was only a shadow. Now the light is come; all the candles are lighted in the hands of the faithful. "Soon shall the angel of the covenant come into the Temple." The riddle is suddenly unraveled before Simeon's eyes, he grasps this connection between the figure and the reality which is the whole meaning of Scripture. Israel has lived by Scripture without fully possessing the key—and here today it is given to her. Israel may disappear: *"Nunc dimittis."*[28] Simeon holds in the palms of his hands, in the midst of the Temple, the master of the Temple.

This encounter between the old order and the new order is not, absolutely speaking, the first of its kind. For if Jesus is indeed the horizon that divides the two creations, the soul of Mary, because she constitutes a separate order, is already part of the new economy. In the Temple of expectation, she represented already a certain fulfillment. Her presentation in the Temple is the prelude to that of Jesus, and is thus charged with a mysterious meaning. All that was to come to pass was already in her heart. In the Temple she was thus more than a figure and less than the reality; she was the light that comes before day.

Thus the presentations reverberate like a sound which is at first faintly heard, then gradually grows louder—the presentation of Adam in the cosmic Temple and the primeval order; the presentation of Samuel in the Mosaic Temple; the presentation of Mary, who alone constitutes an order apart; the presentation of Jesus, who is the great fulfillment, and who gives himself forth in his turn in the presentation of every Christian in the Temple on the day of his baptism, which is itself only the beginning, in the ritual Temple, of the final presentation in the heavenly Temple, when the Son shall say to the Father: "Father, these are they whom thou hast given me."

The second encounter of Jesus with the Temple is also charged with a mysterious significance. It is that of the temptation. The devil "set him on a pinnacle of the Temple, and said unto him, 'If thou be the Son of God, cast thyself down from hence; for it is written, he shall give his angels charge over thee.'"[29] Notice that the temptation of Jesus is enacted in the three holy places—the wilderness, the Temple, and the mountain; notice also the connection which is established between the Temple and the angels.

And indeed this is Satan's idea too. He imagines that the presence still dwells in the Temple; his Jerusalem, that Jewish order which is to attack Jesus. He profoundly grasps that here is the crux of the whole matter. He knows that while the presence dwells in the Temple of stone, he need fear nothing for his reign—and that the nations are beneath his sway. So he urges Jesus to manifest himself in the Temple. For he knows that this would be for him an entry into the

---

28   "Now you may dismiss ..." Compare Luke 2:29–32.

29   Luke 4:9, 10.

order of the Temple. He offers him the repetition of Moses on a larger scale—not only to make bread fall from heaven, but to make it issue from the stones; not only to contemplate the Promised Land from the summit of Nebo, but to see the whole promised earth from the peak of the highest mountain, *"mons excelsus valde,"* not only to show forth from the Tabernacle the countenance surrounded by the visible Glory, but to manifest in the Temple, surrounded by the angels, the invisible glory of the Lord.

But precisely because Jesus is not of the order of Moses, he is not a higher kind of Moses. Moses and the Temple are figures, but Jesus is the reality. The divine presence is no longer to be found in an enclosure of stone, it dwells in Jesus himself—and the angels draw near to minister to him. It is no longer a question of the "bread that our fathers ate," which is only a temporal inheritance, or of the Temple built by Solomon, which is only the shadow cast on earth by the heavenly Temple of reality. It is not a question for Jesus of beginning again, or repeating a pattern. It was everything else that was only a repetition, and it is now that the day of reality has dawned. The miracle of Jesus will be to distribute real bread at the Last Supper, to build the real Temple at the resurrection, to lead his people into the real kingdom at the ascension. "The devil leaveth him, and behold, angels came and ministered unto him."[30]

All the other encounters of Christ with the Temple are charged with similar meanings—the casting out of the money-changers from the Temple; the well of the Temple, of which Ezekiel had spoken and which, on the day of the Feast of Tabernacles, taking his text from the fresh water of ablutions, Jesus places in its true perspective: "if any man thirst, let him come unto me, and drink."[31] The figurative wells, the ritual ablutions, are abrogated. The well that springs forth in the true Temple is the Holy Spirit that springs forth in the manhood of Jesus. So Jesus brings into relation with himself all the properties of the Temple. He fulfils the Law. And it is not until he has finished this task that all is fulfilled, that the foundations of the new order are finally established—that the old Temple, henceforth rendered useless, sees its veil torn asunder.

With him it is the Mosaic order that comes to an end. This had two characteristic features—the separation between God and man, and the dwelling in a single place. The veil that shut off the Holy of Holies is rent asunder; we are brought into familiar relations with the divine. We have the "boldness to enter into the holiest by the blood of Jesus, by a new and living way, which he hath consecrated for us, through the veil, that is to say, his flesh."[32] This is not simply a

---

30   Matt. 4:11.

31   John 8:37.

32   Heb. 10:19–20.

return to the cosmic Temple, but after the Mosaic purification, access to a higher presence, entry by humanity into the Holy of Holies, not simply the natural presence of God in his creation. And henceforth this presence is no longer bound to a single place. It is connected with the glorified manhood of Christ, the final and conclusive Temple—that is, with the total Christ in his individual reality and in his Mystical Body, the place of worship "in spirit and in truth."

In the Temple of the Church

It is the manhood of Jesus that is the Temple of the new Law, but this manhood must be taken as a whole, that is to say, it is the Mystical Body in its entirety; this is the complete and final Temple. The dwelling of God is the Christian community whose head is in heaven, and whose members are still making their earthly pilgrimage; it is the true Temple of which the Temple of stone was the figure.

> Ye also, as lively stones, are built up a spiritual house, a holy priesthood, to offer up spiritual sacrifices, acceptable to God by Jesus Christ. (1 Pet. 2:5)

> Now therefore ye are no more strangers and foreigners, but fellow citizens with the saints, and of the household of God; and are built upon the foundation of the apostles and prophets, Jesus Christ himself being the chief corner stone; in whom all the building fitly framed together groweth unto a holy temple in the Lord. (Eph. 2:19–20)

There is a basic difference between the Temple at Jerusalem and the Christian Church. Under the old Law, the presence of God is connected with the building of stone; under the new Law, it is connected with the spiritual community. The church of stone is not in the succession of the Temple, but of the synagogue; it is the assembly, the *ecclesia*, the meeting-place. Or rather, at the same time it continues both of them, since it is the normal place for the sacrifice. But it can be dispensed with; it is not necessary that it should be there for the celebration of the Mass. While the community *is* necessary, the Mass cannot normally be celebrated without a server.

> Here is once more a house for us to say our prayers,
> A new house whose lamps Satan shall not put out,
> Neither shall he break asunder the adamantine vaults.

> I see before me the Catholic Church, which is from all the
> world.[33]

Thus is fulfilled the saying of Jesus: "Where two or more are gathered to-gether in my name, there am I in the midst of them."[34] It is the essential condition required for the offering of an acceptable host that is presented in the Sermon on the Mount, where it is written: "If thou bring thy gift to the altar, and there rememberest that thy brother hath ought against thee … first be reconciled with to thy brother, and then come and offer thy gift."[35] No offering is accepted save that which is made in charity, in community. For there the Temple is, the one and only place where man is in the presence of God.

This is an extraordinary fact, as extraordinary in its own order as the pres-ence of God in the Temple at Jerusalem. God enters into relationship not with isolated souls, but with the community, and only the souls who are part of the community. Through the baptismal rites, the entry of the catechumen into the church of stone is a figure of his entry into the living Church, into the community which is the place of his meeting with God.

The Sacrament of Love

Of this meeting, the Eucharist is the permanent sign, being at once the sacrament of the Mystical Body and the sign of the real presence, and bringing about at the same time union with God and the strengthening of the bonds of charity. Sin has the effect simultaneously of alienating the sinner from the presence of God, and of separating him from the community. The primitive discipline of the Church made this clear when it excluded the sinner publicly from the community. He still remains excluded from communion; and reconciliation with God is necessarily required by the community as intermediary. This is the meaning of confession, in which the priest represents the people, which itself represents God.[36]

This is why the Church has the deposit of the living Word of God. It is in her that the Word mysteriously dwells, thus continuing the incarnation of the *Logos*. "We come to faith in Christ not by the study of dead literary documents, but in a preliminary way through the living witness of an organism sustained and animated by Christ, through the teaching of the living apostolic Church; in a full and effec-

---

33   Claudel, *Cinq Grandes Odes*, 176.

34   Matt 18: 20.

35   Matt. 5:23–24.

36   Henri de Lubac, *Catholicisme, Catholicisme: Les Aspects Sociaux du Dogme* [The True Face of Catholicism] (Paris: Cerf, 1947), 56. Eng. trans.: *Catholicism: Christ and the Common Destiny of Man*, trans. Lancelot C. Sheppard and Elizabeth Englund (San Francisco: Ignatius, 1988).

tive way by immediate contact with the living Christ in the Church, through the operation of grace acting in all its fullness in the Sacrament."[37]

Connected with the new Temple which is the community, the presence of God is bound up with charity: "If we love one another, God dwelleth in us."[38] For the Christian community is not the biological community, the maternal medium in which the person, as an insufficiently constituted entity, aspires towards his own dissolution. But it is the community of spiritual persons bound together by love, that is, in which every member holds fast of his own free will to the appetite for existence of the others. It is not a return to the beginning, a nostalgia for an earlier, still undifferentiated condition, but it is that continuous creation of charity praised by St. Paul: "[From Christ] the whole body fitly joined together and compacted by that which every joint supplieth, according to the effectual working in the measure of every part, maketh increase of the body unto the edifying of itself in love."[39]

The proper work of charity is the building of the true Temple. It is present before all creation as ministration, efficacy. Sometimes we confuse it with a certain tenderness and weakness that disarms us before the will and desire of another, making us condescend to him, even to his damnation. Charity knows nothing of this cowardly condescension. It is "strong as death," according to the phrase in Solomon's Song.[40] Pleasing someone is often the opposite of doing him good. True love is pitiless. It does not love weakness; it loves in spite of them and against them, it corrects them. But its strength is that of love, it is trust, help, support. We look for violence in irony or insult, but it is charity that is truly strong—strong to others, but above all strong to itself, hard as a diamond, lucid, transparent, penetrating to the depths; hard, but not inflicting pain. Violence bruises, irony inflicts pin-pricks; charity goes straight to the heart and heals the sufferer.

"Charity suffereth long." It does nothing hastily. Like the father of the prodigal, it awaits the hour chosen by God. It is a faithful watchdog. It prays in silence. It is altogether disinterested, it seeks for no return, it takes pleasure in the well-being of that which it loves; that is its reward; it is forgetful of self. It matters little to it whether good is done by it or by another, so long as it is done. It loves the good for its own sake. It does not take pleasure in its own activity. Where nothing needs to be done, it comes to a halt. It does not take pleasure in spending itself. It is economical. It does not seek for acclaim. It is only interested in the fruits. It has no time to think of itself. It is a realist. All deceit is repugnant to it. It is precise,

---

37   Karl Adam, *Le vrai visage du catholicisme* [The True Face of Catholicism] (Paris: B. Grasset, 1931), 273.

38   1 John 4:12.

39   Eph. 4:16.

40   Song 8:6.

watchful, clear-headed, not to be bluffed. It is not satisfied with words. It is no formalist, no Pharisee.

"Charity never faileth." It is always active, it never ceases, it is always busy. "Charity hopeth all things." It knows that nothing is impossible with God, it hopes against all hope. "Charity believeth all things." It is always deceived, but it is thus that it triumphs over the general distrust, it overcomes evil with good, it demands truth, it works on another level and raises others to it. Souls reveal themselves to it. Its poverty encourages them. Its very nature is a summons. It is no use puffing oneself up before it. One is obliged to confess, to lay bare the most hidden sores, and to know that in spite of this, one is loved with a never-failing love, which plumbs the depths of misery without harm or derision, and which restores the taste of life to the most despairing of souls.

The Temple of the Church that is thus slowly built up by charity is at the same time the fulfillment of the Mosaic Temple and of the cosmic Temple. It is of the Temple of the Church that the Christian may truly affirm what the Jew said of the Temple at Jerusalem: "LORD, I have loved the habitation of thy house, and the place where thine honor dwelleth ... One thing I have desired of the LORD, which I will require, even that I may dwell in the house of the LORD all the days of my life."[41] But henceforth the Temple is no longer the far-off mountain towards which the desire of the exiles is directed; it is ever-present, and it suffices that we enter into ourselves to join in the communion of saints.

> Our Lord Jesus Christ, after dying for our sins on the cross, and ascending on high, left not the world as he found it, but left a blessing behind him. He left in the world what before was not in it—a secret home, for faith and love to enjoy, wherever they are found, in spite of the world around us. ... This is the Church of God, which is our true home of God's providing, his own heavenly court, where he dwells with saints and angels. ... Though thou art in a body of flesh, a member of this world, thou has but to kneel down reverently in prayer, and thou art at once in the society of saints and angels.[42]

This is what Christ declared to the Samaritan woman when he said that "ye shall neither worship in this mountain, nor yet at Jerusalem, worship the Father," but that "the true worshippers shall worship the Father in spirit and in truth"—that is, they shall worship in the true Temple, the spiritual Tabernacle.

---

41 Pss. 26:8; 27:4.

42 John Henry Newman, "The Church a Home for the Lonely," in *Parochial and Plain Sermons*, vol. 4 (London: Longmans, Green, 1900–1902), 190, 198.

This is also the fulfillment of the cosmic Temple, in that the cosmos is affected by the Temple whose every stone is a universe in itself, if it is true that "the Spirit is in some manner all things,"[43] and that "one thought of man's is worth more than all the world."[44] Let us not be misled by the word "Temple" into thinking of some towering edifice, static and stationary. It is an overwhelming vision of expanding universes of the spirit that should be our mental picture of the Temple of the Church, of a Temple growing towards infinity in all directions, thrusting out towards the heavenly regions like the baroque cupola of the St. Johann-Nepomuk-Kirche at Munich, that stupendous cathedral which opens up a vision of the celestial realms of the Church, and gives access to endless vistas of contemplation.

The Church and the New Creation

The creation of the Church is the creation of a new cosmos, of which the first was only the preparation and image. On Calvary, when the ancient world vanished and the new order began, at the same time that the veil of the Temple was rent, announcing the abolition of the Mosaic order and the entry of mankind into the true Temple, the sun was darkened,[45] because it is the new creation of the world that comes into force, and a new sun rises whose brightness infinitely surpasses that of the first. This is the new universe which Isaiah proclaimed, when he declared that there should be a new heaven and a new earth. It is of this that St. John the Divine teaches us in the Book of Revelation, when he says that "the city had no need of the sun," for "the Lamb is the light thereof."[46]

As the sun is the vital principle of the biosphere, so Christ, the sun of spirits, is the vivifying principle of the spiritual universe. It is he whose rising is hailed by Zechariah and Simeon: "*Visitavit nos oriens ex alto*"—"the dayspring from on high hath visited us." As the sun rises in the East, so Christ, according to Scripture. It is in the East that the first Paradise was planted; it is towards the East that ever since then mankind has ceaselessly gazed; it is from the East that the Lord appeared.

He is Paradise regained, the first creation restored. It is still towards the East that we continue to look, because it is in the East that he arose on the day of the ascension, and because it is from the East that he must come again like a flash of lightning on the horizon. So it is towards the East that our churches are

---

43   St. Thomas, *Summa Theologica of St. Thomas Aquinas: First Complete American Edition*, 3 vols. (New York: Benzinger, 1947–1948).

44   St. John of the Cross, *Maxims*, in *The Collected Works of St. John of the Cross*, trans. Kieran Kavanaugh and Otlio Rodriguez (Washington, DC: Institute of Carmelite Studies, 1979).

45   "There was a darkness over all the land" (Matt. 27:45).

46   Rev. 21:23, "And I saw a new heaven and a new earth: for the first heaven and the first earth were passed away. and there was no more sea" (Rev. 21:1), "And there shall be no night there; and they shall need no candle, neither light of the sun, for the Lord God giveth them light" (Rev. 22:5).

oriented; so it is to the East that, drawn by an invisible force of gravitation, longing souls are attracted with all their weight; so it is to the East that, rising before the dawn, watching monks, heirs of the first Christians, await the appearance of the visible sun, as a daily sign and image of that other Light. *"O Oriens, splendor lucis aeternae et sol iustitiae, veni ad illuminandos sedentes in tenebris et umbra mortis."* Every day the sun represents the coming, the parousia, the rising in glory of the light eternal.

This raising of the cosmic Temple to the level of the Temple of the Church is recorded in the liturgy for the Feast of Christmas, which was the *Natale solis invicti* of the Romans.[47] So Christ appears to us as the inheritor, not merely of the Jewish order and the Mosaic Temple, but also of the pagan order and the cosmic Temple.

> He was to inherit earth and Rome,
> The violent sea and bitter Zion.[48]

It is the character of Christmas to reveal this to us; not to be in the line of descent of the Jewish expectation, of the cycle of Passover, Pentecost, and Tabernacles, in the sequence of pastoral cults and the Jewish East, but rather to be in the succession of another expectation, that of the wise men of the pagan world who watched the stars, and who were represented at the manger at Christ's nativity by the Magi, side by side with the shepherds. For the visible sun was the pagan prefiguration in the cosmic Temple and the expectation of the invisible sun and of another illumination, as the annual entry into the Temple by the High Priest was, under the old Mosaic Law, the prefiguration of the true High Priest into the heavenly Temple; and under the new Law it remains the daily ritual representation, according to the measure of our existence which is subject to the rhythm of sleep and night, of the rising—henceforth irrevocably possessed—of the final sun in all its transcendent glory. Some day, indeed, the visible sun will be extinguished, and the true light will shine alone. Then we shall no longer need images and figures; then our eyes shall see, in the heaven of an eternal day, the sun that knows no setting, a perpetual Orient, the ever-renewed arising of the sun of righteousness.

Liturgy in the New Temple

Thus the new Temple finally replaced the Temples of Jerusalem and the cosmos. It was time for these to disappear. The first Law was destroyed because of its weak-

---

47 "The Day of the Birth of the Unconquered Sun." Louis Duchesne, *Origines du Culte Chrétien: Étude sur la Liturgie Latine avant Charlemagne* (Paris: Thorin, 1909), 279. Eng. trans.: *Christian Worship: Its Origin and Evolution: A Study of the Latin Liturgy Up to the Time of Charlemagne* (London: Society for Promoting Christian Knowledge, 1903).

48 Péguy, "Eve," 842.

ness and ineffectiveness, but it saw the introduction of a greater hope, by means of which we have access to the presence of God. The figure has no further part to play, when the fact which it proclaims has come to pass. The new Temple brings with it an infinitely better reality. It is no longer through heavenly signs that man looks for traces of God, but the true sun has finally risen upon a new world. It is no longer in a single place that the living God may be worshipped; it is to the ends of the earth that the new Temple reaches out, and it is enough that two or three are gathered together in the name of Jesus, for him to dwell among them.

But the destruction of the old order is positive; it removes the blemishes of the old order, it preserves all the valuable elements. Nothing is lost, all is retained, organized on a higher level of significance; it is a pure elevation, an absolute progress. Just as the Temple at Jerusalem continued the cosmic Temple while taking over its functions, so the Church continues the Temples of Jerusalem and the cosmos. It offers the new sacrifice according to the ancient ritual patterns.

Thus the Mass contains all the breadth of time and space, cosmos and history. Through it, we have recovered in the depths of our ancestral memory the first religious gesture of mankind, the offering of bread and wine, that of Melchizedek, the high priest of the cosmic Temple—and it is he whose sacrifice becomes a sacrament: "*Sicuti accepta habere dignatus es munera pueri tui justi Abel et sacrificium Patris nostrae Abrahae; et quod tibi obtulit summus sacerdos tuus Melchisedech.*"[49] On the threshold of the Holy of Holies—"*ad sancta sanctorum puris mentibus mereamur introire*"[50]—the Mass inspires us with Mosaic dread in the highest sense: "*Sanctus, sanctus, sanctus, Dominus Deus Sabaoth.*"[51] All is brought together here, restored to its true meaning, rendered to God through Christ: "*Per quem haec omnia, Domine, semper bona creas …*"[52] The Mass bears witness, at the *epiclesis*, to the descent of the fire which, by consuming the victims, shows that they were pleasing to God; it is no longer material fire descending on fleshly victims presented upon the altar by Elijah, but spiritual fire, the Holy Spirit, which comes down to consume the corruptions of which the Host is the sacrament, "*ut quotquot ex haec altaris participatione sacrosanctum corpus et sanguime, sumpserimus omni benedictione coelis et gratia repleamur!*" [53]

---

49   "Look with favor on these offerings as once you accepted the gifts of your servant Abel, the sacrifice of Abraham, our father in faith, and the bread and wine offered by your priest Melchizedech." Eucharistic Prayer I.

50   "That being made pure of heart we may be worthy to enter into the Holy of Holies." Silent prayer said by the priest during the *Confiteor* [Confession] of the Mass.

51   "Holy, holy, holy, Lord God of Hosts."

52   "By whom, Lord, thou dost ever give unto us every good thing." From the prayer of the priest after the consecration during the Mass.

53   "That as many of us as shall receive the most sacred Body and Blood of thy Son by partaking

What is true of the Mass, is true of the whole order of the Church. I shall only take one other example, that if the great liturgical feasts; the Passover, Pentecost, Tabernacles. In origin these are three seasonal feasts, three liturgies of the cosmic Temple. The Passover is the feast of the first grains of barley, and this is why unleavened bread is offered, loaves made before there was a new leaven of fermented yeast. Pentecost, seven weeks later, is the feast of the harvest. Tabernacles, in September, is the feast of fruit and vintage, when huts of leaves are put up. Under Moses, new meanings come to be connected with these feasts, in harmony with the establishment of the religion of Sinai. The Passover, which now receives its name, is the "passing over" of God, the sparing of the Jewish first-born. Pentecost, seven weeks later, is the revelation on Sinai and the vision of the Tabernacle, the theophany of God in thunder and cloud. Finally, Tabernacles commemorates the forty years' pilgrimage in the tabernacles, the tents of the wilderness. Thus the ancient rites develop a new meaning.

The Temple of the Church is written into the continuity of the feasts; it gathers together the various elements and gives them their fresh significance, underlining in this way the fact that they were only images of what was to come. The Passover is the day of deliverance not from Egypt, but from sin; it is the day when the true Lamb is slain; it is the day when the firstborn among the dead is spared; it is the day when the true unleavened bread is distributed. What hand, save that of him who said he had come to accomplish all things, has gathered together with such care every crumb of the ancient feast without losing a single grain, and has made of them signs and sacraments into which he has breathed authentic life?

Pentecost is the pouring out of the Spirit, in thunder and cloud as on Sinai, but for the sake of dwelling not in the Temple made with human hands, but in the new Temple which is the hearts of the faithful. Finally, Tabernacles, which is only reflected precisely in the liturgy of the Ember Days (of fast and abstinence) in September, covers in fact the whole period after Pentecost, representing the long journey across the desert to reach the Promised Land, which is to replace the precarious tents of the nomads with the dwelling of God in the Temple of Moses.

Clearly it is no accident, but a definite divine intention, that brought the great mysteries of the revelation of Christ into relation with the Jewish festivals, emphasizing in this way that the latter were figures of what was to come. However, there is no question whatever of reducing the Christian mystery to what preceded it, for it is completely new; and at the same time this fundamental newness is inscribed in a tradition, asserts the continuity and unity of the divine plan. If the word "history" has any content, if it means at once absolute progress and a continu-

---

thereof from this altar may be filled with every heavenly blessing." Prayer of the priest after the consecration during the Mass.

ity in that progress which makes it intelligible, it is here that it applies, and here alone. It betrays the presence of God. For there is a divine presence in history, as there is in time. There is a divine presence in duration, as there is in space, and that presence is the dwelling of God in the Temple of duration, which one may call the "prophetic Temple," because it is revealed in that perpetual and absolute development which each period, each aeon manifests, the Mosaic age being an absolute advance upon the cosmic age, and the age of Christ upon that of Moses, and at the same time upon that prefiguration, that characteristic form of each period in the preceding period which is, strictly speaking, *prophecy.*

Christ is thus present in the whole of history, at once present and hidden in the Holy of Holies of the prophetic Temple, but revealing himself more and more clearly. The present aeon is to him the figuration of the coming "Day," the week that prepares for the Sabbath. It is this presence of God in time, after that of space, which Rudolph Otto recognizes in his book, *The Idea of the Holy*: "He who devotes himself to contemplation of that great continuity which we call the old covenant up to the time of Christ, will feel, as it were, forcibly awaken in him the intuition that some eternal power presides over it."[54]

This contemplation of the presence of God in history is the reading of Scripture. The cosmos and Scripture are the two great Temples where God hides himself beneath signs, beneath the veil of the Tabernacle. The death of Christ rends the veil, reveals their meaning, shows us his presence hidden beneath signs. This is why meditation on Scripture was the special task of the early Fathers. It is no mere study, but a real contemplation of God as present in his Scripture. Thus, for Origen, Scripture is "the sign, chosen by God, of the presence of the *Logos*, like a word in the world, the precious urn of the spiritual life, the inexhaustible material source of the divine life."[55] In the Bible, the Jews venerated the presence of God, but he remained obscure to them, their eyes were covered with a veil. With Christ, the veil of the twofold Temple is removed—at once of the Temple at Jerusalem and that of the sealed book. The peoples are permitted to penetrate into each of them, to enter into communion with space and duration.

Thus Christianity confers its mysterious nature on history, by showing it the presence of God. We have said this of space in relation to the cosmic Temple. For the Christian it is not that unreal space of the physicists which consists of nothing but mathematical relationships, nor that universe profaned by man which is reduced to an object of pleasure. It is the place where a presence dwells, the house

---

54   Rudolph Otto, *The Idea of the Holy; An Inquiry into the Non-Rational Factor in the Idea of the Divine and Its Relation to the Rational* (New York: Oxford University, 1958), 233. Compare Jean Daniélou, *God and Us* (London: Mowbray, 1957), Chapter 1.

55   Hans Urs von Balthasar, "Le mysterion d'Origène" [The Mystery in Origen] in *Recherches de Science Religieuse*, (December 1936): 545.

of God. It is the same with time. Prophetic intuition confers its mysterious nature on history. It is opposed to the rationalist conception of an entirely quantitative development, in which there is no absolute advance, and thus no real advance at all. It is equally opposed to the irrationalist conception which acknowledges only a sequence of random civilizations, lacking all continuity and supported by no authentic wisdom.[56] In these two conceptions there is no presence, no mystery, but only pure reason or pure chance, while prophecy discloses at once a power and a wisdom—and thus a presence—and does not merely disclose it, but reveals it clearly. Moreover, we are permitted to worship this presence.

But the advance of history is not achieved without rending. The movement from one order to another, if it is a pure fulfillment and preserves in the highest degree all the valuable elements in its predecessor, also demands that the old order should disappear in its particular existence. This is the dramatic aspect of the mystery of history. "Destroy this Temple and I shall rebuild it." The new Temple must appear, in order that the old Temple may be destroyed. "It was necessary that Christ should die" in so far as he was identified with the old order, that by rising again he might establish the new order. That is the mysterious meaning of the passion. The death of Christ is the destruction of the old order, that of the Law, with which he must identify himself so that it might be destroyed in him, because this destruction was the necessary condition for the establishment of the new order and the coming of the kingdom. The death of Christ marks the break in continuity between the two orders, their incompatibility. This is the mystery that reproduces for every Christian the baptism, death, and resurrection, by which the mystery of history takes place in every destiny. The mystery of Christ is at once the fulfillment of the figure and the destruction of the figure as such; it condemns him who is attached to the figure.

Such, too, is the meaning of hostility of the Jews to Christ; it shows the resistance of the old order to the new order, and thus their discontinuity. This is also the exemplary meaning of the condemnation of Israel. It means that Israel as a figure is abolished—and this is expressed historically by the condemnation of the Jews. This is one of the deepest mysteries of history, on which St. Paul meditates at length in the Epistle to the Romans: "For I would not, brethren, that

---

56　All the interpretations of history apart from the prophetic perspective lead either to the eternal recurrence of Nietzsche, or to the purely quantative progress of Karl Marx, or to the pure irrationalism of Oswald Spengler. See on this subject the well-justified remarks of Raymond Aron, *Introduction to the Philosophy of History: An Essay on the Limits of Historical Objectivity* (Boston: Beacon, 1961). This would seem to show that the modern idea of history as qualitative progress, of which the ancient world knew nothing, and which is born with Christianity, is an idea of the religious order, which loses its content in any other perspective. Compare Jean Daniélou, *The Lord of History: Reflections on the Inner Meaning of History* (Chicago: Regnery, 1957).

ye should be ignorant of this mystery, lest ye should be wise in your own conceits; that blindness in part is happened to Israel, until the fullness of the Gentiles be come in. And so all Israel shall be saved."[57] For the gifts and the calling of God are without repentance. Thus the condemnation of Israel appears to be required by the necessity of demonstrating visibly the destruction of the old order. It forms part of the same economy as the destruction of the Temple. It strikes us all the more because it affects a living race. "It was necessary," wrote Origen, "that the elders of the Jerusalem of the lower regions and their scribes—a living incarnation of the figure—should rise up against Jesus, in order that the elders of heaven and the spiritual princes and the scribes concerned with the letter graven in all hearts by the Holy Spirit should render grace to him."[58]

The sign of the Temple appears to us, therefore, under a new aspect. It is the "sign of contradiction" proclaimed by Simeon on the day of the presentation in the Temple, as he grasped the dramatic relationship which was to unite the child whom he held in his hands with the Temple in the midst of which he stood. This prophecy was strangely fulfilled; for it is by declaring his relationship with the Temple, by pronouncing the mysterious words, "Destroy this Temple, and I will build it again in three days," that Christ was condemned to death. This is the very accusation that was made against him. And it is just because the Pharisees had calculated its scope, that they had understood that it meant that the old order was abolished and that the new Temple stood before them. But the mystery is precisely that they refused to acknowledge him, that they refused the death that was the condition of the resurrection, that to maintain at all costs the old Temple which they felt to be threatened, they sought to destroy the new Temple—and that in doing so, they were on the contrary the means of its construction, themselves pronouncing the sentence of death on the old order, destroying with the manhood of Jesus the whole Mosaic order with which he sought completely to identify himself, and by this very means permitting the establishment of the new order in the resurrected Jesus.

This drama is also that of the pagan world, the inheritor of the cosmic order. Although the new creation had appeared, and the old had perished, it too sought desperately to maintain the cosmic Temple, which was henceforth without an object, and to venerate the visible sun, whose brightness had been darkened since the time of Calvary. It remained subject to the cycle of the stars and their fatalism without understanding that the chain of necessity was irrevocably broken,

---

57   Rom. 11:25–26.

58   Origen, *Commentary on the Gospel of Matthew.* Text in *Patrologiae Cursus Completus, Series Graeca*, ed. J. P. Migne (Paris: Garnier and J. P. Migne, 1857–1866), 1027 B, 1029 B. Herafter, *PG*.

that man had escaped from the round of births and had entered once for all into eternal life. So, as for Israel, what had been until then a prefiguration became death and corruption. It was no longer the innocence of the cosmic world "and the first sunrise on creation's morn,"[59] but in the heart of the Temple of the Church the anachronistic presentation of a cult that no longer existed. Thus Julian sinned against history when he abandoned the God who had lightened the day of his baptism, to return to the pagan god of the solstice and force himself to re-establish a paganism now transformed out of all recognition.

The mystery of history continues to develop today. It provides the key to that dramatic relationship which never ceases at once to attract and repel the three worlds—pagan, Jewish, and mankind. At the same time, the pagan world and the Jewish world are secretly attracted by the Christian world, as if towards their fulfillment, and at the same time they oppose it, for that fulfillment could only take place if they renounced their own existence. Sometimes the Christian world sees them as precursors, whose riches it possesses in their integrity—the Bible and the virgin, Rome and Jerusalem—and sometimes as enemies who refuse to receive Christ and, like the Jews of old, take up stones to drive him and his followers from the Temple. The fact is that it is necessary, according to the profound view of Pascal, that there should be manifested at once the continuity and the separation of the figure and the reality—and this preeminently in the case of the Jewish people, on account of their special relationship with Christianity, but in an equally special manner in relation to all races and empires. Thus the tragedy of Jerusalem continues throughout history, which is *crisis* and resolution, at the same time as it is fulfillment and *pleroma*.

Into the Temple of the Mystics

> Christ, the Son of God, has built for God, for himself, and for us, an eternal Ark and Tabernacle; and it is none other than he himself or the Church and every man of goodwill whose prince and head he is. ... When a man seeks to obey God with an undivided heart, he is freed and discharged from every sin, by the blood of our Lord. He is bound and united to God, and God with him. And he becomes himself the Ark and Tabernacle where God wishes to dwell, not in a figure but in reality. For the figure is past, and the reality is revealed to those who wish to turn towards it.[60]

---

59 Péguy, "Eve," 707.

60 John von Ruysbroeck, *Le Tabernacle Spirituel*, [The Spiritual Tabernacle], in *Oeuvres de*

So John of Ruysbroeck writes, at the beginning of his treatise on the spiritual Tabernacle. The true Temple, which is the manhood of the Word, presents a threefold aspect. It is at the same time the manhood of Jesus, the Church, and every soul in particular. Every soul is thus the authentic Temple of God, of which the Mosaic Temple was the figure; and Ruysbroeck, after Gregory of Nyssa, before Teresa of Avila, described the spiritual splendor of this interior Tabernacle.

Christ had proclaimed the dwelling of the three divine persons in those who should be incorporated into his manhood. "If a man love Me ... we will come unto him, and make our abode with him."[61] The saints have known the fulfillment of this promise. St. Teresa herself wrote: "This person sees clearly that the three persons are in the interior of her soul, and in the inmost place as in a very deep abyss. This person cannot say what this very deep abyss is. It is there that she feels within herself this divine company."[62]

Thus every Christian soul is a consecrated Temple, which must not be profaned: "Know ye not that ye are the Temple of God, and that the Spirit of God dwelleth in you? If any man defile the Temple of God, him shall God destroy; for the Temple of God is holy, which Temple ye are. ... Know ye not that your body is the Temple of the Holy Ghost which is in you, which ye have of God, and ye are not your own? ... Ye are the Temple of the living God; as God hath said, I will dwell in them; and I will be their God, and they shall be my people."[63]

The interior Temple is the pattern which was prefigured by the Mosaic Tabernacle. Like the latter, it consists of three parts. First of all, there is the outer court, which is exterior man. "The outer court of the Tabernacle is a life conformed to morality according to the exterior man, with all that is connected with it. ... It is surrounded by a curtain of fine twined linen: by this is understood purity of manners and life."[64] Thus the practice of virtue is the outside of the spiritual tabernacle; it is its most conspicuous feature. In the outer court there was the altar of burnt sacrifice. "This signifies the unity of the senses and the recollection of the powers of the senses, through withdrawal from earthly preoccupations."[65] Then there is a second, more interior enclosure, which is the holy place. "The life of virtue is not only on this level the practice of the virtues, but also the theological virtues which

---

Ruysbroeck L'Admirable (Bruxelles: Vromant, 1928).

61   John 14:23.

62   St. Teresa of Avila, *Interior Castle*, (the seventh mansion). Text in *The Collected Works of St. Teresa of Avila*, vol. 2, tran. Kieran Kavanaugh and Otilio Rodriguez (Washington, DC: Institute for Carmelite Studies, 1980).

63   1 Cor. 3:16–17; 6:19; 2 Cor. 6:16.

64   Ruysbroeck, *Le Tabernacle spirituel*.

65   Ruysbroeck, *Le Tabernacle spirituel*.

are of a more excellent order than the virtues, since they unite us directly with God."[66]

Thus we penetrate more and more into the interior, and in proportion as the soul thus enters into herself, God draws near to her. "For it is in the interior man that truth dwells." The right way to find God is thus to detach oneself from the exterior man, from this foreign life in which we alienate ourselves, in order to recover our real life, the image of God, which is the center of the soul. This progressive entry into oneself is the very movement of the spiritual life; it withdraws from the illusory world of appearances in order to find its reality in its own depths. This movement of return does not withdraw the soul from others. On the contrary, it is when she is most at the center of herself that she is nearest to them; it is through the center of our soul that we communicate with others. In this way above all, the soul once more finds God. For the movement from exterior to interior is at the same time an entrance and an exit. It is an entrance because it withdraws us from the world in order that we may find ourselves, but it is an exit because beyond ourselves, but in the inmost place, we must find God, who is nearer to us than we are to ourselves, "in me, more myself than I." At the deepest level, it enables me to discover the source from which my existence springs.

At the beginning of this abandonment of the world, this return into oneself, prayer appears to the soul as an act of pure will, a struggle against a carnal weight. Little by little the soul grows accustomed to it—and it is this carnal weight that becomes alien. She rediscovers her true nature. But then she encounters other obstacles—pride, vanity—which she must renounce. Then it is images themselves and concepts from which her understanding must be purified—and this is a more excellent purity. Finally it is the very root of her ontological being, the *amor sui*, the love of self, that she must renounce. And this is the most painful effort of all. But beyond it there is rest, the peaceful ocean of the divine beatitude. The soul wanders there eternally, ever abandoning herself in ecstasy. But ecstasy is no longer anguished. It is the renunciation of Love[67] that would be intolerable to her. Ecstasy is what we move towards. In heaven we shall be totally disappropriated, brought into God. (This should not be represented as possession, since it is a perpetual and beautifying dispossession.) But the difference is that this renunciation is a costly process here below, because it corrects our fallen nature, while in heaven it will no longer be so, since we shall be totally restored to our true being.

This is the Holy of Holies, the *adyton*, the most secret place in the sanctuary. It is the depth of the soul of which John Tauler speaks, its center, the deepest abyss of which St. Teresa tells us. This place cannot be known by the soul. It is a dark-

---

66 Ruysbroeck, *Le Tabernacle spirituel.*

67 1 John 4:16.

ness which her glance cannot penetrate. And it is there, hidden from profane eyes, in the utmost depth of the sanctuary of the soul, that the Trinity dwells. Or rather it is there that the Trinity perpetually communicates itself to the soul that lies before it, leading her to the very heart of her own life, through the communication which the Father makes to her of the Word who by the Spirit draws her into the Father, bearing her within the cycle of the trinitarian life, within the movement of eternal love. Through this, in an ecstasy which carries her beyond the world and beyond herself, the soul truly succeeds in being transformed into God.

The presence of God at the center of the soul is not a static reality. It is an ever-renewed coming, a perpetual generation of the Word. This is the mystery of the nativity of the Word in souls—*"Dum medium silentium teneret omnia."*[68] It is in the night of the divine darkness that God engenders the Son, proffers the Word from all eternity; it is in the deepest of silences that he proffers the one *Logos*. It is in the silence of the night of Bethlehem that the Word is born into his historical existence; it is likewise in that darkness of the soul which is unknowable to it, at the center where there are no longer images or acts, in the midmost silence, in the recollection of all the powers of the soul, at its very core, which is a window that opens upon God, the deep root that originates in him—it is in this silence of the night that the Word is engendered in the soul.

The interior man, great and noble, comes from the pure depth of divinity. He is made in the image of God, the noblest, the most spiritual of beings, and he is called to enter into that depth from which he sprang in order that he may there become the sharer in all goodness. If anyone could, deep within himself, find, know, and contemplate God as he is established in himself, hidden mysteriously in the depth of that soul, certainly such a man would be happy. No doubt man turns away the inward gaze of his soul and lets it wander among outward things, he scatters himself and is lost among creatures. Yet he is always brought back, sought out by God, who is present in his own depths, within his inmost soul.[69]

> O Mary, bring together all the powers of my soul,
> and establish me at the center of my soul.
> In the silence beyond all desires, in the night beyond all images,
> make my soul flow into itself towards that mysterious center
> where the Word is to be born;
> make my soul flow entirely into the Word
> and enter into the unity of the trinitarian life.

---

68   "While earth was rapt in silence and night only half through its course, your almighty Word, O LORD, came down from his royal throne." Compare Wis. 18:14–15.

69   Tauler, *Oeuvres Complètes*, vol. 2 (Paris: Tralin, 1911), 49.

May it be lost entirely, may it lay aside all activity,
may it be transformed into thee, O Word of God.
O Mystery of the Word present from the beginning,
present once more in my heart: "*et Verbum caro factum est*"
—"and the Word was made flesh,"
grant me the power to become a child of God,
bestowing sonship upon me: "*dedit eis potestatem filios Dei fieri*"
—"to them gave he power to become the sons of God."
Draw me into that center of my soul, make me present at that
    birth.
All heaven is assembled there as at Bethlehem;
Mary bows down with the angels, Joseph and all the saints.
Together they worship him who comes down for us, in us,
    among us.

The Mass Is Open to Heaven

In the Temple at Jerusalem, the Holy of Holies was divided from the rest of the Temple by a veil, woven of four colors, which none ever passed through, unless it was the high priest once a year. The very repetition of the act indicated that it was only a question here of a symbolic gesture, of an effort which had not reached its goal: "The Holy Ghost thus signifying, that the way into the holiest of all was not yet made manifest."[70] All was figurative here—Temple, High Priest, entry. And the reality that was thus figuratively given, was the consummation of the work of salvation, the final entry of Christ, the High Priest of mankind, into the heavenly Temple on ascension day. "Christ being come a High Priest of good things to come, by a greater and more perfect Tabernacle, not made with hands, that is to say, not of this building; neither by the blood of goats and calves, but by his own blood he entered in once into the holy place, having obtained eternal redemption for us."[71]

All the words here are charged with mystery, and describe the greatest act of history, the unique act, of which the action of the Mass is only the sacramental possession: "*Jube haec preferri per manus sancti Angeli tui in sublime altare tuum.*"[72] For it is the ascension that is the consummation of the mystery of salvation. Christ is the High Priest, that is to say, he is the representative of total humanity—and with him the whole of "human nature" is finally brought into the heavenly Temple. With him, it is the heavenly Temple that humanity penetrates, that is to say, into

---

70 Heb. 9:8.

71 Heb. 9:11–12.

72 "Command these offerings to be borne by the hands of thy holy angels to thine altar on high." Prayer of the priest at the consecration during the Mass.

the *pleroma* of the spiritual creatures which are the Temple, the glory, in the midst of which dwells the Holy Trinity. "The perfect unity of heavenly spirits bound together without any division, constitutes the total and proper dwelling of divinity."[73]

St. Gregory of Nyssa compares this total, heavenly creation with a symphony, with a chorus mingled with songs and dances, celebrating a perpetual feast around the leader: "There was a time when the chorus of spiritual creatures was one, all looking towards the single leader and putting forth the harmony of their dances, following the measure given by him. But the Fall supervened, marring that inspired harmony. It was a cause of stumbling to the first men who danced amid the angelic powers."[74] Since then, the latter have kept watch at the heavenly gates, awaiting the return of the hundredth sheep, their sister humanity. The ascension is the return of the lost sheep borne on the shoulders of the shepherd, and the angels joyfully hail Christ, the conqueror of death, who brings man back into the chorus, now once more complete.

This entry of mankind into the heavenly Temple is achieved once for all. It is no longer the High Priest alone who is admitted once a year to the figurative Holy of Holies—a fact, as St. Paul profoundly remarks, which showed by its very repetition that it was only a question of a figure and not of an achievement; but it is mankind as a whole that now dwells there permanently. This again is a proclamation of the highest importance. It means that salvation is irreversibly achieved, that henceforth it is on longer exposed to a relapse. And how could it be otherwise, since it is in the very person of the Son of God that humanity is united with divinity? This declaration disperses any mirage of eternal recurrence, with its cycle of salvation and relapse. It gives Christian hope the solidarity of the Word of God who never fails. The divine plan is fulfilled, the world has achieved its end and object, it has found its meaning. We are at the end of all times: "So shall my

---

73   St. Bernard, *The Word of Isaiah*, 3. Compare a passage from St. Ignatius beloved by Newman: "In your unanimity and concordant charity Jesus Christ is sung. And one by one you take your parts in the choir, so as to sing with one voice through Jesus Christ to the Father that he may hear your petitions (from Ignatius' *Epistle to the Ephesians*, 4).

74   Gregory of Nyssa, *Commentary on the Psalms*, PG 44, 508 B, 509 A. This image refers to the type of dance known as a singing round. It makes a circle by singing and dancing round the altar of the god. But the center may be occupied by a leader bearing a lyre. The symbol recurs in Plotinus, *Enneads*, Bk. 6, Chap. 9, 38. It is not a question strictly speaking, as in Origen, of an angelic prehistory of mankind, but of a participation in the privileges of the angels, that is to say, "in familiarity with God, in the contemplation of divine realties." Moreover, these privileges are not present as having historically existed, but as representing God's plan for humanity which is only fulfilled historically in and through Jesus Christ.

Word be that goeth out of my mouth, it shall not return unto me void, but it shall accomplish that which I please."[75]

Indeed it is "by his own blood" that Christ enters the heavenly sanctuary. Salvation is achieved for all time, for eternity, through the sacrifice of the Lamb. This is why the sacrifice of the Lamb is coextensive with all periods of history. It fills Holy Week. It is the same way that the Book of Revelation presents to us the same scene of the entry into the heavenly Temple: "And I beheld, and lo, in the midst of the throne and of the four beasts, and in the midst of the elders, stood a Lamb as it had been slain."[76] Here is a supreme dramatic effect. The angels are expecting the Lion of Judah, the triumphant King—and it is a sacrificial Lamb who appears.

Gregory of Nyssa describes their astonishment: "The angels of earth went in procession and demanded that the celestial gates should be opened to him, so that he might be glorified afresh. But he was not recognized, clothed as he was in the shabby garment of our nature, his tattered clothes bedraggled with human grime."[77] This is the new element that is introduced into the celestial choir; the red robe of the redeemed mingles with the white robe of the heavenly host. There is something else for which the angels can envy mankind—the fact that it shared in the passion of Christ. In the midst of the angelic choir, here to the eternal Temple come the martyrs bathed in the blood of the Lamb, that blood in which St. Catherine of Siena saw the whole Church steeped.

Henceforth, humanity's place is in heaven; it is there that man dwells already through Christ, the head of the Mystical Body, and through the glorified Church. It is there that henceforth there is a uniquely valuable liturgy, no longer beside the waters, nor in the Temple of stone. It is this liturgy that St. John the Divine describes in the Book of Revelation: "The elders fell down before the Lamb, having every one of them harps, and golden vials full of odors, which are the prayers of saints."[78] It is in this heavenly liturgy that we share at the Mass, which is the offering of the heavenly sacrifice. It is the real presence of the event commemorated, which is granted by a special privilege—and that is, strictly speaking, a mystery, abstracted from time. But it is also placed sacramentally in space and time; and that is this, on the ritual side, that the sacrifice which we offer differs from the heavenly sacrifice with which it is substantially identical. So it is the same reality which is symbolized by the entry of the High Priest into the Holy of Holies, fulfilled by the entry of Christ into heaven on ascension day, possessed invisibly

---

75   Isa. 55:11.

76   Rev. 5:6.

77   Gregory of Nyssa, *The Ascension*. Text in *PG* 46, 693 C.

78   Rev. 5:8.

on earth under the eucharistic species; and it is the entry of human nature into the heavenly Temple. The Mass is open to heaven, and this is why the angels are present. It is filled with the echo of their songs, from the *Gloria* of the nativity to the *Sanctus* of the hidden mystery.

But it remains to be said that this entry of mankind into the heavenly Temple, if it is achieved for all men, if it is already real for every member, must nevertheless be gained by each of them. It is real—and that is the fundamental difference from the Mosaic situation—but it is still veiled: "Christ being come a High Priest of good things to come."[79] Every present economy, if it is a reality in relation to the Mosaic figure, is itself a figure in relation to the consummation of all things. It is prophecy, waiting. The real life, the real dwelling, are elsewhere. Here there are only passing tents, which we must always be ready to fold up. "While we are at home in the body, we are absent from the Lord."[80] The total presence is like an inward weight that irresistibly attracts the Christian towards the divine presence: "*Pondus meum, amor meus.*"[81] St. John the Divine in the Book of Revelation shows us mankind as a procession advancing towards the heavenly Temple; "A great multitude … stood before the throne, and before the Lamb, clothed with white robes, and palms in their hands."[82]

Thus the Christian life is altogether an act of waiting. The Christian knows that he is made for greater things. He feels acutely the misery of his present condition. He aspires to be relieved of the weight of animal life and its servitude. "I desire to depart, and to be with Christ."[83] Whilst carnal man grasps desperately at his pleasures and possessions, the Christian lives already in the order of being, detached, free, making use of time, so long as it is given, to perform works of charity towards all—an activity invisible to the eyes of the world. The Christian life is a hidden life. But when the world is folded up like a tent, the reality that has been hidden until that moment will be clearly revealed.

This does not mean, all the same, that the Christian is not interested in the world, but he sees in it only a beginning, only a crucible where immortal souls are in the making. The only work that interests him is, at every moment, making the life of Christ grow in himself and others. The world is indeed for him "a machine for making gods." But it is in this world that gods are made; so he takes part eagerly in temporal struggles, not for their own sake, and without believing in the establishment of a perfect human city, for he knows that Christ said, "My

---

79   Heb. 11:11.

80   2 Cor. 5:6.

81   "My love is my weight." St. Augustine, *Confessions*, Bk. 13, Chap. 9.

82   Rev. 7:9.

83   Phil. 1:23.

kingdom is not of this world," but because the salvation of many souls is bound up with the temporal conditions of life.

This is not to say that there is for him, as it were, a devaluing of earthly realities, a weakening of the instinct for life, a desire to escape from the wicked world, a morbid taste for death. This attitude, which inspires the "Hymns to Night" of Novalis, the *Nirvana* of Arthur Schopenhauer, the "Tristan" of Richard Wagner, is foreign to him. It is the return of the individual to the original stream of life, to an undifferentiated primordial state. For the Christian, on the contrary, death is the full reality of all for which he has imperfectly lived on earth, the liberation of the person with regard to the mortal shedding of blood. "Through death, we offer ourselves to that for which we lived on earth."[84]

This does not mean, either, that the Christian blurs the frontiers of life and death, as a Rilke seems to do. "The living all make the mistake of establishing vast differences. The angels, for their part, do not know if they are passing among the living or the dead."[85] Certainly there is for the Christian a continuity between the Christian life that has begun, and its consummation in eternity. But it remains true that the human act by which the free soul ratifies his detachment from mortality and adheres to eternal life is the most serious of all. Not that he could change anything. We know that the faithful soul could not deny what has always been his life. But it is then that he reaps the fruits. It is to prepare himself for this solemn act, which is the entry of every man into the heavenly Temple, through the veil that still conceals it, that man's whole life must be devoted.

That life consists for the Christian in endowing himself little by little with divine manners. And the education that proceeds till the hour of death—for all life is only an adolescence—consists, as Jean Guitton says, "In that discipline by which we prepare the child for temporal life, the adult for eternal life, so that whatever he sees, he feels he has seen it already."[86] We must not be without a country on our arrival in heaven. Our life is an apprenticeship. It is a matter of learning the rudiments of what we shall have one day to do. So let us already try in prayer to stammer what will later be the "conversation in heaven" with God and his angels; so we must try to make less crude this intellect of ours, which is so immersed in the world of time and space, and to acclimatize it gradually to heavenly things through the action of the gifts of the Holy Spirit. Thus charity itself is the clumsy beginning of that complete communion which will embrace all the saints. So doing, we

84   Gabriel Marcel, *La Soif* [The Thirst] (Paris: Desclée de Brouwer, 1938), 161.

85   *Duino Elegies.*

86   Jean Guiton, *La Pensé Moderne et le Catholicisme* [Catholicism and Modern Thought] (Paris: Aubier, 1938), 3:57.

begin to do what we have always to do. It is our real life which is being mapped out. Let us begin it.

This apprenticeship is not only that of our life with God, it is also that of our life together. Death will not only be the revelation of our mysterious unity—that is to say, something still hidden. Just as beneath the appearances of our mortal body is hidden our glorified body, so beneath the appearance of the visible Church is hidden the Mystical Body, the unity of man. Both are revealed at the same time. The two great signs of the present decadence of mankind are the corruption of death and the rupture of unity. The restoration of incorruptibility and of unity will mark the return of mankind to its true condition. Of this, the Eucharist is at once the sign and the instrument. It is essentially viatic, the bread of the traveler, which keeps him going till he reaches home. It communicates the principle of the glorified life and maintains it; it symbolizes the unity of the Mystical Body and begins to put it into effect. Finally, for our poor human race, so prone to earthly food, it is already the bread of heaven, of which it gives us the foretaste, besides which earthly things lose their savor, and which slowly awakens in us a longing for the life of reality, and draws our souls towards the Father.

Letter & Spirit 4 (2008): 289–317

CHURCH, KINGDOM, AND THE ESCHATOLOGICAL TEMPLE

~: Yves M.-J. Cardinal Congar, O. P. :~

When the Book of Revelation, or the Apocalypse, speaks of the Temple, it uses the words *skēnē* and *naos* exclusively and never the other expressions found in the New Testament.[1] It describes the Temple of which it speaks, in terms and images that refer to the Temple of Jerusalem. If we follow the attractive hypothesis put forward by M. E. Boismard, the Temple was still standing when St. John wrote these descriptions.[2]

But the Apocalypse speaks of two temples: one heavenly, the other earthly. In one whole section of the visions, there is a Temple in heaven and events take place there while the history of the world continues, and there is even a Temple on earth, in which also certain events occur. On the other hand, at a given moment, the end of history is proclaimed and John sees the judgment of the nations (Rev. 20: 11–15), a new heaven and a new earth (Rev. 21:1) and the New Jerusalem coming down from heaven (Rev. 21:2). An entirely different situation is then inaugurated as regards the Temple or dwelling of God. There is a city, Jerusalem, but John declares: "I saw no Temple in it; its Temple is the Lord God Almighty, its Temple is the Lamb" (21:22).

Thus, in a *literary* form which is a combination of two texts placed side by side rather than fused into one, somewhat as a Galician and Roman text have been juxtaposed in the ordination ritual, we find in the text of the Apocalypse as it is presented to the meditation of the faithful, a real division corresponding to two moments in the history of God's dwelling among men. We shall divide our study of the text by reference to these two moments.

The Temple in History

In the first moment, we are concerned with earthly events. The Apocalypse offers us a view of history entirely dominated by the reality of heaven, and also the image of a Church still on earth and entirely ruled by the virtue of him who is in heaven and is ultimately shown to us as her Bridegroom. It is because Christ, having

---

1   *Hieron* (Rev. 11:2 however, does provide an equivalent), and *oikos* never appear. *Topos* is used, but not in the sense of "a holy *place*." On the other hand, *naos* occurs fifteen times: Rev. 3:12; 7:15; 11:1, 2, 19; 14.:15, 17; 15:5, 6, 8 (twice); 16:1, 17; 21:22 (twice). *Skēnē* occurs three times (Rev. 13:6; 15:5; 21:3) and in its verbal form, four times (Rev. 7:15, in which the meaning is simply "to spread a tent"; Rev. 12:12; 13: 6; 21:3).

2   See M. E. Boismard, "'L'Apocalypse' ou 'les Apocalypses' de S. Jean'" ["The Apocalypse" or "the Apocalypses" of St. John], *Revue Biblique* 56 (1949): 507–46.

obtained the victory, has taken his place by his Father on the Father's throne, that the faithful are kings reigning with Christ and priests also entering with him into the very presence of God.[3]

The Church of the Apocalypse is a community of kings and priests, that is, of the faithful who share in the dignity and activity of Christ as king and priest.[4] As kings, they share in the Kingdom of God and its struggles throughout history, and they will share God's eschatological reign in the world to come. As priests they share in the worship of thanksgiving and in the praise offered to God in heaven by the elect, but which begins in the Church on earth (Rev. 1:6); they surrender themselves to the work of purification which God wishes to accomplish in them ("He has proved his love for us by washing us clean from our sins in his own blood" Rev. 1:5); their voices ring out with the *Amen* that stands for the inmost substance of worship and sacrifice and is at the same time the final word of every doxology and blessing.[5]

The Apocalypse sees the historical and earthly life of this royal and priestly Church as an extremely bitter struggle between the reign of God and the reign of God's adversary. To expound and explain all that this prophetic book tells us in this connection would be tantamount to providing a complete commentary. Here we can only confine ourselves strictly to what concerns the Temple.

First of all we are shown "the beast," which symbolizes the Roman Empire, and through it, all the powers which fight against the Kingdom of God, uttering "blasphemy against God, blasphemy against his name, against his dwelling-place (*skēnē*), and all those who dwell in heaven (*tous en tō ouranō skēnountas*)" (Rev. 13:6). There is an obvious resemblance between the beast blaspheming against God's dwelling-place, that is God himself in his heavenly transcendence, and the adversary of 2 Thessalonians 2:4 "lifting himself above every divine name, above all that men hold in reverence." But the similarity, although it indicates a connection, does not imply a rigorous identification. We should note also, the role assigned by the Apocalypse to the "false prophet."[6] Under the guise of a lamb, he speaks in fact the language of the "dragon," that is, of Satan. He works wonders and labors to bring the world to the worship of power.

The Church herself is represented under the image of the Temple of God (*naos*), that is, the Temple of Jerusalem (Rev. 11:1). John is commissioned to measure

---

3   See Brooke Foss Westcott, *The Epistle to the Hebrews: The Greek Text with Notes and Essays* (London: Macmillan, 1899), 215. Heb. 8:1 is the basis of Rev. 3:21.

4   Rev. 1:6; 5:10 (compare 1 Pet. 2:9); Rev. 20:6 (the reign of a thousand years).

5   See Heinrich Schlier, "*Amen*," in *Theologisches Wörterbuch zum Neuen Testament*, 10 vols., eds. Gerhard Kittel (Stuttgart: W. Kohlhammer, 1932–1979), 1:339–342. Eng. trans.: *Theological Dictionary of the New Testament*, 10 vols., ed. Gerhard Kittel, trans. and ed. Geoffrey W. Bromiley (Grand Rapids, MI: Eerdmans, 1964–1985).

6   Rev. 13:11–17; 16:13; 19:20; 20:10. See the discussion in Yves Congar *The Mystery of the Temple* (London: Burns and Oates, 1962), 193–196.

the Temple and the altar and to count the worshippers who are there, so that he may number and make a record of those who are to be spared from punishment. "But leave out of your reckoning," John is told, "the court which is outside the Temple; do not measure that, because it has been made over to the Gentiles, who will tread the holy city under foot for the space of forty-two months" (Rev. 11:2).

John here uses imagery that has a reference to the persecution of Antiochus Epiphanius, which had become the type of all persecution of the faithful by a hostile ideological and political power. Hence the period of forty-two months. But the point that interests us here is the image of the Church as Jerusalem, or rather, as the sacred area the evangelists call the *hieron*, which includes the terrace and the courts of the Temple. In this area John observes two zones—one, exterior (*tēn aulēn tēn exōthen*), is more or less given over to the Gentiles who will tread it underfoot, as they did the holy city during those three years and a half which are the "type" period of persecution.[7]

It is in this city of Jerusalem where too "their Lord was crucified" (Rev. 11:8), that the beast will slay the two faithful witnesses, that is, in this sacred area given over to the pagans so that they may tread it underfoot.[8] The other zone is a protected one. It is represented by the Temple of God, the altar, and the worshippers in the building—that is, the true faithful, those who conquer the seductions, threats, and violence of the dragon and his ministers. The Apocalypse often speaks of those who conquer, using terms which awaken a great desire to be among their number.[9] In particular it utters this promise:

> Who wins the victory? I will make him a pillar in the Temple of my God, never to leave it again. I will write on him the name of my God, and the name of the city my God has built, that new Jerusalem which my God is even now sending down from heaven, and my own new name (Rev. 3:12).

---

7   This "treading underfoot," therefore, is not of exactly the same kind as that mentioned in Luke 21:24, where it is above all providential and beneficial. The Gentiles' adoration will, in a sense, replace that of the Jews who have refused Christ. In the Apocalypse, they tread the courts underfoot, not as they come to adore, but in order to trample upon and destroy the worship of the true God.

8   It seems to us that, under these conditions, "there, too, their Lord was crucified" does not indicate the geographical Jerusalem, but the spiritual Jerusalem given over to the hostility, the persecution, and the temporary victory (forty-two months) of the beast. This does away with the chief difficulty that has been raised against the interpretation which takes the two witnesses to be Peter and Paul martyred at Rome under Nero ("Their bodies will lie in the open street, in that great city which is called Sodom or Egypt in the language of prophecy" Rev. 11:8). John is simply combining a direct reference to Jerusalem (v. 8), indicating the section of the Church (the Temple) which the Gentiles are allowed to tread underfoot, with another symbolizing the actual city of Rome.

9   See, for instance, Rev. 2:7, 11, 17 (and esp. Rev. 2:26); 3:5, 12, 21; 12:11 (and, in particular, Rev. 15:2); 21:7. We have emphasized the passages that are most interesting from the point of view of our theme. Compare Rev. 14:1–5 and, as far as Wisdom is concerned, Wis. 10:12–14.

This promise has in view the final reward and membership of that Jerusalem from on high of which we shall have something to say later. But there is a continuity between the Temple on earth, the Church, and the Temple on high. Further, if the victor is to be a pillar in the Temple of God, it is above all in reference to the Church, for in the heavenly Jerusalem there is no Temple.

We therefore retain two points in connection with this passage (Rev. 11:1). First, the Temple of God is the Church, as in the other apostolic writings, and it is made up of the faithful themselves in their fidelity and unity.[10] Then, in the center of an area, sacred in itself but trodden underfoot and profaned by the pagans, a Temple of God remains in being and is composed of the true faithful, the pure whom John sees later (Rev. 14:1–5) accompanying the Lamb wherever he may go. Since they have kept true "to God's commandment and the faith of Jesus" (Rev. 14:12), since they have refused to worship the beast, that is, to serve God's adversary (Rev. 20:4), they are not only sharers in the kingship of Christ, but also have the privilege of attending him, wherever he goes (Rev. 14:4). As in the prophets, God's presence is linked with his reign, and friendship with him in his Temple to faithful observance of his commandments (compare John 14:23).

The Liturgy of Heaven

While on earth the struggle unfolds between God's reign and his adversary, in heaven there is a Temple. Sometimes St. John calls it the *naos*,[11] occasionally adding "in heaven," at others the *skēnē*.[12] Both words indicate the same reality and the term might be translated "the tabernacle that bears record in heaven" (Rev. 15:5).[13]

For John the heavenly temple is modeled on the Temple of Jerusalem. He even sees in it the Ark of the Covenant which appears when the Kingdom of God is about to be reestablished.[14] He sees an altar which is both that of the burnt-offerings and the altar of incense, but chiefly the latter.[15] Under the altar, John sees

---

10   This is clearly stated in Rev. 3:12 and is implied in Rev. 11:1.

11   Rev. 7:15; 11:19 (in heaven); 14:17 (which is in heaven); 15:5 (in heaven) 6, 8; 16:1, 17.

12   Rev. 13:6; 15:5 (the temple of the tent of witness); compare Rev. 21:3.

13   This is how J. Comblin translates it in his, "La Liturgie de la Nouvelle Jérusalem (Apoc. 21:1–22:5)" [The Liturgy of the New Jerusalem], *Ephemerides Theologicae Lovanienses* 29 (1953): 5–40, at 21, n. 41. He observes that in Rev. 21:3 the two words have the same sense.

14   The source here may be the legend revived in 2 Macc. 2:5–8 according to which Jeremiah hid the Tabernacle, the Ark, and the altar of incense in a cave on Mount Nebo when Jerusalem was captured in 586 B.C. The belief was that God would reveal the whereabouts of these sacred objects when he had gathered his people together again and shown his mercy towards them.

15   The majority of the exegetes distinguish between the two uses of the altar of which the Apocalypse speaks—its use as an altar of holocausts and as an altar of incense. But they do not always agree. (For a fuller discussion, see Congar, *Mystery of the Temple*, 208, n. 1.) It is no doubt true that the evidence is inconclusive. It is impossible to distinguish clearly two altars, an altar of holocausts and an altar of incense. Moreover, we should note that if we turn to the Hebrew equivalent of these expressions, the altar of gold in Heb. 9:4 and in Rev. 8:3; 9:13, is identical with the altar of incense (in Luke 1:11, for instance). It is not due to a slip that Heb.

the "souls of all who had been slain for love of God's word and of the truth they held" (Rev. 6:9 see also Rev. 8:3; 6:7): we shall shortly see what role these martyrs play and with them the altar from which their prayer rises like incense (Rev. 8:3).[16] If John thus sees the heavenly Temple in the shape of the Temple of Jerusalem, it is not so much because he imagines the sanctuary on the model of the sanctuary he had seen on earth at Jerusalem, it is principally because the latter, as the successor of the Mosaic tabernacle, had been constructed according to the heavenly proto-type shown to Moses on the mountain.[17] If the Apocalypse sometimes mentions "a tent of witness" at the same time and with the same meaning as "Temple," it is, in our opinion, to recall the Exodus on the one hand, and so to demonstrate the continuity of God's divine purposes and the continuity of the mystery of his dwell-

---

9:4 puts the golden altar, which is the altar of incense, in the Holy of Holies. It is because, as in Rev. 8:3, the Temple in question is the heavenly Temple, where all the faithful enter and go to the throne of God. In the Mosaic liturgy, only the high priest did this. And, generally speaking, we ought not to look for a rigorously accurate succession of images in the Apocalypse. John is not copying from a model, he is seeing a vision. But above all, Robert H. Charles, whose knowledge of the apocalyptic literature was unrivaled, has shown that in this literature only one altar is intended and that the word "the altar" (Hebrew: *hammizbah*) which elsewhere means the altar of holocausts, here indicates rather the altar of incense. See his *A Critical and Exegetical Commentary on the Revelation of St. John*, 2 vols. (Edinburgh: T. & T. Clark, 1920), 1:172, 227–30. The Apocalypse has "the altar" (*to thysiastērion*) and when it adds a clarifying detail, it mentions that this is the golden altar standing before the throne (Rev. 8:3; 9:13). The exegetes then admit that the altar of incense is meant, and in fact this is clear enough. But we think, with Charles, that it is impossible to distinguish clearly between this altar and another, namely, the altar of holocausts, and that there is in reality one altar with certain characteristics of the altar of holocausts, and others, much more clearly marked, of the altar of incense. Further, as Charles remarks, since there are in the heavenly Temple no more animal sacrifices of the type offered in the Mosaic ritual but only the offering of the spiritual sacrifice which is that of man himself, it is normal that there should be only the one altar of incense, from which the praise, thanksgiving, and prayer of the saints rise like the smoke of incense (*thysia* is derived from *thyō*, meaning to smoke or to cause smoke to rise): Rev. 8:3; 5:8; 6:9; see also Ps. 141:2. It is also noteworthy that previous Jewish apocalyptic literature mentioned only one altar in heaven. Certain rabbis even held that after the messianic restoration, expiatory sacrifices would cease and the sacrifice of praise alone remain. See Joseph Bonsirven, *Le Judaisme Palestinian au Temps de Jésus-Christ*, 2 vols. (Paris: Beauchesne, 1935), 1:456; Eng. trans.: *Palestinian Judaism in the Time of Jesus Christ*, trans. William Wolff (New York: Holt, Rinehart, and Winston, 1964). In the context of Christianity, this view is essential. See Yves Congar, *Lay People in the Church: A Study for a Theology of the Laity*, trans. Donald Attwater (Westminster: Newman, 1957), 72.

16   Some explain the presence of the martyrs under the altar (and they make it clear they think it is the altar of holocausts) by the fact that the soul is in the blood and the blood flows under the altar (see Ernest-Bernard Allo, *Saint Jean: L'Apocalypse*, Études Bibliques [Paris: J. Gabalda et Cie, 1933], 103). We should be better advised with Charles (*Revelation*, 1:29) and Allo to think rather of the Jewish concept of the souls of the just as beneath the throne of God. With Joachim Jeremias, we may also bear in mind the ideology which held that the rock of the Temple was the highest point on earth and contact was made there not only with the heavenly world but also with the subterranean world of the souls of the dead. See his "Golgotha und der Heilige Felsen eine Untersuchung zur Symbolsprache des N. T." [Golgotha and the Holy Rock: An Investigation of New Testament Symbolism], *Angelos* 2 (1926): 74–128.

17   Exod. 25:40.

ing among his people from the time of the Exodus, in the earthly Jerusalem, in the Church, and finally in heaven;[18] and, on the other hand, it is because the oracles of God were revealed in the tent of meeting and now his judgments are pronounced from within his heavenly Temple.

Once more, this heavenly Temple assumes into itself the presence of God in the historical life of his people in their passage through time. This is why, at the moment of final consummation, we shall again meet the themes that have occurred throughout the process of biblical history: "He will dwell with them, and they will be his own people" (Rev. 21:3) and "I will be his God, and he shall be my son," with a reference to the prophecy of Nathan (Rev. 21:7; compare 2 Sam. 7:14).

Who will be the celebrant in the heavenly Temple? The Apocalypse nowhere calls Christ priest or high priest as does the Epistle to the Hebrews. Yet he makes his appearance as a priest, clothed with a long robe and wearing a golden girdle. Thus he who makes us kings and priests is himself priest and king.[19] But the image in which Christ chiefly appears in the Apocalypse is that of the Lamb (this name is given to him twenty-nine times). The word reveals him in his character of victim, but as a victim who is alive again (Rev. 5:6; Rev. 1:18).

He is, therefore, the Christ of Easter, the Christ who said: "Destroy this Temple, and in three days I will raise it up again," and who called himself the stone rejected by the builders but precious in the sight of God and so made the cornerstone.[20] The Lamb of the Apocalypse is therefore not merely the paschal lamb as *immolated*. Already as the immolated paschal lamb, he is revealed as the victor, for it is by his blood that the faithful are separated from the unfaithful and rescued from the plagues God sends upon the world.[21]

However, it may be admitted that, either on the strength of the double meaning of the Aramaic word for *arnion* ("lamb"), or even by reference to a certain number of uses of the word "Lamb" in Jewish apocalyptic literature, where it implies triumph, the term can bear the meaning of Christ's sovereignty dominating history and the world.[22] It is a fact that, in the Apocalypse, "Lamb" is the name of

---

18   See Rev. 15:3, where those who have triumphed over the beast sing the song of Moses and of the Lamb; compare Exod. 15:1.

19   Compare François-Marie Braun, "In Spiritu et Veritate" [In Spirit and Truth], *Revue Thomiste* 52 (1952): 494 and also *Revue Thomiste* 52 (1952): 258. The long robe was the High Priest's vestment (Exod. 28:4; 29:5; Zech. 3:4. The golden girdle is one of the insignia of royalty, compare the golden clasp in 1 Macc. 10:89; 11:58. Christ has made us kings and priests: Rev. 5:10; 1:6.

20   John 2:19; Matt. 21:42.

21   Rev. 5:6, 9, 12. Notice how, once again, the "type" event in Exodus, the lamb that is slain, is here "recapitulated."

22   See Hans Wenschkewitz, "Die Spiritualisierung der Kultusbegriffe Tempel, Priester und Opfer im N. T." [The Spiritualization of the Notions of Temple, Priest, and Sacrificial Victim in the New Testament], *Angelos* 4 (1932): 70–230, at 214–215, who refers to Friedrich Spitta regarding the Jewish apocalyptic literature and to C. F. Burnay for the two meanings of the Aramaic word corresponding to *arnion*, namely, lamb and child or servant (of God), *pais*. In the Apocalypse,

Christ as associated with God in the exercise of his sovereignty and in the glorification of the elect.

Heaven, where the Lamb sits upon the throne, is a palace as well as a Temple.[23] A liturgy is celebrated in which the angels have their part to play[24] together with the elect and the mysterious twenty-four elders. We are given frequent glimpses of this heavenly liturgy.[25] It is a liturgy of praise and prayer, with no sacrifice save that of "the tribute of lips."[26] J. Comblin has shown fairly convincingly that the liturgy celebrated in heaven while the history of the world unfolds (Rev. 7:9) is the same as the liturgy of eternity (Rev. 21–22), but that this liturgy is conceived on the model of the liturgy of the great Jerusalem pilgrimages, and on the model, too, of the liturgy of the Feast of Tabernacles. Thus, the image we are given of the heavenly Church is that of a great host of pilgrims who have reached the Temple at Jerusalem and are in God's presence. With palms in their hands, they acclaim with vibrant voices the royal and saving power of God: "To our God, who sits on the throne, and to the Lamb, all saving power belongs" (Rev. 7:9–12).

Heaven in History

One of the most remarkable features of the Apocalypse is the connection it reveals between events on earth and events in heaven. In the Epistle to the Hebrews also, the Christian liturgy which is both earthly and heavenly, is that of a great assembly (*panegyris*) in which we join with the angels, and of a joyful feast, whose center is the living God (Rev. 12:22).

From one point of view, heavenly events determine the great events in the earthly history of God's people. It is from the heavenly Temple that the decrees

---

"Lamb" in fact does stand for the suffering Servant as risen, victorious, and henceforth reigning with God.

23 Rev. 4; 7:9–10; 11:16–17.

24 See Jean Daniélou, *The Angels and their Mission according to the Fathers of the Church*, trans. David Heimann (Westminster, MD: Christian Classics, 1988 [1956]); on the idea of the monastic life as angelic, see Jean Leclercq, *La Vie Parfaite: Points de Vue sur l'Essence de l'État Religieux* [The Life of Perfection: Viewpoints on the Essence of the Religious State] (Paris: Turnhout, 1948); L. Bouyer, *Le Sens de la Vie Monastique* [The Meaning of the Monastic Life] (Paris: Turnhout, 1951).

25 See Rev. 4; 5; 7:9–12; 14:1–2; 19:1–2.

26 Wenschkewitz, "Die Spiritualisierung," 217. On the sacrifice of praise, see Ps. 50:14, 23; Hosea 14:2; Isa. 57:19; Heb. 13:15. The messianic-eschatological Temple of the prophets was a place of thanksgiving and not of expiation: see Jer. 33:11; Ezek. 20:40–41; 37:27–28; compare Isa. 51:3. The fact that in heaven there can be only the sacrifice of praise, may be explained in the light of the magnificent prospect described by St. Augustine below (see n. 88). We may then say with Florus of Lyons, a ninth-century ecclesiastical writer, that there is "a sacrifice of praise" at the precise moment when "*nulla nostra merita agnoscimus, sed solam Dei gratiam collaudamus*" [we recognize that our worth is nothing, but we praise highly the singular grace of God] (*Opusculum De Expositione Missae* [Explanation of the Mass], 53. Text in *Patrologiae Cursus Completus, Series Latina*, ed. J. P. Migne [Paris: Garnier and J. P. Migne, 1844–1864], 119, 48C.) Hereafter, *PL*.

ordering the execution of God's judgments are promulgated.[27] John sees the seven angels who are to bear the seven plagues come out from the heavenly Temple. They have been given golden cups full of the wrath of God who lives for ever and ever (Rev. 15:5–8). It is from the heavenly Temple that a voice cries to these seven angels: "Go and pour out the seven cups of God's vengeance on the earth" (Rev. 16:1), and then, when the last cup is emptied, the voice cries: "It is over" (Rev. 16:17). When history has come to an end, it is once more from the heavenly Temple that an angel goes forth, sickle in hand, to "gather the grapes from earth's vineyard" (Rev. 14:18).

But from another point of view, the carrying out of God's judgments and the decision to begin the harvesting of the grapes are in part determined, or in any case, hastened, by men, by the faithful and the elect who in their turn are assisted by the angels. It is from the altar whence the prayer of the saints rises like the smoke of incense that the angel takes the burning coals which he throws upon the earth (Rev. 8:3–5). Again, it is from the horns of the heavenly altar that there comes a voice ordering the release of the four destroying angels "who were waiting for the year, the month, the day, the hour" (Rev. 9:13–16). And when the angels with the golden cups have poured all the wrath of God upon the earth, it is also the altar which John hears saying: "Yes, the judgments you do pronounce, Lord God Almighty, are true and just" (Rev. 16:7).

The altar which speaks these words is the same as that which asked for the just punishments of God to be unleashed, the same again from which the angel took the fire of justice and of final purification. It is the altar of prayer and praise, of supplication and thanksgiving, and under it those who had been slain for God's Word and the witness they had borne, cried out with all their might: "Sovereign Lord, the holy, the true, how long now before you will sit in judgment, and exact vengeance for our blood from all those who dwell on earth?"[28] It is clear that the voice of the altar was the very voice of the martyrs and the faithful witnesses (compare Rev. 19:1–3). The judgments of God are therefore hastened and, in part, set in motion by the prayers of the saints.

But the Church militant, the Church on earth, herself has her part in the decrees of Providence. It seems very likely that the invitation to gather the grapes and harvest the corn comes from two angels who go forth from the earthly Temple of God—that is, from the Church (see Rev. 14:15, 18, where the "Temple" is clearly distinct from that in heaven, Rev. 14:17). Angels from heaven gather the grapes and harvest the corn (Rev. 14:14, 17), but they are invited to do so by the angels who are given charge over the Church militant, God's earthly Temple. Should we be

---

27   Isa. 66:6.

28   Rev. 6:9–10. There is a parallel passage in Luke 18:7: "Will not God give redress to his elect, when they are crying out to him day and night?" We have to remember, too, that the apostles had been promised that they would judge the twelve tribes of Israel (Matt. 19:28; Luke 22:30), and that it is written that we shall judge even the angels (1 Cor. 6:3; compare Wis. 3:8; 1 Cor. 2:15), and that in the Apocalypse itself, the faithful sit upon thrones and receive the right to judge: Rev. 20:4.

justified in thinking that some angels follow the progress of the Church, that is, the growth of the body or the building-up of the Temple,[29] and then tell the angels serving God in heaven that "the crop of earth is dry and the time has come to reap it" (Rev. 14:15), that it is time to gather the grapes from earth's vineyard for "its clusters are ripe" (Rev. 14:18)?

Such a theme need cause no surprise if we remember the prospects opened up by the Epistle to the Ephesians.[30] In our opinion, the theme is not out of key with the context of the Apocalypse in which both the Spirit and the bride say "Come" (Rev. 22:17). The prayer of the Church seeks to hasten the Second Coming. The sacraments, in a sense, "desire" to be swallowed up in the reality they mediate, and the Temple of time "desires" to be engulfed in the Temple of eternity.

The New Heavens and the New Earth

Beginning with Revelation 20:11, we enter the purely heavenly order: the order of eternity. The order of the present creation has passed away. Heaven and earth have vanished without a trace (Rev. 20:11; 21:1), the sea and hell give up their dead (Rev. 20:13), the books are opened, and the dead are judged in the light of their contents, each man according to his works (Rev. 20:12). It is at this point that St. John, in Revelation 21 and 22, offers us the astonishingly beautiful vision of the heavenly Jerusalem.

The passages that concern us here are Rev. 21:1–4, 9–11, 22–24, 27; 22:1.[31]

---

29   In the vocabulary and imagery of the Apocalypse, we should say: "until their companions in God's service and their brethren who are to be slain as they were, have reached their full number" (Rev. 6:11) and join them "beneath the altar" (Rev. 6:9). See also Rev. 22:11–12.

30   Because of its ideas on the growth of the body (or building) until it reaches its perfect stature (see Eph. 2:21; 4:13, 15–16) and on the manifestation of the mystery of salvation made to the heavenly principalities and powers by the apostolate and by the life of the Church (see Eph. 3:18–19; compare 1 Pet. 1:12). Then there are the angels of the churches in Rev. 1:20.

31   We shall consider these passages as a single, complete whole, without prejudice, however, to the problems of literary criticism and their solution. Our two chapters obviously give two parallel descriptions and this fact is one of Boismard's arguments in favor of distinguishing "two Apocalypses" in St. John ("'L'Apocalypse' ou 'les Apocalypses'"). According to Boismard, the first text (written in Domitian's reign) follows Rev. 20:13–15 and comprises Rev. 21:9–22:2, plus Rev. 22:6–15; the text (written in Nero's reign) follows Rev. 20:11–12 and comprises Rev. 21:1–4, plus Rev. 22:3–5;1-4, plus Rev. 21:5–8. We are quite willing to accept this scheme, but we cannot agree with Boismard when he interprets it as showing that Rev. 21:9–22:15 is a description of the messianic Jerusalem and therefore of the Church in her state of pilgrimage on the earth, and not of the heavenly Jerusalem which is described in Rev. 22:1–8. We do not deny that some details in Rev. 21:9–22:15 refer to the Church on earth, but those instanced by Boismard are not all very clear and in some cases can be otherwise explained. Does Rev. 21:10 make it essential that the earth should still be in existence? Rev. 21:24–6 may be understood eschatologically. Also, with Henry Barclay Swete (*The Apocalypse of St. John: The Greek Text with Introduction, Notes, and Indices* [New York: Macmillan, 1906]) and Allo (*L'Apocalypse*), we may note that the Church in her earthly phase and the Church of eternity are fundamentally identical (compare St. John's concept of eternal life): Rev. 21–22, taken as a whole, describe the new creation ("the new aeon in time and in eternity" [Allo, *L'Apocalypse*, 339]), but more particularly, the eschatological

Then I saw *a new heaven and a new earth* (Isa. 65:17). The old heaven, the old earth had vanished, and there was no more sea. And I, John, saw in my vision that holy city which is the new Jerusalem, being sent down by God from heaven, all clothed in readiness, like a bride who has adorned herself to meet her husband. I heard, too, a voice which cried aloud from the throne, "Here is God's Tabernacle pitched among men; *he will dwell with them, and they will be* his own *people, and he will be among them,* their own God. *He will wipe every tear from their eyes* (Isa. 25:8), and there will be no more death, or mourning, or cries of distress, no more sorrow; those old things have passed away." ...

And now an angel came and spoke to me, one of those seven who bear the seven cups charged with the seven last plagues. "Come with me," he said, "and I will show you that bride, whose bridegroom is the Lamb." *And he carried me off in a trance to a great mountain* (Ezek. 40:2), high up, and there showed me the holy city Jerusalem, as it came down, sent by God, from heaven, *clothed in God's glory* (Isa. 60:1). The light that shone over it was bright.[32] ...

I saw no Temple in it; its Temple is the Lord God Almighty, its Temple is the Lamb. Nor had the city any need of sun or moon to show in it; the glory of God shone there, and the Lamb gave it light. *The nations will live and move in its radiance* (Isa. 60:3); the kings of the earth will bring it their tribute of praise and honor. ... Nothing that is unclean, no source of corruption or deceit can ever hope to find its way in; there is no entrance but for those whose names are written in the Lamb's book of life.

He showed me, too, a river, whose waters gave life; it flows, clear as crystal, from the throne of God, from the throne of the Lamb.

All the details in this description are borrowed from the Old Testament or the Jewish apocalyptic literature. This fact shows once again the continuity be-

---

conditions of life, while they include some details that are relevant to our present condition or perhaps with the reign of a thousand years. But we have no wish to enter here into the question of the meaning of this latter mysterious fact. Finally, some details at least in Rev. 21:9–22:5 are relevant to the heavenly Jerusalem, such as Rev. 21:10, 20; 22;3, 4, 5.

32   Here follows a description of the city, with its twelve gates on which were inscribed the names of the twelve tribes of Israel (v. 12) and a great wall resting on twelve foundation stones each bearing the name of one of the twelve apostles of the Lamb (v. 13); the length, breadth and height of the city are equal (v. 16).

tween Christianity's fulfillment of the prophecies and the promises or hopes which preceded it. We shall briefly review these themes, but the passages we have quoted prophecy a new state and a transcendent consummation as complete as were the assumption into and the accomplishment by Christianity of the Old Testament prophecies. We shall therefore attempt later to show clearly what is meant by this new state and this transcendent consummation.

The New Jerusalem Is Identical with the Church

The vision we are studying returns to the theme of Jerusalem, linked with the whole pattern of the history of salvation and with the messianic hope since the time of David.

In this general restatement, a number of details are combined in a remark-able way. Since the days of Ezekiel and the third section of Isaiah,[33] Jerusalem had been considered as the place and the realization of Israel's hopes at the end of the world. It is, therefore, this hope as a whole which is taken up into the idea of a new, glorious, fruitful Jerusalem at peace with itself and secure from all evil. The commentators point out the parallels in the Old Testament and the Jewish apocalyptic literature for all the details in this description. Even the changeover from the image of a city to that of a woman and a bride was common.[34] For St. John, the whole city is seen as a sanctuary. This is clear from the measurements, which are odd and baffling if taken as referring to a building existing in space,[35] but they in fact represent a cubic space such as that of the Holy of Holies (compare 1 Kings 6:10).

The city is truly the city of God, the city in which he reigns, the holy city. It is in direct contrast to Babylon, the courtesan,[36] the city of the reign of the adversary, the city of Antichrist. On the one side is the bridal city, on the other the harlot city. The harlot city is also the persecuting city, Babylon. It is made up of the worshippers of the beast who blasphemes the name of God, his dwelling-place, and those who dwell in heaven (Rev. 13:6). The bridal city is made up of those whom

---

33 See Ezek. 40 and the chapters that follow; also Isa. 60:1–6, 14; 65:18–25. On the biblical theme of Jerusalem, see Congar, *The Mystery of the Temple*, 83–90.

34 The extra-biblical book, 4 Ezra 10 (25–7), which dates from the late first century A.D., is a classic example. (It is quoted, for instance, by Allo, *L'Apocalypse*, 335). See also, the *Sibylline Oracles* (Bk. 5, 420–425), which dates to the late first or early second century A.D. Texts in *The Old Testament Pseudepigrapha*, 2 vols., ed. James H. Charlesworth (Garden City, NY: Doubleday, 1983), 1:403, 547. For the Bible, see Gen. 2:22 (in the Septuagint translation, the creation of Eve is worded literally as "he built her as a woman"). St. Augustine had already noted this expression (*The City of God*, Bk. 22, Chap. 17); Gen. 16:2; 30:3; Ruth 4:11; Jer. 31:4 (the "virgin-Israel is built"); Isa. 62:5 ("thy builder shall wed thee"); compare Rev. 19:7; 21:2, 9–14.

35 Nevertheless, Allo attempts to do this, *L'Apocalypse*, 347, 349. The language of the Apocalypse is symbolical rather than "plastic." We must not succumb to the repeated use of the word "vision." John *sees* yes, but spiritually, and he uses the imagery of symbols.

36 In biblical language, the words "adulterous" and "prostitute" or "courtesan" (harlot) indicate infidelity to God. See Rev. 2:14; 14:4–5.

the Lamb gathers on Mount Zion—here John returns to a traditional theme of messianic hope[37]—the souls whose faith is undefiled (Rev. 14:4–5), who are always with the Lamb and with God and serve him day and night—that is, always—in his Temple.[38] Thus revelation comes to an end as it brings together the themes which had inspired the preaching of the prophets—the themes of the bride, the city, the reign, the persecutor and, finally, the Temple.

John sees the bridal city coming down from heaven. He thus returns once again to a theme which, if not found in the Old Testament, at least belongs to the Jewish apocalyptic literature. But he treats it in so novel a fashion that the parallelism or the borrowing is very slight indeed. But the aim of Jewish apocalyptic writers is very different; their aim is specifically Old Testament and Jewish in character. The city in question is a material one and the Temple is one of stone, even though the stones are precious.[39] In the Apocalypse, external imagery is used only to give expression to a spiritual reality. The city is identical with the Church—that is, with the community of the faithful, and its foundations are the apostles.[40] Once again, the bridal city is made up of faithful men, while those who are impure are excluded (compare Rev. 21:8, 27; 22:15). The theme of the purity of the city as Temple and Church is also restated in the Apocalypse and with exactly the same meaning we have met in St Paul.[41]

Besides these restatements of more or less traditional material, we should note that in the new Jerusalem of the Apocalypse, major themes of the Old and the New Testament are brought to fulfillment. There is a complete recapitulation, as Comblin observes:

> The introduction of Jerusalem, as the type of the final stage of God's work, involves also the introduction of the covenant, the chosen people, the inheritance, the twelve tribes, the divine espousals, God's dwelling among his people. Everything is given a new meaning.[42]

But we must confine ourselves to the question of the Temple. The great promise found throughout the times of the old dispensation now becomes a complete

---

37 2 Kings 19:30–31; Joel 3:5–7, 20–21.

38 Rev. 14:4; 7:15 (which is a restatement of Isa. 4:5–6).

39 Ps. 122 is often quoted. See Hermann L. Strack and Paul Billerbeck, *Kommentar zum Neuen Testament aus Talmud und Midrasch* [Commentary on the New Testament in Light of the Talmud and Midrash], 5 vols. (München: Beck, 1922–1956), 3:573, 852 (on the Temple).

40 As in Eph. 2:20—one more instance of the similarity between the two books.

41 Rev. 21:7–8 should be compared with 1 Cor. 6:9; 15:50; Gal. 5:21.

42 Comblin, "La Liturgie de la Nouvelle Jérusalem," 19.

reality. It is the promise that God will have his dwelling among men, that he will be God-with-them, and so make of them his own people.[43] But John is so imbued with the idea that all the nations are to enjoy the presence of God and communion with him and so become Jerusalem,[44] that he breaks with the traditional formula and writes: "he will dwell with them and they will be his own people*s* (the Greek is plural: *laoi*).[45] We shall shortly see how genuinely and how fundamentally this central promise in the history of our salvation is to be realized in the kingdom of the life to come.

The Davidic Messiah and the Temple of the Church

The promise is quoted again a little later on (Rev. 21:7) in a slightly different form which it is important to note: "Who wins the victory? He shall have his share (inheritance) in this; *I will be his God, and he shall be my son.*" In the Old Testament, God calls his people his sons on more than one occasion.[46] But the passage referred to here is from the prophecy of Nathan, that decisive moment in the story of the Temple theme and the source of the whole Davidic theme of the Messiah.

The Apocalypse makes specific reference to these themes, by echoing Psalm 89:34–37 (Rev. 1:5) or Isaiah 11:1, 10 when it calls the victorious Christ "the offspring of David's race" (Rev. 5:5; 22:16). The victorious king seated on the throne of God is, in his ultimate reality, that royal lineage which God had promised David would last forever in his sight. But if this "offspring" is associated with God's own royal estate, so too the faithful, who have conquered also, are associated with his royal estate and his kingship.[47]

The title "Son of God" goes with this royal dignity. As with Abraham's lineage in St Paul (Gal. 3:16), so that of David issues in one and in several simultaneously. There is only one heir, one man who fulfils the promise made to David, just as there is only one heir, one man who fulfils the promise made to Abraham, but in both cases the faithful are included in him. The Temple of God is this unique person, both Son and King, Jesus Christ, and ourselves in and with him.[48]

In actual fact, therefore, the whole meaning of the Temple as it is understood by the Gospel and the apostles is restated in the Apocalypse. The Gospel meaning

---

43   The principal texts in order of importance are: Ezek. 37:26–8; Zech. 2:14–17; Lev. 26:11–12; Exod. 29:45; Zech. 8:8; Jer. 31:33. For the theme of "God-with-us," see Isa. 7:14; 8:8; Matt. 1:23.

44   Rev. 5:9; 7:9; 15:3–4; 21:26; 22:2.

45   Compare Isa. 45:22.

46   See Hos. 11:1; Jer. 31:9; Isa. 43:6.

47   See Rev. 2:26–8; 3:21; 5:10; 22:5.

48   It is worth noting that the words of 2 Sam. 7:14, which are here applied to the faithful Christian are used in Heb. 1:5 to show the divine sonship of Christ and are quoted in 2 Cor. 6:18 as proof of the fact that we "are the Temple of the living God."

is that Christ (immolated and risen from the dead) is the Temple. The meaning in the teaching of the apostles is that the Temple is the community of the faithful. The synthesis provided in 1 Peter combined these two statements.[49] The Apocalypse, in its own key and with its own resonances, repeats the same theme.

Christ in the Apocalypse is the Christ of John's Gospel—the Lamb slain and victorious, from whose side flows, as from the new Temple, the water of life, that is, the Spirit, the specific gift of the new and definitive covenant.[50] The community of the faithful, represented as militant on earth and in heaven as the liturgical assembly of those whose pilgrimage has ended in joy, is now God's dwelling-place.

This idea could not be more strikingly expressed than in Revelation 22.[51] John sees the bridal city coming down from heaven—sees the new Jerusalem—and the voice (of an angel?) which explains what is taking place, does so in very significant terms: "Here is God's Tabernacle pitched among men; he will dwell with them" (Rev. 22:2–5). Yet, as in 1 Peter and Ephesians, the Church is the Temple only through Jesus Christ; likewise the faithful are victors, kings and priests, only through him who, before them, offered himself, won the victory, and now reigns;[52] they are purified and made strong only by his blood.[53]

As we shall see in a moment, the whole Church lives her own pasch of death, resurrection, rejection, glory, and does so in union with and through the pasch of the Lamb that was slain, but is now victorious (Rev. 1:18; 2:8; 5:6). This is another image which expresses exactly what is heard in the words of our Lord and read in the writings of St. Peter, when they used the image of the stone once rejected which has become the chief stone, the first cell, of the new Temple of God.[54]

Eschatological Cosmic Restoration

Finally, the Apocalypse includes and fulfils the cosmic aspect of the mystery of the Temple. In it, as in the epistles of the captivity, Christ is the source of a new creation.[55] The final prospect is that of a new creation (Rev. 21:1, 5; 22:1–2) whose

---

49 See 1 Pet. 2:4–10.

50 Rev. 21:6; 22:1–2, 17; see also Rev. 2:7; 7:17. Compare these passages with John 4:10–15; 7:37–39; 19:34.

51 In Rev. 19:8 the linen of shining white in which the bride of the Lamb clothes herself is "the merits of the saints"; compare Rev. 7:9, 14, where the robe of the bride is made from those of the martyrs and of the faithful.

52 Rev. 1:6; 5:10 (kings and priests); Rev. 2:27–28; 3:31; 17:14; 22:5.

53 Rev. 12:11; 7:14–15: "They have washed their robes white in the blood of the Lamb. And now they stand before God's throne, serving him day and night in his Temple."

54 Mark 12:10; 1 Pet. 2:4, 7.

55 See Rev. 1:5, where Christ is called "the firstborn from the dead" (*prōtotokos tōn nekrōn*); compare Col. 1:18.

source is the kingship of God (Rev. 21:5) which is shared by the Lamb who sits upon the same throne (22:1; 3:21). While in the past the Church lived under conditions of struggle and affliction due to the serpent of the primal age and to sin,[56] God will now wipe away all tears[57] and make the brightness of his own glory shine in the new Jerusalem.[58] The fact that the word *doxa* (glory), is closely connected with the theme of God's presence or dwelling among his people, already justifies us in suspecting that the eschatological cosmic restoration—corresponding to the "new birth" in Matthew 19:28 or to the "time when all is restored anew" in Acts 3:21—is the fruit not only of the perfect reign of God, but also of his perfect presence; if, that is, a distinction between the two can have any meaning.

But there is no need to make suppositions or deductions, since in Revelation 21:3–5 it is expressly stated that there is a link between the establishment of God's dwelling[59] among his people or his presence, and the creation of a new, reconciled and glorious universe. At the root of all this, obviously, is the theology of the prologue to St. John's Gospel.[60] The key-word to that prologue ("Word" [of God]) appears in Revelation 19:13. And the longing for cosmic redemption is only fulfilled in the concrete economy of the incarnate Word, the Cross, and Easter.

In the new state and the transcendent consummation, the new Jerusalem comes down from on high, from God. This idea is not found in the Jewish apocalyptic literature.[61] St. John, however, sees the holy city, the new Jerusalem, coming down from heaven, from the home of (her) God (Rev. 3:12; 21:2, 12). We must note that he *sees* it. In this life, the true dimensions of God's Temple remain unknown to us, yet this Temple is being built in the souls of men. But, at the last day, these dimensions will be clearly revealed to give joy to God's friends. And his work transcends all our reckoning. John *sees* the new Jerusalem coming down from God's home, when all that has been built in the field of creation by grace from on high at length becomes manifest. And this Jerusalem *comes down from heaven.*

---

56 Rev. 12:2, 6, 9, 13.

57 Rev. 7:17; 21:4.

58 Rev. 21:11, 23; 22:5. Swete (*Apocalypse*) refers also to 2 Cor. 3:8, an evocative verse. There is also a parallel between Rev. 21:1, 5 and 2 Cor. 5:17.

59 *Skēnē*; there is perhaps an allusion here to the cloud of the divine presence, the *Shekinah*. See Swete, *Apocalypse*, 278.

60 See John 1:14.

61 See Strack and Billerbeck, *Kommentar zum Neuen Testament*, 3:796. The idea is nonexistent among the ancient rabbis and is rare in more recent midrashim. It is found in apocalyptic literature only in writings dating from the end of the first century A.D., such as 4 Ezra (7:26). Compare also Comblin, "La Liturgie de la Nouvelle Jérusalem," 10–11, n. 12. He makes it quite clear that we are dealing here with something very different from the restoration of a former reality, or something from the "*religionsgeschichtlich*" [history of religions] theme of a city preexisting in heaven. The latter theme, in any case, appears at a relatively late date.

No *"religionsgeschichtlich"* [history of religions][62] parallel or so-called parallel can explain this original idea—an idea given to us by revelation, by the Word of God, and whose profound meaning must be sought in the Word of God itself.

The first value expressed in this concept is that of the gratuitous nature of the gift. During the Exodus, or under David or Ezekiel, no human initiative could force God to be present among his people. His presence remained his mystery and a gift of his grace. The new Jerusalem comes down from God because it is composed of "those whose names are written in the Lamb's book of life" (Rev. 21:27). True, if our names appear in this book it is because of our deeds (Rev. 20:12), but our names may be blotted out (Rev. 3:5) and, at the very root of the fidelity and heroism which have earned a place for our names, there is a movement on God's part which we must call gratuitous predestination (see Rev. 13:8; 17:8). In one sense, there is a celestial Jerusalem because, "ever since the world was made"[63] the elect have existed in God's thought and predestination. The preexisting Church of which some authors have written genuinely exists only in this way.

The second value expressed in this concept is that of the absolute purity demanded by God's Temple. All the ritual, all the regulations with which the Mosaic Law surrounded everything that concerned the Temple and the worship of God, were figures of the true, interior, spiritual purity, as a quality in man himself that was to be required in the new spiritual Temple of which John tells us "nothing that is unclean … can ever hope to find its way in" (Rev. 21:27).[64] John tells us this just after he has shown us the kings of the earth bringing their treasures into the city whose gates therefore always remain wide open.

Some time ago, we ourselves showed that the catholicity of the Church as-sumes into itself— "recapitulates"—all that is of value in the unlimited evolution

---

62   Hence the celestial city is given twelve gates, not by deduction from geophysics as is the case in modern Cambodian or Burmese symbolism, or in that of Muslim Baghdad with its twelve palaces. No, it is because there were twelve sons of Jacob, twelve tribes of Israel; and also twelve foundations since there were twelve apostles of the Lamb: Rev. 21:12–14. A genuine cosmic value is implied and parallel teaching can be quoted from the study of the history of religions, but in the Apocalypse, this value is incorporated into the positive facts of the history of salvation, itself dependent on a free act of God's will, by which, moreover, the world has been created as an ordered and measured whole.

63   Rev. 13:8. It is erroneous to translate this image as that of the "Lamb slain in sacrifice *ever since the world began.*" The words in italics do not refer to the Lamb, but to the names written in the book of life, as is made clear in the parallel passage, Rev. 17:8. The notion of the Church as preexisting is explained in the Fathers by that of predestination; compare Heb. 12:23; 2 Tim. 1:9. On the Church as coming down from heaven because she is a free gift of grace, see St. Augustine, *The City of God,* Bk. 20, Chap. 17. Text in *The Nicene and Post-Nicene Fathers,* First Series, vol. 2, ed. Philip Schaff (Grand Rapids, MI: Eerdmans, 1997), 436–437.

64   See also Rev. 21:8; 22:15. Compare Isa. 35:8; Ezek. 44:9. For the new form of purity according to Christ, see Matt. 15:1–20; Mark 7:1–23.

of the energies of the first Adam.[65] We also noted above that the dimensions of the spiritual Temple which are unknown to us include, in a certain sense, the entire world and a multitude of men who in their own little lives have had no explicit knowledge of Jesus Christ, his Church, or even of God himself.

What then shall we say of the "good deeds," the "merits" of the faithful and of the saints themselves, those deeds out of which are woven the robe of shining white that clothed the bride for her wedding feast, as St. John showed us, (Rev. 19:8)? If we turn to the prophet Isaiah, we hear him say, "We were all of us like those that are impure, and all our acts of justice were like filthy linen."[66] We can only cleanse ourselves in a spring from on high, by receiving something that comes from God who alone is holy. This is the biblical idea of sanctity:[67] it comes from God and belongs to God. In the Mosaic system, a thing was from God and belonged to God through an act of consecration, that is, by being set apart. Under the dispensation of the incarnate Word and of the Holy Spirit as given to man, man comes from God and belongs to him because of the communication of a genuinely "spiritual" gift.[68]

Jesus baptizes with the Holy Spirit because he himself came from on high (John 3:13, 31) and the Holy Spirit came down and rested upon him (John 1:32–3). The New Testament can indeed link together the words "spiritual," "pleasing to God," and "not made by man's hands."[69] The dispensation of the new and eternal covenant is that of a truly heavenly and specifically divine gift of grace, a dispensation where circumcision is not the work of man's hands (Col. 2:11; Eph. 2:11). Nothing that is not heavenly can enter heaven, as St. John declares in the Apocalypse. But the Church, the new Jerusalem, is wholly compounded of heavenly grace, of gifts that have truly come from on high.[70] Our high priest purifies us within, from the

---

65   See Yves Congar, *Chrétiens Désunis, Principes d'un "Oecuménisme" Catholique* (Paris: Éditions du Cerf, 1937); Eng. trans.: *Divided Christendom: A Catholic Study of the Problem of Reunion*, trans. M. A. Bousfield (London: G. Bles, 1939). See esp. Chap. 3.

66   See the Septuagint translation of Isa. 64:6 (*ōs rakos apokathēmenēs pasa he dikaiosynē ēmōn* = like the soiled sanitary towel of a woman [compare Lev. 12:2; 15:19–20]). In Rev. 19:8, the word used is *dikaiōmata tōn hagiōn* ("righteous deeds of the saints"). Swete rightly draws attention to the wedding garment in Matt. 22:11. See also, Pope St. Gregory the Great (*Morals in Job*, Bk. 17, 15, 21): "*Humana quippe justitia auctori comparata injustitia est*" [Man's righteousness when compared to his Maker is unrighteousness.] Text in *Morals on the Book of Job by St. Gregory the Great*, 3 vols., trans. James Bliss (Oxford: J. H. Parker, 1844–1850).

67   See Otto Procksch, "*Hagios*," in *Theologisches Wörterbuch*, 1:88–97.

68   For this contrast, see John 1:17 and 6:31–3; compare Gal. 3:1–4; Heb. 3:1–66.

69   See C. F. D. Moule, "Sanctuary and Sacrifice in the Church of the New Testament," *Journal of Theological Studies* 1 (1950): 29–41.

70   "*De coelo descendere dicitur ista civitas, quoniam coelestis est gratia qua Deus eam fecit, propter quod ei dicit etiam per Isaiam: Ego sum Dominus faciens te (45:11)." [This citizenship is said to*

Holy of Holies he has entered and which is the sanctuary of God himself, not made by man's hands.[71]

The Easter of the Church and of the World

These ideas lead us back to the theme of the spiritual Temple brought into being by Christ's Easter experience.[72] And indeed, the fundamental significance of the fact that the new Jerusalem must be sent down to us from on high is identical with the fundamental significance of Easter. And what we are saying of the new Jerusalem, we must—and in this we are following St. John—also say of the whole creation, of those new heavens and that new earth which the visions of the Apocalypse link with the appearance of the new Jerusalem. We must say it of all that the Apocalypse and the whole of the New Testament call "new."[73]

The idea of restoration, of making anew what has been overthrown or profaned, was frequent in the Old Testament and in Jewish thought. But for the latter, it was most often simply a matter of recalling to life what had previously existed.[74] During his pasch, Christ passed through death; the body which came out of the tomb is a Temple not made by human hands. It is the source of a truly new creation, of a truly new man. The whole of St. Paul's thought is relevant here. So also is the whole theology of the new covenant, made as it was in the blood of Christ and in his pasch. This new covenant is the very act by which the new Jerusalem is founded.[75]

What the Apocalypse proclaims is, therefore, the Easter of the Church and of the world. "The Most High does not dwell in temples made by men's hands."[76] It is not merely each man's individual body which will be given back to him from on high ("not made by human hands") to be his everlasting dwelling-place (2 Cor. 5:1);

---

descend from the sky because heavenly grace is made in the same manner in which God makes them, wherefore, indeed, he says through Isaiah: "I am the Lord, your Maker."] Primasius of Hadrumentum (circa 540 A.D.), *Commentary on the Apocalypse*, Bk. 5. Text in *PL* 68, 921. The passage is repeated verbatim by St. Bede (d. 735), *The Explanation of the Apocalypse* (*PL* 93, 194). Compare James 1:17: "Every good gift and every perfect gift is from above, and cometh down from the Father of lights."

71   Heb. 9:11–28, where the expression "not made by human hands" occurs twice, vv. 11, 28.

72   Compare Mark 14:58; John 2:19–22.

73   Heaven and earth (Rev. 2:1, 5; 2 Peter 3:13; Isa. 43:19; 65:17). Jerusalem (Rev. 3:12; 21:2). Wine (Mark 14:25 and parallels). Name (Rev. 2:17; 3:12; compare Isa. 62:2; 65:15). Song (Rev. 5:9; 14:3; compare Isa. 42:10; Ps. 95:1). See also 2 Cor. 5:17; Gal. 6:15 (new creature); Rom. 5:12–14; 1 Cor. 15:21–22; Eph. 2:15 (man). See also, Johannes Behm, *"Kainos"* [New, Renewal] in *Theologisches Wörterbuch*, 3:451–2.1.

74   See Strack and Billerbeck, *Kommentar zum Neuen Testament*, 3:840.

75   Luke 22:20; 1 Cor. 11:25; compare 2 Cor. 3:6; Heb. 8:8–9; 9:15.

76   Acts 7:48 (Stephen); 17:24 (Paul); compare Heb. 9:11, 24.

it is the whole spiritual Temple, the Church as the Body of Christ, which will be restored from on high, made anew in the image of the Lord who, in his own pasch, was its first stone.

In short, we are here confronted with the decisive mystery of the identity of the Alpha and the Omega (Rev. 1:8; 21:6; 22:13), of the identity of the mysteries of Easter and the *parousia*, or "coming" of the Lord.[77] John is describing for us the final Easter of the Church and of the world which, in its own way, is to be modeled on the Easter of Jesus. He who, by his pasch is the source of a new creation is indeed Jesus, son of Mary; but he has had to pass through death—the death of all in him which belonged to the former world for which he "took birth from a woman, took birth as a subject of the law" (Gal. 4:4) "in the fashion of our guilty nature" (Rom. 8:3). So, in the same way, all which in the Church as God's Temple is in the fashion of our guilty nature, must die, for "the Kingdom of God cannot be enjoyed by flesh and blood."[78]

The Church must have her pasch, she must pass through death, as did Christ, and a body wholly pure must be given back to her so that she may be united to God and receive him as the Temple and bride described in the Apocalypse. She cannot be the perfect bride unless she is perfectly virginal in the deepest sense, as we find it in the New Testament, the Fathers and the monastic tradition—unless, that is, she lives entirely by a life from on high and not from below, unless she is wholly heavenly, not earthly. "Only the spirit gives life; the flesh is of no avail" (John 6:63).

It is only after she has passed through the death of the flesh that Christ can take to himself his bride "in all her beauty, no stain, no wrinkle, no such disfigurement ... holy ... spotless" (Eph. 5:27). But if this is accomplished first of all in baptism, which is the principle and the very substance of our Easter, it will only be perfectly accomplished, as will also our baptism and Easter, through an actual

---

77   On this point cf. F. X. Durrwell, *La Résurrection de Jésus, Mystère de Salut: Étude Biblique* (Paris: Cerf, 1954); Eng. trans.: *The Resurrection, A Biblical Study* (New York: Sheed and Ward, 1960). See also, Yves Congar, "Le Purgatoire" [Purgatory], in Centre de Pastorale Liturgique, *Le Mystère de la Mort et sa Célébration* [The Mystery of Death and its Celebration], (Paris: Editions du Cerf, 1951), 279–236.

78   See Jacques Benigne Bossuet, "Assumption" (1660 A.D.): "Such flesh (*caro peccati*: Rom. 8:3) must be destroyed, even, I say, in the elect; because, as sinful flesh, it does not deserve to be united to a blessed soul or to enter the kingdom of God: *Caro et sanguis regnum Dei possidere non possunt* [flesh and blood cannot inherit the kingdom of God] (1 Cor. 15:50). So it must change its first form in order to be made new, and it must lose entirely its first being in order to receive a second from the hand of God." Text in *Bossuet on Devotion to the Blessed Virgin: Being the Substance of all the Sermons for Mary's Feast throughout the Year*, trans. F. M. Capes, introd. William T. Gordan (New York: Longmans, Green, 1899), 141. But it is St. Irenaeus (early second century A.D.) still more than Bossuet, who should be quoted in this connection. See *Against the Heresies*, Bk. 5, Chap. 9, 4. Text in *Ante-Nicene Fathers*, vol. 1, ed. Alexander Roberts and James Donaldson (Peabody, MA: Hendrickson, 2004), 535.

death, through an actual purification from the flesh, through an actual and total resurrection according to the Spirit; in a word, at the last day. We have previously attempted to look at the fact of Purgatory from this paschal point of view, and in so doing we believe we have been faithful to the thought of the Fathers.[79]

The purification prophesied by Malachi (3:1) and wrought by Jesus by means of an act which was prophetic and therefore both real and symbolic in its proclamation of a spiritual truth (John 2:13–18), is to be fully accomplished in the mystery of the *parousia*, which the Apocalypse, after the Gospels, describes as follows—judgment, hell giving up its dead, the new heavens and the new earth, the new Jerusalem coming down from heaven and from God, adorned like a young bride for her husband (Rev. 20:11; 21:2).

The Fathers here as elsewhere show a remarkable understanding of the mystery of the Scriptures. Tertullian shows us Christ in the glory of his second coming, no longer the stumbling-block but the keystone crowning the completed Temple.[80] Origen, commenting upon the episode of the cleansing of the Temple, in the context of this eschatological theme of judgment, wrote:

> The Church is a Temple built of living stones. Among her chil-
> dren, there are some who live as though they were not in the
> Church. They fight their battles in human strength (2 Cor. 10:3).
> These make the house of prayer, composed of living stones, into
> a den of thieves …

Origen then explains how it is that some men make the Temple into a den of thieves through the selling and buying of doves and the like. He goes on to warn them to beware when Jesus comes into the Father's house of prayer, for he will drive them from their seats.

> When I examine this passage of Scripture, I ask myself whether
> Jesus will not bring all this to pass when he comes for the second
> time, the time of that long-awaited divine judgment. Then he
> will enter the Temple wholly, the Church now complete … and
> he will drive out all those who, though they are reputed to have

---

79 See Congar, "Le Purgatoire."

80 See Tertullian, *Against Marcion*, Bk. 3, Chap. 7. In his second coming "he shall no longer remain 'a stone of stumbling and a rock of offense,' but after his rejection become 'the chief corner-stone,' accepted and elevated to the top place of the Temple, even his Church, being that very stone in Daniel (7:13–14), cut out of the mountain which was to smite and crush the image of the secular kingdom." Text in *Ante-Nicene Fathers*, vol. 3, 326.

their place in the Temple of God, in reality behave as mere traffickers.[81]

If we call to mind what was said above about the dimensions of the Church as Temple, of the mixture of the pure and the impure within her, if we remember all those who apparently live beyond her bounds but in reality belong to her, we shall then understand something of the pasch through which the Church as Temple must pass. She will be purified and united, built at last of living and precious stones and completed in the fullness of her dimensions only when she has been gathered together from the whole earth and when God takes her to himself from on high, recreated as she will be according to the Spirit, and able fully to be the bride because, by grace, she will be made utterly virginal.

Does all this mean there will be no kind of continuity between earthly life and the life of the world to come? Will there be an entirely new creation in which a body, a Church that is wholly new is to take in some sort the place of the body, the Church which has struggled in the mire and suffered in the night of this earth? We are more and more inclined to think[82] that all of divine revelation and the Apocalypse, its final chapter, are against such a supposition.

To confine ourselves to the Apocalypse, we see that the continuity between the earthly and heavenly phases of the Church's existence is clearly and abundantly obvious. The holy city which comes down from God is the bride adorned for her wedding-feast. But her robe, as we have seen, is woven from the good deeds of the saints (Rev. 19:8), for their deeds go with them (Rev. 14:13). Those who are clothed in white robes—whom God will lead to the living waters and from whose eyes he will wipe away all tears (Rev. 7:13–17)—are also those who have come through great tribulation. If we bring together all the promises made to the "victor" in the seven letters to the churches (Rev. 2:1–3:21), we see that they correspond to the bliss that is given to the new Jerusalem which comes down from God's home, and whose name, moreover, is written upon this "victor" (Rev. 3:12).

And thus every effort made in time and within the framework of earthly history is taken up into heaven. The new song does not do away with the Song of Moses (Rev. 15:3; Exod. 15:1). Here, as in the rest of the New Testament, the theme of the Exodus is always present.[83] We are shown a liturgical pilgrimage reaching its climax in the Temple in the celebration of the liturgy of the Feast of Tabernacles.

---

81 See Origen, *Commentary on the Gospel of Matthew*. Text in *Patrologiae Cursus Completus, Series Graeca*, ed. J. P. Migne (Paris: Garnier and J. P. Migne, 1857–1866), 13, 1444 and 1452–3. Hereafter *PG*.

82 More and more, that is, in relation to what we have already written in *Lay People in the Church*, 56–61, 81–102.

83 See the thought-provoking note by Jeremias in "Golgotha," 123, n. 1. For St. Paul, see Harald

But we are shown equally, at least, a final Exodus across the Red Sea and the desert. As with the first Exodus, the time of trial is also the time of betrothal. The Church clothes herself with her fine robe of white linen so that when she celebrates her eternal wedding-feast she finally fulfils the ideal of the Exodus, the ideal of love and fidelity in the midst of poverty.

It is clear, therefore, that the new life given from above is not a creation discontinuous with what was already in existence. Moreover, in the New Testament, whenever something new is given gratuitously, we are never dispensed from the effort to retain possession of it and to make it bear fruit.[84] The view we have put forward above and which we share with Swete and Allo, is particularly favorable to these ideas. The new Jerusalem is also the Church in time. Already in time, she comes down from heaven, as new, as from God. In her activity she is a reality in the order of grace. What she does depends entirely upon what has been *given* to her. But at the last day, all impurity in her actions will be eliminated, or washed clean and transfigured. In the Temple, there will remain only what has been built in gold or in a substance that resists decay (1 Cor. 3:10–15). The city which is both Temple and bride is composed entirely of precious stones (Rev. 21:11, 18–21).

"I Saw No Temple In It"

In eternity there is no Temple other than God himself. When he was shown the new Jerusalem in its glorious state (Rev. 21:10–11), St. John was astonished, for he had visited every part of it, yet he wrote, "I saw no Temple in it" (Rev. 21:22). For a Jew this was inconceivable—Jerusalem without a Temple! This enables us to sense how new was a "revelation" which incorporated so many elements from the Old Testament or from Judaism, but which also went beyond them.

Condren makes a pertinent comparison. He reminds us of Isaac's astonishment when he saw no victim for the sacrifice his father was about to offer on the mountain. God was to provide for the sacrifice, and become himself the victim.[85] The answer here is similar: *Its Temple is the Lord God Almighty. Its Temple is the Lamb* (Rev. 21:22). This, then, is the final word of the revelation given to the Church concerning the mystery of the Temple and of God's presence. We must do our best to hear and understand it.[86]

Sahlin, "The New Exodus of Salvation according to St Paul," in *The Root of the Vine: Essays in Biblical Theology*, ed. Anton Fridrichsen (New York: Philosophical Library, 1953), 81–95.

84   Behm (*"Kainos,"* 452), says it well: "Für den einzelnen ist der neue Mensch Gabe und Aufgabe zugleich" [For individuals, the "new man" is a gift and, at the same time, a task]. See Eph. 4:24. Compare Gal. 6:15; 2 Cor. 5:17.

85   Charles de Condren, *L'Idée du Sacerdoce et du Sacrifice de Jésus-Christ* [The Idea of the Priesthood and Sacrifice of Jesus Christ] (Paris: Douniol, 1901), 127). Compare Gen. 22.

86   The commentators we have consulted are not very satisfactory. Swete, excellent though he is, has

The first point to note is that the words are used of the Lord (*kyrios*) God Almighty (*ho Theos ho Pantokratōr*) and of the Lamb. The title *Pantocrator* occurs nine times in the Apocalypse, although it appears only once in the rest of the New Testament and then as a mere rider to a quotation.[87] These uses of the word show that in the Apocalypse the writer is not so much concerned with stating an attribute of God for its own sake (as is done in theodicy) as with revealing his royal sovereignty. In fact, the title *Pantocrator* is very clearly linked either with the character of absolute existence dominating time as a whole from beginning to end (see Rev. 1:8; 4:8); or with the affirmation of the power God possesses and exercises in order to establish his kingdom (Rev. 11;17; 15:3; 9:6) and to execute his judgments (Rev. 16:7, 14; 19:15). In two places the word also includes an act of praise of God's transcendent holiness (Rev. 4:8; 15:3). We may therefore conclude that the eternal Temple of the faithful is God in his sovereign reign. The fact that the name of the Lamb is added after the word *Pantocrator* does not alter this conclusion, since it indicates Christ precisely as associated with the sovereign and saving reign of God.

For the prophets, God was present where he reigned. The first meaning of the passage we are studying is that in eternity there will be no Temple other than God himself and his holy will. God is in his Temple because he dwells in himself and in his own holy will. There is also a sense in which he is in his Temple in the believer and the people who love and do his will (compare John 14:21, 23).

By the same token, the believer is in God just as God is in him.[88] In the Temple of God's presence and God's will, the believer or the people—it is not

---

little to say (*Apocalypse*, 295); Allo (*L'Apocalypse*, 348) confines himself to a reference to the final phrase in Ezek. 48:35. This is a valid reference but leads him to remark that the whole city is a temple. But John did not say that; instead his words were: God is the Temple. Wenschkewitz (pp. 148-9) senses the novelty of the statement but sees in it an example of "spiritualization". Finally, Boismard (in his introduction to the installment version of the Jerusalem Bible; see *La Sainte Bible, Traduite en Francais sous la Direction de L'École Biblique de Jérusalem* [Paris: Éditions du Cerf, 1961]) limits Rev. 21:9 to a description of the messianic Jerusalem (the Jerusalem before the *parousia*) and gives to the text above a commonplace meaning: there is no longer any temple, since the Church is the Temple. Once again, this is not what St. John says at this point.

87 See 2 Cor. 6:18. *Pantocratōr* is the usual Septuagint rendering for "*Yahweh Sabaoth*" in the Hebrew text. (Hence Rev. 4:8 compared with Isa. 6:3.) According to J. N. D. Kelly (*Early Christian Creeds* [London: Longman, Green, 1950], 132) the word should not be translated by "Almighty," but by "All-Ruling," or "All-Sovereign."

88 "*Cum vero habitationem ejus cogitas, unitatem cogita, congregationemque sanctorum: maxime in coelis, ubi propterea praecipue dicitur habitare, quia ibi fit voluntas ejus perfecta eorum, in quibus habitat obedientia.*" [And when you think of his indwelling, think of the unity of the gathering of saints, especially in heaven, where he is said to dwell in a unique manner, because his will is done there by the perfect obedience of those in whom he dwells] St Augustine, *Letter* 187, 14 (*PL* 33, 848). Eng. trans. in St. Augustine, *Letters (165–203)*, trans. Wilifrid Parsons (Washington, DC: Catholic University of America, 1964), 254.

possible to differentiate between them, and the Apocalypse speaks at times of the victor as a person and at others, with obvious preference, as the people, as the "*tota redempta civitas*" [whole redeemed city], in the words of St. Augustine[89]—are like priests at the altar: "And now they stand before God's throne, serving him (*latreuousin autō*) day and night in his Temple" (Rev. 7:15). "God's throne (which is the Lamb's throne) will be there, with his servants to worship him."[90] The liturgy of the Apocalypse is essentially a liturgy of loving and enthusiastic obedience to God's royal will for our salvation.[91] It may be summed up in the *Amen, Alleluia!* (Rev. 19:4) and as a commentary upon it, we may take these words of St. Augustine: "They shall say Alleluia! Because they shall say *Amen!*"[92]

There is, therefore, no need to pause to consider Comblin's remark, perfectly correct though it is, that in the new Jerusalem the elect are no longer called "priests" but are simply said "to reign" (Rev. 22:5).[93] The only conclusion that need be drawn from this is that the elements of outward ceremony, of preparation and of mediation in the worship and the priesthood of the messianic Temple have

---

89   *The City of God*, Bk. 22, Chap. 17. See n. 63 above.

90   Rev. 22:3. St. John uses exactly the same expression as in Rev. 7:15, *latreuousin autō*, to denote the public worship given to the living God by his people, Israel. Therefore, as was said in Rev. 21:3: "He will dwell with them, and they will be his own people, and he will be among them, their own God." Compare Acts 26:7; Phil. 3:3; Rom. 12:1. Note that in all these passages worship is offered before the throne of God and of the Lamb; the Temple is a palace; God *reigns* there—an absolutely essential fact—and the worship offered is the worship offered to the sovereign will from which grace comes.

91   Rev. 4:8–11; 5:8–14; 7:9–12; 14:1–5; 19:1–5.

92   "... *Tota actio nostra, Amen et Alleluia erit ... Quid est enim Amen? quid Alleluia? Amen est verum; Alleluia, laudate Deum. Quia ergo Deus veritas est incommutabilis. ... Quam ergo insatiabiliter satiaberis veritate, tam insatiabili veritate dices; Amen ... amore ipsius veritatis accensi et inhaerentes ei dulci et casto amplexu, eodemque incorporeo, tali etiam voce laudabimus eum et dicemus; Alleluia. Exultantes enim se ad parilem laudem flagrantissima charitate invicem et ad Deum, omnes cives illius civitatis dicent Alleluia, quia dicent Amen!*" [Our whole activity will consist of Amen and Alleluia. ... What does *Amen* mean, and what is *Alleluia? Amen*, "It is true"; *Alleluia*, "Praise God." So now, God is unchangeable truth. ... When we say this, we shall of course be saying *Amen*, but with a kind of never satisfied satisfaction. ... We shall be fired with love of this truth and cling to it with a sweet and chaste embrace—a non-bodily one, of course; and so we shall also praise him with the same kind of voice, and say, *Alleluia*. All the citizens of that city, you see, will be urging each other to equal heights of praise with the most ardent charity toward God, and so they will be saying, *Alleluia*, because they will be saying, *Amen*] Sermon 362, 29 (PL 39, 1632–1633). Eng. trans. in: *The Works of St. Augustine: A New Translation for the 21st Century*, 3:10 (Sermons, 341–400), ed. John Rotelle (Brooklyn, NY: New City, 1995), 265–266. On the Alleluia as the canticle of the heavenly life, see the splendid pages of Augustine in his *Exposition of the Psalms*, 148, 1 (PL 37, 1938); Sermon 243, 8 (PL 38, 1147); Sermon 252, 9 (PL 38, 1176-7); Sermon 255, 1, 5 (PL 38, 1186, 1188); Sermon 256 (PL 38, 1190).

93   See Comblin, "La Liturgie de la Nouvelle Jérusalem," 25, n. 53: "All idea of offering and sacrifice has disappeared; similarly the idea of priesthood has been removed from the traditional formula *basileian hiereis* and is now changed to *basileusousin*."

disappeared. There remains only the ultimate reality of worship, sacrifice, and priesthood—namely man's perfect and filial surrender of himself to God,[94] of which these elements were the sign. But this is the quintessence of sacrifice and of priesthood.[95] At the same time it explains the royal character of our priesthood in the sense of 1 Peter (2:5, 9).[96]

As they adore the throne of God and of the Lamb, that is, their royal will for our salvation, the elect, God's servants, are with him; they are his people and he is their God. By the same token, they see his face, his name is on their foreheads (Rev. 22:4), his dwelling in them, becomes a fact (Rev. 21:3); and this priestly service, this wholly spiritual sacrifice of obedience and union which they offer, is a royal sacrifice. By obedience to him as reigning, they share in his reign and are themselves kings of glory:

> The Lord God will shed his light on them, and they will reign for ever and ever. (Rev. 22:5)

> Who wins the victory? I will let him share my throne with me; I too have won the victory, and now I sit sharing my Father's throne (Rev. 3:21).[97]

They are in full partnership with Christ as king, and with him share the kingship of God, for they are sons not only after the manner of David (2 Sam. 7:14), but through and in Jesus Christ, the Son in the absolute and perfect sense. Hence, they are sons in the way David's Lord is Son, the Lord of whom David himself said: "The LORD said to my Lord: Sit on my right hand" (Ps. 110:1; Matt. 22:42–44). Henceforth, if the Temple is the will of God, that is, his throne, it is not enough to say that the elect are in him as worshippers or as celebrating priests. We must recognize that there is a sense in which they themselves are the Temple and no

---

94 Rev. 21:7. The final and communal perfection of the Church, as such, is to say "Pater *noster*" [*Our Father*] and to end by uttering Christ's own *Amen*.

95 See Chap. 4 of Congar, *Lay People in the Church*. It is self-evident that the sacrificial worship of sinful men and of the Church during her earthly pilgrimage must have expiatory value and a visible, collective, sacramental character. In heaven, says St Thomas, there will no longer be anything but "*gratiarum actio et vox laudis* [the act of thanksgiving and the voice of praise] (compare Isa. 51:3)." See *Summa Theologiae*, Pt. 1a-2ae, Quest. 101, Art. 2; Pt. 1a-2ae, Quest. 103, Art. 3. In *Summa Theologica of St.Thomas Aquinas: First Complete American Edition*, 3 vols. (New York: Benzinger, 1947–1948), 1:1052, 1085.

96 See *Mystery of the Temple*, 178.

97 Compare Georges Bernanos' novel, *Journal d'un Curé de Campagne* (1937), the scene in which the countess who is quite willing to pray, "Thy kingdom come," but not "Thy will be done": "The kingdom whose coming you have just prayed for is both yours and his." See *The Diary of a Country Priest*, trans. Pamela Morris (Garden City, NY: Image, 1954), 134.

longer merely as the community of the faithful, as the Temple in which God dwells, but in the very sense in which in eternity there is no more Temple because the Lord God Almighty is the Temple, as is also the Lamb. *God himself* has become truly a house of prayer for all nations (Mark 11:17).

Not that we are to imagine some kind of fusion of existences, a confusion in the order of being. The victor, God, and the Lamb, are, in the Apocalypse, persons with well-defined characters. It is not a question of fusion but of communion, a communion divinely real and profound. We cannot study here the reality of this communion as taught by the New Testament as a whole, by St. John ("life") and by the Apocalypse. A whole book would be needed. But one short text sums it all up: "What is it, this fellowship of ours? Fellowship with the Father, and with his Son Jesus Christ" (1 John 1:3). All we have to do is to consider the reality and the depth of this communion from the point of view of the truth that God himself is eternity's Temple.

God Becomes the Temple of Humanity

This communion is, first of all, a mutual exchange. This is already implied in the very notion itself of a covenant and in the theme that is constantly repeated: *I will be their God and they shall be my people.* We live in God. He is our dwelling-place. But we, too, are his dwelling-place and he lives in us.[98] "*Templum hominis Deus, templum Dei fit homo.*"[99] Between God and ourselves there is, we may venture to say, reciprocal hospitality and indwelling, because there is between us both communication and communion (*koinonia*). It is not for nothing that Jesus has described our final bliss under the image of a meal[100] and that the Apocalypse returns to this image—not only to point out that all hunger and thirst will forever be satisfied (Rev. 7:16–17) but to insist on this intimate communication and reciprocity:

---

98 This is shown by the New Testament uses of the verb *menein*, to remain, and the noun *monē*, a dwelling. For the latter, compare the two (only) examples in John 14:2: "There are many dwelling-places in my Father's house"; and 14:23: "If a man ... and make our continual abode with him." For the verb, compare on the one hand, God (1 John 4:16) and Christ (John 15:4–7; 1 John 3:24) dwelling in the faithful and, on the other, the faithful dwelling in God (1 John 2:24; 4:16) and in Christ (John 6:56; 15:4–7; 1 John 2:6, 27–28; 3:6, 24).

99 [And so God becomes the Temple of man and man becomes the Temple of God]. St. Peter Damian (d. 1072), *Letter* 49, 16 (*PL* 144, 265). Text in Peter Damian, *Letters (31–60)* (Washington, DC: Catholic University of America, 1989), 280.

100 Luke 14:15–24 (Matt. 22:2–24); 22:29–30 (where we find the same connection between a meal and kingship). The same image occurs as far back as Isa. 25:6. For the idea of the messianic banquet in rabbinical circles, see Joshua Bloch, *On the Apocalyptic in Judaism*, Jewish Quarterly Review Monograph Series 2 (Philadelphia: Dropsie College for Hebrew and Cognate Learning, 1952), 96–100.

> See where I stand at the door, knocking; if anyone listens to
> my voice and opens the door, I will come in to visit him, and
> take my supper with him, and he shall sup with me. Who wins
> the victory? I will let him share my throne with me; I too have
> won the victory, and now I sit sharing my Father's throne. (Rev.
> 3:20–21)

There is a reciprocal presence. The friends enjoy one another's company, they entertain one another, one in his cottage, the other in his palace. And this is in imitation of the relations between the Father and the Son, for the Father is in the Son and the Son in the Father (John 10:38). And where the Son is, he wishes that those should be with him who have been given to him by the Father (John 17:24). But it is clear that, in this mutual interchange, it is we who receive and are filled. God is no richer for possessing us. He receives nothing he did not already have. Yet he delights in giving, for he is good, and in communicating himself to us, for he loves us. But for us to possess God is to be filled and filled to overflowing.

That God is our Temple means that there is between him and ourselves a mutual indwelling, a communion, an intercommunication in which we find our hunger satisfied and our joy filled to the uttermost.[101] What is true in eternity of the relations between the Father and the Son, "all I have is yours, and all you have is mine" (John 17:10), is henceforth true also and eternally of the relations between the Father and his sons by adoption. It is they who return to their Father's house and are filled. They know the truth of that familiar relationship which Jesus in the parable of the prodigal son expressed in these words: "My son, you are always at my side, and everything that I have is already yours" (Luke 15:31).

In this way then, our inherent desire for a complete inward life, a desire which corresponds exactly to God's plan of grace, will at last be satisfied. If there is one obvious direction in the great story of God's presence to his creatures as it has been made known to us by revelation, if this story has one overall movement, it is surely this—it begins by momentary contacts and visits, then passes through the stage of external mediations that draw God ever nearer to mankind, and finally reaches the state of perfectly stable and intimate communion. Whether it be through the Temple, the sacrifice, or the priesthood, God's plan moves towards a communion of such intimacy that the duality between man and God, and therefore their external separation from one another, are both overcome in so far as this is possible without a meaningless confusion of beings or pantheism.

---

101 "*Ipse Deus erit electis aeternae beatitudinis praemium, quod ab eo possessi possidebunt in aeternum.*" [The chosen gift of eternal happiness will be God himself, and in his possession they will dwell in eternity] St. Bede, *The Explanation of the Apocalypse*, 21, 3 (PL 93, 194). This fact was already indicated in the image of the betrothal, so closely allied to the theme of Zion and its Temple.

In harmony with this divine plan, the religious soul has always longed that God himself should be all in all to her, that he should be her light,[102] that he himself should be her guide,[103] that he should utter within her, beyond all the ideas of our human mind, one of those creative words that are strength and sweet- ness, certitude and light[104]—"May the Lord Jesus and the Holy Spirit speak in us. May he sing hymns in us unto thee!"[105]—that he should be her peace (Eph. 2:4), her justice, her holiness,[106] her strength and her refuge;[107] that he should be her prayer—"Do thou thyself pray in the depths of my being!"[108] May the *opus Dei* [work of God] which I perform be above all *Operans in me Deus* [the work of God in me]!, that he should love in us, that he should set his love in us in the place of our hard, self-centered hearts.[109]

If only we could love through his will present in us.[110] This is the profound meaning of St. Thérèse of Lisieux's act of consecration to the merciful love of God[111]—that the whole city lying within us should, like the Jerusalem of Ezekiel, have no other name but "Yahweh-is-there" (Ezek. 48:35). Not only may God dwell in us and fill our being, may he also himself be our Temple, and the place of our prayer as he was for the exiles in Babylon! (Ezek. 11:16). Beyond his dwelling in us by faith and by love, may we have no other dwelling but that wherein he dwells himself![112]

---

102 2 Sam. 22:29; Isa. 60:20; Rev. 21:23.

103 Ezek. 34:11, 15; 37:22.

104 See Thomas á Kepmis (d. 1471), *The Imitation of Christ*, Bk. 1, Chap. 3, trans. Leo Sherley-Price (New York: Viking Penguin, 1987); St. John of the Cross (d. 1591), *The Ascent of Mount Carmel*, Bk. 2, Chap. 32, in *The Collected Works of St. John of the Cross*, trans. Kieran Kavanaugh and Otlio Rodriguez (Washington, DC: Institute of Carmelite Studies, 1979).

105 The anaphora or eucharistic offering-prayer of Serapion (d. 364 a.d.). Text in *Springtime of the Liturgy*, ed. Lucien Deiss (Collegeville, MN: Liturgical Press, 1979 [1967]), 194.

106 Jer. 23:6; 1 Cor. 1:30; compare Isa. 43:25.

107 2 Sam. 22:2; Isa. 28:6 and the entire theme of "Yahweh my Rock" so frequent in the Bible, especially in the Psalter. Refuge: Ezek. 17:17.

108 Rom. 8:26–7.

109 Rom. 5:5. Compare, in the life of St. Catherine of Siena (d. 1380), the episode in which she "exchanged hearts" with Christ. See her *Dialogue*, trans. Suzanne Noffke (New York: Paulist, 1980), 4.

110 See St John of the Cross, *The Spiritual Canticle*, Stanza 37, in *The Collected Works*.

111 On St. Thérèse of Lisieux's "Act of Oblation to the Merciful Love of God" (June 9, 1895), see her *Story of a Soul*, 3d. ed. trans. John Clarke (Washington, DC: Institute of Carmelite Studies, 1996 180–181; 276–277 (text of the Act). See the analysis of this act of consecration by André Combes, *The Spirituality of St. Thérèse; An Introduction* (New York: P.J. Kenedy, 1950), Chap. 5.

112 St Thomas, *Commentary on the Gospel of Johnn*, Chap. 14, Lect. 1, 1853: Com. in Ev. Joann., c. 14, lect. 1: "Deus autem habitat in sanctis ... per fidem. ...Duplex est ergo domus Dei. Una est militans Ecclesia, scilicet congregatio fidelium. ... Inhabitat Deus per fidem. ... Alia est

triumphans, scilicet sanctorum collectio in gloria patris; Ps. 64:6: replebimur in bonis domus tuae. Sanctum est templum tuum, mirabile in aequitate. Sed domus patris dicitur non solum illa quam ipse inhabitat, sed etiam ipsemet, quia ipse in seipso est. Et in hac domo nos colligit." [Now God dwells in his saints ... by faith. ... Accordingly, God has two houses. One is the Church militant, that is, the society of those who believe. ... God dwells in this house by faith. ... The other is the Church triumphant, that is, the society of the saints in the glory of the Father: "We shall be satisfied with the goodness of thy house, thy holy temple" (Ps 65:4). Yet the house of the Father is not only where he dwells, but he himself is the house, for he exists in himself. It is into this house that he gathers us.] Eng. trans.: *Commentary on the Gospel of John, Part 2: Chapters 8–21*, trans. Fabian R. Larcher (Albany, NY: Magi, 1998).

Letter & Spirit 4 (2008): 319–336

REVIEWS & NOTICES

Christopher J. H. Wright

The Mission of God: Unlocking the Bible's Grand Narrative
(Downers Grove, IL: InterVarsity, 2006)

Canonical exegesis, which insists that individual biblical texts be read in the light of the whole canon, has restored the Church's original sense that these texts form a single "book" that tells of God's plan for humanity revealed in Jesus Christ. In other words, this school of exegesis has returned us to the guiding assumptions of the earliest Christian interpreters—namely, that there is a unified, "grand narra- tive" to the Bible.

Acknowledging that, however, the question then becomes: how do we best characterize that narrative; what does the Bible, taken as a whole, intend to tell us? Christopher Wright has written a big book that seeks to answer that question in two words—*missio Dei*, the mission of God. For Wright, the Bible tells the story of God's mission in history. What is that mission? To bestow his divine blessing on the nations of the world through a people he elected and called to be his special possession—first, Israel, and later the "new Israel," the Church.

This is not a book that seeks to articulate the biblical foundations of the Church's mission to evangelize the world. It is rather something more ambitious—a "missional hermeneutic of the Bible." Wright proposes that the divine mission of blessing is the hermeneutical key for understanding and interpreting the content and unity of Scripture. Thus, he uses this divine mission as the interpretative matrix through which to look at such foundational biblical themes as monotheism, creation, humanity, election, covenant, ethics, and future hope.

Wright roots his "missiological hermeneutic" in the foundational preaching of the New Testament Church. He calls attention to Jesus' own post-resurrection interpretation of "everything written about me in the law of Moses and the proph- ets and the psalms"—that is, in the entire Old Testament. "Thus is written," Jesus said, not only that the Messiah would suffer and rise, but that repentance would be preached in his name "to all the nations" (Luke 24:44–47). St. Paul, too, in his speech to King Agrippa, likewise reads the Old Testament as foretelling a mission to the nations: "The prophets and Moses said that the Christ would 'proclaim light both to the people [Israel] and to the Gentiles'" (Acts 26:22–23).

Following the teaching of Jesus, the New Testament Church read the Old Testament as proclaiming the universal mission of God, according to Wright. At the heart of that divine mission is the call of Abraham and the subsequent Abrahamic covenants, which promise that through Abraham's seed the families of the earth shall be blessed. In his close reading of the Abrahamic materials, Wright helps us to hear an original hermeneutic of the New Testament writers, who believed the Gospel was "preached ... beforehand to Abraham" (Gal. 3:8). Wright draws subtle canonical connections between the account of Abraham's call in Genesis 12 and the primordial history that goes before it in Genesis 1–11, underlining the "new creation" that Abraham represents.

The primordial history culminated in the sin of the tower builders at Babel. Wright notices that, as the people at Babel sought to "make a name" for themselves apart from God, God promises to make Abraham's "name" great (Gen. 11:4; 12:2). Wright sees this echo between the texts as "undoubtedly deliberate." In addition, he notes that the Babel narrative five times repeats the expression "the whole earth" (Gen. 11:1, 4, 8, 9), while similar language is used in God's promise that Abraham will be a blessing for "all the families of the earth" (Gen. 12:3).

Wright also sees the importance of the "sequence of covenants" in the Old Testament as giving shape and direction to the divine mission entrusted to Abraham, and the biblical narrative. He rightly identifies the central significance of the covenant with David—especially for the New Testament authors' understanding of the Church's mission. He describes the New Testament's vision this way:

> [I]n the resurrection of the Messiah, the promised restoration of David's kingdom and rebuilding of the Temple had also taken place. But since the Davidic Messiah would be king for all nations, and the Davidic Temple would be a house of prayer for all nations, the restoration of these things must now move forward to their appointed purpose—the ingathering of the nations as the subjects of his kingdom and the stones in his Temple. The resurrection of Jesus is not just the fulfillment of [the] words of David in the psalms, it is also the restoration of the reign and Temple of David, no longer for ethnic Israel only but for all nations.

Wright also senses that there is a liturgical consummation to the Scripture's grand narrative, marshalling a copious array of Scriptures that speak of all the nations worshipping the God of Israel.

Ultimately, however, Wright's interpretative framework does not provide the full explanatory power that it might. One can agree that the *missio Dei*—what St. Irenaeus and other early interpreters called the "economy of salvation"—forms the narrative of Scripture. And Wright helps us to see that the mission of God, his plan of salvation, is a plan for the blessing of the nations. But Wright does not provide an adequate explanation of either the nature of the blessing that God seeks to bestow on the nations or how he intends that blessing to be communicated to all the families of the world.

The New Testament answer would seem to be clear. St. Paul and St. John speak of the blessing in terms of divine filiation—eternal life as children of God and heirs of Abraham. Believers receive this blessing through the sacramental economy of the Church, that is, through baptism and the Eucharist. The Word of the Gospel is intended to culminate in the sacrament by which the Word is actualized in the life of the believer. This is what Christ commanded and this is what we see the apostolic Church doing over and over again: preaching the Gospel and baptizing those who repent and believe in the Gospel. By this movement of Word and sacrament, they are made children of God and incorporated into the Church, the "new Israel," described as the family or household of God and entrusted with carrying out the mission of God until the end of the age.

Wright, who is the author of the very helpful *Knowing Jesus through the Old Testament* (1995), here too displays his impressive command of biblical motifs and intertextual connections. Yet perhaps because of Wright's own evangelical presuppositions, he never provides a coherent explanation of the identity of the Church, its relation to the kingdom preached by Jesus, or the relation of the Church to the divine mission. It is also to be regretted that not once in this more than 500-page book does he discuss baptism, the Eucharist, or the sacramental economy.

Aidan Nichols, O.P.

*Lovely Like Jerusalem: The Fulfillment of the Old Testament
in Christ and the Church*
(San Francisco: Ignatius, 2007)

Aidan Nichols has written a first-rate introduction to the Old Testament canon and its interpretation in the New Testament and early Christian tradition. His comments on each individual book of the Old Testament are perceptive and insightful. His point throughout is that without a strong knowledge of these books, the fullness of the Gospel can never be understood; nor is it possible to grasp the meaning of "the entire divine plan that stretches between, and over, the two testaments."

Along the way, in a measured, non-polemical fashion, Nichols takes up hot-button scholarly issues such as the hypothesis that the Bible's first five books, the Pentateuch, had four original "sources": J (the Yahwist writer), E (the Elohist), D (the Deuteronomist), and P (the Priestly).

Taking up such matters, Nichols is consistently fair in laying out the arguments before weighing in with his own opinions, which tend towards the more conservative scholarly camps. For instance, he identifies some weaknesses in the JEDP theory, and goes on to make a good case for "the immense antiquity of the source material in Genesis." He also argues for a tenth-century B.C. dating of the whole Pentateuch, which, in his opinion, reflects "ancient traditions, the nucleus of which goes back to Moses."

In his treatment of modern New Testament scholarship, Nichols takes aim at the pervasive influence of what he calls "a resurgence of the heresy of Marcion," the second-century teacher who wanted to cast off the Old Testament as completely incompatible with the New Testament. Critiquing the neo-Marcionite assumptions in such crucial figures in modern exegesis as Adolf von Harnack and Rudolf Bultmann, he argues forcefully that the New Testament cannot be read apart from the Old, anymore than the Old can be read apart from the New. On this point, he quotes Joseph Ratzinger, now Pope Benedict XVI: "For the Christian, the Old Testament represents, in its totality, an advance towards Christ. ... Hence we only interpret an individual text correctly ... when we see it as a way that is leading us ever forward, when we see in the text where this way is tending and what its inner direction is."

Nichols believes that "the messianic hope, broadly conceived," is the unifying theme of the Old and New Testaments. And his treatment of this theme is marked by a timely retrieval of the underappreciated twentieth-century Anglican, A. G. Herbert, especially his book, *The Throne of David: A Study of the Fulfillment of the Old Testament in Jesus Christ and his Church* (1941).

The messianic hope that animates the Bible is expressed in various biblical subthemes. Nichols studies these: the gift of the Spirit, the restoration of Paradise, the faithful remnant of the people, the bride of the Lord, the new covenant, the servant of the Lord, the Son of David, the new Temple, and the homecoming to Mount Zion. He is especially strong in identifying God's "universalist" intentions in the election of Israel and the influence of this universal mission on the self-understanding of the New Testament Church.

Nichols aptly describes his own approach to the sacred page as "a markedly ecclesial exegesis." By that he means a "typological" exegesis that reflects the manner of interpretation found within the Bible and carried forward into the Church's liturgy and the teachings of the Church Fathers. To illustrate this brand of ecclesial exegesis, he turns first to Jean Cardinal Daniélou's classic treatments (in *From Shadows to Reality* [1960]) of the christological and sacramental typologies of Adam's sleep, Noah and the flood, the sacrifice of Isaac, and the Exodus. Nichols then provides chapter-length studies of St. Augustine's exegesis of Genesis, St. Gregory the Great's reading of the Book of Job; Origen's interpretation of the Song of Songs; and Thomas Aquinas' rendering of the Torah.

Describing this great tradition, Nichols concludes:

> The fundamental promise-fulfillment format of the Bible is why
> the kind of exegesis we call "typological" best befits its unique
> genius. That is something recognized within Scripture itself,
> since in the Old Testament the prophets interpret typologically
> the founding events of the history of Israel, and in the New
> Testament, the various inspired writers interpret typologically
> both the ancient Old Testament history and the comments on
> that history made by the writing prophets. The Fathers of
> the Church will continue this typological reading of the Bible,
> which was found in the official catechesis taught by the bishops,
> notably to those preparing for Christian initiation by baptism,
> chrismation (or confirmation), and first Holy Communion.
> Indeed, such typological exegesis is the chosen method of un-
> derstanding Scripture found in the liturgy itself.

Robert Louis Wilken, trans. and ed.

Isaiah: Interpreted by Early Christian and Medieval Commentators, The Church's Bible (Grand Rapids, MI: Eerdmans, 2007)

Prior to his conversion, St. Augustine asked St. Ambrose which books of the Bible he should read. Ambrose told him to read Isaiah. Why? Ambrose never explained, but Augustine later surmised it was because Isaiah "more clearly than others ... foretold the Gospel and the calling of the Gentiles."

The Book of Isaiah has long been regarded in the Church as a sort of "fifth gospel." Already in the New Testament, we can readily see its importance for understanding the person and mission of Jesus. St. Jerome called Isaiah "an evangelist and apostle" and said his prophecy "contains all the mysteries of the Lord." St. Isidore of Seville was able to create a little book on the life of Christ that was composed entirely of citations from Isaiah.

Thus, the arrival of the *Isaiah* volume in Robert Louis Wilken's The Church's Bible series is truly an important and welcome event. Drawing from more than fifty ecclesial writers, as well as from ancient liturgies, Church councils, and manuals, Wilken has woven a grand catena of Christian commentary and interpretation on the Greek text of Isaiah.

As Wilken notes in his finely observed introduction, Isaiah is not only important for understanding the Gospel—the prophet's words have also become part of the daily worship of the Church. The "Holy, Holy, Holy" that Catholics sing in every Mass (also known as the *sanctus* or *trisagion* [lit. thrice-holy]), comes from Isaiah's vision of the Temple of heaven and the throne of God (Isa. 6:3; compare Rev. 4:8). The scene of the seraphim purifying Isaiah's lips with a burning coal (Isa. 6:6–7) is interpreted in the Syriac liturgy as a sign of the Eucharist; before communion, the priest declares to the faithful: "The propitiary live coal of the Body and Blood of Christ our God is given to the true believer for the pardon of offenses and the forgiveness of sins forever."

The liturgical appropriation of Isaiah is part of a broader interpretative tradition that only begins in the New Testament. "[I]t was only as Christians lived the book, heard it read in public worship, sang its 'canticles' (for example, Isa. 12:1–6), pondered its words and images, and debated difficult passages, that its fuller meaning was uncovered," Wilkens writes. "The actual text of Isaiah is the beginning of what Isaiah means for Christians, not the ending."

In bringing us the fruits of this interpretative tradition, Wilken presents an English translation of the Septuagint text along with citations of the text in the New Testament and generous selections from the four complete commentaries on Isaiah that survive from antiquity—those of Eusebius, Jerome, St. Cyril of Alexandria, and St. Theodoret of Cyrus. He also gathers shorter reflections on the text by commentators ranging from the well-known, such as Origen, to the relatively obscure likes of Venantius Fortunatus, a seventh-century Latin poet and hymn writer.

The result is a commentary of rare breadth, offering fresh exegetical and spiritual insights. To point out just a few examples: There is a beautiful meditation on baptism by St. Gregory of Nyssa in which he connects Isaiah's oft-quoted lines about the foundation stone to be laid in Zion with the story of Jacob's well (Gen. 29):

> For from earliest times it was by means of water that salvation came to someone who was perishing. ... When Jacob was looking for a bride, he met Rachel unexpectedly at the well. A great stone was placed over the well, and it required many shepherds to roll it away to provide water for them and their flocks. Jacob, however, moves the stone away by himself and waters the flocks of his betrothed. This stone is a type pointing to what is to come. For what is the stone lying over the well but Christ himself? For of him Isaiah says: "I will lay for the foundation of Zion a stone that is precious, costly, chosen" (Isa. 28:16). And Daniel also says: "A stone was cut without hands" (Dan. 2:34, 45). ... Over the well then, was lying the spiritual stone Christ, concealing in the

depth of the mystery the washing of regeneration that needed much time—one might say a long rope—to bring it to light. And no one was able to move the stone except Israel [Jacob], who signifies the mind that sees God. He draws up the water and also gives drink to the sheep of Rachel. That is, he reveals the hidden mystery and gives water to the flock of the Church.

Elsewhere, Isaiah's reference to "a plan formed of old" (Isa. 25:1) is taken by Cyril of Alexandria to evoke "the mystery of the incarnation" referred to in Ephesians 1:9–10 ("a plan for the fullness of time"). He goes on to read Isaiah's prophecy of the redeemed drinking wine on God's holy mountain (Isa. 25:6, 9–10) as a reference to the Church and the Eucharist.

Wine refers to the mystical oblation, to the unbloody sacrifice which we celebrate in the churches. ... For his plan is for all peoples. ... They confess that "God will give rest on this mountain" (Isa. 25:10). It seems to me that here, mountain refers to the Church, for it is there that one finds rest. For we heard the words of Christ: "Come to me, all who labor and are heavy laden, and I will give you rest" (Matt. 11:28).

And commenting on the passage of the seraphim and the burning coal (Isa. 6), Origen is moved to eucharistic prayer: "Bring down from the heavenly altar, O Lord, tongs carrying a burning coal to touch my lips, for if the tongs of the Lord touch my lips, they will be cleansed! And if the Lord cleanses my lips and burns out my faults ... the Word of God will be in my mouth and no unclean word will escape my lips."

We are witnessing a tremendous period of patristic retrieval and revival. Eerdmans' The Church's Bible series now has volumes on Isaiah, Corinthians, and the Song of Songs. InterVarsity's Ancient Christian Commentary on Scripture series has published volumes covering almost all of the biblical canon (to date, all but Psalms 1–50 and Jeremiah and Lamentations). In this volume, Wilken has made an important contribution to that ongoing revival, giving us a treasure trove for future scholarship, prayer, and homiletics.

Cornelius a Lapide, S. J.

Commentary on the Four Gospels, 4 vols.
(Fitzwilliam, NH: Loreto, 2008; available from www.loretopubs.org)

Cornelius a Lapide, S. J. (1568–1637) is a giant figure in the history of Catholic biblical interpretation. Born in a tiny Catholic enclave in the Calvinist Netherlands in the bloody generation after the Reformation, Lapide grew to be one of the Church's most gifted scholars and spiritual interpreters of the sacred page.

Ordained as a Jesuit priest in 1595, he became a spell-binding lecturer in Scripture and Hebrew, first at Louvain and later at the Roman College. He was known for weaving in topical allusions and references to classical literature, philosophy, and history, along with quotations from the Church Fathers and insights into the Greek, Hebrew, and Latin texts. These were also characteristics of his writing, which was nothing short of prodigious. Between 1614 and 1645, Lapide wrote commentaries on every book of Scripture except Job and Psalms.

Yet despite his historical importance, Lapide today is largely unknown. His works have long been out of print and hard to find; many remain untranslated. Loreto Publications has now published the first complete translation of his commentaries on the four gospels as the launching point for a planned thirty-volume reissue of Lapide's exegetical writings that will also be made available to subscribers online.

To read Lapide four hundred years later is to enter a nearly forgotten world of biblical interpretation—where there are no clear lines between the historical, the literary, and the spiritual reading of the text; where philosophy, archeology, philology, and even the natural sciences are brought to bear in illuminating the divine meaning of the text.

Lapide's reading of the parable of the wise and foolish virgins (Matt. 25:1–13) includes: a discussion of numerology in Philo and Plato; a study of the possible Arabic background to certain expressions in the text; detailed considerations of Virgil's fourth *Ecologue* and *Aeneid*, Catallus, Martial, and Pliny (all in relation to the symbolism of "nuptial lamps and torches"); not to mention citations of more than two dozen Church Fathers along with a quotation from Rabbi Achabia and the Mishnah. It is hard to say what is more striking—the sheer breadth and density of Lapide's interpretative matrix or his audacity in summoning all these resources to the interpretation of the sacred text.

Lapide himself takes a breathtakingly high view of Scripture's purposes:

> The dignity, usefulness, and majesty of sacred Scripture are so great that it surpasses the books of all philosophers and theologians, among the Hebrew and the Greek and Latin authors, as much as divine wisdom surpasses all human wisdom. For sacred Scripture is the Word of God. It is the very utterance and speech of God, by means of which God enunciates his wisdom to us, and shows us the way to virtue, salvation, and eternal happiness. Wherefore St. Augustine (*Epistle* 3) ... asserts that sacred Scripture is an encyclopedia of all the sciences. ... Sacred Scripture is the art of arts, the science of sciences: it is the Pandora and the encyclopedia of wisdom.

Lapide prefaces his commentary with thirty-eight "canons of interpretation," which reflect a wise and prayerful method. Canon 35, for instance, explains the "marvelous ... and wondrously consonant ... harmony of the New Testament with the Old" in the economy of salvation. This hermeneutical presupposition has consequences for Lapide's method. "Hence, in order to explain a Scripture passage of the New Testament from its roots and foundations, examine and trace the figure, the prophecy or thought of the Old Testament to which it alludes. For the old Law was the prelude to the new, and the new is the completion of the old."

It is clear that the Fathers hold of pride of place for Lapide in his interpretative work. He systematically catalogues all the Fathers' comments on individual verses of Scripture. In places, his commentary recalls the beautiful and rich chain of patristic wisdom found in St. Thomas Aquinas' famous *Catena Aurea*. Lapide's four-volume work should be a welcome addition to the libraries of scholars and pastors alike.

Jonathan T. Pennington

Heaven and Earth in the Gospel of Matthew,
Supplements to Novum Testamentum 126 (Leiden: Brill, 2007)

Jonathan Pennington succeeds in what he sets out to do in this book—to unsettle a long-settled scholarly consensus. From the earliest days, New Testament interpreters have noticed that Matthew uses different terminology to describe the core of Jesus' preaching. While the other evangelists recount Jesus preaching about the "Kingdom of God," Matthew prefers the term "Kingdom of heaven." In the modern period, scholars are all but agreed that the difference is due to Matthew's sensitivity to his Jewish audience, which supposedly would have expected some reverential circumlocution to avoid pronouncing the divine name.

There have always been holes in this scholarly commonplace. What about the use of the word "God" throughout the rest of the gospels and New Testament, which presumably were also heard and read by Jews? Then there is the fact that Matthew's Jesus does use the expression "Kingdom of God" on four occasions; what explains that inconsistency? Pennington rightly sees that something deeper is going on in Matthew's Gospel.

He begins by noting that almost one-third of all the New Testament uses of the word *ouranos* ("heaven") are in Matthew; moreover, a larger "heaven and earth" motif is at work in Matthew, a motif not found in the other gospels. As Pennington notes:

> The proclamation of God's coming is not just the Kingdom of God, it is the Kingdom of *heaven* (Matt. 3:2; 4:7; 13:11). The follower of Jesus does not just have God as Father, but as his or her Father in *heaven* (Matt. 5:16; 6:1; 10:32). The way to practice righteousness (Matt. 6:1) is described in terms of laying up *heavenly* treasures rather than fading *earthly* rewards (Matt. 6:19–20). The follower of Jesus should call no one *on earth* his father; but only the *heavenly* Father (Matt. 23:9). The Christian prayer is for the kingdom of the Father *in heaven* to manifest itself *on earth* (Matt. 6:9–10). And as the Church awaits the kingdom, they are given doctrinal and ecclesial authority *on earth* that receives sanction *from heaven* (Matt. 16:19; 18:18–19). Over and over again, Jesus' message in Matthew is put in terms of a dualistic heaven and earth contrast.

The pastoral and theological importance of this theme for Matthew emerges in Pennington's close reading and comparison with Old Testament and other texts. For one, this theme emphasizes that God's reign is universal—that is, that the Creator of heaven and earth is the ruler of all that is on earth and in heaven. Likewise, this theme legitimates the status of the Church as "the true people of God." For Matthew, Jesus' disciples are "a heavenly people in that they alone have a kingdom that is from heaven and a Father who is in heaven. The people of God are defined by Jesus as the ones who 'do the will of my Father who is in heaven' (Matt. 7:21; 12:50). There is also a profound connection between the creation of heaven and earth and the creation of the true people of God."

Pennington makes a good contribution in establishing persuasively that Daniel 2–7 forms the backdrop to both the heaven and earth theme and the "Kingdom of heaven" motif in Matthew. He is not, of course, the first scholar to see the influence of Daniel on Matthew, or even the influence of Daniel on Matthew's understanding of the kingdom; all told, there are more than thirty allusions to the prophetic text in his gospel. But in Pennington's patient analysis, the depth of this influence is made clear. Daniel and Matthew share a preoccupation with heaven (in Daniel 2–7, the word is used twenty-eight times), and both stress the opposition between God's reign in heaven and the reign of the kingdoms of the earth.

Indeed, in Daniel, God is called "the King of heaven" (Dan. 4:37). The prophet foretells the coming of a kingdom on earth to be established forever by "the God of heaven" (Dan. 2:44–45). There are anticipations of the Lord's Prayer, as Daniel looks forward to God's "will" being done in heaven and on earth (Dan. 4:35). Then there is the oft-quoted vision of the Son of Man who is "given dominion and glory and the kingdom" (Dan. 7:13–14).

To build his case, Pennington offers a useful survey of the Kingdom of God in the Old Testament, the Apocrypha, the Pseudepigrapha, and the documents of the Qumran. While various of these texts interweave the same themes we find in Matthew—heaven, earth, and kingdom—"no text combines and appropriates these themes to the extent and degree that we find in Daniel 2–7," Pennington concludes.

For Pennington, the Danielic background offers us clues to the meaning of the Kingdom of heaven in Matthew. Like Daniel, Matthew sees the heavenly kingdom as a sign of God's reign over all the nations and as a "counterpoint of earthly kingdoms and earthly ways of operating a kingdom."

He also makes the interesting observation that the kingdom in Matthew is not understood in abstract terms of God's reign or rule. Rather, Matthew depicts the heavenly kingdom as having "spatial" dimensions as well. While acknowledging that "the ancient notion of heaven as a place is to modern, 'enlightened' scholars either a source of embarrassment or derision," he argues that Matthew clearly believes heaven to be "a dwelling place distinct from the earth"—the site of God's throne (Matt. 5:34) and his angels (18:10; 22:30; 24:36; 28:2).

Matthew uses the genitive "of heaven" in order to criticize existing empires and to deflate Jewish expectations of an earthly kingdom. On this point, Pennington quotes the late-nineteenth century scholar Hermann Cremer (*Biblico-theological Lexicon of New Testament Greek*), who is among the few to see the influence of Daniel on Matthew's Kingdom theology:

> It is a kingdom which has not its origin in the present earthly
> order of things, but which comes down to earth from heaven as
> a new order, molded not after the pattern of this earthly life; a
> kingdom wherein what hitherto was heavenly and beyond this
> world is manifested, and to which also the future brings.

Pennington agrees: "Matthew's choice to regularly depict the kingdom as *tōn ouranōn* [of heaven] is designed to emphasize that God's kingdom is not like earthly kingdoms, stands over against them, and will eschatologically replace them (on earth)."

One might have hoped for Pennington to explain better the relationship between the heavenly kingdom and the earthly Church in Matthew. Nor does he sufficiently explain the "son of David" and Davidic Kingdom typology in Matthew as it might relate to the heavenly kingdom. But he does help us see how the conflict between the heavenly kingdom and the earthly rulers begins immediately in Matthew, in the conflict between Herod and Jesus, which established the latter as "the true King of the Jews (and the world)." Pennington also does a good job of relating the Kingdom of heaven with the Church's mission to the nations.

His research also sheds light on how Matthew intended his book to be "a new Genesis," portraying Jesus as "the culmination of God's redemptive purposes." There are quotations from Genesis (Matt. 19:4–5; 22:24), and allusions to the creation in Matthew's description of the Holy Spirit's work (Matt. 1:18–20; 3:16). Matthew's reference to the beloved son (Matt. 3:16) evokes the Abraham and Isaac story (Gen. 22), and there are other references to Abraham as well (Matt. 1:1–2; 3:9; 8:11; 22:32). Sodom (Matt. 10:15), "the days of Noah" (Matt. 24:37), and the Cain and Abel story are considered (compare Gen. 4:1–16; Matt. 5:21–5; 18:21–22; 23:34–36). The darkness of the world at Jesus' death compares to the darkness before the world was created (Matt. 27:54; Gen. 1:2). And as the gospel begins by calling Jesus the son of Abraham, it ends with an allusion to God's covenant promise to Abraham—that in him all the nations of the world would be blessed (Matt. 28:18–19; Gen. 22:18). Finally, there is Matthew's use of the rare term *palingenesia* (19:28: "rebirth," "regeneration") another sign of his concern to depict a new creation.

Scholars have long noted this intention, apparent in the first two words of the gospel— *Biblos geneseōs*, which is the Greek rendering of "the Book of Genesis" in the Septuagint translation. And Pennington's study, by focusing on the centrality of the heaven and earth motif, illuminates Matthew's intention in all its splendor:

> The prominence of heaven and earth in Genesis 1:1 (and beyond) connects with the heaven and earth theme throughout Matthew, with its climax in 28:19. … It is also very significant that the final five words of Matthew … likewise show his book-ending intentions. Reference to "the end of the age" seems clearly to form an *inclusio* with both Matthew 1:1 and Genesis 1:1, spanning from the creation to the end. Matthew 1:1 also highlights the role of Abraham, as does 28:19 with its reference to the Gospel going forth to "all nations." This clearly alludes to Genesis 11–12 and the introduction of Abraham as the one through whom God will bless "all the nations of the earth" (Gen. 12:2–3). This connection is very significant because in Genesis God's authority

as creator over heaven and earth (Gen. 1–2) is the basis for his redemptive purpose for all the nations, worked out through the person of Abraham (Gen. 12 and beyond). Matthew's structure shows sensitivity to this redemptive narrative, with its strong theme of heaven and earth throughout, culminating in Jesus' own authority over heaven and earth (God's prerogative in Gen. 1:1) *with the result that* his disciples may go and bring the blessings of the Gospel to all nations—the purpose and zenith of the process begun in Genesis 1–2. Therefore ... there is a good reason to believe that Matthew interwove his gospel with the heaven and earth theme and structured his narrative ... to connect his own gospel with the larger narrative of Genesis, thereby proclaiming that Jesus is the one in whom God's foundational purposes are consummated.

Matthew Levering

Participatory Biblical Exegesis: A Theology of Biblical Interpretation
(Notre Dame, IN: University of Notre Dame, 2008)

Modern biblical interpretation is in need of new philosophical and theological foundations. The biblical-exegetical guild in the academy has for too long been dominated by a belief that the Scripture scholar's basic task is limited to reconstructing the historical origins and intentions of individual texts. This job description reflects a set of deep philosophical, epistemological, and historical assumptions—assumptions that mark a radical departure from the original and formative traditions of biblical interpretation in the Church.

At the heart of the problem is a false understanding of history, writes Matthew Levering in his fine new book. Moderns look at history as a linear succession of moments continuing from the past through the present and into the future. In the modern view of history, human intention and action exist autonomously along this continuum, quite apart from any design or plans that God might have. By contrast, the "patristic-medieval" approach, which Levering seeks to retrieve in this book, sees history as a "participatory" project in which we partake of the life of God, through Christ and the sacraments of his Church, as part of the economy of God's on-going self-revelation.

Levering has written an engaging and fair-minded intellectual history which aims to return modern biblical interpretation to its philosophical and theological source in the practice of the Church Fathers and medieval interpreters. The story Levering tells in this copiously annotated book is a familiar one, and he draws effectively from the best of recent scholarship on the rise of modernity, especially Anthony Levi's *Renaissance and Reformation: The Intellectual Genesis*, and Louis Dupré's *Passage to Modernity* and *The Enlightenment and the Intellectual Foundations of Modern Culture*.

He locates the decisive moment in the "nominalist" drift in late medieval metaphysical philosophy. By the fourteenth century, as Levering explains, nominalist ways of the thinking had helped to undermine the patristic-medieval understanding of God's relationship with his human creatures and their history. St. Thomas Aquinas and earlier thinkers had proposed a radical interpenetration of the heavenly design and earthly realities, the divine will and the human will —with the human person created for the "final cause" of finding his or her happiness in God, and human history being a "participation" in the salvific plan of God and the very life and presence of God.

The thought of latter day "nominalists," exemplified for Levering by Blessed Duns Scotus, severed this participatory understanding of the divine-human relationship. In effect, a kind of parallel universe was created with a large gulf between heaven and earth—between the plans and purposes of God and the plans and purposes of men and women.

This, in turn, changed the way people read the Bible. As Levering writes, Scripture came to be seen "*primarily* as a linear-historical record of dates and places rather than as a providentially governed (revelatory) conversation with God in which the reader, within the sacramental and doctrinal matrix of the Church, is situated."

To illustrate this shift, Levering makes a creative narrative move. He traces the history of the interpretation of a single passage of Scripture, John 3:27–36, through ten Catholic interpreters, ranging from the "radically participatory" exegesis of Aquinas in the Middle Ages to the exclusively literary and historical reading of Raymond Brown, the dominant figure in late twentieth-century Catholic exegesis.

Levering dramatizes a remarkable change in perspective. Aquinas reads the text in a way that reflects his belief that Scripture describes a divine reality that believers experience and participate in through their baptism. Further, his exegesis aims at inviting readers into an ever greater sharing in this trinitarian life of God through what Levering describes as the "transformative movement of deification and eschatology." By Raymond Brown's time, the job of biblical interpretation has been reduced from this kind of sublime cooperation in God's revelation, to a kind of archeological recovery of the text's "historical" meaning, understood as what the text meant for its original first-century A.D. audience.

Levering wants to renew Catholic exegesis through reclaiming the approach found in Aquinas and before him in St. Augustine, especially in Augustine's *De Doctrina Christiana* (On Christian Doctrine).

This approach, as Levering synthesizes and explains it, has three prongs. The first is the return to an understanding of history as the locus of our participation in the divine life and in the economy established by God's creative and redemptive work. Second, he wants us to return to an understanding of the interpreter's task as a sharing in the divine pedagogy of "God the Teacher," and a bringing of others into "fellowship" with God through the encounter with Jesus Christ in Scripture (see 1 John 1:2–3). Finally, Levering wants to reaffirm biblical exegesis as an "ecclesial" task in which the exegete participates in the divine mission of passing on the *sacra doctrina* entrusted to the Church

Levering has thus made an important contribution to our understanding of the task of the biblical exegete. And he demonstrates how this approach does not detract from historical and literary study, rather it deepens it.

> [W]hat can be learned about the ancient Near East, the transmission of the texts, and so forth belong to the historicity of salvation. The difference is simply that such historical work cannot, in the case of biblical interpretation, exhaust the meaning of the "historical," because we know in faith other realities operating in history—among them, for example, the triune God's creation of the world, the providential shaping of God's people Israel, the working of the Holy Spirit, the divinity of Jesus, the Church as Christ's Mystical Body, the spiritual mediation accomplished by the sacraments, and the eschatological promise of divinization. Without negating historical research into the biblical texts, it is these realities that guide interpretation of the historical meaning of Scripture, since these realities enable us to understand the historical aspects in their fullness and with proper perspective.

Levering's argument would be stronger had he offered an account of the inspiration and inerrancy of Scripture. There is no question that he presumes the central importance of inspiration and inerrancy for a true understanding of Scripture, but his theology of interpretation remains incomplete without an explanation of how, in the economy of salvation, the human authors participate with God in the "authorship" of the sacred texts, and what that cooperation means for our reading of Scripture.

One thinks, too, that Levering's account of exegesis and ecclesial authority might benefit from a deeper engagement with the early Church's establishments of apostolic succession, the canon, and the rule of faith (*regula fide*). And one senses, as well, that his treatment of the task of exegesis is unfinished without any account of the liturgy and the relationship between the interpretation of Scripture and the sacraments by which the "hearers" of Scripture are brought into fellowship with God. Finally, to fully ground a new theology of biblical interpretation, we need a greater reflection on the relationship of faith and reason and the problems that stem from what Pope Benedict XVI has called "the self-limitation of reason" since the Enlightenment and Kant.

Levering is to be credited, however, with advancing a Catholic approach to Scripture within the broadly ecumenical context of the ongoing public theology debate. There is much to recommend and to think about in this book, which offers an inspiring vision that will hopefully find wide readership in the academy.

> [T]he missions of the Son and the Holy Spirit enable the Church to participate in and mediate God's salvific *sacra doctrina* for the whole world. … [T]he Church, as Christ's Bride, receives interpretive authority by sharing in Christ's Spirit. Both the Church and the divinely inspired Scripture in the Church are thus "sacramental" realities whose purpose is the salvation of the human race. In the Holy Spirit, Christ the teacher gives his authority to the mediations—the interrelated offices, charisms, and vocations that form his visible Body—in and through which he is efficaciously embodied and proclaimed in the world. Christ has won historically the victory over the principalities and powers; through his *doctrina*, the wisdom that is kenotic love, he frees human beings from the principalities and powers. Exegetes are called to this freedom. It is precisely the christological and pneumatological authority of the Church that allows individual exegetes the freedom of self-dispossession, the confidence that the grace of the Holy Spirit is in charge of the exegesis of the Son.

G. K. Beale and D. A. Carson, eds.

Commentary on the New Testament Use of the Old Testament
(Grand Rapids, MI: Baker Academic, 2007)

G. K. Beale and D. A. Carson have assembled a superb team of Protestant exegetes to produce this unique commentary that sets itself to the task of analyzing every Old Testament citation and probable allusion in each book of the New Testament. In addition, contributors have provided extensive bibliographies, making this an excellent reference guide to the best of current New Testament scholarship.

While the format for individual commentaries varies, each contributor was asked to systematically address the following questions: What is the context in which the New Testament writer makes use of the Old Testament reference? What is the original Old Testament context for these quotes and allusions? How were these same Old Testament passages treated in the literature of Second Temple Judaism? What are the textual sources for the citations (for example, is the New Testament writer quoting the Masoretic or Septuagint text)? How and why is the New Testament writer using the Old Testament text? And finally, what theological purpose is being advanced by the quotation or allusion?

The results of this format and method are often intensely close readings that yield new insights on the texts. Beale's commentary on Colossians, for instance, is one of the first full studies of the epistle's use of the Old Testament. He includes an unexpected excursus on Temple Wisdom traditions as a possible background to Colossians 1:19. He shows how "early Judaism viewed 'Wisdom' as having its 'headquarters' in the Temple." Beale continues:

> This background about the association of "Wisdom" and the "Temple" points further to a Temple reference in Colossians 1:19 and may even make more sense of why Colossians 1:9 alludes to Exodus 31:3; 35:31, where God filled people with the Spirit in order to have "Wisdom" to be able to build the Tabernacle. Paul may already subtly be anticipating the Old Testament Temple allusion of Colossians 1:19. ... Thus, one reason why Christ should "come to have first place in everything" (Col. 1:18b) is that he is God and is the inauguration of the eschatological Temple, in which God's fullness and Wisdom have begun to dwell.

In their excellent contribution on Revelation, Beale and Sean McDonough include a long and rich consideration of the world-Temple symbolism in Revelation 22.

The rationale for the worldwide encompassing nature of the paradisal Temple lies in the ancient notion that the Old Testament
Temple was a microcosmic model of the entire heaven and earth.
One of the most explicit texts affirming this is Psalm 78:69:
"And he built the sanctuary like the heights, like the earth which
he founded forever." ... Josephus and Philo discuss various ways
in which the Tabernacle or Temple or parts of it symbolically reflect the cosmos. Jospehus refers to priests as leading the "cosmic
worship" [kosmikē thrēskeia]. ... Likewise, both writers understand the garments of the High Priest to symbolize the cosmos.
Philo, even says explicitly that the High Priest "represents the
world" and is a "microcosm" (or "small world" [brachys kosmos]).
... Since the Old Testament Temple was the localized dwelling
of God's presence on earth, the Temple's correspondence with
the cosmos pointed to an eschatological goal of God's presence
tabernacling throughout the earth, an eschatological goal that
Revelation 21:1–22:5 appears to be developing (compare Rev.
21:3). This imagery ultimately appears to be traceable back to
the garden of Eden itself (note the proliferation of Eden imagery
in chaps. 21–22), if one accepts the likely argument that the
garden was understood as a kind of proto-Temple that was to be
expanded to cover the whole earth.

This landmark commentary promises to bring to pastors, scholars, and
ordinary believers the fruits of more than a generation of intertextual scholarship.
The seeds sown by C. H. Dodd and a few other scholars a generation ago have
borne their fruit. What this volume shows is how the New Testament writers
were not only careful readers of the Old Testament but also profound theologians
themselves.

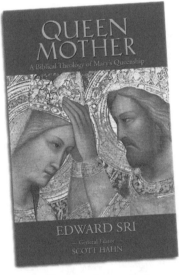

THE ST. PAUL CENTER
FOR BIBLICAL THEOLOGY
Reading the Bible from the Heart of the Church

Promoting Biblical Literacy for Ordinary Catholics . . .

- Free Online Bible Studies—*for beginners, intermediate, and advanced students*
- Online Library of Scripture, Prayer, and Apologetics—*more than 1,000 resources*
- Online Bookstore—*hundreds of titles*
- Popular Books & Textbooks—*on the Bible, the sacraments, and more*
- Workshops—*including parish-based training for Bible-study leaders*
- Pilgrimages—*to Rome and other biblical sites*

. . . and Biblical 'Fluency' for Clergy, Seminarians, and Teachers

- Homily Helps—*lectionary resources for pastors, and RCIA leaders*
- Reference Works—*including a comprehensive Bible dictionary*
- *Letter & Spirit*—*journal of biblical theology*
- Scholarly Books and Dissertations—*on topics of Scripture, liturgy, and tradition*
- Studies in Biblical Theology and Spirituality—*reissues of classic works in the field*
- Seminars and Conferences—*including ecumenical dialogues and themes*

ST. PAUL CENTER
FOR BIBLICAL THEOLOGY

2228 Sunset Boulevard, Suite 2A
Steubenville, Ohio 43952-2204
(740)264-7908
www.SalvationHistory.com

Contemporary Catholic Classics

The St. Paul Center Studies in Biblical Theology and Spirituality is a series of reissues of classic works—many of which have been out of print for decades. Each book is selected and introduced for a new generation by Dr. Scott Hahn. The series is co-sponsored by the St. Paul Center for Biblical Theology and St. Anthony Messenger Press.

The Divine Family: Life in the Trinity
by William McDonough

Path to Freedom: Christian Experiences and the Bible
by Jean Corbon

Pathways in Scripture:
A Book-by-Book Guide to the Spiritual Riches of the Bible
by Damasus Winzen

Transformed By Grace: Scripture, Sacraments and the Sonship of Christ
by Wulstan Mork

Holy Spirit of God: An Essay in Biblical Theology
by François-Xavier Durrwell

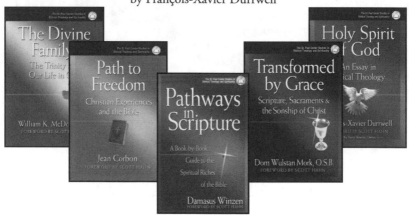

Available at bookstores or from the
online book shop at www.SalvationHistory.com